INVESTMENT PLANNING

2018

D1302349

(Ted) Kexi Zhou

2018 Iowa City

kexi-zhou@uiowa.edu

Published by:
KEIR FINANCIAL EDUCATION, LLC
1-800-795-5347
1-800-859-5347 FAX
E-mail customerservice@keirsuccess.com
www.keirsuccess.com

ISBN PRINT #978-1-945276-48-4
ISBN EPUB # 978-1-945276-49-1

INTRODUCTION

For over 40 years, Keir Financial Education, LLC has helped hundreds of thousands of insurance and financial professionals to obtain their professional designations. Over the last 20 years, Keir has produced supplemental study materials to help students complete the required courses at local universities and colleges in order to qualify to sit for the CFP® Certification Examination. Keir also has comprehensive review materials for the CFP® Certification Examination that have helped thousands of students to pass the CFP® Certification Examination.

While working with numerous program directors and instructors from universities and colleges across the country, Keir Financial Education, LLC often receives requests for a book that can serve as the primary textbook for each course that is required by CFP Board Registered Programs. Program directors and instructors involved with these programs are frequently looking for textbooks focused specifically on the topics and learning objectives outlined by CFP Board. **Keir is pleased to offer textbooks designed specifically for each of the courses included in CFP Board Registered Programs.**

Keir's textbooks are designed using our well proven methodology of structuring each book to follow the Principal Knowledge Topic List provided by the CERTIFIED FINANCIAL PLANNER Board of Standards. The topic list is the current basis for the CFP® Certification Examination, and, along with the Student-Centered Learning Objectives released by CFP Board in 2015, is the basis for student learning in Registered Programs. This textbook covers Investment Planning (Topics 33 – 41). **Since this textbook is designed to follow the CFP Board's topic list and Learning Objectives, we are confident that students and instructors will find this unique format to be the most effective way to learn the skills required of a successful financial planner. While written with CFP Board Registered Programs in mind, this Income Tax Planning textbook is comprehensive and flexible enough to be used in non-CFP Board programs as well.**

This textbook includes over 500 multiple choice questions and case questions to help reinforce each topic. The multiple-choice questions included in this textbook cover the full range of cognitive levels of questions that students will experience on the CFP® Certification Examination. These include: (1) Knowledge/Comprehension, (2) Application, (3) Analysis/Synthesis, and (4) Evaluation. Although the CFP® Certification Examination emphasizes higher level cognitive questions, a student needs to master lower level knowledge and comprehension questions in order to become proficient at answering the application, analysis, and evaluation questions.

To provide the experience of working on cases, as will be required of students when taking the CFP® Certification Examination, we have included comprehensive cases with multiple choice questions in the Appendix at the end of this textbook. Each of the topics contains a table identifying cases and questions covering material in that particular topic. Students should read the case in the Appendix and attempt to answer the case questions identified for that topic. The cases range from a few paragraphs of facts to comprehensive cases with 5 to 10 pages of detailed client information. The short cases are similar to the mini-cases that appear on the CFP® Certification Examination, and allow students to start to build their ability to answer case questions. The comprehensive cases provide the student with the same level of difficulty as the comprehensive cases on the CFP® Certification Examination.

Although most of the multiple choice questions in this textbook were written by Keir Financial Education, LLC, some of the questions have appeared on past CFP® Certification Examinations and are reprinted here with permission.

EDITORIAL BOARD

Sherri Donaldson, CFP®, ChFC®, MSFS, CASL®, CAP®, EA, Editor and Lead Instructor, received her B.S. in Business from The Pennsylvania State University and a Master of Science in Financial Services from The American College. Ms. Donaldson started her career in financial services with Nationwide Retirement Solutions working in the retirement plans field, after which she moved into a position as a Financial Specialist with Nationwide Insurance. In 2001, Ms. Donaldson began working with M&T Securities as a Financial Consultant, then in 2003 moved into a training position with M&T Investment Group. As a Senior Training Specialist, Ms. Donaldson was responsible for the company's internal CFP® certification training program, where she administered and instructed the undergraduate courses required for candidates to be eligible to sit for the CFP® Certification Examination, as well as instructing elective courses for the ChFC® designation, and other advanced designations. She was also responsible for developing and instructing training courses on advanced planning topics such as business succession planning and insurance, estate, and retirement planning for small business owners. In 2007 Ms. Donaldson began working as an independent contractor for Keir as an instructor for CFP® exam review courses. Over the next five years, she also worked for Keir on various writing and editing projects related to CFP® coursework and FINRA licensing. Ms. Donaldson joined Keir full time in 2012. She has over 30 exam cycles of experience helping students to pass the CFP® Certification Exam.

John Keir, J.D., Author, received a B.A from Williams College and a J.D. from Villanova University School of Law. Mr. Keir practiced law in Philadelphia, including a federal court clerkship and public service in the District Attorney's office. Mr. Keir has been writing and editing materials for the company primarily in insurance, risk management, claims, securities law, retirement planning, and estate planning.

Ms. Donaldson and Mr. Keir serve as the Editorial Board of the following nine college textbooks related to the CFP® Certification Examination and education:

General Financial Planning Principles
Risk Management and Insurance Planning
Investment Planning
Tax Planning
Introduction to Financial Planning

Retirement Savings and Income Planning
Estate Planning
Financial Plan Development
Practical Applications for your Calculator

They are also editors and authors of Keir's Comprehensive Review materials for the CFP® Certification Examination.

TABLE OF CONTENTS

Securities Information Essentials exam begins October 1, 2018

Improve your resume by completing the SIE exam after this Investments Course. Employers are looking for candidates that can hit the ground running! A quick exam prep class will have you prepared to pass the exam. Sponsorship not required. Call us to learn more!

Keir Financial Education
800-795-5347
www.keirsuccess.com

INVESTMENT PLANNING

Topics 33–41

[**Note:** This textbook, along with the other Keir textbooks (General Financial Planning Principles, Risk Management and Insurance Planning, Tax Planning, Retirement Savings and Income Planning, and Estate Planning), is structured to follow CFP Board's 72 Principal Topics list. Investment Planning consists of Topics 33-41 in that list. Therefore, this publication, rather than being broken into chapters and starting with chapter 1, will be presented as Topics 33-41.]

800-795-5347

INVESTMENT PLANNING

Characteristics, Uses, and Taxation of Investment Vehicles (Topic 33)

CFP Board Student-Centered Learning Objectives

(a) Describe and compare the characteristics, including risk and return, of all asset classes including cash-equivalent securities, individual bonds and stocks, real estate, other tangible assets, all pooled asset categories, and derivatives.

(b) Select the appropriate use for each asset class and investment vehicle based upon its risk/return characteristics and expected cash flows.

(c) Advise clients on the tax implications of holding and disposing of each security type or asset class.

Characteristics, Uses, and Taxation of Investment Vehicles
- A.   *Cash and equivalents*
    - 1)   *Certificates of deposit*
    - 2)   *Money market funds*
    - 3)   *Treasury bills*
    - 4)   *Commercial paper*
    - 5)   *Bankers' acceptances*
    - 6)   *Eurodollars*
- B.   *Individual bonds*
    - 1)   *U.S. Government bonds and agency securities*
        - a)   *Treasury notes and bonds*
        - b)   *Treasury STRIPS*
        - c)   *Treasury Inflation-Protected Securities (TIPS)*
        - d)   *Series EE, HH, and I bonds*
        - e)   *Mortgage-backed securities*
    - 2)   *Zero-coupon bonds*
    - 3)   *Municipal bonds*
        - a)   *General obligation*
        - b)   *Revenue*
    - 4)   *Corporate bonds*
        - a)   *Mortgage bond*
        - b)   *Debenture*
        - c)   *Investment grade*
        - d)   *High-yield*
        - e)   *Convertible*
        - f)   *Callable*
    - 5)   *Foreign bonds*
    - 6)   *Term structure of interest rates*
        - a)   *Yield curve*

Characteristics, Uses, and Taxation of Investment Vehicles, Continued

    C.   Promissory notes
    D.   Individual stocks
         1)   Common
         2)   Preferred
         3)   American Depositary Receipts (ADRs)
    E.   Pooled and managed investments
         1)   Exchange-traded funds (ETFs)
         2)   Unit investment trusts
         3)   Mutual funds
         4)   Closed-end investment companies
         5)   Index securities
         6)   Privately managed accounts
         7)   Separately managed accounts
    F.   Guaranteed investment contracts (GICs)
    G.   Derivatives
         1)   Options
             a)   Puts
             b)   Calls
             c)   Long-Term Equity Anticipation Securities (LEAPS®)
         2)   Futures
         3)   Warrants and rights

Cash and Equivalents

Cash Equivalents

The term "cash equivalents" refers to investment vehicles that are so liquid as to be almost like cash itself, the most liquid of all assets. Examples of cash equivalents are money market funds, short-term T-bills, commercial paper, CDs, and repurchase agreements.

Certificates of Deposit

A certificate of deposit or CD is a time deposit at a bank. It has a specified interest rate and maturity date. If redeemed prior to maturity, a penalty in the form of a reduced interest rate is imposed. The FDIC insures CDs up to $250,000.

Negotiable CDs are issued in large denominations at rates negotiated between the bank and a large depositor, often a business firm. Maturities are usually three months or less. They may not be redeemed before maturity, but they may be sold in the secondary market.

Brokered CDs

Brokered CDs are certificates of deposit sold through a brokerage firm. The broker can offer access to banks around the country, so the rate is often higher than the rate offered by the local bank. The brokered CD can be held to maturity, or it can be redeemed before maturity at the prevailing market rates. Since rates can rise or fall, there is interest rate risk; however, the investor will not have to pay a penalty for early withdrawal. Brokered CDs are insured by the

FDIC as are other CDs. The FDIC insures depositor accounts in banks and most types of nonbank thrift institutions up to $250,000 per depositor and per bank.

Money Market Funds

Money market mutual funds invest in highly liquid assets, such as Treasury bills, commercial paper, and bankers' acceptances. and they generally produce very low yields. Due to their high liquidity and low yields, money market funds have very low interest rate risk.

Money market funds offer check writing, and investors are able to write an unlimited number of checks against the funds in their account. Money market mutual funds are not FDIC insured.

Traditionally, money market funds have been known to consistently maintain a net asset value (NAV) of $1 per share. The interest earned on investments is not added to the net asset value; rather, the investor receives additional shares of the fund.

As a result of investor "runs" on money market funds during the economic downturn in 2008, the SEC developed new regulations to help funds to control and mitigate similar runs in the future.

Beginning October 14, 2016, rather than maintaining a stable $1 NAV, institutional money market funds have a floating value. **Note that the new rules requiring a floating rate do not impact retail money market funds (those limited to ownership only by individual investors) or U.S. government money market funds; these funds will maintain a stable $1 per share value.**

In times of extreme market volatility (defined as when the fund's weekly liquid assets fall below 30% of its total assets), institutional **and retail** money market funds are permitted to temporarily suspend withdrawals for up to 10 days in a 90-day period (these temporary suspensions may be referred to as "gates") and/or to impose liquidity fees of up to 2% on redemptions. U.S. government bond funds are exempt from fees and gates but can choose to adopt them if disclosed to investors.

As a result of these changes, planners need to evaluate whether it is acceptable for clients to remain in funds that may impose fees and gates, or whether it is in the client's best interest to move to a U.S. government money market fund that has elected not to impose fees and gates.

Money Market Deposit Accounts

Money market deposit accounts are highly liquid accounts set up with banks. A depositor can write a limited number of checks, and the deposits are FDIC insured.

Treasury Bills

U.S. government Treasury bills (T-bills) are direct debt obligations of the federal government. T-bills are short-term securities with original maturities of from 4 weeks up to 1 year. Denominations are $100 at a minimum. They are actively traded in the secondary market and do not have coupons.

Commercial Paper

Commercial paper is a short-term promissory note issued by a corporation. The denominations of these notes are very large, and the paper is unsecured, so only firms with the highest credit quality are usually able to market such paper.

Bankers' Acceptances

Bankers' acceptances are promissory notes guaranteed by a bank. They are used in international trade to ensure that payment is made for the goods delivered. The debt is guaranteed by the bank, and the corporation is no longer the primary obligor. The risk is that the issuing bank may not be able to fulfill its guarantee. The identity of the issuing bank, the size of the instrument, and the currency in which it has been issued are the factors influencing liquidity. They usually have maturities of less than one year.

Eurodollars

Eurodollars are dollar-denominated deposits in banks in foreign countries. They provide a source from which foreign banks can make loans in dollars, rather than in their own currencies.

Eurodollar instruments involve greater risk than investments in U.S. money market instruments. While the yields are higher on Eurodollar instruments, only the aggressive investor will want to accept the increased risk.

Income Taxation of Money Market Instruments

The interest income from money market funds, T-bills, commercial paper, CDs, and repurchase agreements is ordinary income taxed at individual income tax rates.

Individual Bonds

Bond Concepts

When a corporation or government is in need of additional funding, it can raise money by issuing bonds, whereby investors will loan money to the issuing entity in exchange for periodic interest payments (called coupon payments) plus return of the original loan amount at a particular date (called the maturity date).

Par value is the dollar amount shown on the face of the bond and the amount the issuing entity is obligated to pay the bond owner at the bond's maturity. The par value of a bond is usually $1,000.

Bond prices are generally quoted as a percentage of par. For example, if a bond is selling at 98, it is priced at 98% of par value. 98% x $,1000 = $980.

A *coupon* bond is a bond that pays interest, usually semi-annually. The amount of interest is stated as an annual rate and is a percentage of par. For example, a bond with a 10% coupon would pay annual interest of $100 (10% x $1,000 par value), but one-half of that amount is actually paid every six months.

Zero-coupon bonds pay no semi-annual interest. Instead, the full amount of interest is paid at maturity. The bonds are issued at a substantial discount. Thus, a $1,000 bond may be issued to the investor for $600. The bondholder receives no coupon payments and will be paid the full $1,000 par value when the bond matures.

A serial bond is a bond issue in which individual bonds within the total issue mature at different periods. For example, some of the bonds would have a maturity in the year 2025, some would have a maturity in the year 2026, some would have a maturity in the year 2027, and so on.

Premium and Discount Bonds

The internal rate of return (IRR) or the bond's yield to maturity (YTM) calculates the semiannual cash flows, as well as the original purchase price and the final payment (maturity). Bonds are priced at a **premium** when coupon rates are higher than comparable market rates. When coupon rates are lower than market rates, the bond will sell at a **discount**.

Government Bonds

U.S. Government Bonds and Agency Securities

U.S. government bonds are direct debt obligations of the federal government. Some of these debt instruments are nonmarketable (Series EE and HH bonds cannot be sold to other investors), but most U.S. government bonds are marketable, meaning that there is a ready market to buy and sell these bonds.

Treasury Notes and Bonds

U.S. Treasury notes (intermediate-term, 2 – 10 years) and bonds (long-term, 10 years +, 30 years is typically the maturity at issue) also are marketable debt securities. The minimum denomination is $100. They usually have coupons, and all have an active secondary market.

Editor's Note: For practice question and exam purposes, students should assume a par value of $1,000 unless stated otherwise in the question.

Treasury Floating Rate Notes

Treasury Floating Rate Notes (FRNs)have a 2-year maturity, are offered for a minimum purchase price of $100, and pay a varying amount of interest quarterly until maturity. The rate of interest rises and falls each week based on the discount rates in auctions of 13-week Treasury bills, plus a spread. The FRNs can be held until maturity or can be sold prior to maturity. Like other Treasury notes, interest income is taxed at the federal level, but is not taxed at the state or local level. Investors may find these FRNs attractive when short-term interest rates are expected to rise rapidly. In addition to the potential for an increasing interest rate, the price of floating rate securities tends to remain relatively stable versus the price of fixed-rate securities, which go down when interest rates go up.

Treasury STRIPS

STRIPS are U.S. Treasury-issued bonds with two components: interest and repayment of principal. These components are separated and sold individually by financial institutions and government broker/dealers as zero-coupon bonds. The acronym stands for Separate Trading of Registered Interest and Principal Securities.

Treasury Inflation-Protected Securities (TIPS)

An inflation-adjusted security is any security that adjusts its income stream with inflation, as measured by the CPI. If held to maturity, these securities should maintain the purchaser's real rate of return and purchasing power.

In the case of a Treasury Inflation-Protected Security (TIPS), the interest rate is a "real" rate in that coupon payments increase (or decrease) directly with any change in the Consumer Price Index. The bond's par value is linked to the comparable prices. For example, a TIPS bond with a real coupon rate of 4%, expiring in one year, with inflation at 5% has a realized return of approximately 9%. The par value of the bond would then be $1,050 (5% inflation added onto the principal) with the additional 4% coupon yield. TIPS are different from Series I bonds, which just adjust the interest rate every six months for inflation. TIPS pay interest semi-annually at a fixed rate.

Series EE, HH, and I Bonds

The U.S. government savings bonds include Series EE, HH, and I. Series EE bonds issued in paper form prior to 2012 were offered at one-half of face value. As of January 1, 2012, EE bonds must be purchased electronically from TreasuryDirect at face value. Bonds issued between May 1997 and April 2005 have a variable rate of interest and bonds issued after April 2005 have a fixed rate of interest. Bonds redeemed less than 5 years after issue will have a penalty equal the last three months of interest earned).

Series HH bonds pay semiannual interest. However, the Treasury stopped issuing Series HH bonds after August 2004, and investors are no longer able to reinvest in HH bonds or to exchange EE bonds for HH bonds.

Series I bonds pay interest which consists of a fixed component and a variable rate that is adjusted every six months for inflation.

The interest on EE bonds is tax-deferred until the bonds are redeemed or reach their final maturity date. Moreover, for EE bonds purchased after 1989, the interest earnings may be free of federal income taxation for qualifying taxpayers (subject to AGI limitations and other restrictions) who use the proceeds to pay college tuition and fees.

Taxation of Treasury Bonds, Notes, and Bills

Interest on Treasury bonds, notes, and bills is subject to federal income tax but not state or local income tax. The interest is taxed as ordinary income at individual income tax rates.

Taxation of STRIPS

The interest on U.S. Treasury STRIPS is accrued and taxed on an annual basis, even though no income has actually been received. It is also referred to as imputed or phantom income.

Taxation of TIPS

In addition to the taxes on interest payments, the increased principal of the bond is also taxable as ordinary income even though the bond has not matured.

Mortgage-Backed Securities (Ginnie Mae, Freddie Mac, and Fannie Mae)

The Government National Mortgage Association (GNMA, or Ginnie Mae) issues securities consisting of a pool of FHA/VA guaranteed mortgages. The unique feature of Ginnie Mae securities is that they are backed by the full faith of the U.S. government. Each month, Ginnie Mae distributes interest and principal payments to the investors. The interest component of each monthly payment is subject to both state and federal income taxes and is taxed as ordinary income at each individual's income tax rate. The return of principal in each monthly payment is not taxable.

The minimum size of individual GNMAs sold to the public is $25,000. An investor can invest smaller amounts in Ginnie Maes through the purchase of mutual fund shares.

Federal Home Loan Mortgage Corp. (Freddie Macs) and Federal National Mortgage Association (Fannie Maes) are other examples of mortgage-backed securities. Historically, principal and interest on Freddie Macs and Fannie Maes are not guaranteed by the federal government; however, on September 6, 2008, the Federal Housing Finance Agency (FHFA) assumed a conservator role over both Freddie Mac and Fannie Mae in order to help bail out both organizations.

The biggest risk with mortgage-backed securities is that, if interest rates fall, the mortgages will be repaid early, so the bonds will be retired early, leaving the investor with a reinvestment problem.

Municipal Bonds – General Obligation and Revenue Bonds

Municipal bonds are debt securities issued by state and local governments. Some are general obligation bonds, backed by the taxing authority of the entire governmental unit; while others are revenue bonds, backed only by the revenues from the project financed by the bond issue. For this reason, they are considered slightly more risky than GO bonds and generally will offer a higher yield.

If the bonds are used for a public purpose, the interest on them is free of federal income taxes as well as the 3.8% Medicare Contribution tax on investment income (see Topic 36 for additional details regarding the Medicare Contribution tax and calculation of taxable equivalent yield). Hence, municipal bond yields are lower than the pretax yields on most taxable securities. They are often insured by the Municipal Bond Insurance Association (MBIA) or American Municipal Bond Assurance Corporation (AMBAC).

Although the interest on public purpose municipal bonds is free of federal income tax, any capital gain on the sale of the bonds is subject to capital gains tax. The interest may also be subject to state tax, but residents are generally not taxed on bonds issued in their own states.

Zero-Coupon Bonds

A zero-coupon bond is one that pays no interest from issue date to maturity date. The full amount of accumulated interest is paid at the date of maturity. Thus, in effect, the investor is purchasing a very deep discount bond. Zero coupon bonds may be issued by the U.S. government (STRIPS, discussed previously), by state or local governments (zero coupon municipal bonds), or by corporations.

The zero-coupon bond presents the following three main disadvantages for investors:

- The investor is deprived of annual cash flow during the investment period.
- The investor is taxed annually on the assumed interest income at the investor's individual rate, although the investor does not receive any income. For example, if the bond is purchased for $600 and the yield is 10%, then the bondholder will be taxed on $60 of income (10% x $600) the first year. For the second year, the bond principal has grown to $660 so the interest is 10% x $660 = $66. The investor is taxed on that growth even though he or she will not actually receive it until the bond matures.

- The investor is at risk for greater price fluctuation compared to investors who purchase bonds that pay coupons.

⚡ **REMEMBER:** *AS WITH OTHER BONDS, INTEREST ON ZERO-COUPON BONDS ACCRUES ON A SEMIANNUAL BASIS, AND EFFECTIVE YIELDS ON SUCH BONDS SHOULD REFLECT SUCH ACCRUAL.*

Practice Question

What is the yield to maturity on a zero-coupon bond purchased for $500 if it matures in 13 years?

    A. 1.9%
    B. 2.7%
    C. 3.8%
    D. 5.4%

Answer:
The face value of the bond is $1,000. To solve for the yield to maturity, input the following variables into your financial calculator:

N = 13 x 2 = 26
PV = ($500)
PMT = 0
FV = 1,000

Solve for I, which is 2.7%. However, you need to multiply this answer by 2 to get the annual yield to maturity rate of 5.4%.
The answer is D.

Corporate Bonds

Corporate Bonds

When not issuing stock, companies also can borrow money by a bond offering. The bonds sell in units of $1,000 and are sold through bond dealers. All are registered to the purchaser, unlike bearer bonds, which have no recorded owner and trade like cash.

Interest is paid semiannually and is expressed in the stated coupon rate as a percentage of the bond's face value (for example, 6% of $1,000). Interest on corporate bonds is taxable at individual ordinary income tax rates both for federal and state income tax, and any capital gain is taxed at capital gains rates.

Accrued Interest When Trading Bonds

When investors buy and sell corporate bonds, it is necessary for the settlement to include a payment from the buyer to the seller for interest accrued during the time between the previous coupon payment and the settlement date of the trade when the new owner takes possession. This interest payment occurs because the new owner will receive the entire amount of the next coupon payment, even though he did not own the bond for the entire period. Interest due to the seller of the bond accrues up to but not including the settlement date. Regular way settlement occurs 2 business days after the trade date. For corporate bonds, interest is assumed to accrue based on a 30-day month / 360-day year.

Keir editor's note: In 2017, the SEC amended Rule 15c6-1, effective September 5, 2017, to shorten the standard settlement cycle from 3 days (T+3) to 2 days (T+2) for securities such as stocks, corporate bonds, UITs, some mutual funds, ETFs, and ADRs. Securities that already settled in less than 3 days are not impacted by the change.

Example:

Ted buys a $1,000 par value, 6% corporate bond at 90 in a regular way trade on Monday, April 3rd. The bond pays interest on January 1st and July 1st. At settlement, Ted will be required to pay the seller for 94 days of accrued interest.

Monday, April 3rd – trade date
Wednesday, April 5th – settlement date

Interest accrues up to, but not including the settlement date for the month of April, so Ted owes the seller for 4 days of accrued interest in April. Plus, Ted also owes the seller for 30 days of accrued interest for each month of January, February, and March, for a total of 94 days of accrued interest.

94 days/360 days = 26.11% x $60 annual coupon = $15.67

The accrued interest that Ted pays to the seller will be taxable income to the seller, but will not be taxable income to Ted for the year (even though Ted receives the full coupon payment on July 1st, only his portion of that amount is taxable to him).

Note, however, that U.S. government bonds are treated differently for calculating accrued interest. U.S. government bonds settle on the business day after the trade date in a regular way settlement, and are based on actual-days-per-month and actual-days-per-year (as opposed to the 30-day month and 360-day year used for corporate bonds).

Mortgage Bond and Debenture Bond

Bonds are long-term debt instruments. The two main types are mortgage bonds (secured by specific collateral) and **debenture bonds** (secured only by the general earning power of the issuing corporation). They have a stated face value (usually $1,000), a specified maturity date, and a specified coupon rate of interest, usually payable semiannually.

Most corporate bonds are debentures, backed only by the full faith and credit of the issuing corporation. Therefore, bond purchasers must be concerned with the credit rating of the issuing corporation.

Bond Ratings

A credit rating is an informed evaluation of the credit-worthiness of the issuer of a bond, and thus it is an evaluation of the investment quality of the bond. Bond ratings are indicated by letter grades assigned to the bonds only after subjecting them to a thorough financial analysis by professional rating agencies, such as Moody's and Standard and Poor's. The analysis seeks to determine the risk of default and the investment quality of the bond. The letters of the alphabet A through D are used to signal the conclusions of the rating agencies. In descending order of quality (from the highest to the lowest), the ratings run from AAA, AA, A, BBB, etc., until the last rating of D, which indicates default.

Investment-Grade

Investment-grade bonds are high-quality bonds rated by the rating agencies as BBB, Baa, or better. The coupon rates on investment-grade bonds are lower than the coupon rates on non-investment grade (junk) bonds.

High-Yield (Junk Bond)

High-yield (non-investment grade) or junk bonds are bonds rated below investment-grade by the rating services. The high coupons offered by these bonds compensate the investor for the inherent risk.

Convertible

A convertible bond gives the bondholder the right to exchange the bond for a specified number of shares of the issuing company's common stock; hence, the bond has two values, a value as straight debt (present value of future cash flows) and a value as a convertible (number of common shares that can be obtained multiplied by the market price per share). The bond's floor value is the higher of the two values.

The conversion value of a bond formula is as follows:

Conversion Value of a Bond

$$CV = \frac{Par \times P_s}{CP}$$

Where:

CV = Conversion value of the bond
Par = Par value of the bond
CP = Conversion price
P_s = Price per share of stock

Practice Question

What is the conversion value of a bond that can be converted at a $50 per share price if the stock is currently trading for $52 per share?

A. $1,000
B. $1,040
C. $2,080
D. $2,600

Answer:
The par value of a bond is always $1,000. Thus, the conversion value is $1,040 ($1,000/$50 x $52)
The answer is B.

Callable

A callable bond includes a feature that gives a corporation the right to redeem the bond before it matures at a stated price, usually par plus a call premium (also called a call penalty). This feature is most likely to be exercised after interest rates have fallen, allowing the corporation to reissue the debt at a lower rate.

Sinking Fund

The sinking fund is an obligation of the bond issuer to redeem a specified amount of the bond issue each year prior to maturity, either by calling them or buying them in the open market.

Floating Rate Bonds

With floating rate bonds, coupon rates are adjusted periodically and tied to some market instrument (for example, T-bill rate plus 2.5%). Changing economic conditions and/or the financial stability of the corporation must always be monitored. If the company's position deteriorates, a greater risk premium will be demanded above what the "floater" rate is yielding.

Put Bonds

The owner of a put bond can choose to hold onto the bond if its coupon rate is higher than comparable market yields. However, the bond can be "put" (sold) to the issuer for its par value at a specified time should the coupon be lower than market rates. The bond principal can then be reinvested at current market yields. The ability to change to a bond bearing a higher rate of interest makes a put bond attractive, so the issuer is generally able to sell the bond at a lower initial rate of interest.

Foreign Bonds

Foreign government bonds are not guaranteed by the U.S. government, but are generally safer than foreign corporate debt. Both are subject to exchange rate risk and political risk. Due to the increased risks, foreign bonds will generally have higher yields than domestic bonds. Foreign bonds denominated in dollars are bought and sold in dollars, so investors are not subject to exchange rate risk. These bonds are less risky than those denominated in a foreign currency. In particular, **Yankee bonds are less risky because the bonds are issued in the U.S. by foreign banks, and the bonds are denominated in U.S. dollars.** When foreign bonds are included in a portfolio of U.S. stocks, diversification is enhanced.

Term Structure of Interest Rates

Differences in maturity among various securities may account for differences in the interest rate on them. The phrase "term structure of interest rates" refers to the relationship between the rates of interest on securities that have similar characteristics but different terms to maturity, as illustrated in a yield curve relating interest rates to maturities.

Yield Curve

A **yield curve** is a diagram that plots yield to maturity against term to maturity for similar securities. Usually, the yield curve is upward-sloping, indicating that the longer the time until maturity of a security, all other things being equal, the higher will be its interest rate.

The main theories to explain the term structure of interest rates are the market segmentation theory, the expectations theory, and the liquidity preference theory.

- The market segmentation theory holds that the more distant the maturities of two different securities are from each other, the lower the probability that the two securities will be substitutes for each other. Thus, interest rates for short-term securities are determined by the supply of and the demand for short-term funds. The same is true for the interest rate for long-term securities. Most investors prefer short-term securities over long-term securities because of the greater liquidity of short-term securities. Therefore, short-term rates generally are below long-term rates, though this is not necessarily the case.

- The unbiased (rational) expectations theory holds that the shape of the yield curve is a function of expectations concerning future interest rate movements. For example, assume that the average of one-year rates is expected to be 8 percent, and the two-year rate is 7 percent. With these expectations, the rational investor will elect to purchase two successive one-year securities. Business firms seeking funds prefer the 7% and will try to market the two-year securities. The two parties will negotiate, and, in the end, the long-term rate of interest will tend to equal the average of expected short-term rates for the time period. An upward-sloping yield curve will prevail if short-term rates are expected to increase in the future. The yield curve will be downward-sloping if short-term rates are expected to fall in the future.

- The liquidity preference theory holds that there is more uncertainty over the long term than the near term, so investors will demand a premium for giving up liquidity for a longer period. Therefore, the yield curve will usually be rising.

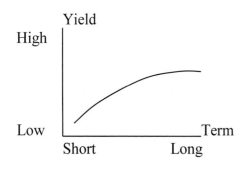

Normal Yield Curve

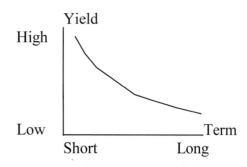

Inverted Yield Curve

Normal Yield Curve   The normal yield curve (positive yield curve) slopes upward to the right to show that the yield increases as the term to maturity becomes longer. Investors generally require greater yields to compensate them for the increased risk of the longer term to maturity. The normal yield curve typically has a slight upward slope. A steep upward slope (as the spread between short-term and long-term rates gets wider) is thought to predict a rapidly approaching expansionary period in the economy.

Inverted Yield Curve   An inverted yield curve (negative yield curve) will slope down to the right to show that the yield is higher for short-term maturities than for longer maturities. An inverted yield curve usually occurs when the Fed has raised short-term interest rates to restrain inflation and to cool an overstimulated economy. The inverted yield curve is usually associated with a peak in the business cycle, and is thought to predict an upcoming recession.

Promissory Notes

Promissory notes are documents signed by a borrower promising to repay a loan under stipulated terms. They can be short or long in duration but have no backing of assets behind them as security.

Taxation of Discount and Premium Bonds

Taxpayers who buy OID (original issue discount) bonds and zero-coupon bonds at a discount will receive more than what they paid for the bonds when they mature and will have to pay taxes on a pro-rata amount each year they hold the bond. This imputed interest will increase the client's basis in the asset and reduce the capital gain on the sale of the asset.

On the other hand, if a taxpayer pays a premium for a bond, he or she has the option of amortizing the bond premium over the years remaining until maturity or including the bond premium as part of basis.

Individual Stocks

Common Stock

Common stock is an equity security that represents the residual ownership interest in a corporation. When it comes to sharing in the earnings of the firm or its assets in a liquidation, common stockholders are the lowest in order of priority, behind creditors and preferred stockholders. Common stock usually has a par value that is significant only for accounting purposes. The book value per share, in contrast, is the difference between the firm's total assets and total liabilities, divided by the number of shares.

As residual owners, common stockholders bear most of the risks of the business, with no legal claim to dividends and possible loss of their entire investment. Offsetting these disadvantages are the right to vote for the board of directors (for most investors, this is done by proxy), the preemptive right to buy into new issues of common to retain their proportionate voting control, and the right to reap most of the rewards if the firm is successful (those rewards taking the form of dividends and capital appreciation).

Classifying Common Stock

Common stocks of companies whose earnings have consistently grown at a significantly higher rate than average and where the company is expected to continue experiencing consistently high growth rates are known as *growth stocks*. Some growth stocks rate as blue-chip stocks (very large, highly reputable companies), while other growth stocks are highly speculative. Growth stocks typically pay little or no dividends. Low payout ratios are typically designed to facilitate reinvestment of earnings to finance growth. The major source of investor return is market price appreciation. It is generally agreed that growth stocks represent greater risk for the investor than would an investment in income stocks. Of course, growth stocks may offer a higher expected return.

An *income stock* is one that is attractive principally because it offers a relatively high dividend yield and a record of regular payment of dividends. Such stocks appeal to an investor who seeks a relatively safe and high level of current income. Dividends can be expected to increase over time, unlike fixed-income securities, such as bonds or preferred stock. Several electric light and power companies fit in this group, for example.

Earnings of *cyclical stocks* tend to vary widely over the course of a business cycle. Naturally, the market prices of such stocks also vary widely over the business cycle. Producers and processors of basic metals are exposed to cyclical fluctuations in earnings, as are automobile manufacturers, steel companies, and machine tool companies. Such stocks are generally marketable, but most investors would not consider cyclical stocks liquid because to realize cash, a substantial capital loss may have to be taken in recession years. In 1932, for example, the common stocks of many blue-chip cyclical companies were poor sources of liquidity.

Defensive stocks are stocks that are affected less by downswings in the business cycle than is the average stock, and for this reason, they are sought by the defensive investor. Defensive shares are a shelter from adverse economic periods. Defensive stocks include utilities, banks, and food companies (for example, Coca Cola). Defensive stocks have little market risk, but those stocks classified as defensive, by reason of their regularly paying dividends, will have some interest rate risk.

Blue-chip stocks are high-quality stocks that have a long and stable record of earnings and dividends. Blue-chips are attractive to investors who seek quality investments, offering respectable dividend yields and modest growth potential. Investors buy blue-chips as long-term investments because of their relatively low level of business risk, reasonable liquidity, and excellent marketability. However, severe market declines that have occurred on particular days in the last few years demonstrate some degree of market risk even for blue-chip stocks.

Speculative stocks are issued by companies that lack proven records of operations success, and earnings are uncertain and unstable. Generally, few or no dividends are paid by these companies, and prices for their stocks can swing widely. Speculative stocks are purchased as investors seek capital gains on a short-term basis.

Such stocks have high market risk and poor liquidity. Many high-tech and dot-com stocks fall into this category.

Preferred Stock

Preferred stock has the following basic characteristics:

- It is a fixed-income security (pays a dividend often stated as a percentage of par, usually the dividends do not increase).

- It can sell at a premium if interest rates are low or at a discount when interest rates are high, much like bonds. The market price for preferred stock is usually more volatile than prices of long term bonds, possibly because preferred stock is an equity investment and may be viewed as riskier.

- It is a perpetuity (no maturity date).

- It is an equity security, but with a prior claim to income and assets ahead of the common stock.

- Failure to pay the preferred is not a default (unless the firm pays a dividend on the common stock).

- It has a claim to income and assets that is junior to all creditors.

- It may be cumulative. (Unpaid dividends are carried over and must be paid in full before any dividend may be paid on the common stock.)

- It may be convertible to common.

- It may have a sinking fund provision.

- It may be participating. (Preferred receives its stated dividend plus a share of the dividends scheduled to be paid to the common stockholders.)

- For corporations that own at least 20% of a dividend-paying company, a dividends received deduction allows 65% of the dividends to be received tax free. For corporations that own less than 20%, the dividends received deduction is 50%.

- Currently, the majority of dividends received from preferred stock are taxed at ordinary income rates.

- Qualifying dividends on preferred and common stock paid to individuals are taxed at the same rate as long-term capital gains, with a maximum of 15% for most taxpayers (20% for taxpayers above certain income thresholds).

Practice Question

Which of the following statements comparing preferred stock and bonds is not correct?

    A. Bonds have a shorter duration than preferred stock.
    B. Both bonds and preferred stock pay a fixed rate of income.
    C. Both bonds and preferred stock may be convertible to common stock of the issuing company.
    D. Distributions on bonds and preferred stock are always deductible by the corporation paying them.

Answer:
Bonds have a fixed maturity, while preferred stock has a perpetual existence. Both bonds and preferred stock pay a fixed rate of income. Both may be convertible. Distributions on bonds are deductible interest, but dividends on preferred stock may or may not be deductible.
The answer is D.

American Depositary Receipts (ADRs)

Investing in foreign securities can add diversification to a portfolio, as long as the returns on those securities are not perfectly positively correlated with those of the domestic stocks in the portfolio. However, differences in terminology and business and accounting practices in some foreign countries add some complexity to the investing process. Also complicating the process is exchange rate risk, the possibility of loss due to adverse fluctuations in the value of the foreign currency versus the U.S. dollar. For example, if the Thai baht falls in value against the dollar (that is, if the dollar strengthens), the bahts produced by an investment in Thailand will buy fewer dollars than formerly, so the U.S. investor's rate of return will fall below its nominal rate of return measured in Thai bahts.

Instead of buying foreign securities directly or through a mutual fund, an investor can obtain American Depositary Receipts (ADRs). These receipts are issued by a bank in a foreign country, representing an ownership interest in foreign securities on deposit at the bank. The bank collects the income from the securities, converts it into dollars, and pays dollars to the ADR holders.

ADRs are a way for domestic investors to invest in non-U.S. companies without going into a foreign market.

Pooled and Managed Investments

Exchange-Traded Funds

Exchange-traded funds are index-type shares that offer investors the ability to invest in a basket of stocks that mirror closely an underlying benchmark index (for example, NASDAQ 100). They trade daily just like stock shares and, unlike mutual funds whose net asset value (NAV) is calculated at day's end, are priced in real time throughout the trading day.

How they operate. Specialists (usually AMEX-based) create and redeem exchange-traded shares based upon the demand and supply factors. When an index basket of stocks changes, the exchange-traded funds may sell off shares to match that change. Because of the relative infrequency of this occurring, exchange-traded funds are thought to be extremely tax-efficient.

Types. Exchange-traded funds come in different forms. Domestic exchange-traded funds, known as SPDRs (Standard & Poor's Depositary Receipts), trade on the NYSE Amex Equities, NYSE Arca Exchange, NYSE, Nasdaq, and represent ownership in a unit investment trust comprised of stocks in the underlying index. SPDRs trade as 1/10th the value of the S&P 500. DIAMONDS (Dow Jones Industrial Monthly Dividend Series) trade as 1/100th of the DJIA's quotation. Sector choices are also available.

Exchange-traded funds pricing is kept fairly stable through the arbitrage pricing mechanism, helping minimize large premiums or discounts to NAV. They offer style consistency, minimum costs, and tax-efficiency. For these reasons, exchange-traded funds are steadily becoming more popular and may represent a challenge to traditional index-type funds.

Exchange-traded funds can be bought on margin and can be sold on a "downtick" (at a price lower than that of the last transaction price).

Unit Investment Trust

A unit investment trust (UIT) is an investment company formed under a trust document to administer specified assets. The unit trust maintains a fixed portfolio of assets that does not change, so active management by an investment adviser is not required. Investors in a unit investment trust may sell their interest back to the trust at net asset value. The secondary market for units is typically not active. The portfolio of the trust is self-liquidating, as the trust distributes cash rather than reinvesting the funds.

Mutual Fund (Open-End Investment Company)

The largest and by far the most important type of investment company is the open-end company, also called a mutual fund. These companies offer shares for sale continuously and agree to buy back or redeem shares at their net asset values. The net asset value of a share in an investment company is calculated at the end of each trading day by determining the total value of the investment securities in the investment portfolio, subtracting the liabilities, and then dividing the result by the total number of shares outstanding. Shares redeemed receive the NAV calculated at the end of the trading day, so the actual redemption price is not known at the time the order is placed. An open-end investment company often actively manages the portfolio and charges investors a fee to cover the cost of the professional management.

Investment companies, and particularly mutual funds, provide a number of advantages for individual investors: professional management, diversification, liquidity, record-keeping services, and brokerage commission savings. On the other hand, there are certain disadvantages associated with mutual funds, notably the fees that are involved. No-load funds do not charge a sales fee, while load funds do, with these ranging as high as 8.5%. The sales fee is expressed as a percentage of the offering price, as opposed to the net asset value. Some funds charge a back-end load instead of a front-end load.

Then, too, all funds, both closed- and open-end, have operating expenses, such as management fees, administrative fees, investment advisory fees, and 12b-1 fees. The 12b-1 fee is a charge to cover the costs of marketing and distributing the shares. Many of these fees are not directly visible on the shareholder's account statement, but are instead reflected in the fund's rate of return.

Types of Mutual Funds

There are dozens of different kinds of funds based on different investment objectives. The following are some of the common mutual fund objectives:

A *growth fund* has an investment objective of high capital appreciation, with little or no emphasis given to dividend yield. Securities are selected for the investment portfolio based upon their growth potential. This means the fund invests mainly in the common stocks of growth companies.

Income mutual funds seek securities that produce an above-average current annual return. Safety of principal is emphasized, so the investment risk is usually minimal. They provide the investor with both good marketability and good liquidity.

Growth-and-income funds generally are more conservative than growth funds and are likely to acquire growth-oriented blue-chip stocks that pay dependable dividends. The stated investment objective is typically to obtain both reasonable dividend income and reasonable prospects for market price appreciation. The emphasis, though, is on capital gain.

Balanced funds seek to allocate investments so that the portfolio is spread among equity and debt securities. Portions of the fund's assets typically are invested in common stock, preferred stock, bonds, and cash. This is a defensive approach to investing, with an emphasis on capital growth and income stability.

A *tax-exempt fund* invests exclusively in tax-free municipal securities. The objective is to provide an investment that will appeal to the investor in a high marginal income tax bracket.

Money market funds are no-load mutual funds that invest in short-term money market instruments. The money market is where short-term instruments or securities are bought and sold. Money market instruments include U.S. government short-term obligations, negotiable bank certificates of deposit, and commercial paper (short-term debt of large, stable corporations). Money market funds have low investment risk and excellent marketability and liquidity. Obviously, yields on money market mutual funds depend on the short-term money market rates existing at the time the money market fund acquires its short-term assets. The vast majority of money market mutual funds for individual investors are designed to maintain a stable net asset value (NAV) of $1. However, as of October 14, 2016, new SEC rules require funds for institutional investors to use a floating NAV, which can result in price fluctuations.

A *mortgage-backed securities fund* invests exclusively in mortgage-backed securities (GNMAs and Freddie Macs). These fund shares are attractive to investors seeking stable income and low risk for the principal sum.

A *sector fund* is a fund that specializes in a particular industry, such as drug companies or biotechnology firms. A sector fund tries to put its money "where the action is." Examples of sector funds include "travel and leisure" funds and "biotechnology" funds.

An *index fund* attempts merely to equal the overall return that would be achieved by investing in the securities comprising some well-known market index, such as the S&P 500. For example, the fund could invest the same proportion of its money in each of the S&P 500 stocks that each represents of the total value of the 500 stocks.

Index funds are popular because of their comparatively low management fees versus actively-managed mutual funds.

When an investor is considering putting money into a mutual fund, he or she should first define his or her investment objectives and select the fund that meets those objectives. Having done so, other factors to consider are the past performance of the fund, the riskiness of its portfolio, the continuity of the fund's management, the fees and expenses that will be charged to the investor, and the services offered by the fund.

Mutual Fund Prospectus

The mutual fund prospectus is the document that provides the investor with all of the information he or she would need to make an informed decision regarding purchase of the fund. The prospectus includes a vast amount of information, including:

- The fund's investment objectives or goals (and strategies for achieving those goals)
- The principal risks of investing in the fund
- The fund's fees and expenses
- The fund's past performance (including year-to-date, 1-year, 3-year, 5-year, 10-year, and since inception)
- Information relating to the fund's investment advisers and portfolio managers
- Details on how to purchase and redeem shares

A mutual fund prospectus must be delivered to the client at or before the confirmation of sale (**note:** the same delivery requirement also applies to variable life and variable annuities). Registered representatives are prohibited from writing in, circling information, or highlighting any particular information in the prospectus.

Practice Question

Which one of the following statements is true of open-end investment companies?

A. The investment portfolio may be actively managed.
B. Shares may be bought and sold in the secondary market.
C. Purchases will include sales charges and broker commissions.
D. The number of shares that can be offered for sale is generally fixed.

Answer:
Open-end investment company shares are not bought or sold in the secondary market. They are issued and redeemed only by the fund

itself. Purchases do not include broker commissions, only sales charges. The number of shares offered for sale is not fixed because each sale is a new offer. The investment portfolio may be actively managed.

The answer is A.

Closed-End Investment Companies

A closed-end investment company is a fund that, in contrast with open-end funds, sells only a fixed number of shares. The fund makes a stock offering much like a public offering for a corporation, and then the capitalization for the issue is complete or "closed." The fund does not continue to offer more shares, and it does not redeem shares. The shares of some closed-end investment companies are actively traded in the major security markets, where their prices are determined, not by the company's net asset value, but, rather, by the forces of demand and supply. The shares may sell above (at a premium) or below (at a discount to) the net asset value. A closed-end investment company actively manages the portfolio.

Taxation of Investment Companies

Closed-end and open-end investment companies distribute the capital gains, dividends, and interest received from the securities in their investment portfolio. The investment company is a pipeline for passing investment income to shareholders, so the shareholders report the capital gains, dividends, and interest on their individual returns. Each item of income retains its characteristics and holding period when distributed to shareholders, so long-term capital gains will be reported by the shareholder as long-term capital gains, qualifying dividends will continue to be qualifying dividends in the hands of the shareholders, and tax free interest will be tax free to the shareholder.

> ### 🔑 KEY SUMMARY 33 – 1
> #### Investment Companies

	Unit Investment Trust	Open-End Investment Company	Closed-End Investment Company
Common name	Unit trust	Mutual fund	Publicly traded fund
Capitalization	Fixed	Constantly changing	Fixed
Management of investments	Passive; portfolio is fixed	Active; portfolio changes	Active; portfolio changes
Purchases	Units offered by trust require a prospectus	Prospectus required; each sale is an offering by the fund	After initial offering, buying on exchanges through a broker does not require a prospectus
Sales	Units are redeemable with a trust at NAV	Shares are redeemed by a fund at NAV, no trading on exchanges	Shares trade on exchanges above or below NAV; shares are not redeemable
Transaction costs	Sales charges by fund	Sales charges by fund	Commission to broker

Index Securities

A portfolio of securities can be selected to mirror the performance of a particular index. The employment of an index fund is part of a passive investment strategy seeking returns and risk characteristics similar to the index. For example, the Vanguard 500 Fund is a mutual fund index of securities. Due to the cost of operating the funds, index funds tend to return slightly less than the index.

Privately Managed Accounts

Privately managed accounts are an alternative to mutual funds for an investor wanting a diversified portfolio of stocks. Similar to mutual funds, the investment firm running the privately managed account will have an investment objective such as long-term appreciation or current income. The account manager will select the most appropriate stocks and/or bonds to meet this investment objective. The account manager is also responsible for making all buy and sell decisions within the account. The main advantage of the privately managed account is that the investor actually owns the underlying shares of stock rather than shares of a mutual fund. The main disadvantages are typically the higher minimum investment required to participate in such an account (which can be $100,000 or higher) and potentially higher investment advisor fees.

Separately Managed Accounts

A separately managed account provides an investor with even more options or control compared to a privately managed account. With a separately managed account, the account manager selects stocks to meet the individual client's investment goals and preferences. For example, if the investor's father died from lung cancer after smoking three packs a day, the investment manager can exclude tobacco stocks from the account.

Similar to privately managed accounts, the main advantage of separately managed accounts is that the investor actually owns the underlying shares of stock rather than shares of a mutual fund. The main disadvantages are also the same with the higher minimum investment required to participate in such an account (which can be $100,000 or higher) and potentially higher investment advisor fees.

Guaranteed Investment Contracts (GICs)

A guaranteed investment contract (GIC) is a contract typically issued by an insurance company that guarantees that the principal will be repaid and interest will be paid as required under the terms of the contract for a set period of time. Due to the decreased risk of failure to pay the interest, GICs typically pay a lower interest rate than bonds; however, the rate is typically higher than money market instruments. GICs may also be referred to as stable value funds, and are frequently offered as an investment selection in retirement plans. Since the guarantees in a GIC are backed by an insurance company, it is a good idea to periodically check the financial stability rating of the company issuing the guarantee.

Derivative Investments

Derivative investments are contracts whose value is derived from another underlying security, index, interest rate, commodity, or financial asset. Derivative investments include options, futures, and warrants.

Options

An option is a contract between two parties (a buyer and a seller) which allows the buyer a set period of time during which to exercise the option to either buy or sell a stock, commodity, or financial instrument. If the buyer of the option chooses to exercise, the seller is then obligated to fulfill his promise to either buy or sell according to the contract. The buyer of the option benefits from having time to experience what is actually happening to the underlying security before making a decision. Because there is value associated with this opportunity, the buyer (holder) of the option must pay a premium to the seller (writer) of the option to compensate him for taking on the risk of being obligated to fulfill the contract at a later date. In this textbook we will focus primarily on options for the purchase or sale of a stock.

The decision to enter into an options contract can speculation (the client has not yet taken a position in is speculating that the price will increase, decrease, or remain unchanged), or can be based on a desire to either protect an existing stock position or add income to a portfolio during a period when the stock price of an existing position is expected to remain flat.

At any given time while the option contract exists, the holder of the option has 3 choices: to exercise the option, to sell the option to another investor, or to allow the option to expire with no action taken.

A Put is an Option to Sell

An investor who buys a put option will have a choice to exercise the option or to allow it to expire without exercise. A put is an option to sell a specified number of shares during a specified period at a specified price. **The investor who buys a put will profit if the underlying stock declines in price.** After the market price declines below the price specified in the put, the investor can profit by buying the stock in the market. The investor will buy at the lower market price and sell that stock at the higher price specified in the put. The writer (seller) of the put is obligated to buy the stock at the higher specified price. The investor will have a gain that is the difference between the price paid for the stock and the higher specified price of the put.

Example:

An investor buys a put option on XYZ Company stock with an exercise (strike) price of $50 per share. The investor pays a premium of $2 per share for the put, or a total of $200.

If the price for XYZ Company stock falls to $35 per share, the buyer of the option will purchase the stock at $35 and then exercise the option to sell the stock (will "put it to" the seller of the option) at $50 per share.

Alternatively, an investor can buy a put for protection when the investor already owns the underlying stock. The investor may have a gain in the stock but is worried about the price of the stock dropping. An investor can use a put to offset the loss because a drop in the stock price will increase the value of the put. When a stock price drops below the specified price of a put option, the put option will increase in value to the same extent as the stock drops in value. The gains from the put option provide an offset to the loss on the underlying stock, so the investor is provided with protection against the price drop of the stock. If the buyer of the put option no longer desires to hold the stock, he could also choose to exercise the option and sell at the exercise price.

The investor who is a buyer or holder of a put will benefit when the underlying stock price drops, so a buyer of a put is said to be bearish. The seller or writer of the put option will benefit when the price of the underlying stock remains steady or rises. If the stock price rises, the seller will have received the buyer's payment for the option, the option will expire worthless, and the seller has no further obligation.

A Call is an Option to Buy

A call is an option to <u>buy</u> a specified number of shares during a specified period at a specified price. **The investor who buys a call will profit if the underlying stock rises in price.** After the price rises above the specified price in the call, the investor can exercise the option and buy the stock at the specified price. Since the specified price is below the market price, the investor can immediately sell the stock for a gain.

Example:

An investor buys a call option on BCD Company stock with an exercise (strike) price of $40 per share. The investor pays a premium of $1 per share for the call, or a total of $100.

If the price for BCD Company stock rises to $50 per share, the buyer of the option will exercise the option to buy the stock (will "call it to" himself) at $40 per share, then sell it in the market at $50 per share.

The investor who is a buyer or holder of a call option benefits when the underlying stock price rises, so a buyer of a call is said to be bullish. The seller or writer of the call option will benefit when the price of the underlying stock remains steady or declines. The seller will then have received the buyer's payment for the option, the option will expire worthless, and the seller has no further obligation.

Options Vocabulary

Some terms you need to know in connection with options:

- The buyer of an option may be referred to as the buyer, the holder, or the long position. The buyer has the right to choose whether to exercise the option.

- The seller of an option may be referred to as the seller, the writer, or the short position. If the buyer chooses to exercise the option, the seller must either buy (put option) or sell (call option) at the strike price.

- Strike price (also called exercise price) – the price specified in the option at which the stock may be bought or sold.

- Expiration date – the last date on which the option may be exercised (European-style options can be exercised only on the expiration date, unlike American-style options, which can be exercised at any time prior to expiration).

- Premium – the price paid by the buyer to the writer of a put or call option. Premium = intrinsic value + time value.

- Intrinsic value – the difference between the market price of the stock and the exercise price of the option. It is determined from the viewpoint of the holder of the option, and is never less than zero. Intrinsic value will be positive if the option is "in the money," meaning there is immediate gain to be made by buying or selling the stock at a bargain price relative to the market price (ignoring the premium paid for the option).

- Time value – the excess of the premium over the intrinsic value. It declines to zero as the expiration date approaches because there is less time for price volatility.

- "In the money" means that the exercise price is below (call) or above (put) the market price of the underlying stock. In other words, intrinsic value is greater than zero.

- "Out of the money" means that the exercise price is above (call) or below (put) the market price of the underlying stock.

- "At the money" is when the exercise price of either a call or a put option is equal to the market price of the underlying stock.

- A naked call is a call option written by an investor who does not own the underlying security on which the call is written. If the writer owns the underlying security, it is a covered call. The covered call is a much less risky strategy for the call writer than a naked call.

- A naked put is a put option written by an investor who does not hold an offsetting short position in the underlying security.

Practice Question

IBM September calls with an exercise price of $87 are selling for $4 per share. IBM shares are selling for $90 per share. Which of the following statements are correct?

(1) The intrinsic value of the call is $4 per share.
(2) The intrinsic value of the call is $3 per share.
(3) The time value of the call is $1 per share.
(4) The time value of the call is $0 per share.

    A. (1) and (3) only
    B. (2) and (4) only
    C. (2) and (3) only
    D. (1) and (4) only

Answer:
The intrinsic value of the call is the difference between the market price of $90 and the exercise price of $87, or $3 per share. The time value is the difference between the selling price of the call and the intrinsic value, or $1 per share.
The answer is C.

Option Exchanges

Options may be exercised, expire worthless, or be sold in the secondary market. Options are traded on a continuous basis, and most options are traded on major exchanges, including the American Stock Exchange (NYSE AMEX), Chicago Board Options Exchange (CBOE), NASDAQ Philadelphia Stock Exchange (PHLX), and New York Stock Exchange (NYSE Arca Options). The option exchanges own the Options Clearing Corporation (OCC), where option transactions are cleared. The OCC guarantees option contract delivery should an option writer default.

Option Contracts

Option contracts are sold in 100-share increments. Each contract gives the holder the right, but not the obligation, to purchase or sell 100 shares. Twenty-five contracts would give the buyer or seller access to 2,500 shares of the underlying stock. A call option gives the owner the right to purchase (at the exercise price), and a put option gives the owner the right to sell an underlying security for the exercise price within a predetermined period.

An investor who buys an option is not entitled to the dividends paid on the underlying stock, and the investor does not become entitled to the stock's voting rights.

An investor who buys a call is optimistic about the future price of a security, and an investor who buys a put is pessimistic. An investor who writes a call is pessimistic about the price for a security, and an investor who writes a put is optimistic.

EXHIBIT 33 – 1 **Buying or Selling Options**		
	Put	**Call**
If investor expects market price to rise:	Sell (write)	Buy (hold)
If investor expects market price to fall:	Buy (hold)	Sell (write)

Leverage with Options

Options afford investors a way to leverage an investment because an investor can control a large amount of value in stock for a relatively small amount of money. With just the payment of the small premiums for call options, an investor buys the right to future gains from the underlying stock. The gains that the investor earns can be multiplied many times over the gains that could be earned by investing in the stock. For example, if a stock sells for $100 per share an investor can buy 100 shares for $10,000. The call option for the same stock may be only $5 per share. For the same $10,000, another investor can buy options on 2,000 shares. If the stock increases in price by $7 per share, the investor who bought the 100 shares of stock will have a gain of $700. The investor who bought the call options on 2,000 shares would have a gain of $14,000. The leverage is 20 to 1.

The risk of trading options is that the leverage works to enlarge both the gains and the losses. In our example, if the stock declines by $1 per share, the investor who bought 100 shares will lose only $100. The investor who bought options in 2,000 shares will lose his entire investment of $10,000. The risk for the investor in options is accentuated by the limited amount of time the holder has for achieving a gain.

Valuing an Option

Options are usually bought and sold without ever being exercised, and they have a value defined by: (a) the relationship between their exercise price and market price, (b) the underlying stock's volatility, and (c) the time until expiration.

Break-Even Price

The intrinsic value of an option is not the same thing as profit because it does not factor in the premium. For a call option, the break-even price will be the strike price plus the premium amount. For example, if the strike price on a call option is $35 and the premium is $4, the break-even price will be $39. For a put option, the break-even price is the strike price minus the premium amount. For example, if the strike price is $28 and the premium is $3, then the break-even price will be $25.

Maximum Potential Gain and Loss

Since the buyer of the option has the right to choose whether to exercise, the buyer's maximum potential loss with an option is limited to the cost of the premium. The maximum potential for profit can be quite large. For the buyer of a call option, profits will increase as the price of the stock rises, so the maximum potential gain is unlimited. For the buyer of a put option, profits will rise as the price of the stock falls, and the maximum potential gain will occur when the stock price falls to zero. If the strike price is $28 and the premium to purchase the option is $3, then the maximum potential gain is $25. The buyer of the put is in the money when the stock price goes below the strike price; however, the price must go down by $3 in order to cover the cost of the premium paid to purchase the option. The remaining $25 that the price could drop is the maximum potential gain. Since $25 is the price at which the buyer of the put will break even, we can say that the buyer's maximum potential gain will be equal to the break-even price. The break-even price is the exercise (or strike) price less the premium paid.

Writers of options are interested in income and believe that a stable, less volatile market will make it likely that the option will not be exercised. A seller's gains are restricted to the size of the premium, but the losses can be very large. Any gain for the buyer of the option will result in a loss for the seller of the option; therefore, the maximum potential loss for the writer of a call option is unlimited, and the maximum potential loss for the writer of a put option is equal to the break-even price.

Long Call Strategy

When an investor buys a call option, the investor will profit in a rising market and is pursuing a "bullish" strategy. The buyer or holder of a call is long for the call, and the seller or writer is short for the call. The long call strategy offers the investor an unlimited potential for gain. The only downside risk for the buyer is the premium paid for the call option.

Example:

An investor buys a call option on ABC Company stock, with an exercise (strike) price of $60 per share. The current price of ABC Company stock is $61. The investor pays a premium of $4 per share for the call, or a total of $400. The intrinsic value of the option is only $1 per share because the market price is $1 above the exercise price. The remaining cost of the option is the time value of the option.

If the price for ABC Company stock rises above $64 per share, the investor will profit by exercising the call option at $60 per share. The investor has the right to buy the stock from the call writer at $60 per share. The breakeven point is $64, which is the exercise price plus the premium. The investor has an unlimited potential for gain because the investor achieves more and more profit as the price for ABC stock rises above $64 per share.

If the price for ABC stock falls below $60 per share, the investor will not exercise the option, and the investor has lost the amount of the premium paid for the call. The investor can lose no more than the amount of the premium, even if the stock goes to zero.

If the price of ABC stock is between $60 and $64 per share at the time the call option expires, the investor should exercise the option (or sell it) to offset a portion of the premium cost.

REMEMBER: *THE INTRINSIC VALUE OF AN OPTION WILL NEVER FALL BELOW ZERO. THE OPTION BUYER CAN NEVER LOSE MORE THAN THE PREMIUM.*

Long Put Strategy

When an investor buys a put option, the investor will profit in a falling market and is pursuing a "bearish" strategy. The investor who buys a put is long for the put, and the seller or writer is short for the put. The long put strategy offers the investor a potential for gain that will be the difference between the break-even price and the market price. The only downside risk for the buyer of the put is the premium paid for the put option.

Example:

An investor buys a put option on ABC Company stock with an exercise (strike) price of $62 per share. The current price of ABC Company stock is $61. The investor pays a premium of $4 per share for the put, or a total of $400. The intrinsic value of the option is only $1 per share because the market price is $1 below the exercise price. The remaining cost of the option is the time value of the option.

If the price for ABC Company stock falls below $58 per share, the investor will profit by exercising the put option at $62 per share. The investor exercises the right to sell the shares to the put writer at $62 per share. The breakeven point is $58, which is the exercise price less the premium. The investor's maximum potential gain will result from the ABC stock price dropping to zero. Then, the gain will be the exercise price of $62 per share less the premium paid.

If the price of ABC stock is between $58 and $62 per share at the time the put option expires, the investor should exercise the option (or sell it before expiration) to offset a portion of the premium cost.

EXHIBIT 33 – 2
Wins and Losses with Options

	Breakeven	*Max. Gain*	*Max. Loss*
Buy a Call	Exercise price + Premium	Unlimited	Premium
Sell a Call	Exercise price + Premium	Premium	Unlimited
Buy a Put	Exercise price – Premium	Exercise price – Premium (if stock price is zero)	Premium
Sell a Put	Exercise price – Premium	Premium	Exercise price – Premium (if stock price is zero)

☞ *K Study Tip* – **The "breakeven point" for a call option is the exercise price plus the premium. The option is "in the money" as soon as the market price is above the exercise price, even though it is not yet at the "breakeven point."**

	KEY SUMMARY 33 – 2 Options	
	Call	**Put**
Reason to buy (hold)	Greed – Buyer is bullish; expects rise in stock price.	Fear – Buyer is bearish; expects drop in stock price.
Reason to sell (write)	Writer expects stock price will not rise – writer is neutral or bearish. Writer receives premium income.	Writer expects stock price will not drop – writer is neutral or bullish. Writer receives premium income.
Potential gain for holder	Unlimited in bull market.	In bear market, difference between market price and exercise price less premium.
Potential gain for writer	Premium.	Premium.
Potential loss for holder	Premium.	Premium.
Potential loss for writer	Unlimited in bull market.	In bear market, difference between market price and exercise price less premium.

Index Options

Put and call options are also available on various stock indices, such as the S&P 500, allowing investors to speculate or to hedge portfolios based on broad market (or market sector) movements rather than a specific stock. When an index option is settled, the settlement is in cash (based on the change in value of the underlying index), relieving the writer from the obligation to purchase or sell every underlying security in the index.

Combining Options

Investors have used options in various combinations as part of an investment strategy. Some of the more common combinations are spreads, and straddles. Strategies in which a combination of an option (or options) and an existing stock position in the portfolio are used for protection or to produce additional portfolio income are discussed in Topic 40.

Spread

A spread is the combination of two or more of the same kind of options in one transaction, such as the simultaneous purchase and sale of two calls or the simultaneous purchase and sale of two puts. The options may have different exercise prices and may expire on different dates.

Straddle

A straddle occurs when an investor combines a put option and a call option on the same stock, with both options having the same strike price and date of expiration. Anticipation of a very volatile market is conducive to owning a straddle. An investor would sell a straddle when anticipating a market with little volatility.

Long-Term Equity Anticipation Securities (LEAPS®)

Investors are most familiar with short-term options, which have from three- to nine-month terms to expiration. Another type of option is the long-term equity anticipation (LEAP) option, which has a maturity of up to three years. LEAPs operate in a manner similar to short-term options but are restricted to a much smaller number of stock selections. There are two principal types of LEAPs: Equity LEAPs and Index LEAPs. LEAPs are often used to provide investors with a long-term hedge.

Be aware that American-style options are exercisable at any time during their term, while European-style options may be exercised only on their expiration date.

Taxation of Options

The writer of an option does not report taxable income at the time the option is written and the premium paid. The writer has taxable income only when the option is exercised, lapses, or is closed out. If the option is not exercised, the writer has capital gain on the date of the lapse. The gain will be short-term capital gain, which is taxed as ordinary income, unless the option is a LEAP of more than 12 months.

Call Writer:
Capital Gain = Exercise Price + Premium – Basis

If a call option is exercised, the buyer adds the premium cost to the exercise price plus the commissions to determine the buyer's basis in the stock. The holding period for the stock begins after the option is exercised. The writer of the call option will report capital gain that is the difference between the exercise price and his or her adjusted basis in the stock. The writer will add the call premium received to the sale proceeds.

Example:

An investor purchased 100 shares of ABC Company stock for $45 per share. Ten months later, the investor wrote a call for the 100 shares at $60 per share. The investor received a premium of $4 per share. The call is exercised 9 months later.

The writer recognizes long-term capital gain that is calculated as the exercise price of $6,000, plus the premium of $400, less the basis of $4,500, or a gain of $1,900.

The holder (buyer) will have a basis in the ABC stock of the exercise price $6,000 plus the premium of $400.

Put Buyer:
Capital Gain = Exercise
Price – Premium – Basis

If a put option is exercised, the writer is obligated to purchase the underlying stock from the owner and takes a basis that is the exercise price less the put premium received. The holder who exercises the put option sells the underlying stock and reports a gain that is the exercise price less the put premium paid and less the investor's adjusted basis.

Example:

An investor purchased 100 shares of ABC Company stock for $45 per share. Ten months later, the investor bought a put option for 100 shares of ABC Company stock at a premium of $4 per share. The exercise price was $62 per share. The investor exercised the put four months later when ABC stock was selling at $55 per share.

The holder (buyer) of the put sold the ABC stock and will report a capital gain of $6,200 less the $400 premium and the cost basis of $4,500, for a total long-term capital gain of $1,300.

The writer (seller) of the put purchased ABC stock and will have a basis that is the exercise price of $6,200 less the $400 premium received, for a total of $5,800.

Futures, Warrants, and Rights

Futures Contracts

Futures contracts are commitments to buy or sell a specified amount of a commodity, financial instrument, or currency at a specified future date at a specified future price. They are bought through brokerage houses, and a clearinghouse guarantees the fulfillment of the contract. The contract is fulfilled either by taking or delivering the physical subject matter or by making an offsetting or opposite transaction (for example, by entering a short position to offset a long position). By becoming both a buyer and seller in the same contract, the investor has closed the position.

Futures contracts may be used as a form of hedging. With a long hedge, an investor who is short the underlying commodity will take a long position in the futures contract. For example, in the spring of the year a baker may use a long hedge to help protect against adverse changes in the price of wheat between the spring of the year and in the fall when the wheat is harvested and the baker needs to purchase wheat. The wheat farmer may use a short hedge to help protect against adverse price changes. He is long on the wheat when he plants it in the spring and uses the short hedge to protect against

800-795-5347

adverse changes in the price of wheat between the spring of the year and in the fall when the wheat is harvested and he is ready to sell it.

Warrants

A warrant is a certificate most often attached to a bond or preferred stock, enabling the buyer to purchase a specified amount of securities at a set price (the subscription price). This right to purchase, usually above the current market price at time of issuance, can last for 2, 3, or more years. Warrants are said to be dilutive in that their exercise all at once could affect shareholder value.

As for warrants, they are similar to and different from options. Warrants give the holder the right to buy stock at a specified price. However, they are issued as a "sweetener," along with another security, usually a bond. They have long maturities and non-standardized terms, unlike options. They have an intrinsic value of not less than zero and may or may not be "in the money." If detachable, they may be bought or sold in the secondary market without buying or selling the bond to which they are attached.

Practice Question

Which of the following statements comparing call options with warrants is correct?

A. Corporations are the issuers for warrants and call options.
B. Warrants and call options typically last for 2, 3, or more years.
C. The exercise of warrants and call options will result in creation of new shares of stock.
D. The exercise price for warrants and call options is generally set above the market price at issuance.

Answer:
Corporations are the issuers of warrants, but individuals write call options. Warrants typically last for 2, 3, or more years, but call options expire generally within 9 months. The exercise of warrants will result in creation of new shares of stock, but exercise of call options does not create shares. The exercise price for warrants and call options is generally set above the market price at issuance.
The answer is D.

Rights

Unlike warrants, which have long terms to expiration, rights offerings typically expire within 30 days. Rights offerings are issued to existing shareholders when newly issued shares are created, allowing the current shareholders to purchase an additional number of shares that is proportionate to their current ownership interest in the corporation. The subscription price at which the shares can be purchased is usually below the current market price of the stock. This discount in pricing creates intrinsic value in the rights offering. A shareholder who does not wish to exercise the rights offering to purchase additional shares can sell the rights to another investor.

Alternative Assets

Alternative assets such as real estate investments, hedge funds, limited partnership interests, collateralized debt obligations, and tangible assets are discussed in Topic 41.

TOPIC 33 – APPLICATION QUESTIONS

1. Which of the following is <u>not</u> one of the advantages of owning exchange-traded funds in a well-diversified portfolio?

  A. They offer ease of trading similar to stocks.

  B. They may be shorted; therefore, investors may speculate on a downturn.

  C. Arbitrage pricing mechanisms do <u>not</u> apply, so exchange-traded funds have more stable pricing and are less volatile.

  D. Pricing is real time and is available throughout the day.

2. (Published question released December, 1996)

Which of the following best describes a debenture?

  A. A long-term corporate promissory note

  B. An investment in the debt of another corporate party

  C. A long-term corporate debt obligation with a claim against securities

  D. A corporate debt obligation that allows the holder to repurchase the security at specified dates before maturity

  E. Unsecured corporate debt

3. Which one of the following products can provide both growth and income for a moderate risk tolerance investor?

  A. Blue-chip stock fund

  B. Zero-coupon bond

  C. Aggressive growth mutual fund

  D. High Yield corporate bond fund

4. Lambda Corp. recently issued a series of callable first mortgage bonds. In which of the following situations are these bonds most likely to be called?

  (1) Interest rates in general rise sharply.

  (2) Lambda's credit rating is improved substantially by the rating agencies.

  (3) The company must fulfill a sinking fund commitment.

  A. (1) and (2) only

  B. (1) and (3) only

  C. (2) and (3) only

  D. (1), (2), and (3)

  E. Neither (1), (2), nor (3)

5. (Published question released December, 1996)

Your client is designing an educational investment program for her eight-year-old son. She expects to need the funds in about ten years, when her AGI will be approximately $45,000. She wants to invest at least part of the funds in tax-exempt securities. Identify which investment(s) would yield tax-exempt interest on her federal return if the proceeds were used to finance her son's education.

(1) Treasury bills
(2) EE bonds
(3) GNMA funds
(4) Zero-coupon Treasury bonds

    A. (3) and (4) only
    B. (1), (3), and (4) only
    C. (2) and (3) only
    D. (2) and (4) only
    E. (2) only

6. (Published question released November, 1994; updated)

Municipal bonds that are backed by the income from specific projects are known as:

A. Income bonds
B. Revenue bonds
C. General obligation bonds
D. Debenture bonds

7. (Published question released December, 1996)

Municipal bonds are frequently insured. One of the insurers is the:

A. Federal Insurance Guarantee Corporation
B. Resolution Trust Corporation
C. Associated Municipal Bond Corporation
D. Municipal Insurance Group
E. Municipal Bond Insurance Association

8. Which of the following is not a characteristic of warrants attached to bonds?

A. May have an intrinsic value
B. May be detachable from the bonds
C. Usually have long maturities
D. Written in standardized terms
E. May be "out of the money"

9. (Published question released November, 1994)

Which of the following is (are) characteristics of a municipal bond unit investment trust?

(1) Additional securities are <u>not</u> added to the trust.
(2) Shares may be sold at a premium or discount to net asset value.
(3) Shares are normally traded on the open market (exchanges).
(4) The portfolio is self-liquidating.

    A. (1) only
    B. (1) and (4) only
    C. (2) and (3) only
    D. (2) and (4) only
    E. (1), (2), (3), and (4)

10. Which of the following is a characteristic of common stock?

    A. Gives the holder the preemptive right to buy new issues of preferred stock of the company
    B. Is last in order of priority in its claim on the assets of the firm in time of liquidation
    C. Has a prior claim to dividends over preferred stockholders
    D. Gives the holder the right to vote for members of the board of directors only in person at the stockholders' annual meeting
    E. Has a par value that establishes a floor under its market price

11. Which of the following features added to a bond will generally mean a decrease in the coupon that must be offered by the issuer?

(1) Put
(2) Call
(3) Convertible
(4) Warrant

    A. (1) only
    B. (1), (3), and (4) only
    C. (2) and (4) only
    D. (1), (2), (3), and (4)

12. (Published question released November, 1994)

Which of the following types of investor benefits most from the tax advantage of preferred stocks?

    A. Government
    B. Individual
    C. Corporation
    D. Mutual funds
    E. Nonprofit institution

******

(Three published questions released January, 1999)

Match the investment characteristics listed below with the appropriate type of investment company in the items that follow:

A. Passive management of the portfolios
B. Shares of the fund are normally traded in major secondary markets
C. Both A and B
D. Neither A nor B

13. __B__ Closed-end investment companies

14. __D__ Open-end investment company

15. __A__ Unit investment trust

******

16. (Published question released November, 1994)

American Depositary Receipts (ADRs) are used to:

(1) Finance foreign exports
(2) Eliminate currency risk
(3) Sell U.S. securities in overseas markets
(4) Trade foreign securities in U.S. markets

A. (1) and (3) only
B. (1) and (4) only
C. (2) and (4) only
D. (4) only
E. (1), (2), and (4) only

17. A bond investor comes to you and asks why it may be a disadvantage to invest in individual bonds. Which of the following would be a good first response to this question?

A. Bond mutual funds are the superior alternative.
B. High-yield bonds suffer periods of large capital losses.
C. Bond index funds have essentially replaced the need for individual bond purchases.
D. Yield spreads are difficult to calculate.
E. Excessive transaction costs may pose a problem.

18. XYZ stock is selling for $53 per share, and a call option with three-month expiration may be bought for $3 per share, with a strike price of $55. This option may be said to be:

A. At the money
B. In the money
C. Without a time premium
D. Valued at fair market
E. Out of the money

19. Dan Hope has come to you asking about stock options in general. He is confused about what he has heard about puts and calls. Which of the following statements about puts and calls is not correct?

    A. Both call and put option writers receive premiums.

    B. A put writer has a positive view of future market movements.

    C. An investor who believes market prices will be stable is likely to write calls.

    D. The seller of a call or put option forfeits the premium once the exercise price has been attained.

    E. The buyer of a call option anticipates a stock price increase.

20. A long-term equity anticipation security (LEAP) may have an expiration date of no longer than:

    A. One year

    B. Two years

    C. Three years

    D. Five years

21. Janet wants to write an uncovered, or naked, call. She will succeed in making income from this strategy if:

    A. She offsets with a covered put.

    B. The price of the stock falls or remains unchanged.

    C. She increases her initial margin to lessen any sharp drop in stock price.

    D. The stock price increases beyond the cost of the premium to the buyer.

    E. She writes another call for a stock whose price she anticipates will rise sharply.

22. The intrinsic value of a put option whose exercise price is $32 at a time when the underlying stock is priced at $35 is:

    A. 3

    B. 2.5

    C. 0

    D. –3

    E. None of the above

23. George Demos bought 100 shares of General Motors stock at $30 on February 15. On December 1, the stock had risen to $38, so George wrote a 9-month call option, with an exercise price of $40. The premium was $3 per share. The call was exercised just before it expired. What gain will George report for income taxes? (Ignore commissions.)

    A. $1,000 long-term gain

    B. $1,300 short-term gain

    C. $300 short-term gain and $1,000 long-term gain

    D. $1,300 long-term gain

    E. $300 short-term gain

24. Kelly has a call option with a strike price of $30. The stock subject to the option is currently selling for $27. In this situation:

    A. The option has an intrinsic value of $3 because it is "in the money."

    B. The option has an intrinsic value of zero because it is "out of the money."

    C. The option has an intrinsic value of $3 because it is "on the money."

    D. The option has an intrinsic value of zero because it is "on the money."

    E. The option has an intrinsic value of zero because it is "in the money."

25. Campbell has a put option with a strike price of $30. The stock subject to the option is currently selling for $27. In this situation:

   A. The option has an intrinsic value of $3 because it is "in the money."

   B. The option has an intrinsic value of zero because it is "out of the money."

   C. The option has an intrinsic value of $3 because it is "on the money."

   D. The option has an intrinsic value of zero because it is "on the money."

   E. The option has an intrinsic value of zero because it is "in the money."

26. Which of the following statements concerning the writing of a call option is (are) correct?

   (1) The writer expects the price of the stock subject to the option to go down or remain unchanged.

   (2) The primary advantage of writing a call option is the revenue produced by selling the option.

   (3) Writing a naked call option presents a smaller loss potential than writing a covered call option.

   A. (2) only

   B. (3) only

   C. (1) and (2) only

   D. (2) and (3) only

   E. (1), (2), and (3)

27. Stanley writes a put for $8 with a strike price of $30. The stock has a current market price of $28. In this situation, which of the following statements is (are) correct?

   (1) Stanley's expectation is that the market price of the stock is going to plummet.

   (2) Stanley will break even if the market price of the stock settles at $22.

   (3) Stanley's maximum profit will occur if the market price of the stock reaches $30 or more.

   A. (1) only

   B. (2) only

   C. (3) only

   D. (1) and (2) only

   E. (2) and (3) only

28. (Published question released November, 1994)

   A call option with a strike price of 110 is selling for 3.50 when the market price of the underlying stock is 108. The intrinsic value of the call is:

   A. 0.00

   B. 1.50

   C. 2.00

   D. 3.50

   E. –2.00

29. (Published question released November, 1994)

With the same dollar investment, which of the following strategies can cause the investor to experience the greatest loss?

A. Selling a naked put option
B. Selling a naked call option
C. Writing a covered call
D. Buying a call option
E. Buying the underlying security

30. A Eurodollar is:

A. A U.S. dollar printed by a foreign government
B. A European currency held on deposit in a U.S. bank
C. A U.S. dollar held on deposit in a foreign bank
D. A U.S. dollar held on deposit in a European bank

31. All the following statements concerning the maturity date of bonds are correct, EXCEPT:

A. It is the date when the principal or par value is usually paid back to the investor.
B. A zero-coupon bond pays all interest at a single maturity date.
C. A serial bond may have many maturity dates on which a certain portion of the bond issue expires.
D. A bond's maturity date is a fixed date, and a bond is not callable before that date.

32. All the following statements concerning bond ratings are correct, EXCEPT:

A. They are assigned by a staff of professional bond analysts after a thorough study of the underlying company.
B. The two major rating services are Moody's and Standard and Poor's.
C. The purpose of the credit analyst's financial analysis of the bond is to assess default risk and investment quality.
D. Only those bonds that receive one of the top four ratings are considered investment-grade securities; the rest are deemed speculative.
E. Bonds rated AAA have an extremely low risk of default and are only minimally affected by interest rate risk.

33. Which of the following correctly describes accrued interest?

A. Interest accrued since the last payment of the coupon
B. Interest accrued since the bond was rerated by Moody's
C. Interest accrued since the sinking fund payment was made
D. Interest accrued since the issuer paid a dividend

34. All the following statements concerning the rights of preferred stockholders are correct, EXCEPT:

   A. In a liquidation, preferred stockholders have a claim on the corporate assets before the common stockholders, limited to a maximum of the par or stated value of the stock.

   B. The minimum dividend payment is fixed and has priority over the common dividend.

   C. The corporation is legally obligated to declare and pay the preferred dividend.

   D. Preferred stockholders normally are not given voting rights in the running of the corporation.

35. Which of the following statements correctly describe differences between preferred stock and long-term bonds?

   (1) Preferred stock is more risky for the investor than long-term bonds issued by the same company.

   (2) The market price of preferred stock fluctuates more than the market price of long-term bonds.

   (3) Long-term bonds usually have a longer maturity than preferred stock.

   (4) Preferred stock pays a fluctuating dividend, while long-term bonds pay a fixed rate of interest.

   A. (1) and (2) only

   B. (3) and (4) only

   C. (1), (2), and (4) only

   D. (2), (3), and (4) only

36. Stockholders who are entitled to recover dividends missed in prior years, as well as the right to receive the current year's dividend, are owners of which of the following type of stock?

   A. Preferred stock

   B. Cumulative preferred stock

   C. Participating preferred stock

   D. Convertible preferred stock

37. All the following statements concerning preferred stock are correct, EXCEPT:

   A. Preferred stock has an infinite life.

   B. The issuing corporation has no obligation to buy back its outstanding preferred stock.

   C. The preferred dividend rate is often stated as a percentage of par value.

   D. The preferred dividend is legally binding on the corporation and must be paid as long as earnings are sufficient to cover the required dividend.

   E. Preferred stock may be convertible into common stock.

38. Which of the following statements correctly identify a difference between bonds and preferred stock?

(1) Bond interest must be paid as promised, while a corporation is not legally required to ever pay a preferred dividend if it pays no dividend on its common stock.
(2) Preferred stockholders are paid before bondholders in the event of bankruptcy of a firm.
(3) The principal on bonds must be repaid by the issuing corporation at maturity, but an ongoing company need never repay a preferred stockholder the par of the instrument or the amount originally paid to acquire the instrument.
(4) Price fluctuations of bonds generally exceed those of preferred stock.

    A. (1) and (2) only
    B. (1) and (3) only
    C. (2) and (3) only
    D. (2) and (4) only
    E. (1), (3), and (4) only

39. Which of the following statements concerning newly issued U.S. government securities and their maturities is (are) correct?

(1) Treasury bills have maturities varying from four (4) weeks up to two (2) years.
(2) Treasury notes have maturities varying from two (2) years to ten (10) years.
(3) Treasury bonds have maturities varying from ten (10) years to thirty (30) years.

    A. (1) only
    B. (2) only
    C. (2) and (3) only
    D. (1), (2), and (3)

40. Which of the following statements concerning U.S. government Series EE bonds is (are) correct?

(1) They are actively traded in secondary markets.
(2) Their interest earnings may be free from federal income taxes.
(3) Their interest earnings are fully taxable at the state and local levels.

    A. (1) only
    B. (2) only
    C. (3) only
    D. (1) and (2) only
    E. (2) and (3) only

41. All the following statements concerning federal agency debt are correct, EXCEPT:

    A. Federal agency bonds are considered very safe.
    B. Federal agency debt is issued by federally-sponsored corporations.
    C. Federal agency bonds offer slightly higher yields than U.S. Treasury debt.
    D. Federal agency bonds are issued by and backed by the full faith and credit of the U.S. government.

42. All the following statements concerning types of municipal bonds are correct, EXCEPT:

    A. General obligation bonds are secured by the full faith and taxing authority of the issuer.

    B. Revenue bonds are only as secure as the project's ability to generate and collect revenues from its own activities.

    C. Private activity municipal bonds are issued to finance private projects that are not government operations and thus may not be tax-free.

    D. Interest as well as capital gains from buying and selling municipal bonds are tax-free.

43. Convertible bonds offer all the following features to an investor, EXCEPT:

    A. Convertible bonds permit the holder to convert bonds into common stock of the issuing company.

    B. Convertible bonds have a floor value that is their value as debt.

    C. Convertible bonds have call provisions which can be used by the issuing firm to force conversion.

    D. Investors have downside protection if the stock of the underlying company falls rapidly.

44. Which of the following statements concerning the value of convertible bonds is (are) correct?

    (1) The value of a convertible bond is related to the value of the stock into which the bonds may be converted.

    (2) The value of a convertible bond is related to the value of the bond as debt.

    A. (1) only

    B. (2) only

    C. Both (1) and (2)

    D. Neither (1) nor (2)

45. The conversion value of a convertible bond as stock depends on all the following, EXCEPT:

    A. The face value (or principal amount) of the bond

    B. The conversion price or exercise price of the bond

    C. The price of the convertible bond

    D. The market price of the common stock

46. Which of the following statements best describes the conversion ratio as it applies to a convertible bond?

    A. It is the bond price times the conversion price of the stock.

    B. It is the number of shares of stock into which the convertible bond may be converted.

    C. It is the value of the bond as if it were nonconvertible debt.

    D. It is the sum of the value as stock and the value as a bond, divided by two.

47. The investment value of a convertible bond is also called its intrinsic value (or value as debt). All the following are components of intrinsic value, EXCEPT:

A. The annual interest or coupon rate the bond pays
B. The current interest rate that is paid on comparable nonconvertible debt
C. The requirement that the principal or face value be retired at maturity
D. The price of the underlying common stock

48. Bill Camp owns an XYZ Corporation convertible bond. The bond has a 10% coupon rate paid semiannually and matures in 12 years. Comparable debt is yielding 12%. Bill's bond is convertible at $18 a share, and the current market price of XYZ common stock is $28 a share. What is the conversion value of Bill's convertible bond?

A. $504
B. $1,236
C. $1,455
D. $1,556

49. Bill Camp owns an XYZ Corporation convertible bond. The bond has a 10% coupon rate paid semiannually and matures in 12 years. Comparable debt is yielding 12%. Bill's bond is convertible at $18 a share, and the current market price of XYZ common stock is $28 a share. What is the approximate bond value of Bill's convertible bond?

A. $975
B. $875
C. $1,011
D. $1,236

50. All the following statements describe differences between convertible bonds and convertible preferred stock, EXCEPT:

A. Convertible preferred stock is traded like an equity, and bonds are not.
B. The firm is under no legal obligation to pay preferred dividends, but it must pay bond interest or go into default.
C. Bonds have a stated maturity, whereas preferred stock is perpetual.
D. Premiums are not paid for convertible preferred stock but are paid for convertible bonds.

51. Which of the following statements best describes put bonds?

A. At the firm's option, these bonds will be exercised.
B. Owners of put bonds have the option to sell the bonds back to the issuing company at market prices.
C. Like a put option on stock, the bondholder has the right to sell the bonds back to the issuer at a specified date for its principal.
D. Put bonds have more price risk than non-put bonds.

52. Assume that an investor owns a convertible bond with a 7.5% coupon rate, paid semiannually, that matures in 12 years. Comparable bonds (rating and maturity) are currently yielding 9%. The bond is convertible at $40 per share, and the current market price of the stock is $47. What is the conversion value of the bond?

A. $860
B. $1,233
C. $1,455
D. $1,175

53. Which of the following statements concerning bond pricing is correct?

    A. If the coupon rate is less than the prevailing market rate, the bond will logically be selling at a premium.

    B. As a premium bond moves closer to maturity, it increases in price toward par value.

    C. If the coupon rate is less than the prevailing market rate, the bond will logically be selling at a discount.

    D. As a discount bond moves closer to maturity, it decreases in price toward par value.

54. Which of the following statements concerning the intrinsic value of listed options is correct?

    A. The premium of a call tends to approach its intrinsic value as the option approaches its expiration date.

    B. The intrinsic value of a call sets the maximum premium for the option.

    C. The intrinsic value of a put is the difference between the market price of the underlying stock and the strike price, multiplied by 100.

    D. A call has no intrinsic value, as long as the market price of the underlying stock remains above the strike price.

55. Which of the following statements concerning the effect of leverage in option investing is correct?

    A. It magnifies both gains and losses.

    B. A small percentage change in the market price of the underlying stock will usually result in a smaller percentage change in the premium of the option.

    C. The potential leverage for an option tends to be lower than the potential leverage for the underlying stock.

    D. The greater the intrinsic value of an option, the greater its potential leverage.

56. Which of the following indicates a basic difference between warrants and calls?

    A. Warrants expire within one year; calls have a longer expiration date.

    B. Calls offer leverage potential; warrants do not.

    C. Warrants are issued by corporations; calls are issued by individuals.

    D. Calls result in the issuance of new stock when exercised; warrants result in the purchase of stock in the market when exercised.

57. Which of the following indicates a basic similarity between puts and calls?

    A. Both are issued by corporations.

    B. Both allow the investor the right to purchase the underlying security.

    C. Both are traded in secondary markets.

    D. Both usually sell below their intrinsic values.

58. Which of the following correctly describes the premium for a call?

   A. The intrinsic value of the call
   B. The market price of the call
   C. The exercise price of the stock
   D. The basis price of the stock

59. A stock sells for $60, the exercise price on the call is $64, and the premium on the call is $2. What is the intrinsic value of the call?

   A. $0
   B. $2
   C. $4
   D. $6

60. A stock sells for $60, the exercise price on the put is $64, and the premium on the put is $7. What is the intrinsic value of the put?

   A. $0
   B. $2
   C. $4
   D. $7

61. Which of the following are disadvantages of investing in options?

   (1) No dividend income available
   (2) Limited time frame to make profit
   (3) Large margin deposits required
   (4) No voting rights available

   A. (1), (2), and (3) only
   B. (2), (3), and (4) only
   C. (1), (2), and (4) only
   D. (1), (3), and (4) only

62. A call option is said to be in-the-money when:

   A. It is first purchased.
   B. The market price exceeds the exercise price.
   C. The exercise price exceeds the market price.
   D. The value of the stock goes down.

63. Which of the following statements correctly distinguishes between most open-end and most closed-end investment companies?

   A. An open-end company offers a specified number of shares; a closed-end company does not.
   B. A closed-end company pays dividends; an open-end company does not.
   C. A closed-end company's shares trade on national stock exchanges; an open-end company's shares do not.
   D. Shares of an open-end company may sell at a discount from net asset value; shares of a closed-end company do not.

64. Which of the following statements concerning mutual funds are correct?

    (1) They provide diversification for investors who have only a small amount to invest.

    (2) From the initial purchase of mutual fund shares, an investor is assured of a minimum income level and a stated redemption price.

    (3) They do not charge sales fees on initial investments.

    (4) Their earnings are exempt from federal income taxes at the corporate level.

    A. (1) and (2) only
    B. (1) and (4) only
    C. (2) and (3) only
    D. (3) and (4) only

65. Which of the following statements correctly identifies a similarity between most open-end and most closed-end investment companies?

    A. Both usually involve brokerage commissions in the sale of their shares.
    B. Both charge management fees.
    C. Both sell redeemable shares.
    D. Both provide a high degree of liquidity.

66. Which of the following statements concerning open-end investment companies are correct?

    (1) They may continually issue new shares.

    (2) They must redeem shares at net asset value.

    (3) They pass income, capital gains, and capital losses through to shareholders.

    (4) They generally utilize financial leverage to achieve their objectives.

    A. (1) and (2) only
    B. (1) and (3) only
    C. (1), (3), and (4) only
    D. (2), (3), and (4) only

67. Which of the following statements concerning mutual funds is correct?

    A. They are conduits through which income passes to shareholders tax-free.
    B. Purchases and redemptions of shares are made directly with the fund.
    C. The portfolio of securities held by these funds is usually selected by the board of directors.
    D. There are no restrictions on the investment policies that the fund must follow.

68. Which of the following statements concerning closed-end investment companies is correct?

    A. Investors must sell their shares to the funds when they liquidate their investment.
    B. The capitalization of these funds is constantly changing.
    C. Share prices are determined by the forces of supply and demand.
    D. They never utilize financial leverage.

69. Which of the following considerations are important for investors to consider in selecting a mutual fund?

    (1) Sales charges, fees, and 12b-1 charges
    (2) Their services, such as exchange privileges
    (3) The size of the fund
    (4) Whether the board has independent directors

    A. (1) and (4) only
    B. (1), (2), and (3) only
    C. (1), (2), and (4) only
    D. (2), (3), and (4) only

70. Which of the following statements concerning no-load mutual funds is (are) correct?

    (1) These funds do not charge a sales commission, but they may collect a redemption fee.
    (2) These funds may charge 12b-1 fees for marketing expenses.
    (3) Shares of these funds may be sold without a prospectus because they are sold by direct mail and media advertising.

    A. (1) only
    B. (2) only
    C. (1) and (2) only
    D. (1), (2), and (3)

71. All the following statements about the offering price and net asset value of mutual fund shares are correct, EXCEPT:

    A. The offering price of no-load fund shares is the same as the net asset value.
    B. The difference between the offering price and the net asset value is the maximum sales commission charged.
    C. The offering price of fund shares includes an amount for brokerage commissions.
    D. Net asset value is the value of the securities in the fund's portfolio, less liabilities, divided by the number of shares outstanding.

72. Which of the following statements concerning a unit investment trust is correct?

   A. It has an unmanaged portfolio.
   B. It usually consists of common stocks.
   C. It is most appropriate for young people.
   D. It requires constant management attention.

73. All the following are factors to consider when buying a mutual fund, EXCEPT:

   A. Portfolio management
   B. Fees and charges
   C. Fund age and size
   D. SEC compliance

74. Which of the following corporate bond funds is likely to have the highest current income?

   A. Junk bond funds
   B. Short-term funds
   C. Investment-grade funds
   D. Adjustable-rate funds

75. Which of the following statements correctly describes a GNMA fund?

   A. These funds purchase zero-coupon bonds that all have the same maturities and produce compound returns for investors.
   B. These funds purchase Treasury bills, notes, bonds, and U.S. government agency debt and seek slightly higher yields than government-guaranteed funds.
   C. These funds sell options on the securities in their portfolio, which consist mainly of U.S. agency debt instruments.
   D. These funds purchase mortgage-backed securities whose principal and interest payments are direct obligations of the U.S. government.

76. Which of the following statements concerning puts and calls is (are) correct?

   (1) A call obligates the writer to sell securities at an exercise price that may be below market.
   (2) A put obligates the writer to buy securities at the current market price.
   (3) Puts and calls are generally only sold on short-term bonds and income-producing stocks.

   A. (1) only
   B. (1) and (2) only
   C. (2) and (3) only
   D. (1), (2), and (3)

77. Which of the following statements concerning foreign bonds is (are) correct?

(1) They generally have higher yields than domestic U.S. bonds.
(2) These bonds are denominated in U.S. dollars.
(3) Although these securities are not directly guaranteed by the U.S. government, most experts believe the government would not permit defaults.

   A. (1) only
   B. (2) only
   C. (1) and (2) only
   D. (1), (2), and (3)

78. Which of the following statements concerning bankers' acceptances is (are) correct?

(1) They are promissory notes, guaranteed by a bank, and are typically used in foreign trade.
(2) They usually have maturities of less than one year.
(3) They are a primary debt of the corporation that imports goods.

   A. (1) only
   B. (2) only
   C. (1) and (2) only
   D. (1), (2), and (3)

79. Which of the following statements concerning money market mutual funds is (are) correct?

(1) Return on investment is reflected in additional shares, not in increased net asset value.
(2) They typically have no purchase or redemption fees.
(3) Their interest rate risk is relatively high because of their low liquidity.

   A. (1) only
   B. (2) only
   C. (1) and (2) only
   D. (1), (2), and (3)

80. Which of the following correctly describes a straddle?

   A. A combination of a put and a call on the same stock with different expiration dates and exercise prices
   B. A combination of a put and a call on the same stock with the same expiration dates and exercise prices
   C. Sale of a stock short and sale of a put
   D. Purchase of a stock (long) and a put (short)

81. Which of the following correctly describes a spread?

   A. A combination of a purchase and sale of calls on the same stock with different expiration dates and exercise prices
   B. A combination of a put and a call on the same stock with the same expiration dates and exercise prices
   C. Sale of a stock short and sale of a put
   D. Purchase of a stock (long) and a put (short)

82. Which of the following correctly describes a long hedge position?

  A. The investor is short the underlying commodity and short the futures contract.

  B. The investor is long the underlying commodity and long the futures contract.

  C. The investor is short the underlying commodity and long the futures contract.

  D. The investor is long the underlying commodity and short the futures contract.

83. Which of the following is an example of achieving an offsetting position?

  A. The seller of a March cattle futures contract buys a December cattle futures contract.

  B. The seller of a March cattle futures contract buys a March pork belly futures contract.

  C. The seller of a March cattle futures contract buys a March cattle futures contract.

  D. The seller of a March cattle futures contract makes a delivery of live cattle in January.

84. A manufacturer of bacon wants to protect against an increase in the cost of raw materials, that is, pork bellies. What type of hedge position should the manufacturer enter?

  A. A long position; the manufacturer should buy pork bellies futures contracts to hedge against higher prices.

  B. A short position; the manufacturer should sell pork bellies futures contracts to hedge against lower prices.

  C. A long position; the manufacturer should buy pork bellies futures contracts to hedge against lower prices.

  D. A short position; the manufacturer should sell pork bellies futures contracts to hedge against higher prices.

85. Clayton Jones owns a diversified stock portfolio worth $100,000. He is afraid that the market is heading downward, and he does not want to liquidate his portfolio, but he would like some kind of protection against falling stock prices. Which of the following correctly states the position Clayton should enter in the S&P 500 futures contracts and the reason for that position?

  A. A long position to hedge against higher stock prices

  B. A short position to hedge against higher stock prices

  C. A long position to hedge against lower stock prices

  D. A short position to hedge against lower stock prices

86. A farmer's wheat crop will be ready for sale in September. The farmer wants to protect against the possibility of falling wheat prices. Which of the following correctly states the type of hedge position the farmer should enter in wheat futures contracts and the reason for that position?

    A. A short position to hedge against higher wheat prices

    B. A long position to hedge against higher wheat prices

    C. A short position to hedge against lower wheat prices

    D. A long position to hedge against lower wheat prices

87. All the following money market instruments are likely to be acquired by a conservative money market fund, EXCEPT:

    A. Eurodollars

    B. Certificates of deposit

    C. Repurchase agreements

    D. Federal agency securities

For practice answering case questions related to Topic 33, please answer the following questions in the cases included in the Appendix at the back of this textbook.

Case	Questions
Donaldson	1, 2, 3, 4, 14, 15, 16, 17, and 18
Hilbert Stores, Inc.	1, 2, and 3
Maxwell	1, 2, 3, and 4
Beals	1 and 2
Mocsin	4
Eldridge	
Young	1
Johnson	1, 2, 3, and 4
Thomas	1, 2, 3, and 4
Jim and Brenda Quinn	1, 2, 3, 4, 5, 6, 29, and 31

Types of Investment Risk (Topic 34)

CFP Board Student-Centered Learning Objectives

(a) Identify, measure, and differentiate between types of investments risks including systematic, unsystematic risk, interest-rate risk, liquidity risk, credit risk, inflation risk, operating and financial risk, reinvestment-rate risk, exchange-rate risk, and political risk in a client's portfolio.

(b) Explain the impact of low-probability economic events on clients' welfare.

Types of Investment Risk
- A. *Systematic/market/nondiversifiable*
- B. *Purchasing power*
- C. *Interest rate*
- D. *Unsystematic/nonmarket/diversifiable*
- E. *Business*
- F. *Financial*
- G. *Liquidity and marketability*
- H. *Reinvestment*
- I. *Political (sovereign)*
- J. *Exchange rate*
- K. *Tax*
- L. *Investment manager*
- M. *Low-probability economic events*

Types of Investment Risks	**Risk is the probability that the actual or realized rate of return will be less than the expected return.** Risk comes in several forms or from several types of causes.
Systematic/Market/ Nondiversifiable	**Systematic risk is a broad category or composite encompassing various risks that tend to affect all securities to some extent, rather than being unique to a particular company.** In effect, all securities tend to move together in a systematic manner in response to these risks. As a result, systematic risk is nondiversifiable, as it affects the entire market, regardless of which stocks an investor owns. Examples of systematic risk include market risk, interest rate risk, reinvestment rate risk, purchasing power risk, and exchange rate risk. Each of these is covered in greater detail in the definitions that follow.
Market Risk	Market risk is the loss possibility arising from factors affecting the market as a whole (recessions, loss of confidence, etc.).
Purchasing Power Risk	Purchasing power risk (also called inflation risk) is the risk of reduced purchasing power of principal and income. Purchasing power risk will particularly affect cash equivalents and fixed

income investments, such as bonds and mortgage backed securities.

Interest Rate Risk

Interest rate risk is derived from two components: the impact on principal (price risk) and the reinvestment opportunities (reinvestment risk) as interest rates change. There is an inverse relationship between the price of fixed income securities and changes in interest rates. If interest rates rise, the values of securities tend to fall, and vice versa.

Interest rate risk is one of the major risks associated with investing in fixed income securities, including bonds and mortgage-backed securities. Bonds with shorter durations (discussed in topic 38) will have less price volatility when interest rates change, versus bonds with longer durations. For a coupon-paying bond, the duration will be shorter than the number of years to maturity, but a zero-coupon bond will have a duration equal to the number of years to maturity. Therefore, a zero-coupon bond with the same time to maturity as a coupon-paying bond will experience greater price fluctuation when interest rates change.

However, if interest rates rise, the returns from reinvesting periodic income received from the investment (such as bond coupon payments) rise, and vice versa.

Reinvestment Risk

Reinvestment risk is the risk that interest or earnings from a selected investment will not be reinvested at current rates of return. For example, a bond whose coupon pays more than rates today will have its cash flow invested at lower rates. Zero-coupon bonds do not experience this risk, as all payments are made at the time of maturity.

Exchange Rate Risk

Exchange rate risk is the loss possibility arising from adverse fluctuations in the value of the dollar relative to a foreign currency.

For example: After an investor makes an investment in a business in Mexico, the dollar strengthens against the peso, or the peso is devalued; either of these events will mean the pesos generated by the investment are not worth as many dollars as had been expected.

To compute the rate of return on a foreign security after a change in the exchange rate, the following formula for total return is used. Note that the use of this formula requires that the foreign currency be stated in U.S. dollars. For example, if 100 yen buys 1 USD, then the value of the yen would be stated as $.01.

$$TR = NRR \ x \ \frac{EOP \ val. \ of \ foreign \ currency}{BOP \ val. \ of \ foreign \ currency} - 1$$

Where:

NRR = Nominal return relative
EOP = End of period
BOP = Beginning of period

Example:

If an investment in Canada produces a nominal rate of return of 8%, the nominal relative return (NRR) is 1.08. If the Canadian dollar fell from $.80 U.S. (beginning of period) to $.70 U.S. (end of period), the actual total return (TR), adjusted for the exchange rate change, is:

$$TR = 1.08 \ x \ \frac{\$.70}{\$.80} \ - 1$$

$$= (1.08 \ x \ .8750) - 1$$

$$= -5.5\%$$

That is, exchange rate risk causes the yield to be not +8%, but –5.5%.

Viewing this from a logical analysis: If $100 U.S. dollars were originally exchanged for Canadian dollars with an exchange rate of .80, the result would be an investment of 125 Canadian dollars (100/.8 = 125). The investment then grew by 8% to 135 Canadian dollars (125 x 1.08 = 135). To convert back to U.S. dollars, multiply 135 x .70 = $94.50.

Unsystematic/Nonmarket/ Diversifiable Risk

Unsystematic risk arises from some specific or unique circumstance of a business or industry. Since this risk is not a risk of the entire market, unsystematic risk can be eliminated through proper diversification.

REMEMBER: *SYSTEMATIC RISK CANNOT BE REMOVED BY DIVERSIFICATION; UNSYSTEMATIC RISK IS DIVERSIFIABLE.*

Business Risk

Business risk is the risk associated with how the individual company earns its income. For example, a competitor could introduce a "better mousetrap." The business could also have problems purchasing raw materials, or their union workers could go on strike.

Financial Risk

Financial risk is the loss possibility due to use of leverage (heavy debt financing). Leverage is beneficial to a company when the money borrowed can be invested to earn greater returns than the cost of the loans. Excessive leverage is likely to cause a reduction in profits due to the additional interest payments required to service the debt.

Default Risk

Default risk is the loss possibility arising from a borrower's failure to pay interest and principal on a timely basis; it is also called credit risk.

Liquidity Risk

Liquidity risk is the loss possibility due to an inability to convert an investment into cash quickly and without loss of value. An investment such as real estate generally requires many months to sell in order to convert the investment to cash, and in that time, there may be loss of value. By contrast, a money market fund can be converted to cash almost immediately without loss of any value.

Marketability Risk

Marketability risk is the loss possibility because of inability to sell an asset easily due to absence of an organized market in which to sell it. Marketability and liquidity are similar, but liquidity suggests that the value of the investment is preserved while marketability indicates only ease of buying and selling. For example:

- T-bills are liquid and marketable.
- Options may be illiquid but marketable.
- A person's mansion may be illiquid and not very marketable.

Prepayment Risk

Prepayment risk is the risk that investments such as mortgage-backed securities may be retired or repaid early if interest rates decline. The investor will then be subject to reinvesting the funds at a lower rate.

Call Risk

Call risk is the possibility that the issuer will call a bond, so the owner must return it to the issuer and lose a favorable interest rate. An issuer is likely to call a bond when interest rates have declined because the issuer wants to pay off the debt and replace the bond with a lower yielding bond.

Political (Sovereign) Risk

Political (country) risk is the loss possibility due to factors related to the government and its stability in foreign countries, for example, confiscation of assets or change in government leaders.

Tax Risk

Tax risk is the loss possibility due to changes in tax laws. For example, Congress could change the tax treatment of municipal bond interest or the currently favorable taxation of qualified dividends. In addition, products subject to "sin" taxes (tobacco, alcohol, etc.) are subject to tax risk.

Investment Manager Risk

Investment manager risk is the loss possibility due to a change in investment managers on a particular mutual fund or managed account. Investment manager risk can also include the risk that the investment manager does not act in the best interests of the investors when managing the assets.

🔑 KEY SUMMARY 34 – 1
Systematic and Unsystematic Risks

Systematic Risks	*Unsystematic Risks*
Market	Business
Interest rate	Financial
Purchasing power	Default
Reinvestment	Liquidity
Exchange rate	Marketability

Risk-Return Trade-off

Investors generally require additional return for taking additional risk. The higher the risk, the more return required by investors. This is the risk-return trade-off. We saw in Topic 33 that the yield curve for interest rates reflects the increased interest return that investors require in exchange for taking the greater risk of investing for longer periods of time. The longer the investor must wait for a return of principal, the greater is the purchasing power risk, so the investor will require greater compensation for taking this additional risk.

T-bills are often identified as risk-free investments because the investor does not have the risks associated with other bonds. The T-bill is a short-term investment, typically 60-180 days, so there is little or no purchasing power risk over such a short time period. Changes in interest rates will have no impact on the T-bill, so reinvestment and interest rate risks are avoided. Finally, there is no risk of default by the federal government.

EXHIBIT 34 – 1
Major Risks for Bond Investors

Corporate Bonds	*Government Bonds*
Purchasing power risk	Purchasing power risk
Interest rate risk	Interest rate risk
Reinvestment risk	Reinvestment risk
Default risk	

Bond Ratings

Default (or credit) risk is present in corporate and municipal bonds. For this reason, rating agencies rate the quality of bonds according to the risk of default. Bonds that receive the top four ratings are considered investment-grade, and the next level down is considered speculative. Speculative bonds are also sometimes called junk bonds. Bonds below the speculative level are in default or near default.

Some of the different ratings provided by the rating services are shown in the following chart:

Bond Grade	Standard and Poor's, Duff & Phelps, Fitch Inv. Service	Moody's
Investment-grade	AAA AA A	Aaa Aa A
Minimum	BBB	Baa
Speculative-grade	BB B	Ba B
Default or near	CCC	Caa
Default		D

Low Probability, High Impact Economic Events

Low probability, high impact economic events are sometimes referred to as "black swan" events. (The concept dates back to the 17th century when it was discovered that black swans do exist, refuting the centuries-old belief that all swans were white, thus revealing that shortcomings in knowledge and imagination often lead to flawed conclusions and decisions.) Retroactive studies of black swan events imply that many catastrophic economic events should have been predictable but were not predicted due to design flaws in the models. Rational investors make decisions based on available information and personal perspective, often omitting the possibility of a black swan event. Other investors may consider the possibility, but ultimately determine that the likelihood of the event is so low that it is unreasonably costly to protect against it. These random and unexpected events, however, can have a devastating impact on clients' financial plans.

Recent studies of low probability, high impact events indicate that people have a tendency to deal with them poorly: whether the event is a natural disaster, premature death, living to age 100+, or a market bubble. Many people have a tendency to be overconfident and/or feel that these things will never be a problem for them. People also have the tendency to protect themselves immediately following a disastrous event, but within a few years the recency of the event has diminished, and protection no longer seems worth the cost. In cases where these psychological biases are causing clients to make irrational and potentially costly decisions, it is up to the planner to serve as the voice of reason and remind clients to continue following sound planning principles even when it may not "feel" right at the time. These principles include maintaining adequate insurance coverages, ensuring essential retirement expenses are covered with guaranteed life income streams, and diversifying investment portfolios and/or using hedging strategies to protect investment portfolios. (Additional information regarding recency, overconfidence, and other behavioral finance issues can be found in Topic 37).

TOPIC 34 – APPLICATION QUESTIONS

1. Assume that an American's investment in the stock of a French company yielded a nominal rate of return of 18% in the past 12 months. Assume also that the euro was worth $.20 at the start of the period and $.25 at the end of the period. In this case, the true rate of return for the investor was:

A. −5.6%
B. 11.3%
C. 22.5%
D. 43.0%
E. 47.5%

2. (Published question released January, 1999)

Mortgage-backed securities may contain which of the following risks?

(1) Purchasing power risk
(2) Interest rate risk
(3) Prepayment risk

A. (2) only
B. (1) and (2) only
C. (1) and (3) only
D. (1), (2), and (3)

3. Which of the following statements concerning the risk-return trade-off is (are) correct?

(1) Investors tend to demand higher rates of returns for greater risk.
(2) Investors accept a lower return on T-bills because of the low degree of risk.
(3) To earn higher rates of return, investors usually must be willing to accept a higher degree of risk.

A. (1) only
B. (1) and (2) only
C. (1) and (3) only
D. (2) and (3) only
E. (1), (2), and (3)

4. Which of the following statements concerning interest rate risk is <u>not</u> correct?

A. The owners of fixed-income securities experience a decline in the market prices of their securities when the market rate of interest increases.
B. The market prices of fixed-income securities move, so that their yields to maturity are consistent with the market rates of interest.
C. The market price variation for short-term, fixed-income securities is greater than the market price variation for long-term securities.
D. The market prices of some common stocks and preferred stocks tend to move inversely to the market rates of interest.
E. When market rates of interest decline, the owners of GNMA mortgage-backed securities may be forced to reinvest at the low market rates of interest.

5. Which of the following statements concerning unsystematic risk is (are) correct?

(1) It is associated with a particular security or company.
(2) It is related to such factors as business risk and financial risk.
(3) The investor who owns three listed blue-chip common stocks can reduce unsystematic risk by buying several additional listed blue-chip common stocks.

    A. (1) only
    B. (1) and (2) only
    C. (1) and (3) only
    D. (2) and (3) only
    E. (1), (2), and (3)

6. Which of the following statements concerning systematic risk is correct?

    A. It can be greatly reduced by owning a diversified portfolio of common stocks.
    B. It covers those types of risk that cause all securities to move together in a systematic manner.
    C. Business risk, such as a strike at an individual firm, is considered a systematic risk.
    D. It includes financial risk, or risk arising when the firm borrows heavily to finance its activities.

7. (Published question released November, 1994)

Which of the following are nondiversifiable risks?

(1) Business risk
(2) Management risk
(3) Company or industry risk
(4) Market risk
(5) Interest rate risk
(6) Purchasing power risk

    A. (4), (5), and (6) only
    B. (1), (2), and (3) only
    C. (2), (5), and (6) only
    D. (1), (3), and (4) only
    E. (1), (4), and (6) only

8. All of the following statements concerning market risk are correct, EXCEPT:

    A. Market risk exposes individual common stocks to the uncertainty of the performance of the stock market as a whole.
    B. The market prices of listed common stocks tend to move in tandem.
    C. An astute program of diversification of common stock ownership is very helpful in reducing market risk.
    D. The stock market crash following the terrorist attacks on the World Trade Center on September 11, 2001, is a good example of market risk.

9. All of the following statements concerning purchasing power risk are correct, EXCEPT:

A. Purchasing power risk is uncertainty concerning the future buying power of the investor's total return.
B. During inflation, a bond's fixed annual interest and fixed maturity value lose purchasing power.
C. Inflation tends to increase market rates of interest, and this depresses the market prices of fixed-income securities.
D. During most of the past inflations, the market prices of bonds followed the market prices of common stocks as the latter moved upward.
E. Real estate, precious metals, and certain other commodities are considered better hedges against inflation than fixed-income securities.

10. Which of the following statements concerning business risk is (are) correct?

(1) Business risk is the uncertainty of an investor's total return associated with the unique problems of a specific industry or company.
(2) An example of business risk is a company's exposure to bankruptcy because of the interest charges on its enormous amount of debt.

A. (1) only
B. (2) only
C. Both (1) and (2)
D. Neither (1) nor (2)

11. All of the following statements concerning financial risk are correct, EXCEPT:

A. It is the possibility of loss due to the overuse of debt financing: issuers of debt securities that are overextended, along with the holders of their bonds, risk losing some or all their investment.
B. If a firm had no debt, there would be no financial risk for the investor.
C. When referring to the debt of a business firm, debt is synonymous with financial leverage.
D. The greater the percentage of debt in a firm's total capital structure, the greater the probable variation in the firm's net profits.
E. Given two firms in the same industry, with equally competent managements, an investor would be wise to buy the common stock of the company with no debt, rather than the common stock of the company with debt.

12. All of the following statements concerning the liquidity of investment-quality assets are correct, EXCEPT:

A. Liquidity is measured by the rapidity of converting to cash, without a significant price sacrifice or price concession.
B. Real estate has poor liquidity.
C. Stocks that can be traded on organized stock exchanges have good liquidity since they can be sold by a mere telephone call to a broker.
D. Money market funds have excellent liquidity since their investments are of high quality and very short maturity.

13. All of the following statements concerning the systematic risk associated with the ownership of investment-quality assets are correct, EXCEPT:

A. Market risk, interest rate risk, and financial risk are all systematic risks.
B. The market prices of listed common stocks tend to move uniformly in reaction to the inflation risk.
C. Diversification, achieved through increasing the number of different companies' common stocks owned by an investor, will not reduce the investor's systematic risk.
D. Systematic risk cannot be eliminated, even when diversifying with different types of assets, such as bonds, real estate, and stocks.

14. All of the following statements concerning systematic risk are correct, EXCEPT:

A. Reinvestment rate risk, or the inability to obtain the same attractive yields after a decline in interest rates as before the decline, is considered a systematic risk.
B. Purchasing power risk, or the chance that rising inflation will damage the future purchasing power of an investment, is considered a systematic risk.
C. Market risk, as exemplified by the stock market crash on October 19, 1987, which affected almost every stock, is considered a systematic risk.
D. Exchange rate risk, or the inability to exchange a senior security into common stock, is considered a systematic risk.

15. Which of the following statements concerning marketability is (are) correct?

(1) An investment that can be quickly and easily converted into cash has excellent marketability.
(2) Investments that exhibit excellent marketability always possess excellent liquidity.

A. (1) only
B. (2) only
C. Both (1) and (2)
D. Neither (1) nor (2)

16. Which of the following correctly describes interest rate risk?

A. Interest payments will have less purchasing power in the future.
B. Bond prices decrease as interest rates increase.
C. Interest payments may not be paid if the issuer goes bankrupt.
D. The bond may be called because interest rates have decreased.

17. All of the following could negatively affect an investor's gain from foreign investing, EXCEPT:

A. Systematic risk
B. Devaluation of the dollar
C. Nationalization and expropriation of assets
D. Exchange rate risk

18. If an American buys a British stock, he or she could lose money if which of the following occurs?

   A. The security rises and the pound rises.
   B. The security rises and the dollar falls.
   C. The security is constant and the pound falls.
   D. The security is constant and the pound rises.

19. Bonds of the GHI Corporation were recently issued to yield a 7.3% rate of return. Bonds of the JKL Corporation were issued on the same day to yield a 6.8% rate of return. Which of the following factors may have accounted for this difference?

   (1) Differences in the risk-free rate of return
   (2) A shorter time to maturity for the GHI bonds
   (3) A lower degree of default risk for the JKL bonds
   (4) The presence of collateral underlying the GHI bonds

     A. (1) only
     B. (3) only
     C. (2) and (4) only
     D. (1), (2), and (4) only
     E. (2), (3), and (4) only

20. (Published question released January, 1999)

   Which of the following best describes the investment characteristics of a high-quality long-term municipal bond?

   A. High inflation risk; low default risk
   B. Low inflation risk; high market risk
   C. Low inflation risk; low default risk
   D. High inflation risk; high market risk

21. Which of the following statements concerning the risk-return trade-off is (are) correct?

   (1) Investors tend to demand higher rates of return for greater risk.
   (2) Investors accept a lower return on T-bills because of their low degree of risk.
   (3) To earn higher rates of return, investors usually must be willing to accept a higher degree of risk.

     A. (1) only
     B. (2) only
     C. (1) and (3) only
     D. (2) and (3) only
     E. (1), (2), and (3)

22. Which of the following statements correctly describes the risk-return trade-off?

   A. Investment vehicles with a great potential for capital appreciation also tend to have a great potential for loss of purchasing power.
   B. Investment vehicles with a great variability in returns tend to have lower growth potential.
   C. Investment vehicles with a great potential for reward through capital appreciation also tend to have a great potential for loss of principal.
   D. Both risk and return tend to be highest for investors who trade frequently.

For practice answering case questions related to Topic 34, please answer the following questions in the cases included in the Appendix at the back of this textbook.

Case	Questions
Donaldson	4
Hilbert Stores, Inc.	
Maxwell	5
Beals	3
Mocsin	
Eldridge	
Young	
Johnson	5
Thomas	
Jim and Brenda Quinn	7, 8. 9, 10, and 11

Quantitative Investment Concepts (Topic 35)

CFP Board Student-Centered Learning Objectives

(a) Calculate and interpret statistical measures such as mean, standard deviation, z-statistic, correlation, and R^2 and interpret the meaning of skewness, and kurtosis.

(b) Estimate the expected risk and return using the Capital Asset Pricing Model for securities and portfolios.

(c) Calculate Modern Portfolio Theory statistics in the assessment of securities and portfolios.

(d) Explain the use of return distributions in portfolio structuring.

(e) Identify the pros and cons of, and apply advanced analytic techniques such as forecasting, simulation, sensitivity analysis and stochastic modeling.

Quantitative Investment Concepts
- A. *Distribution of returns*
  - 1) *Standard deviation*
  - 2) *Normal distribution*
  - 3) *Lognormal distribution*
  - 4) *Skewness*
  - 5) *Kurtosis*
- B. *Semi-variance*
- C. *Coefficient of variation*
- D. *Combining two or more assets into a portfolio*
  - 1) *Covariance*
  - 2) *Correlation coefficient*
  - 3) *Two-asset portfolio standard deviation*
- E. *Beta*
- F. *Modern portfolio theory (MPT)*
  - 1) *Mean-variance optimization*
  - 2) *Efficient frontier*
  - 3) *Indifference (utility) curves*
- G *Capital market line*
- H. *Capital asset pricing model (CAPM)*
  - 1) *Security market line*
  - 2) *Limitations of CAPM*
- I. *Arbitrage pricing theory (APT)*
- J. *Other Statistical Measures*
  - 1) *Coefficient of determination (R^2)*
  - 2) *Z-statistic*
- K. *Probability analysis, including Monte Carlo*
- L. *Stochastic modeling and simulation*

Variability of Returns
Risk is the possibility that actual results will be less favorable than anticipated results. The greater is this probability, the greater is the risk. Obviously, then, investment assets whose prices or returns fluctuate widely (percentage wise) over time are more risky than those with less variable prices or returns. Two commonly used measures of a security's variability and volatility are its standard deviation and its beta.

Distribution of Returns
Standard deviation is an absolute measure of the variability of results around the average or mean of those results.

Standard Deviation Calculation
The standard deviation can be calculated manually, but to save time, you should use a financial calculator. To illustrate, assume that an investment has produced the following results in recent years:

Year	Rate of Return
1	–3.6%
2	7.0%
3	9.0%
4	14.0%
5	–2.2%
6	11.0%

You could compute the mean of these results by adding up the numbers and dividing by 6. You will find it to be 5.87% doing it this way. However, use your financial calculator for both the mean and standard deviation. For example:

On the HP-10B II, press the orange shift key (hereinafter referred to simply as shift), CL$\sum$, 3.6, +/–, $\sum$ +, 7, $\sum$ +, 9, $\sum$ +, 14, $\sum$ +, 2.2, +/–, $\sum$ +, 11, $\sum$ +, shift, and xy (to get the arithmetic mean of 5.87), shift, σxσy (to get the population standard deviation of 6.56), shift, SxSy (to get the sample standard deviation of 7.19).

The population standard deviation is for the entire series of numbers given. The sample standard deviation is a statistical estimate for a larger universe of numbers of which the numbers given are a subset, such as an historical set of returns. In this course, we will focus primarily on the calculation of the sample standard deviation.

If you use the HP-12C, press yellow f, CLX, 3.6, CHS, $\sum$+, 7, $\sum$+, 9, $\sum$+, 14, $\sum$+, 2.2, CHS, $\sum$+, 11, $\sum$+, blue g, and $\bar{\times}$ (to get the arithmetic mean of 5.87), blue g, S (to get the sample standard deviation of 7.19). Note that the HP-12C does not calculate a population standard deviation directly.

On the HP-17B II+, press sum, shift, CLR DATA, Yes, 3.6, +/–, INPUT, 7, INPUT, 9, INPUT, 14, INPUT, 2.2, +/–, INPUT, 11, INPUT, EXIT, CALC, and MEAN (which will give you the answer of 5.87), STDEV (which will give you the answer of 7.19).

If you use a BA-II Plus calculator, press 2nd data, 2nd clear work, 3.6, +/–, enter, ↓↓, 7.0, enter, ↓↓, 9.0, enter, ↓↓, 14, enter, ↓↓, 2.2, +/–, enter, ↓↓, 11.0, enter, ↓↓, 2nd stat, 2nd clear work, and 2nd set (until you see 1 – V on your screen), ↓ (you will see n = 6 on your screen), ↓ (you will see X = 5.87 on your screen), and ↓ (you will see Sx = 7.19 on your screen).

Normal Distributions

In a normal (bell-shaped) distribution, 68% of all results will fall within ± one standard deviation of the mean. 95% of all results will fall within two standard deviations of the mean and 99% of all results will fall within three standard deviations of the mean. Likewise, 50% of the results will be higher than the mean and 50% of the results will be lower than the mean.

This diagram shows the normal (bell-shaped) distribution and the standard deviations:

Exhibit 35 – 1

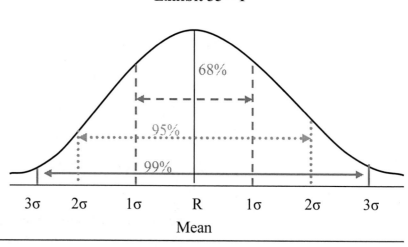

σ = Standard Deviation

Lognormal Distributions

A lognormal distribution differs from a normal distribution in that the shape is not necessarily symmetrical. The underlying factors affecting the distribution are, however, normally distributed. For financial planning purposes, a lognormal distribution is used on models when the distribution of certain variables, such as how long clients will live or how much income they will earn, is expected to be skewed.

Skewness

Skewness measures the symmetry of the bell curve. For example, if the tail to the right of the mean is larger than the tail to the left of the mean, the curve has positive skewness. In a normal bell curve, the two tails are equal, which means the curve has no skewness.

Investors generally are risk averse and will prefer positive skewness to negative skewness because negative skewness means increased downside potential and positive skewness means increased upside potential.

Kurtosis

Kurtosis measures the tallness or flatness of the bell curve. Bell curves with distributions concentrated around the mean and fat tails have a high kurtosis (these are called leptokurtic), while bell curves with evenly spread distributions around the mean and skinny tails have a low kurtosis (called platykurtic). Investors who are risk averse generally prefer low kurtosis to high kurtosis. High kurtosis (with "fat tails") means that there is increased probability of surprise upside and downside returns such as the "black swan" events mentioned in Topic 34. While the tails are fat on both the upside and the downside, investors tend to react more to the increased downside potential and prefer to avoid such increased downside risk.

Exhibit 35 – 2

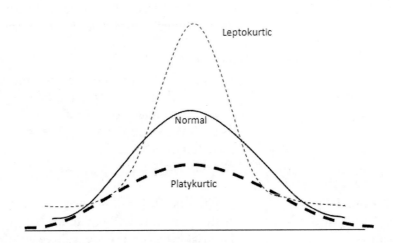

Semi-variance

Semi-variance is a risk measurement of only the downside returns in a portfolio. Only the downside from the mean is averaged since investors seem to fear losses much more than they enjoy positive returns. Morningstar Publications uses this measurement in its star-rating system.

Coefficient of Variation

As discussed at the start of this topic, standard deviation is the absolute measure of variability. The greater the standard deviation, the greater the variability (and, so, riskiness). But, which is more variable, Asset A or Asset B?

Asset A, with an average return of 5.87 and a standard deviation of 7.19

Asset B, with an average return of 6.87 and a standard deviation of 7.59

To answer this, we need a relative measure of variability. That relative measure is the coefficient of variation, which is the standard deviation expressed as a percentage of the mean. In this case, A is riskier because it has a higher relative degree of variability or coefficient of variation.

$$A = 7.19 \div 5.87 = 1.22\%$$

$$B = 7.59 \div 6.87 = 1.10\%$$

Practice Question

Which of the following four investments will provide the least variability and risk?

A. Investment A: Average return 24%, standard deviation 12
B. Investment B: Average return 6%, standard deviation 3
C. Investment C: Average return 12%, standard deviation 5
D. Investment D: Average return 8%, standard deviation 3

Answer:
The coefficient of variation for these investments is the standard deviation divided by the average return. The investment with the lowest coefficient of variation will be the least variable and least risky. Investment D has the lowest coefficient, with a coefficient of variation of 3/8 = .375.
The answer is D.

Combining Two or More Assets into a Portfolio

When a portfolio of securities is assembled, each of the securities in the portfolio will, of course, have its own standard deviation. The riskiness of the overall portfolio will, therefore, have some relationship to the standard deviation of each of the securities in it, as well as to the proportion of the total portfolio that each security represents within it. However, the riskiness of the portfolio is not simply the weighted average of the standard deviations of the securities in the portfolio. Another factor has to be taken into account, namely, the degree to which the stocks tend to move together. Covariance is one way of measuring this movement. A positive covariance means the stocks tend to move in the same direction, whereas a negative covariance means they tend to move in opposite directions.

Covariance

Covariance is the relationship between and among stocks that includes not only the individual stock's variability, but also its effect on and interaction with other portfolio securities. Covariance is the reason the calculation of a portfolio's standard deviation cannot simply be its weighted average.

EXHIBIT 35 – 3
Covariance

$$\text{COV.}_{ij} = P_{ij}\, \sigma_i\, \sigma_j$$

Where:
σ_i = Standard deviation of Asset "i" returns
σ_j = Standard deviation of Asset "j" returns
P_{ij} = Correlation coefficient for Assets "i" and "j"

Correlation Coefficient

The correlation coefficient is another measure of how two assets move in relation to each other. The correlation coefficient measures the relationship between stocks, which is found by dividing the covariance (see below) by the product of the separate standard deviations. The correlation coefficient can be anywhere between +1.0 (perfectly positive correlation) and –1.0 (perfectly negative correlation). A correlation coefficient of 0 means there is no relationship between the returns for the two investments (they move independently of one another).

EXHIBIT 35 – 4
Correlation Coefficient

$$P_{ij} = \frac{\text{COV.}_{ij}}{\sigma_i \times \sigma_j}$$

Where:
σ_i = Standard deviation of Asset "i" returns
σ_j = Standard deviation of Asset "j" returns
COV._{ij} = Covariance of Assets "i" and "j"

Unless the securities are all perfectly positively correlated (meaning that they all move in the same direction at the same time to the same extent), the standard deviation (riskiness) of the portfolio will be less than the weighted-average standard deviation of the individual securities. That reduction in standard deviation is what diversification is all about.

Diversification can be accomplished within an asset type by adding different stocks to a portfolio. For example, the addition of foreign stocks will reduce portfolio risk if the portfolio securities are negatively correlated with the foreign stocks. Diversification can also be accomplished across asset types by adding stocks, bonds, and risk-free assets (cash) to a portfolio. Diversification across asset types is thought to be more effective.

Two-Asset Portfolio Standard Deviation

If a client has a portfolio with just two assets, the standard deviation of that portfolio will not be the average of the standard deviation of the two assets. The reason is not only the weighting of each asset in the portfolio, but also how these two stocks interact together, or their covariance. The standard deviation of the two-asset portfolio will be equal to or less than the weighted standard deviation, depending upon the covariance between the assets.

Unfortunately, there are no shortcuts on the financial calculators to solve for the two-asset portfolio standard deviation. As a result, you will need to use the following formula to solve for the two-asset portfolio standard deviation:

Two-Asset Portfolio Standard Deviation

$$\sigma_p = \sqrt{W_i^2 \sigma_i^2 + W_j^2 \sigma_j^2 + 2W_i W_j COV_{ij}}$$

Where:

σ_p = Standard deviation of the two-asset portfolio
W_i = Weight of Asset "i" in the portfolio
σ_i = Standard deviation of Asset "i" returns
W_j = Weight of Asset "j" in the portfolio
σ_j = Standard deviation of Asset "j" returns
$COV._{ij}$ = Covariance of Assets "i" and "j"

Example:

What is the standard deviation of the following portfolio?

Stock I
- $40,000 FMV (40% of portfolio)
- Standard deviation = 2%

Stock J

- $60,000 FMV (60% of portfolio)
- Standard deviation = 3%

Covariance of Stock I and Stock J = 0.5

The standard deviation of the portfolio is 2.0298% which is calculated as follows:

$$2 \sqrt{[(0.4^2 \times 2^2) + (0.6^2 \times 3^2) + (2 \times 0.4 \times 0.6 \times 0.5)]}$$
$$2 \sqrt{[.64 + 3.24 + .24]}$$
$$2 \sqrt{[4.12]}$$
$$= 2.0298\%$$

Beta

The standard deviation of a series of numbers reflects all the **variability** around the mean of those numbers. Consequently, the standard deviation of the returns around the average return reflects all the risks, both systematic (nondiversifiable) and unsystematic (diversifiable), associated with the investment. Beta is quite a different measure of the riskiness of results, one that reflects only the systematic risks, the risks that cannot be diversified away.

Beta measures a portfolio's volatility, not variability, relative to some benchmark. The values for beta will differ depending on whether the benchmark used for the market is the S&P 500, the NYSE composite, or some other benchmark. Beta is calculated using historical data for the returns from the market and for the returns from the asset. Beta can change over time, and different results can be obtained depending on the periods used. The beta is measuring the impact of this new asset when added to an already-diversified portfolio.

 K Study Tip – **Note the distinction between the two key terms –** *variability* **and** *volatility*. **The former refers to fluctuations around the security's own mean or average. The latter refers to fluctuations around the market mean or average. Variability is measured by standard deviation; volatility is measured by beta.**

Beta is the measure of risk to use with a diversified portfolio in which unsystematic risk has been removed by diversification. Standard deviation is the measure of risk to use when a portfolio is not diversified.

🔔 **REMEMBER:** *BETA IS A MEASURE OF SYSTEMATIC RISK; STANDARD DEVIATION IS A MEASURE OF TOTAL RISK (SYSTEMATIC AND UNSYSTEMATIC).*

Calculation of Beta

Beta is a measure of the **volatility** of a particular security's rate of return or price relative to the volatility of the market as a whole (or the average security in the market). Beta can be calculated using the following formula:

EXHIBIT 35 – 5
Beta

$$\beta_i = \frac{P_{im}\ \sigma_i}{\sigma_m}$$

Where:
σ_i = Standard deviation of the individual stock or portfolio
σ_m = Standard deviation of the market
P_{im} = Correlation coefficient between the individual stock or portfolio and the market

---

Example:

The standard deviation for a stock is 15%, and the standard deviation for the market is 10%. The correlation coefficient for the stock and the market is 0.6. The beta will be calculated as:

$$\beta = \frac{(0.6 \times 0.15)}{.10} = 0.90$$

Beta as a Measure of Volatility

The market as a whole has a beta of 1.0, so a security that is just as volatile as the market also has a beta of 1.0. If the betas of securities are more than or less than 1.0, those securities are more or less volatile than the market. For example, Stock A, with a beta of 1.3, is 30% more volatile (risky) than the market. Stock B, with a beta of .8, is only 80% as volatile (risky) as the market. Of course, beta is often based on what has happened in the past, so it may not be an accurate indicator of risk in the future.

Beta for Mutual Funds

For a mutual fund, beta is a measure of the fund's volatility in relation to a market index, such as the S&P 500 Index or another index that more closely resembles the fund characteristics. Funds with betas of more than 1.0 are more volatile than the index, while those with betas of less than 1.0 are less volatile than the index.

Weighted Beta for Portfolios

If a portfolio of securities is assembled that has a weighted-average beta coefficient of 1.0, the variations in the prices and returns should coincide with those of the market as a whole. For example, the following simple portfolio is theoretically a fully diversified one that is exposed only to systematic risk:

Security	Weight		Beta		Wtd. Beta
A	50%	x	1.3	=	.65
B	50%	x	.7	=	.35
					1.00

Practice Question

An investor's portfolio consists of the following funds:

Fund	Amount	Beta
A	$45,000	1.10
B	30,000	.90
C	15,000	.75

What is the beta for the investor's portfolio?

A. 1.00
B. .975
C. .917
D. .900

Answer:
The calculation of the weighted beta is as follows:
Fund A: (45/90) x 1.1 = .55
Fund B: (30/90) x .9 = .3
Fund C: (15/90) x .75 = .125
  Weighted average   =   .975
The answer is B.

Modern Portfolio Theory

In his 1952 article entitled "Portfolio Selection," Harry M. Markowitz laid the foundation for the basic portfolio model. This theory looks at portfolio performance based upon a combination of its assets' risk and return. With the use of modern computers and the refinement of many complicated quadratic-programming formulas, the theory now provides a framework for helping an investor understand the relationship between risk and return.

The set of portfolios that is the foundation of modern portfolio theory is known as the efficient frontier. Here, the investor attempts to achieve one of the following:

- For a given level of expected return, there is no other portfolio characterized by lower risk.
- For a given level of risk, there is no portfolio with a higher expected return.
- The rational investor will choose the highest expected return with the lowest risk.

Mean-Variance Optimization

The primary goal of modern portfolio theory is the optimal asset allocation. The mean-variance optimization is a process that can assist investors in the asset allocation by balancing risks and returns.

Efficient Frontier

Figure 35 – 1

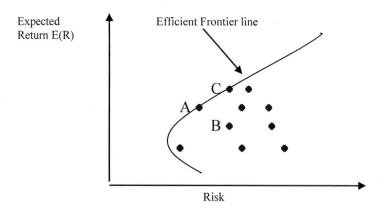

All possible portfolios below the efficient frontier line are attainable, but they may not maximize return for the risk level assumed. **No attainable portfolio can lie above the efficient frontier.** Portfolios outside the efficient frontier are not included in the "feasible set," or array of possible options. This is because no risk and expected return level is attainable at that point. Ultimately, though, it is the individual who will have to decide what combination of risk and return in a portfolio is to be selected. Portfolio A in Figure 35 – 1 is efficient because it lies on the efficient frontier line. For the same level of risk, there is no other portfolio that offers a higher return. Portfolio B is inefficient because for the same level of risk, another portfolio (portfolio C) provides a higher return.

Indifference (Utility) Curves

Investors attempt to find the optimum portfolio, balancing risk and return by using indifference curves (also called utility curves). These measure the risk/reward *preferences* that an investor is willing to make along the efficient frontier. These curves do not intersect with one another since they represent different investor preferences.

The slope of any curve is a function of the risk-averse nature of the investor. The steeper the slope of the curve, the greater is the investor's aversion to risk. Portfolio possibilities are represented all along the efficient frontier, and the investor is indifferent regarding portfolios that lie on the same indifference curve. For example, portfolios B and C in Figure 35 – 2 below both lie on the same indifference curve (I_3), so the investor is indifferent as to these portfolios; he does not perceive one to be of greater value than the other. However, the investor will prefer portfolios on higher curves. The rational investor will seek out the optimum portfolio position. This occurs at a point where the highest indifference curve is tangent to the efficient frontier curve, Portfolio A in Figure 35 – 2. While portfolio C is also on the efficient frontier, this investor prefers portfolio A because it is on a higher indifference curve.

Figure 35 – 2

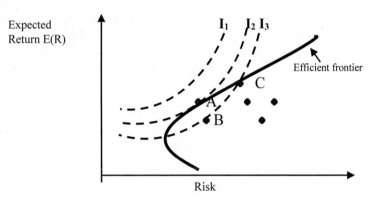

The Addition of the Risk-Free Asset

Notice that in Figure 35 – 1, all assets are "risky" assets. In other words, there are no assets on the far left vertical axis where the level of risk is zero. It wasn't until 1958 when James Tobin expanded on the work of Markowitz and added the concept of a risk-free asset. By combining the risk-free asset with a portfolio on the efficient frontier, the ability to leverage the portfolio can create a risk-return profile that is superior to the portfolios on the efficient frontier.

Capital Market Line (CML)

The capital market line (CML) shows the risk-return trade-off for all combinations of risk-free and risky portfolios. For example, in figure 35-3, if all possible combinations of the risk-free asset and portfolio D (e.g., 100% R_f and 0% D, 80% R_f and 20% D, 50% R_f and 50% D, and so on) are plotted, the result will form a straight line between point R_f and D. However, an investor would not logically choose any combination that includes portfolio D or any other portfolio located to the left of portfolio M, since they are inferior to the returns that can be provided by combining the risk-free asset and portfolio M, which is the market portfolio. The market portfolio M is, conceptually, a portfolio made up of the entire universe of risky assets with the weight of each asset based on its market value. In practicality, the S&P 500 index is often used as a substitute for the market portfolio and U.S. Treasury bills are often used as a proxy for the risk-free asset.

This new efficient frontier line can now extend to the right of point M and into the area that lies above the old efficient frontier by borrowing at the risk-free rate and using the borrowed funds to invest in the market portfolio.

The CML is a tool that facilitates the search for the highest expected returns in relation to various levels of portfolio risk, measured by the standard deviation. When depicted graphically, the vertical axis represents the portfolio's rate of return, while the horizontal axis represents the standard deviation of returns, as shown below in Figure 35 – 3. The CML intercepts the vertical axis of the graph at the rate of return available on a risk-free portfolio, R_f. The line rises to the right to reflect the fact that for all the available efficient portfolios, return rises as riskiness, measured by standard deviation, rises. The slope of the CML reflects how much more return can be achieved with a given increase in riskiness (or how much more riskiness must be accepted in order to achieve a given increase in return).

The market portfolio point (M) lies where the CML and the efficient frontier line are tangent. To the left of that point is a combination of the risk- free assets and the market portfolio (some assets are invested in the market portfolio, with the remainder being lent at the risk-free rate). To the right of the tangency point is the area in which all of an investor's assets are invested in the market portfolio, and the investor borrows to invest additional amounts in the market portfolio thereby using leverage.

Figure 35 – 3

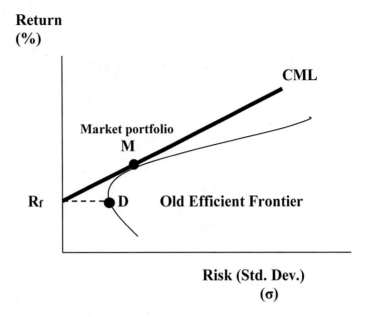

One of the particular goals of the efficient frontier is to select the portfolio with the highest expected return, given a level of risk. The CML model helps investors achieve this goal.

The equation for the CML is:

EXHIBIT 35 – 6
Required Rate of Return – Capital Market Line
$$r_p = r_f + \sigma_p \left[\frac{r_m - r_f}{\sigma_m} \right]$$ Where: r_p = Expected or required rate of return r_f = Risk-free rate of return r_m = Market rate of return σ_p = Standard deviation of the portfolio σ_m = Standard deviation of the market

The expected or required rate of return is the minimum rate of return that will induce an investor to commit funds to a particular risky investment.

Practice Question

What is the investor's required rate of return on a portfolio using the CML model if the market return is 10% with a 4% standard deviation, the risk-free return is 6%, and the portfolio has a standard deviation of 3%?

A. 6%
B. 9%
C. 12%
D. 15%

Answer:
$r_p = 6\% + [3\% \times (10\% - 6\%)/4\%)] = 9\%$
The answer is B.

The excess of the market return over the risk-free return ($r_m - r_f$) is known as the market risk premium. In other words, the market risk premium is the extra return provided by investing in the market versus investing in the risk-free asset.

The slope of the capital market line in Figure 35 – 3 is determined by the part of the formula: $\dfrac{r_m - r_f}{\sigma_m}$

The slope of the line will change when any of the three variables changes (the return of the market, the risk-free rate, or the standard deviation of the market).

It should be noted that, the CML assumes the only risky asset that is held is the market portfolio, which is a diversified portfolio; therefore, the CML is only useful for diversified portfolios.

Capital Asset Pricing Model

The Capital Asset Pricing Model (CAPM) was formulated mostly by William Sharpe (1964) and was built upon the concepts laid down by Markowitz. It relates the risk as measured by beta to the required rate of return or expected level of return on a security and can be used for both diversified and undiversified portfolios (including a single stock). Because of this flexibility, CAPM and the Security market line (SML) is used more frequently than the CML.

Certain assumptions are built into the model and include the following:

- Rational investors use like information to formulate the efficient frontier.

- Investors can borrow and lend at the risk-free rate of return.

- Taxes, inflation, and transaction costs are equivalent to zero.

There is no preference made for investment decisions on capital gains versus dividend distributions.

Security Market Line (SML)

CAPM is represented by the security market line (SML). Here, the slope of the line reflects the risk-return trade-off applicable to individual securities. Though the SML is similar to the CML, there is an important difference. In the SML, riskiness is measured by the beta of the security in question, not by its standard deviation. The beta of the security is based upon that security's impact on the variability of the portfolio.

In the following graph (Figure 35 – 4), point L reflects the choice of a low-risk asset since its return and beta are less than those of the market as a whole. Point H represents the choice of a high-risk asset. Notice that the SML extends to the left of the vertical axis and R_f. An expected return below the risk-free rate could occur if an asset has a negative beta. Securities with a negative beta would be expected to move in the opposite direction of the market, and would, therefore, perform well if the market were to collapse.

Figure 35 – 4

Return of the Individual Security

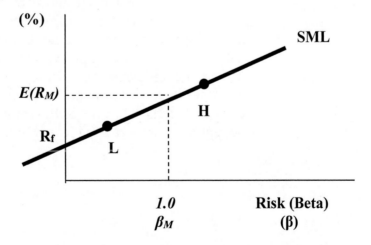

The security market line (SML) is the model for CAPM. It represents the risk/return relationship for efficient portfolios and uses beta as its risk measure. The equation for the SML is:

> **EXHIBIT 35 – 7**
> **Required Rate of Return – Security Market Line**
>
> $$r_i = r_f + (r_m - r_f)\,\beta$$
>
> Where:
>
> r_i = Expected or required rate of return
> r_f = Risk-free rate of return
> r_m = Market rate of return
> β = Beta

This equation shows that the expected or required return rate for a security, or a portfolio of securities, is equivalent to the rate of return required for securities that are risk-free, plus the risk premium ($r_m - r_f$) required by investors for the assumption of a given level of risk as measured by beta. The risk-free rate is generally the T-bill rate. The higher the degree of nondiversifiable risk, the higher is the expected rate of return demanded.

The market is usually represented by the S&P 500 Index and is assigned a beta of 1. This is the number from which beta helps to calculate risk and expected return.

The SML formula defines the expected (or required) rate of return for any given beta, risk-free rate, and market return, *when the asset is in equilibrium.* If the pricing of the security is not in equilibrium, it will fall in a plot point above or below the SML. When a security falls above the SML, such as point A in figure 35 – 5 below, it is underpriced because it is currently providing a return that is higher than would be expected if it were in equilibrium. If markets are efficient, the price of the security will quickly be driven up to force the return back into alignment. If a security temporarily falls below the SML (point B), it is overvalued (priced too high), which is causing its return to fall below the equilibrium rate.

Figure 35 – 5

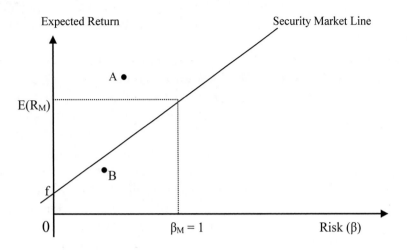

Practice Question

The S&P 500 return for the year is 12%. The 90-day T-bill rate is 2.5%. The investor's common stock fund has a beta of 1.2. What is the expected return for the stock fund?

    A. 11.4%
    B. 13.9%
    C. 14.85%
    D. 17.4%

Answer:
$r_i = 2.5\% + (12\% - 2.5\%)\ 1.2 = 13.9\%$
The answer is B.

Limitations of CAPM CAPM does have some important limitations, including:

- Some results using CAPM may be different, depending upon assumptions used. It is difficult to define investor expectations with any degree of assuredness. Also, since market returns cannot be "observed," they can only be estimated.

- Beta is a very dynamic statistical tool and can shift rapidly over relatively short periods of time. If beta's formula does not have a market proxy closely paralleling that of the one used in CAPM, the results may be skewed.

- The nature of risky investments favors the position that risk-averse investors should expect higher returns for investing in riskier assets. Even before the investment is made *(ex ante)*, this is the investor's expectation. After the fact *(ex post facto)* observations may result in a risk/reward trade-off that does not meet the investor's expectations. Nonetheless, the basic underpinnings of CAPM appear to be supported.

Arbitrage Pricing Theory (APT)

The Arbitrage Pricing Theory (APT) model was developed by Stephen Ross and is predicated upon the law of one price. The premise behind APT is that pricing of securities in different markets cannot differ for any significant length of time. The theory involves few assumptions about investor preferences and states that any unanticipated changes that can cause pricing inefficiencies (arbitrage opportunity: buying in one market to sell immediately in another at a higher price) will be eliminated at some equilibrium point. Most anticipated market changes are said to be already reflected in security values.

A multi-factor model is used in explaining APT in the belief that there are underlying risks that influence both expected and realized security returns. These are "surprise" factors that can occur in the economy and that are not related to any firm or company-specific risk. The following are the factor characteristics:

- The risk factors must have an overriding influence on security returns.

- The risk factors influence expected return. Technical analysis of security returns is used to see what factors have most influenced returns.

- The risk factor must be unpredictable at the beginning of the period analyzed. If it is unexpected, then it cannot be predicted. Inflation could not be an APT risk factor since some reasonable projection of it can be forecast. This factor looks to the difference between real and expected values. Any deviation will be said to have affected the return.

The four primary factors that APT states are key to explaining unexpected changes in security returns are:

(1) Unexpected inflation
(2) Unexpected changes in industrial production
(3) Unanticipated changes in the term structure of interest rates (yield curve)
(4) Unanticipated changes in risk premiums

In the APT formula, the expected value of each factor is zero. The deviation from each of those factors is measured against that base. An error factor is included in the formula to explain any random error term specific to the security. By identifying a few factors that may be influencing most securities and, in turn, portfolio performance, APT suggests an alternative strategy that investors may employ to improve total returns. Depending upon the influence a factor is said to have, a manager might select a weighting of securities based upon a factor realization that favors that factor in relation to other risk factors in the market. If correct, APT suggests that total returns can be superior to market returns.

Other Statistical Measures

Coefficient of Determination (R^2)

The coefficient of determination is represented by the symbol R^2. This is the square of the correlation coefficient, calculated for a given portfolio in relation to the market portfolio. R^2 measures the percentage of variation in a portfolio that is attributable to the market. It reveals the extent of diversification in a fund. A low R^2 (for example, .25) suggests that a fund is not well diversified and has more unsystematic risk exposure than another fund with an R^2 of .70. An R^2 of .70 would mean that 30% of the movement in a portfolio cannot be explained by market movement. An R^2 of less than .70 suggests that a portfolio is not adequately diversified.

The R^2 for a fund is calculated in relation to the most appropriate index for that fund. For most stock funds, the R^2 will be based on the S&P 500 index.

REMEMBER: *R^2 SHOWS THE VARIATION IN A PORTFOLIO THAT CAN BE ATTRIBUTED TO THE MARKET. A WELL DIVERSIFIED PORTFOLIO WILL HAVE AN R^2 ABOVE .70.*

Z-statistic

The z-statistic is a relative measurement that can be used to assess whether a closed-end mutual fund (which trades on the market and can be priced at a discount or premium to NAV) is expensive or inexpensive. If the Z-stat is positive, it indicates that the current discount is higher than the mean for a given period; a negative value, however, indicates that the current discount is lower than the mean for the period. Following a mean reversion theory, the price and return should move back to the average.

Z = (current discount-mean discount)/standard deviation

In the formula for the z-statistic, standard deviation measures the extent to which the discount has varied.

Morningstar assesses a z-score of less than -2 as a signal that a fund is relatively inexpensive, and a score of greater than +2 as a signal that the fund is relatively expensive.

Example 1:

A closed-end fund with a net asset value of $10 is trading at $8.00. The average 1-year discount is -14%. The 1-year standard deviation of the discount/premium is 2.

In absolute terms, the fund is trading at a discount of -20% because you are paying 80 cents for each $1 of NAV.

The z-statistic is:

$$[(-20) - (-14)]/2 = -3$$

With a z-score of -3, this fund would be considered relatively inexpensive. (**Note:** being relatively inexpensive does not necessarily mean undervalued. Additional research will be needed to determine if it is truly undervalued.)

Example 2:

A closed-end fund with a net asset value of $10 is trading at $9.00. The average 1-year discount is -15%. The 1-year standard deviation of the discount/premium is 2.

In absolute terms, the fund is trading at a discount of -10% because you are paying 90 cents for each $1 of NAV.

The z-statistic is:

$$[(-10) - (-15)]/2 = +2.5$$

With a z-score of +2.5, this fund would be considered relatively expensive. (**Note:** being relatively expensive does not necessarily mean overvalued. Additional research will be needed to determine if it is truly overvalued.)

Probability Analysis and Modeling

Probability Analysis

Probability analysis attempts to make sense of historical data and may be used to help predict what has not yet occurred. Gathering data, organizing it intelligently, and then analyzing its significance are all key elements that quantitative analysis relies upon for determining probable outcomes.

Financial planners should be aware of the advantages of probability analysis, without necessarily understanding all the "hows" and "whys" that underlie methodology protocol or probability audits. The planner must always remember that this analysis is but one of many tools that can augment the investment planning process. It is not a predictor of future returns, but simply a means by which simulated returns can be represented over a specific time interval. Utilized properly, probability analysis can serve as another value-added tool in managing client portfolios.

Stochastic Modeling

Stochastic modeling may be used to forecast conditions under different outcomes when one or more of the variables within the model are random.

Modeling and Simulation

One popular form of stochastic modeling used to estimate the probability of outcomes is Monte Carlo simulation. Financial planners should realize that an expected percentage return for a portfolio is simply a point estimate; it is one number in an entire range of possible outcomes. The caveat here for planner and client alike is to be fully aware of GIGO – Garbage In, Garbage Out! Critical elements like input variables, confusion over what the model distribution curve should look like (not likely to be bell-shaped, that is, normal), and the range of distributions can, rather than diminishing uncertainty, contribute to it. Still, the modeling process offers a decided advantage over simply using a benchmark portfolio approach or projecting retirement distribution percentages predicated upon mean (average) returns. By depending too much upon single-point estimates that squeeze the variable range of historical data into one number, the planner may be disregarding the importance of variability characteristics that are exhibited in actual portfolio performance figures.

Monte Carlo modeling can make use of data comprised of estimates of probable cash flows. These estimates can then be altered randomly together with different asset allocation assumptions. A conclusion can then be drawn as to what might be the most useful asset classes or what could be the possible shortfalls that might be encountered after "x" number of years. Whereas "efficient" portfolios based upon traditional input data may not always coincide with client goals and objectives, a decided advantage in employing this methodology is the user's ability to crunch new, random numbers that were never exhibited in historical data. Financial planners will have a better tool for mapping probabilities for targeted returns or client withdrawal expectations in retirement.

Monte Carlo simulation does not attempt to analyze past data but, instead, builds upon what has already occurred. Projections are made in planning for what might occur should the inputted data returns materialize. Repetitive tests of random numbers improve analysis of client goals and objectives, and more intelligent conclusions can thus be drawn. When one collects enough results from repeated "runs," a confidence interval can then be established for each measurement.

This process does seem preferable to reliance upon past average returns over 10 or 20 years or more. There would appear to be too much uncertainty inherent in relying upon single-point estimates for future returns. One only has to review deterministic models that utilize geometric average returns and their corresponding single-point estimate. The problem posed is that the same average annual return can be calculated in whatever order the individual returns appear, but it may have severe consequences on a client's portfolio when needed withdrawals commence. Simulation models like Monte Carlo, however, can test hundreds, even thousands, of different market scenarios and adapt client goals and objectives to the variability in projected portfolio returns that result.

Sensitivity Analysis

Sensitivity analysis (What-if analysis) seeks to analyze an investment based on its sensitivity to various factors such as interest rate changes, inflation rate changes, and tax rate changes. The analysis may include pro forma projections on a best-case, worst-case, and most-likely case scenario basis.

TOPIC 35 – APPLICATION QUESTIONS

1. (Published question released November, 1994)

The standard deviation of the returns of a portfolio of securities will be _____ the weighted average of the standard deviation of returns of the individual component securities.

- A. Equal to
- B. Less than
- C. Greater than
- D. Less than or equal to (depending upon the correlation between securities)
- E. Less than, equal to, or greater than (depending upon the correlation between securities)

2. (Published question released December, 1996)

Which combination of the following statements about investment risk is correct?

- (1) Beta is a measure of systematic, non-diversifiable risk.
- (2) Rational investors will form portfolios and eliminate systematic risk.
- (3) Rational investors will form portfolios and eliminate unsystematic risk.
- (4) Systematic risk is the relevant risk for a well diversified portfolio.
- (5) Beta captures all the risk inherent in an individual security.

- A. (1), (2), and (5) only
- B. (1), (3), and (4) only
- C. (2) and (5) only
- D. (2), (3), and (4) only
- E. (1) and (5) only

3. Stocks X and Y produced the following returns in recent years:

Year	Stock X	Stock Y
1	6%	2%
2	8%	0%
3	4%	10%
4	9%	12%
5	11%	14%
Avg.	7.6%	7.6%

Which of the following are the standard deviations of the returns on the two stocks?

- A. X = 2.7, Y = 6.2
- B. X = 2.7, Y = 4.8
- C. X = 3.8, Y = 6.5
- D. X = 3.8, Y = 5.9
- E. X = 4.1, Y = 5.3

4. Assume that XYZ Corporation's stock has a mean rate of return over the years of 11% and a standard deviation of 3.0. If the historical returns are normally distributed, approximately what percentage of the historical returns have been between 8% and 14%?

- A. 33%
- B. 50%
- C. 68%
- D. 75%
- E. 96%

5. Which of the following investments is less risky: Stock X, with an average expected return of 20% and a standard deviation of 3; or Stock Y, with an average expected return of 27% and a standard deviation of 5?

    A. Stock X, because it has a lower expected return

    B. Stock X, because it has a lower standard deviation

    C. Stock Y, because it has a higher expected return

    D. Stock Y, because it has a higher standard deviation

    E. Stock X, because it has a lower coefficient of variation

    F. Stock Y, because it has a lower coefficient of variation

6. Assume that a portfolio consists of two stocks, X and Y, and each makes up 50% of the total. Also assume that X and Y have identical standard deviations around their rate of return. In this case, which of the following statements is correct?

    A. If X and Y are perfectly positively correlated, the standard deviation of the portfolio will be twice that of either X or Y.

    B. If X and Y are perfectly negatively correlated, the standard deviation of the portfolio will be zero.

    C. If X and Y are perfectly positively correlated, the standard deviation of the portfolio will be zero.

    D. If X and Y are perfectly negatively correlated, the standard deviation of the portfolio will be twice that of either X or Y.

    E. None of the above conclusions can be drawn because we do not know the market prices of X and Y.

7. The stock of Ajax Corp. has a beta of 1.1, while that of Bohunk Corp. has a beta of .85. In this situation, which of the following statements is correct?

    A. Ajax stock is more volatile than Bohunk stock.

    B. Ajax stock is less volatile than an average stock.

    C. Bohunk stock is more volatile than an average stock.

    D. Both Ajax and Bohunk are less volatile than an average stock.

    E. Both Ajax and Bohunk are more volatile than an average stock.

8. Which of the following statements concerning beta is (are) correct?

    (1) It is a measure of a stock's total riskiness.

    (2) It is based on historical data.

    (3) The higher the beta, the greater is the systematic riskiness of a stock.

    A. (1) only

    B. (2) only

    C. (3) only

    D. (1) and (2) only

    E. (2) and (3) only

9. Your client informs you that she read a financial report that listed the beta coefficient of a fund you recently placed in her portfolio as 1.0. Your initial reply to her would be correct if you stated only that:

(1) Beta is a measure of systematic risk.
(2) A beta of 1.0 signifies a risk-free portfolio compared to one with a beta of 2.0.
(3) Beta helps measure the variability of a portfolio's return.

    A. (1) only
    B. (1) and (2) only
    C. (3) only
    D. (1) and (3) only
    E. (2) and (3) only

10. A private investor tells you that he recently learned that a stock he owns has a beta of –2.0 and a standard deviation of 16.3. If the market declines by 5%, he should anticipate that his stock will:

    A. Decline by 10%
    B. Rise by 11.3%
    C. Rise by 10%
    D. Decline by 20%
    E. There is not enough information to perform the calculation.

11. The beta of a security:

(1) Is not the measure of its systematic risk level
(2) Can be measured by standard deviation
(3) Is the slope of the capital market line

    A. (3) only
    B. (2) only
    C. (1) and (3) only
    D. (1) only
    E. None of the above

12. David purchased a stock with a mean return of 5% and a standard deviation of 2%. What percentage of the time should David expect to earn 3% or higher on his investment?

    A. 16%
    B. 32%
    C. 68%
    D. 84%

13. Portfolios selected by investors that are located on the lower left portion of the efficient frontier would most likely be characterized as:

    A. Risk averse
    B. Aggressive
    C. Neutral with a conservative bias
    D. Favoring the use of put options
    E. None of the above

14. A portfolio that is positioned above the efficient frontier line is said to be:

    A. At its optimal point
    B. Attainable, provided its standard deviation is below the point of tangency
    C. Inefficient
    D. Attainable for aggressive investors only
    E. Not in the feasible set

15. Indifference curves along with the efficient frontier line on a graphic display:

    A. Depict capital gains potential for the risk-averse investor
    B. Define the least risky portfolio
    C. Reveal beta coefficients that are greater than 1.0
    D. Measure risk and reward preferences
    E. Cannot cross the efficient frontier at more than one point

16. What is the market risk premium if the market is expected to return 15% on average over the next year, the risk-free rate is 4%, and Company A has a beta coefficient of 1.4 and a past annual return of 26%?

    A. 22%
    B. 30.8%
    C. 21%
    D. 11%
    E. 15.4%

17. Which of the following statements concerning the efficient frontier as developed in the Markowitz model is (are) correct?

    (1) A rate of return represented by a point that is inside the efficient frontier indicates a superior portfolio.
    (2) A portfolio that offers both the highest rate of return and the lowest risk would be represented by a point on the efficient frontier.
    (3) A portfolio represented by a point outside the efficient frontier is not feasible.

    A. (1) only
    B. (2) only
    C. (3) only
    D. (1) and (2) only
    E. (2) and (3) only

18. Based on the Markowitz model, which of the following represents a security that is the most logical for an investor?

    A. Rate of return 9%, beta 1.3
    B. Rate of return 8%, beta 1.4
    C. Rate of return 11%, beta 1.2
    D. Rate of return 12%, beta 1.1
    E. Rate of return 12%, beta 1.2

19. The following information is provided to Martha, who wants to learn what the market risk premium is. The risk-free rate is 5.5%, the market return is 12%, and the beta for ABC stock is 1.3. She correctly calculates that the market risk premium is:

    A. 8.45%
    B. 7.15%
    C. 13.95%
    D. 13.65%
    E. 6.5%

20. (Published question released November, 1994)

If the market risk premium were to increase, the value of common stock (everything else being equal) would:

A. <u>Not</u> change because this does <u>not</u> affect stock values
B. Increase in order to compensate the investor for increased risk
C. Increase due to higher risk-free rates
D. Decrease in order to compensate the investor for increased risk
E. Decrease due to lower risk-free rates

21. (Published question released November, 1994)

Modern "asset allocation" is based upon the model developed by Harry Markowitz. Which of the following statements is (are) correctly identified with this model?

(1) The risk, return, and covariance of assets are important input variables in creating portfolios.
(2) Negatively correlated assets are necessary to reduce the risk of portfolios.
(3) In creating a portfolio, diversifying <u>across</u> asset types (e.g., stocks and bonds) is less effective than diversifying <u>within</u> an asset type.
(4) The efficient frontier is relatively insensitive to the input variable.

A. (1) and (2) only
B. (1), (2), and (3) only
C. (1) only
D. (2) and (4) only
E. (1), (2), and (4) only

22. (Published question released December, 1996)

In analyzing the position of a portfolio in terms of risk/return on the capital market line (CML), superior performance exists if the fund's position is _____ the CML, inferior performance exists if the fund's position is _____ the CML, and equilibrium position exists if it is _____ the CML.

A. Above; on; below
B. Above; below; on
C. Below; on; above
D. Below; above; on
E. On; above; below

23. On the efficient frontier line:

A. No investment in entirely risk-free assets is possible.
B. All risky assets in a market portfolio are not included.
C. The beta coefficient is substituted for standard deviation.
D. According to Markowitz, many portfolios can be efficient.
E. Only individual securities are evaluated.

24. Which of the following statements concerning Arbitrage Pricing Theory (APT) are correct?

   (1) Unlike the Capital Asset Pricing Model, APT adds several more variables to explain the rate of return on securities.

   (2) APT focuses on unexpected changes as being the changes in variables that affect the rate of return on a portfolio.

   (3) APT suggests that two portfolios or securities with the same degree of risk are likely to generate substantially different rates of return over the long run.

   A. (1) and (2) only
   B. (1) and (3) only
   C. (2) and (3) only
   D. (1), (2), and (3)
   E. Neither (1), (2), nor (3)

25. All of the following statements concerning diversification are correct, EXCEPT:

   A. Diversification of an investor's bond portfolio can be achieved by owning the bonds of several corporations.

   B. Diversification would be improved for a wealthy investor who has $10 million spread among three well managed common stock mutual funds by investing some of the $10 million in a bond fund, a real estate investment trust, and CDs.

   C. Diversification of a stock portfolio can be increased by adding stocks with low correlation.

   D. If an investor's broker advises him or her that another September, 2001, stock market crash is imminent, the investor will be wise to sell all his or her common stock mutual fund shares and put the cash in a money market fund.

26. Which of the following statement(s) concerning correlation coefficients is (are) correct?

    (1) A correlation coefficient of –1 for the returns of two securities indicates that both of them should be carefully considered for inclusion in a portfolio since maximum risk reduction could be achieved by including both.

    (2) The returns of Security B would increase 8% when the returns of Security A increased 8% if the correlation coefficient for the returns of the two securities were +1.

    A. (1) only
    B. (2) only
    C. Both (1) and (2)
    D. Neither (1) nor (2)

27. Which of the following is the correct formula for calculating the coefficient of variation?

    A. The standard deviation minus the mean
    B. The mean divided by the standard deviation
    C. The standard deviation divided by the mean
    D. The standard deviation multiplied by the mean

28. All of the following statements concerning matching the betas of specific stocks with an 8% increase in the market prices of all listed common stocks are correct, EXCEPT:

    A. Stock M, with a beta of .4, would have a 3.2% increase in its market price.
    B. Stock N, with a beta of 1, would have an 8% increase in its market price.
    C. Stock O, with a beta of 1.5, would have a 15% increase in its market price.
    D. Stock P, with a beta of 1.8, would have more than a 14% increase in its market price.

29. Which of the following statements concerning a standard deviation is (are) correct?

    (1) A higher standard deviation for a distribution of investment returns suggests higher risk since the expected outcome is more uncertain.

    (2) Standard deviation is a measure of both systematic and unsystematic risk.

    (3) An investor should choose a lower standard deviation of returns over a higher standard deviation, other things being equal.

    A. (1) only
    B. (1) and (2) only
    C. (2) and (3) only
    D. (1) and (3) only
    E. (1), (2), and (3)

30. Beta coefficient is a volatility measure of systematic risk. However, differences in calculating beta may result from which of the following?

(1) Differences in time periods covered
(2) Considering only price changes and not total returns
(3) The use of different measurements of the market
(4) Portfolio standard deviation calculations that are mostly positive

    A. (2) and (4) only
    B. (1), (2), and (3) only
    C. (3) and (4) only
    D. (1) and (3) only
    E. (1), (2), (3), and (4)

31. All of the following statements concerning correlation are correct, EXCEPT:

    A. The coefficient of determination is the square of the correlation coefficient.
    B. The correlation coefficient measures the relationship between two variables.
    C. If the numerical value of the correlation coefficient is −1.0, the variables move exactly opposite to each other, and maximum diversification is achieved.
    D. Foreign diversification reduces portfolio risk only if the foreign and domestic securities are perfectly correlated.

32. Based on the following correlation coefficients between U.S. stocks and foreign stocks, which country's equities would provide the greatest diversification to a U.S. investor?

Canada	.720
UK	.513
Japan	.326
Germany	.209

    A. Canada
    B. Germany
    C. Japan
    D. United Kingdom

33. All of the following statements concerning rates of return are correct, EXCEPT:

    A. According to portfolio theory, the required rate of return is the minimum rate of return an investor must expect that will induce him or her to commit funds to a particular risky investment.
    B. The key words pertinent to a definition of "required rate of return" in portfolio theory are "minimum expectation" and "minimum inducement."
    C. An investor's realized return is only determinable when all the facts are known, after the investment has been liquidated or otherwise terminated.
    D. Investors tend to realize their expected returns on risky securities more often on a short-run basis than on a long-run basis.

34. The tangency point between the efficient frontier of risky assets and the capital market line defines the efficient portfolio of the risk-free asset and the portfolio of all risky assets. According to the modern portfolio theory, an investor:

A. Should never select any proportion of assets from this optimal risky portfolio
B. Should seek the riskiest portfolio, provided there are a minimum of fixed-income instruments available
C. Should always choose the portfolio of risky assets and then move to his or her risk-preference level, regardless of his or her risk aversion
D. Must first determine which type of risk-free asset is being offered

35. Portfolios that offer the highest expected return at a given level of risk constitute the efficient frontier line. These portfolios, in accordance with modern portfolio theory:

A. Are the best ones attainable at any time
B. Are limited in number on the efficient frontier line
C. Do not have indifference curves
D. Have both standard deviation and beta as risk measures on the horizontal axis

36. The risk-free rate of return is 9%, and the market rate of return is 15%. An investor is considering a stock that sells for $50 and pays $1.25 in dividends that are expected to grow by 6% annually. The beta of the stock is .97. Based on the CAPM formula, what is the investor's required rate of return?

A. 8.65%   C. 14.82%
B. 14.55%   D. 15.00%

37. The risk-free rate of return is 7.3%, and the market rate of return is 10.2%. An investor is considering a stock that sells for $40 and pays $.85 in dividends that are expected to grow at 7% annually. The beta of the stock is 1.12. Based on the CAPM formula, what is the investor's required rate of return?

A. 7.30%   C. 10.55%
B. 9.27%   D. 11.42%

******

38. Assume that a stock sells for $50 per share and pays an annual dividend of $3.50, and dividends are expected to grow at 7% per year into perpetuity. The stock has a beta of 1.2. The market rate of return is 16%, and the risk-free rate of return is 9%.

Based on the CAPM formula, the required return for the above stock is _____.

A. 10.80%
B. 14.29%
C. 17.40%
D. 19.20%

39. Which of the following statements correctly describes a case where standard deviation is the best measure of the portfolio's risk level?

A. When the portfolio is well diversified
B. When the portfolio is not well diversified
C. When the portfolio is fully invested
D. When the portfolio is indexed

40. Which of the following statements concerning arbitrage pricing theory (APT) is (are) correct?

(1) APT takes account of more variables as determinants of a stock's return than the Capital Asset Pricing Model (CAPM).
(2) APT focuses only on expected changes in the variables, affecting a stock's return.
(3) APT suggests that differences in the prices of different securities presenting the same degree of risk will be only temporary.

    A. (1) only
    B. (1) and (2) only
    C. (1) and (3) only
    D. (2) and (3) only
    E. (1), (2), and (3)

For practice answering case questions related to Topic 35, please answer the following questions in the cases included in the Appendix at the back of this textbook.

Case	Questions
Donaldson	5 and 6
Hilbert Stores, Inc.	
Maxwell	
Beals	
Mocsin	
Eldridge	1
Young	
Johnson	6, 7, and 8
Thomas	5, 6, 7, 8, 9, 10, and 11
Jim and Brenda Quinn	12, 13, 14, 15, 16, 17, and 18

Measures of Investment Returns (Topic 36)

CFP Board Student-Centered Learning Objectives

(a) Identify, measure and interpret investment returns including after-tax, holding period return, effective annual rate, annual percentage rate, time- and dollar-weighted returns, geometric and arithmetic returns.

(b) Calculate and interpret risk-adjusted performance measures such as the Sharpe, Jensen, and Treynor ratios.

Measures of Investment Returns

A.	Simple vs. compound return
B.	Geometric average vs. arithmetic average return
C.	Time-weighted vs. dollar-weighted return
D.	Real (inflation-adjusted) vs. nominal return
E.	Holding period return
F.	Internal rate of return (IRR)
G.	Yield-to-maturity
H.	Yield-to-call
I.	Current yield
J.	Realized compound yield
K.	Taxable equivalent yield (TEY)
L.	Risk-adjusted performance measures
	1) Sharpe ratio
	2) Treynor ratio
	3) Jensen ratio
	4) Information ratio

Measures of Investment Returns

The following paragraphs contain explanations and illustrations of various ways in which the rate of return on an investment may be measured.

Simple vs. Compound Return

There are two ways of computing interest. Simple interest is computed by applying an interest rate to only an original principal sum. Compound interest is computed by applying an interest rate to the total of an original principal sum and all interest credited in earlier time periods.

To illustrate the difference, assume $100 is deposited in an account that earns 6 percent simple interest per year. At the end of each year, the account will be credited with $6.00 of interest. At the end of five years, there will be $130 in the account. Alternatively, if the account earns 6 percent compound interest per year, it will grow to $133.82 (input the following variables into your financial calculator: n = 5, I = 6, PV = 100, and PMT = 0, and solve for FV). The extra $3.82 in the account when it is credited with compound interest is interest earned on previous interest earnings.

☞ **K Study Tip** – **You should always assume compound interest on the exam unless the exam question specifically tells you otherwise.**

Annualized Return

Rates of return, to be comparable, should be expressed on a per year basis. For example, if a particular investment yielded 3.4% in a calendar quarter, its annualized return could be expressed as four times that rate, or 13.6% per year. This annualized return is what is usually referred to on a loan as the APR, or annual percentage rate.

Effective Annual Rate

Technically, however, it is not quite accurate to multiply a periodic rate by the number of periods per year. Time-value-of-money analysis tells us, for example, that 4% quarterly (expressed as 16% nominal rate) is more than 8% semiannually [$(1.04)^4 = 16.99\%$ and $(1.08)^2 = 16.64\%$]. You could use the interest rate conversion function on your financial calculator to show that 4% quarterly is an effective annual rate of 16.99%, whereas 8% semiannually is an effective annual rate of 16.64%.

Geometric Average vs. Arithmetic Average Return

The discussion of standard deviation and coefficient of variation in Topic 35 dealt with variability around the arithmetic mean, which is simply the sum of a group of numbers divided by the number of numbers in the group. However, the arithmetic mean can give misleading results when some of the numbers are negative, while others are positive.

To illustrate this point, assume that an investment yielded a 6% rate of return in Year 1 and a negative 4% rate of return in Year 2. The arithmetic mean rate of return is $(+6 - 4) \div 2 = 1\%$ per year. If you invested $100 at the start of Year 1, would you have $102.01 at the end of Year 2? No, you would have $101.76 (i.e., $100 x 1.06 = $106 x .96 = $101.76).

The geometric mean, or geometric average, should be used when averaging percentages, including cases with both positives and negatives. Express each of the n percentages as an index number of 1 (a return relative), multiply them together, take the nth root of the product, and subtract 1 from the result. For example, if the rates of return on an investment have been:

Year	Rate of Return
1	70.0%
2	–26.5%
3	20.0%

The geometric mean return per year is:

$$= \sqrt[3]{1.70x \ .735 \ x \ 1.20} \ - 1$$

$$= \sqrt[3]{1.4994} \ - 1$$

$$= 1.4994^{.3333} - 1$$

$$= 1.1445 \ - 1 \quad = \ .1445, \text{ or } 14.45\%$$

The nth root is the same as the 1/nth power, so you can solve for the geometric mean on your financial calculator by using your y^x key, If you are using an HP-12C, press 1.70, ENTER, .735, x, 1.20, x, ENTER, 1, ENTER, 3, ÷, and y^x. This will give you the answer of 1.1445. Subtract 1, and you get the answer of 14.45%.

If you are using an HP 10BII, press 1.70, x, .735, x, 1.20, =, orange key, y^x, .3333, and =. This will give you the answer of 1.1445. Subtract 1, and you get the answer of 14.45%.

If you are using a TI BAII Plus, press 1.70, x, .735, x, 1.20, =, y^x, .3333, and =. This will give you the answer of 1.1445. Subtract 1, and you get the answer of 14.45%.

The geometric mean return formula as it appears on the CFP® exam provided formula sheet is as follows:

$$GM = \sqrt[n]{(1 + r_1) \ x \ (1 + r_2) \ ... \ (1 + r_n)} \ - 1$$

There is an alternative (and easier) method to solve the geometric mean on the financial calculator by inputting the following variables:

N = 3 (the number of observations)
PV = (1)
PMT = 0
FV = 1.4994

Solve for I which is 14.4562%.

🔔 **REMEMBER**: *USE THE GEOMETRIC MEAN, RATHER THAN THE ARITHMETIC MEAN, WHEN AVERAGING POSITIVE AND NEGATIVE NUMBERS.*

Time-Weighted vs. Dollar-Weighted Rate of Return

A time-weighted return is a financial calculation that does not take into consideration an investor's cash flows. It measures an investment's performance without regard to the inflows and, therefore, is the preferred method of evaluating a portfolio manager's actual rate of return. However, in order to compute a time-weighted return, it is necessary to be aware of when the portfolio's cash inflows and outflows occur. The calculation for a portfolio's return commences before any cash flow has been made and terminates whenever the next cash inflow has been made or at the end of the time period. The only cash flows that are recognized in a time-weighted return are those resulting from dividends or capital appreciation. Finally, the annualized rates of return for each period are calculated and geometrically linked, and a compound rate of return for the measurement period is established. By utilizing this type of measurement, the "value-added" component of a portfolio manager's performance may be evaluated since it will not be prejudiced by the cash flow decisions of a client.

The dollar-weighted return, also known as the internal rate of return (IRR), is a financial calculation that measures the total return on a portfolio from its beginning value. It includes all cash inflow and outflow activity until the end of the time period. The final value of the portfolio, along with all intervening cash flows, is equated with its beginning value. Different cash flow amounts can strongly influence the actual return achieved. Therefore, this measurement is preferred when evaluating the rate of return achieved by an individual client. However, since each individual must decide when and how much is invested during any period, this performance measurement is not suitable for comparison with an index fund. It is a more appropriate calculation when attempting to measure the earnings on invested dollars and when projecting what might be acceptable minimum returns for a client.

The following illustration shows the comparison of time-weighted returns vs. dollar-weighted returns:

Example:

An investor deposits $10,000 at the beginning of Year 1. One year later, the investment has earned a total return of 20%, or $2,000. The investor contributed an additional $50,000 to the account at the beginning of Year 2, but earns only 6%, or $3,720. Finally, at the beginning of Year 3, the investor contributes $25,000 and earns a 10% rate of $9,072. The final account value, at the end of Year 3, is $99,792.

In this example, the dollar-weighted, or internal rate of return, was 9.11%. The time-weighted return, which does not consider the yearly cash flows at the beginning of Years 2 and 3, was 11.85%. Both of these calculations are described below. Since the investor made a larger deposit at the beginning of the second year, which saw a subsequent return of only 6%, the timing decision put the bulk of the investment dollars at more risk and resulted in the dollar-weighted return being lower than the time-weighted return.

Dollar-Weighted Return (IRR)

($10,000)	CF_0
($50,000)	Cash Flow 1
($25,000)	Cash Flow 2
$99,792	Cash Flow 3

$$IRR = 9.11\%$$

See the Internal Rate of Return section on page 36.10 for calculator keystrokes.

Time-Weighted Return

$$\sqrt[3]{1.20 \; x \; 1.06 \; x \; 1.10} \; - 1 \quad = \quad \sqrt[3]{1.3992} \; - 1$$

$$= 1.11847 - 1 = .11847 \; x \; 100 = 11.85\%$$

Note: The keystrokes are the same as the geometric mean shown on page 36.3.

KEY SUMMARY 36 – 1
Time-Weighted Returns vs. Dollar-Weighted Returns

- ❑ A time-weighted return measures an investment's performance without regard to inflows and is the preferred method for evaluating a portfolio manager.
- ❑ The dollar-weighted return, or internal rate of return (IRR), measures the total return on a portfolio from its beginning value and includes all cash inflow and outflow. This measurement is preferred for evaluating the return achieved by an individual client.

Real (Inflation-Adjusted) Return vs. Nominal Return

If an investment yielded a nominal rate of return of, say, 12% in a year when inflation was 4.5%, the investor did not gain 12% in purchasing power. To reflect the impact of inflation, a real rate of return is calculated. The formula is:

$$\text{Real rate} = \left[\frac{(1 + \text{Nominal rate})}{(1 + \text{Inflation rate})}\right] - 1$$

In our example, the real rate:

$$= \frac{1.12}{1.045} - 1$$

$$= .0718, \text{ or } 7.18\%$$

Editor's Note: There is a shortcut on a financial calculator to solve for the inflation adjusted rate of return. If you are using an HP 12C calculator, press 1.045, ENTER, 1.12, Δ% (second row from the top, directly under the PMT key). If you are using an HP 10BII calculator, press 1.045, INPUT, 1.12, orange shift, % CHG (third row from the top, two keys under the I/YR key).

🔑 **KEY SUMMARY 36 – 2**
   Adjusting for Inflation

To adjust for inflation, use the formula for the real rate of return:

$$\text{Real rate} = \left[\frac{(1 + \text{Nominal rate})}{(1 + \text{Inflation rate})}\right] - 1$$

Note: Multiply by 100 to compute the percentage rate.

Total Return

The total return from an investment is the income it produced, plus or minus any capital appreciation or depreciation, and minus expenses; divided by the purchase price paid. For example, if a stock was bought one year ago for $52, paid a dividend during the year of $4, and was sold today for $51, the total return:

$$= \frac{\$4 - 1}{\$52}$$

$$= 5.77\%$$

Or, to take a prospective case, the expected total return on a stock can be found by dividing the expected dividend by the stock's current price, plus the expected dividend growth rate. For example, if a stock is selling for $30, is expected to pay a $2 dividend next year, and is expected to have a dividend growth rate of 5%, the expected total return for the year will be:

$$= \frac{\$2}{\$30} + .05$$

$$= 0.0667 + .05 = 11.667\%$$

Holding Period Return

The holding period return is the same as the total return. However, it produces a misleading result because it doesn't take into account the length of time needed to achieve that total return, except in the case where the holding period is exactly one year. For example, if a total return of 12% was achieved during a two-year holding period, that isn't as good as if it were achieved during a six-month holding period.

 KEY SUMMARY 36 – 3
Holding Period Return Formula

$$HPR = \frac{\text{Income} + \text{Appreciation} - \text{Expenses}}{\text{Purchase price}}$$

Editor's Note: The formula for holding period return appears on the formula sheet as follows:

$$HPR = [(1+r_1) \times (1+r_2) \times ...(1+r_n)] - 1$$

Example:

An investor bought 200 shares of GM stock on margin at $25 per share. The margin interest rate was 10%. He received dividends of $0.75 per share and sold the stock after nine months for $32 per share. What was the holding period return?

The investor bought the GM stock on margin. Margin interest is an expense. The margin requirement is usually 50%, and if the question does not state otherwise, you should assume a margin of 50%. Therefore, the investor used only $2,500 of his own money and borrowed $2,500. He paid 10% interest on $2,500 for 9 months, thus:

Margin interest = (9/12)(10%)($2,500) = $187.50

$$\text{Appreciation} = \$6,400 - \$5,000 = \$1,400$$

$$\text{Income} = (\$0.75)(200) = \$150$$

$$\text{Purchase price} = \$5,000 - \$2,500 = \$2,500$$

$$\text{HPR} = \frac{\$150 + 1,400 - \$187.50}{\$2,500} = 54.5\%$$

The **after-tax holding period return** can be calculated by reducing the income and gains by the amount of tax on each item and then using the reduced amount of income and gains in the formula for holding period return.

Weighted-Average Expected Return

The weighted-average expected return on a portfolio is determined by multiplying the return expected for each security included in the portfolio by the proportion of the total funds that the individual security represents in the portfolio and then adding these weighted percentages together. The total of the proportions invested in each security (used as weights) must always equal one. For example, assume an investor owns a stock with a current market value of $12,000 that has an expected return of 9% and owns a bond with a current market value of $7,000 that has an expected return of 11%. The weighted-average expected return for the portfolio is 9.74%, calculated as follows:

Investment Category	Amount Invested	Proportion in Portfolio	x	Expected Return	=	Weighted Return
Stock	$12,000	.632	x	.09		.0569
Bond	7,000	.368	x	.11		.0405
	$19,000	1.000				.0974

The weighted-average expected return can also be used with beta coefficients to help select an appropriate portfolio. Consider the following data for three assets that could be used to construct a portfolio:

Asset	Return	Expected Beta
Treasury Bills	7.0%	0.0
Stock A	12.0%	0.8
Stock B	16.0%	1.2

Assume the investor does not wish to accept a portfolio risk higher than 1.0. One possible portfolio could be 20% invested in Treasury Bills and 80% in Stock B. The following calculations can be made to determine expected return and the portfolio beta.

A Asset	B Weight in Portfolio	C Beta	D = B x C Weighted Beta	E Expected Return	F = B x E Weighted Expected Return
Treasury Bills	.20	0	0	7.0	1.4
Stock B	.80	1.2	0.96	16.0	12.8
			0.96		14.2

Net Present Value (NPV)

Net present value (NPV) and internal rate of return (IRR) are calculations that can be used to analyze the attractiveness of a project, or to compare alternative project choices. The net present value is the present value of all cash inflows minus the present value of all cash outflows. The calculation will require an interest rate to be used for evaluation. This rate may be the required return for the investment based on the amount of risk assumed, the cost of capital required to fund the investment, or the rate that could be earned on an alternative investment (the opportunity cost). If the result of the NPV calculation is positive, the investment is a good investment (PV of cash inflows is greater than PV of cash outflows). If the result is a negative NPV, the investment will not provide the return required by the investor and should not be entered. An NPV of zero would indicate that the investment is providing exactly the return required by the investor or is just barely covering the cost of capital.

Internal Rate of Return (IRR)

The internal rate of return (IRR) of an investment calculates the discount rate at which the present value of the cash inflows equals the present value of the cash outflows. The IRR is the rate at which NPV is equal to zero. If the IRR is larger than the investor's required return or cost of capital, the investment is attractive. If the IRR is below the investor's required return or cost of capital, the investment should not be pursued.

The internal rate of return on an investment is a highly accurate measure of its yield. Thus, IRR takes into account the timing and amount of each of the investment's cash flows, in and out, and reduces them to a true annual rate of return.

To illustrate, assume that a proposed investment is expected to entail the following cash flows:

Beg. of Year	Net Cash Flow
1	$50,000 outflow
2	20,000 inflow
3	10,000 outflow
4	14,000 inflow
5	38,000 inflow

By using the cash flow mode of a financial calculator, one could enter each of the above five cash flows (positive number for cash inflows and negative number for cash outflows) as they occur at the start of each year and compute the IRR, which is 7.27% per year.

TI-BA-II Plus	**HP-12C**
CF, 2nd, CLR Work	f, REG
50,000, +/−, ENTER, ↓	50,000, CHS, g, CFo
20,000, ENTER, ↓, ↓	20,000, g, CFj
10,000, +/−, ENTER, ↓, ↓	10,000, CHS, g, CFj
14,000, ENTER, ↓, ↓	14,000, g, CFj
38,000, ENTER, ↓	38,000, g, CFj
IRR, CPT	f, IRR
IRR = 7.27%	IRR = 7.27%
HP-10B II	
Orange Shift, C ALL	
50,000, +/−, Cfj	
20,000, Cfj	
10,000, +/−, Cfj	
14,000, Cfj	
38,000, Cfj	
shift, IRR/YR	
IRR = 7.27%	

To illustrate the NPV calculation, the same expected cash flows can be used, and the cost of capital is assumed to be 6%. With the same information in the financial calculator, we enter 6 for the interest rate and solve for NPV. The NPV will be $1,822.

Bond Yields

Yield to Maturity

The yield to maturity (YTM) on an investment is its IRR per year throughout a known holding period. It is frequently used to compute the yield on a bond that has been or will be held until it matures.

Example:

An investor buys a $1,000 face amount bond for $895. The bond has a 7% coupon rate with interest payable semiannually, starting in six months, and will mature in 4½ years. One could calculate its YTM using the cash flow mode of a financial calculator and doubling the result.

Alternatively, one could use the calculator's basic time value of money (TVM) mode to produce the same result. Note that ½ of the annual coupon amount is typically paid every 6 months, so the calculation is adjusted for semi-annual compounding. Enter:

> $1,000 as the FV
> $35 as the end-of-period payment PMT
> 9 as the N
> $895 as the PV (input as a negative number)
> and solve for I/YR, which is 4.975%

This is a semiannual rate, so the APR is double that amount, or 9.95%.

A bond's price is related to its yield to maturity, so if the YTM is known, the price can be calculated using the above TVM calculation and inputting the YTM as I/YR (entered as a semi-annual rate), then solving for the present value (PV).

Practice Question

(CFP Board published question released January, 1999)

Assuming that the current market yield for similar risk bonds is 8%, determine the discounted present value of a $1,000 bond with a 7.5% coupon rate which pays interest semiannually and matures in 17.5 years.

A. $504.68
B. $539.78
C. $953.34
D. $968.96
E. $1,653.26

Answer:
Enter $1,000 as the FV, $37.50 as the end-of-period payment, 4 as the value of i, and 35 as the value of n. Solve for PV, which is $953.34.
The answer is C.

☞ *K Study Tip* – **In computing the YTM for a zero-coupon bond, you should assume semiannual compounding unless the question states to the contrary.**

Yield to Call

On a callable security, the yield to call (YTC) is calculated in the same way as its YTM, except that the call price is used as the future value, and the first (or next) date on which it may be called is used to measure the value of n. For example, assume that a $1,000 face amount bond with a 9% coupon rate and interest payable semiannually is now selling for $910. It can be called by the issuer at any time, starting three years from now. The call premium is six months' interest. To find the YTC, enter $45 as the end-of-period payment, -$910 as the PV, 6 as the n, and $1,045 as the FV. Solve for I/YR, which is 7.02% semiannually, or 14.04% on an annual basis. Note PV is entered as a negative number, whereas PMT and FV are positive numbers.

Current Yield

A security's current yield is simply the annual income it provides divided by its current price. This is true for both bonds and for stocks. Capital appreciation or depreciation is ignored. For example, a preferred stock selling at $82.50 and paying an annual dividend of $5.75 has a current yield of:

$$\frac{\$\ 5.75}{\$82.50} = 6.97\%$$

 KEY SUMMARY 36 – 4
Current Yield

$$\text{Current yield} = \frac{\text{Annual income}}{\text{Price}}$$

Yields for Premium and Discount Bonds

The following diagram shows the relationship among interest rates, yields, and prices for bonds that sell at a **premium**. The coupon or nominal yield will be higher than the current yield, which will be higher than the yield to maturity, which will be higher than the yield to call. Interest rates have declined after the bond was issued, so the market price for the bond increased the yield to call has fallen farther than the yield to maturity, which has fallen more than the current yield.

Bond Sells at a Premium

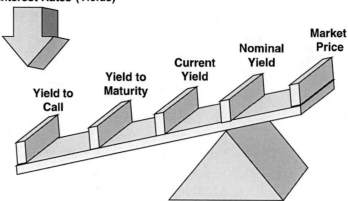

The next diagram shows the relationship among interest rates, yields, and prices for those bonds that sell at a **discount**. The coupon or nominal yield will be lower than the current yield, which will be lower than the yield to maturity, which will be lower than the yield to call. Interest rates have risen and the market price for the bond decreased, so yield to call has risen farther than the yield to maturity, which has risen more than the current yield.

Bond Sells at a Discount

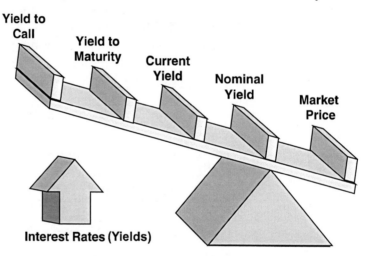

Realized Compound Yield

The realized compound yield is the yield actually earned on an investment, including the earnings on any reinvested interest, dividends, or other cash flows received from the investment. The return actually realized on a coupon-paying bond will equal the yield to maturity only if coupons are reinvested at the same rate as the yield to maturity.

Example:

An investor paid $1,025.56 to purchase a bond with an 8% coupon that matures in 12 years (assume annual compounding). The yield to maturity is calculated as follows:

N = 12
PMT = 80
PV = -1,025.56
FV = 1,000
Solve for I = 7.67%

If interest rates change to 9%, the investor will be able to reinvest each coupon payment at 9%, rather than 7.67%. To calculate the realized compound yield, we must first determine the future value of the reinvested coupons:

PMT = -80
N = 12
I = 9
Solve for FV = $1,611.26

The second step is to determine what interest rate will make the present value equal to the total future value, which includes the total value of the reinvested coupons plus the return of par, when the bond matures:

FV = 2,611.26
N = 12
PV = -1,025.56
Solve for I = 8.10%

This answer makes sense because the coupons were reinvested at a higher rate than the YTM; therefore, the realized yield should be higher than the YTM.

After-Tax Return and Taxable-Equivalent Yield

After-Tax Return

Most investors will be more concerned with the rate of return they earn after taxes than with the pretax rate. Also, a comparison of different investments with different tax treatment requires evaluation on an after-tax basis.

An investment's after-tax rate of return is found by multiplying the pretax rate by the quantity one minus the investor's marginal tax bracket.

For example, if an investment provides a taxable return of 24% to an investor in a 35% combined federal and state marginal tax bracket, the after-tax return is as follows:

$$24 (1 - .35) = 24 \times .65 = 15.60\%$$

Investors should not assume that the return on a tax-free municipal bond will be greater than the return on other bonds. If the investor is not in a high tax bracket, a corporate bond is likely to provide a higher after-tax return than the municipal bond. It is generally important to perform the calculation of after-tax return for corporate and Treasury bonds to make certain which bond will provide the superior return.

Tax Rates on Investments

When calculating the after-tax return on investment income, it is assumed that the income generated from investments is the last income the client receives. In other words, it is taxed at the client's highest marginal rate for the type of income that is generated. Investment income taxed as ordinary income or as a short-term capital gain are taxed at the client's highest ordinary income rate. Qualified dividends and long-term capital gains from the sale of property that was held longer than one year are taxed at rates based on the following breakpoints, which were adjusted by the Tax Cuts and Jobs Act (TCJA) of 2017:

2018 TCJA Long-Term Capital Gain Tax Rates – Married Filing Jointly

Tax Rate	Taxable Income
0%	$0 – $77,200
15%	$77,201 – $479,000
20%	Over $479,000

2018 TCJA Long-Term Capital Gain Tax Rates – Head of Household

Tax Rate	Taxable Income
0%	$0 – $51,700
15%	$51,701 – $452,400
20%	Over $452,400

2018 TCJA Long-Term Capital Gain Tax Rates – Single

Tax Rate	Taxable Income
0%	$0 – $38,600
15%	$38,601 – $425,800
20%	Over $425,800

2018 TCJA Long-Term Capital Gain Tax Rates – Married Filing Separately

Tax Rate	Taxable Income
0%	$0 – $38,600
15%	$38,601 – $239,500
20%	Over $239,500

Unearned Income Medicare Contribution Tax

The Patient Protection and Affordable Care Act (Patient Protection Act) passed in 2010, included a 3.8% tax on investment income for individuals with an adjusted gross income (AGI) above $200,000 and joint filers with AGI above $250,000 ($125,000 MFS). This is in addition to the regular tax imposed on the investment income.

The 3.8% tax is assessed on the lesser of: (1) Net investment income, or (2) the amount by which MAGI exceeds the threshold. For most individuals MAGI will be their AGI unless they are living abroad and have foreign earned income.

The tax applies to investment income from dividends, interest, annuities, royalties, rents, gains from disposition of property, and income from passive activities. It does not apply to income earned in the ordinary course of a trade or business.

The tax is imposed on individuals, self-employed individuals, estates, and trusts. Distributions from qualified retirement plans, including IRAs, SEPs, SIMPLEs, 403(b), and 457 plans are exempt from the tax. Maximizing investments into any qualified plan or IRA as an alternative to other investments will provide for future savings since the income withdrawn from a qualified plan or IRA will not be subject to the Medicare tax. Taking distributions from a Roth IRA rather than a traditional IRA may help keep AGI below the threshold.

 **KEY SUMMARY 36 – 5**
After-Tax Return

After-tax return = Taxable return (1 – Tax bracket)

Taxable-Equivalent Yield

A taxable equivalent yield is calculated for an investment that pays tax-exempt interest, such as a municipal bond. The calculation will tell you what the yield needs to be in a taxable bond to provide the same yield after tax as paid by the tax-exempt bond. Since taxes are going to have to be paid from the taxable bond interest, the yield needs to be higher in the taxable bond to be equivalent after tax to the yield of the tax-exempt bond. So the corporate bond yield will generally be higher than the yield on a municipal bond, because the interest paid by a corporate bond will be subject to tax that will reduce the investor's net income.

Note that some municipal bonds are exempt from federal, state, and local taxes but some are exempt only from federal taxes. If the bond is issued in the taxpayer's state of residence, the interest paid to the bondholder will be exempt from state taxes as well as the federal taxes. If the taxpayer is a resident of the municipality that issued the bond, then the interest is also free from local taxes.

The taxable-equivalent yield can be calculated by dividing the tax-free yield by the quantity one minus the investor's marginal tax rate. For example, if an investor in a 36% federal and state tax bracket can obtain a federal and state tax-free yield of 16.2%, the taxable-equivalent yield is calculated:

$$= \frac{16.2}{(1 - .36)}$$

$$= \frac{16.2}{.64}$$

$$= 25.31\%$$

 KEY SUMMARY 36 – 6
Taxable-Equivalent Yield for Municipal Bonds

Taxable-equivalent yield $= \dfrac{\text{Tax-free yield}}{(1 - \text{Tax bracket})}$

Editor's Note: This formula appears on the formula sheet as follows:

TEY = r/(1 – t)

Practice Question

An investor who is in a 28% combined federal and state marginal tax bracket is considering investing in a tax-free municipal bond offered by the taxpayer's state and yielding 6.75%. What is the taxable-equivalent yield this bond would provide to this investor?

   A. 7.04%
   B. 7.88%
   C. 8.19%
   D. 8.88%
   E. 9.38%

Answer:
The taxable-equivalent yield is found by dividing the tax-free rate of return by the quantity (1 – Marginal tax rate), as follows:

$$.0675 \div (1 - .28)$$

$$.0675 \div .72 = .0938, \text{ or } 9.38\%$$

The answer is E.

For taxpayers who are subject to the additional 3.8% Unearned Income Medicare Contribution Tax on net investment income, the taxable-equivalent yield should also be adjusted to reflect this additional tax savings.

Practice Question

A single investor has an AGI of $245,000, and he is in a 35% marginal federal tax bracket and 3% state tax bracket. He is considering investing in a tax-free municipal bond offered by the taxpayer's state and yielding 6.75%. What is the taxable-equivalent yield this bond would provide to this investor?

    A. 6.96%
    B. 10.88%
    C. 11.02%
    D. 11.60%
    E. 16.15%

Answer:
The taxable-equivalent yield is found by dividing the tax-free rate of return by the quantity [1 – (Federal marginal tax rate + 3.8% + state tax rate)], as follows:

$$.0675 \div (1 - .418)$$

$$.0675 \div .5820 = .1160, \text{ or } 11.60\%$$

The answer is D.

Risk-Adjusted Performance Measures

Performance Measures

At this point, we should again mention a tool used to evaluate a portfolio's diversification: the coefficient of determination, R^2. R^2 is calculated as the square of the correlation coefficient between the portfolio's returns and the market's returns. The closer it is to 1.0, the higher is the degree of diversification. For example, if the correlation coefficient = +.806, so that $R^2 = .65$, then 35% of the portfolio's return was influenced by factors that could have been diversified away, that is, by unsystematic risk. A mutual fund with an R^2 that exceeds 70% is considered highly correlated with the market unless the correlation coefficient is negative. In the latter case, the fund is negatively correlated with the market.

For a common stock fund, the comparison with the market is typically made to the S & P 500. For other portfolios, comparison may be made to other indices that are more comparable. For example, the R^2 for a gold fund might be calculated by comparison to an index of gold stocks or natural resources stocks, rather than to the S & P 500.

Risk Adjusted Return

The process by which the performance of a portfolio is evaluated by combining risk and return in a single calculation or formula produces risk-adjusted returns. Most formulas have at their core the use of beta. Consequently, it is most important that beta be properly measured in order to be a valid tool in calculating risk-adjusted returns. For instance, a beta number might be suspect if the coefficient of determination (R^2) is low, suggesting that the degree of diversification is suspect and that other elements are affecting the portfolio's returns. Only the Sharpe Ratio, sometimes referred to as the Reward-to-Variability Ratio (RVAR), does not make use of beta in its formula. Instead, it employs standard deviation in measuring total risk.

To evaluate whether a return is acceptable or to evaluate which of the returns from different investments is preferable, the degree of risk involved must be taken into account. The investor might specify the rate of return he or she believes reflects the degree of riskiness that is appropriate and compare the investment's return with this rate (see the discussion of IRR and NPV previously in this Topic).

Required Rate of Return (Risk-Adjusted Return)

Another technique is to calculate a required rate of return based on the beta of the security in question. For example, the Capital Asset Pricing Model (CAPM) described in Topic 35 can be used to evaluate the rate of return that should be generated by a stock whose beta (β) is 1.3, when the risk-free rate (r_f) is 4% and the market rate of return (r_m) is 11%, as follows:

$$\text{Required rate } (r_i) = r_f + (r_m - r_f)\beta$$

$$\text{Required rate } = 4 + (11 - 4)(1.3)$$

$$= 4 + (7)(1.3)$$

$$= \ 4 + 9.1$$

$$= \ 13.1\%$$

Still other approaches to accounting for risk in evaluating a rate of return are to rely on measures such as the Sharpe, Jensen, and Treynor performance indices, described below.

Practice Question

A particular stock has a beta of .9, and the risk-free rate of return is 3.5%. The average stock yields 8.25%. What is the required rate of return on this stock, in light of its risk?

    A. 7.4%
    B. 7.8%
    C. 8.2%
    D. 8.5%
    E. 9.0%

Answer:
According to the CAPM model, the required, risk-adjusted rate of return should be:

Required rate (r_i) $= r_f + (r_m - r_f)\beta$

$$= 3.5 + (8.25 - 3.5)[.9]$$

$$= 3.5 + (4.75)(.9)$$

$$= 3.5 + 4.275$$

$$= 7.8\%$$

The answer is B.

Sharpe Ratio

The Sharpe Ratio (Reward-to-Variability Ratio) is a risk-adjusted index based upon William Sharpe's work in capital market theory. It is expressed as the ratio of excess return of the portfolio to its standard deviation.

The formula is expressed as follows:

> **EXHIBIT 36 – 1**
> **Sharpe Ratio**
>
> $$S_p = \frac{\overline{r_p} - \overline{r_f}}{\sigma_p}$$
>
> Where:
>
> $\overline{r_p}$ = Average total return for the portfolio during a selected time period
> $\overline{r_f}$ = Average risk-free rate during the period
> σ_p = Standard deviation of return for the portfolio during the period

Excess return is measured in the numerator and displays the return achieved above a rate of return that could have been earned without taking on any risk (the 3- or 6-month T-bill rate is often used for r_f). This excess return is often referred to as the risk premium. The denominator utilizes the standard deviation, a measure of total risk (systematic and unsystematic) in the portfolio's return. The higher the ratio number, the better is the performance of the portfolio on a risk-adjusted basis.

Practice Question

What is the Sharpe Index for a portfolio that has average returns of 9% and a standard deviation of 6%, when the 90-day T-bill rate is 2.5%?

    A. 1.08
    B. 1.20
    C. 1.33
    D. 1.67

Answer:

$$S_p = \frac{9\% - 2.5\%}{6\%} = 1.083$$

The answer is A.

Sharpe Ratio Measures Excess Return Against Total Risk

The Sharpe Ratio encompasses total risk and is calculated for the market. Therefore, it would be the preferred ratio to employ when considering a portfolio that is not diversified, such as a portfolio with an R^2 of less than .70. The Sharpe Ratio might also be used for an investment that is the only one in the portfolio. The benchmark line for use in a graphic display of the Sharpe Ratio is the capital market line (CML).

🔔 **REMEMBER:** *USE THE SHARPE RATIO TO MEASURE RISK-ADJUSTED PERFORMANCE FOR A PORTFOLIO WITH AN R² BELOW .70.*

Treynor Ratio

The Treynor Ratio (Reward-to-Volatility Ratio) is a risk-adjusted index introduced by Jack Treynor and measures a portfolio's performance, predicated on the assumption that the entire portfolio has diversified away all unsystematic risk. It is expressed as the ratio of the excess return of the portfolio to its beta.

The formula is expressed as follows:

EXHIBIT 36 – 2
Treynor Ratio

$$T_p = \frac{\overline{r_p} - \overline{r_f}}{\beta_p}$$

Where:

$\overline{r_p}$ = Average total return for the portfolio during a selected time period

$\overline{r_f}$ = Average risk-free rate during the period

β_p = Portfolio's beta

Again, as with the Sharpe Ratio, the numerator represents the risk premium or average excess return on the portfolio. However, the denominator is represented by beta, and so a calculation is being made for the excess return per unit of systematic (not total) risk. Other diversified portfolios may be measured against each other. The highest Treynor Ratio number is a measure of the portfolio with the best relative performance. The benchmark line for use in a graphic display of the Treynor Ratio is the security market line (SML).

Comparing Sharpe and Treynor

Which measure is better to utilize when comparing portfolios? The choice ultimately depends upon the definition of risk – total or systematic only – that is employed. If portfolios are perfectly diversified, the two rankings should be identical. Differences between the two rankings are a function of the disparity in portfolio diversification.

If all of an individual's assets are in a portfolio of securities, then the Treynor Ratio would be the more appropriate measure of total return relative to total risk. If an individual has just a small portion of his or her assets in a portfolio, then unsystematic risk may be the relevant measure, and the Sharpe Ratio should be utilized. If a portfolio is diversified with an R^2 of more than .70, the Treynor Ratio should be used, as well as the Jensen Ratio.

Jensen Ratio

The Jensen Ratio is the risk-adjusted performance measure commonly referred to as alpha (sometimes referred to as the differential return measure). This measure calculates the portfolio return actually attained and subtracts from it what the return should have been, based upon the risk taken in the portfolio. The return that should have been achieved is determined by the Capital Asset Pricing Model (CAPM), which is the risk-free rate plus the risk premium multiplied by beta.

The formula is expressed as follows:

EXHIBIT 36 – 3
Jensen Ratio (alpha)

$$\alpha_p = \overline{r_p} - \left[\overline{r_f} + \left(\overline{r_m} - \overline{r_f}\right)\beta_p\right]$$

Where:

$\alpha_p =$ Alpha, the difference between the realized return and the risk-adjusted expected return

$\overline{r_p} =$ Realized return

$\overline{r_f} =$ Risk-free rate

$\overline{r_m} =$ Return of the market

$\beta_p =$ Asset or portfolio's beta

A positive alpha signifies that the portfolio's return was in excess of what should have been expected. A negative alpha signifies that the portfolio's return was less than what should have been expected, given its level of systematic risk.

Some observe that a positive alpha suggests the degree to which a manager is adding value to a portfolio's return. For example, if an alpha score is 4.5, it indicates that, on average, a risk-adjusted rate of return of better than 4% above the market average was achieved.

Both the Sharpe and Treynor Ratios assist in the evaluation of a portfolio's realized performance and may be used to rank portfolios. The Jensen Ratio (alpha), like the Treynor Ratio, uses beta for its risk measure, but it is not normally utilized to rank portfolio performance.

Practice Question

A diversified portfolio of large-company common stocks has a beta of 1.1 and an annual return of 12%. The S&P 500 achieved a 10% return for the year. The T-bill rate is 2.5%. What is the alpha for this portfolio?

  A. –0.75
  B. 1.25
  C. 1.75
  D. 2.95

Answer:
  $\alpha_p = 12 - [2.5 + (10 - 2.5)\, 1.1] = 12 - 10.75 = 1.25$
The answer is B.

Alpha for Mutual Fund Portfolios

A mutual fund's alpha is the difference between its actual performance and its expected performance, given the characteristics of the fund. An alpha of 0.0 indicates that the fund's performance was similar to the overall market for securities of a particular risk level. The return for the market is usually the return on an index, such as the S & P 500. A positive alpha means that the fund showed good performance on a risk-adjusted basis, while a negative alpha means that the fund showed poor performance on a risk-adjusted basis.

There are some limitations involved in the use of risk-adjusted performance ratios:

1. Beta is a very dynamic statistical tool and is subject to change constantly. A change in a market index comparison (for example, from the S&P 500 to the Russell 3000) could alter portfolio rankings from one period to another.

2. The correlation between the relative performance in past and future returns is not as strong as the correlation between the variability of returns from the past to the future.

🔔 **REMEMBER:** *FOR A WELL DIVERSIFIED PORTFOLIO WITH AN R^2 ABOVE .70, BETA WILL BE AN APPROPRIATE MEASURE OF RISK, SO THE JENSEN RATIO (ALPHA) AND THE TREYNOR RATIO SHOULD BE USED TO MEASURE RISK-ADJUSTED PERFORMANCE.*

Information Ratio

William Sharpe developed the Information Ratio, which incorporates a risk adjustment to alpha. This ratio is sometimes called the appraisal ratio, as this ratio provides investors with a way to evaluate the return earned by a fund manager, based on the given risk of the fund.

The formula is expressed as follows:

EXHIBIT 36 – 4
Information Ratio

$$IR = (R_P - R_B)/\sigma_A$$

Where:

IR = Information Ratio
R_P = Portfolio Return or Manager's return
R_B = return of the benchmark
σ_A = the standard deviation of the Active return.

TOPIC 36 – APPLICATION QUESTIONS

1. If an investment has produced a 3.6% holding period return since it was purchased nine months ago, the annualized return is:

A. 2.7%
B. 3.4%
C. 3.8%
D. 4.3%
E. 4.8%

2. Harry is delighted that the return he has realized on his mutual fund has been 13% per year, well ahead of the average annual inflation rate of 3.7%. Which of the following has been Harry's real, or inflation-adjusted, rate of return?

A. 8.16%
B. 8.97%
C. 9.30%
D. 9.81%
E. 12.33%

3. Larry Ryan is considering the purchase of stock now selling for $38 per share and expected to pay an annual dividend of $1.25 next year. He expects the dividend growth rate to be 6%. If he is correct, his expected total return in the next 12 months will be:

A. 3%
B. 6%
C. 9%
D. 12%

4. (Published question released November, 1994)

A $1,000 bond originally issued at par maturing in exactly 10 years bears a coupon rate of 8% compounded annually and a market price of $1,147.20. The indenture agreement provides that the bond may be called after five years at $1,050. Which of the following statements is (are) true?

(1) The yield to maturity is 6%.
(2) The yield to call is 5.45%.
(3) The bond is currently selling at a premium, indicating that market interest rates have fallen since the issue date.
(4) The yield to maturity is less than the yield to call.

A. (1), (2), and (3) only
B. (1) and (3) only
C. (2) and (3) only
D. (4) only
E. (1), (3), and (4) only

******

5. Clarissa bought a zero-coupon bond for $350 that will mature for $1,000 in 9 years. What is the YTM for the bond?

A. 6%
B. 12%
C. 12.18%
D. 12.37%

(Two published questions released December, 1996)

Smith invests in a limited partnership which requires an outlay of $9,200 today. At the end of years 1 through 5, he will receive the after-tax cash flows as follows. The partnership will be liquidated at the end of the fifth year. Smith is in the 28% tax bracket.

YEARS	CASH FLOWS	
0	($9,200)	CF0
1	$600	CF1
2	$2,300	CF2
3	$2,200	CF3
4	$6,800	CF4
5	$9,500	CF5

6. The after-tax IRR of this investment is:

A. 17.41%
B. 19.20%
C. 24.18%
D. 28.00%
E. 33.58%

7. Which of the following statements is (are) correct?

(1) The IRR is the discount rate which equates the present value of an investment's expected costs to the present value of the expected cash inflows.
(2) The IRR is 24.18%, and the present value of the investment's expected cash flows is $9,200.
(3) The IRR is 24.18%. For Smith to actually realize this rate of return, the investment's cash flows will have to be reinvested at the IRR.
(4) If the cost of capital for this investment is 9%, the investment should be rejected because its net present value will be negative.

A. (2) and (4) only
B. (2) and (3) only
C. (1) only
D. (1), (2), and (3) only
E. (1) and (4) only

******

8. Which of the following factors may cause a bond investor's realized compound rate of return to be higher than the investor's expected yield to maturity?

(1) Reinvestment rates rise.
(2) Reinvestment rates fall.
(3) Reinvestment rates remain unchanged.

A. (1) only
B. (2) only
C. (1) and (3) only
D. (2) and (3) only

9. An investor who is single and in a 24% marginal tax bracket (with AGI of $125,000; below the threshold for the 3.8% Medicare tax on investment income) bought a stock one year ago for $86 per share. The stock paid a qualified dividend of $9.10 during the year. The investor still owns the stock, which is now selling for $81 per share. Which of the following is the investor's after-tax current yield?

    A. 4.77%
    B. 5.06%
    C. 6.77%
    D. 7.19%
    E. 9.55%

******

(Two published questions released December, 1996; updated)

The tax bracket and holdings of your client are as follows:

Federal tax bracket = 24% (15% for LTCG)

Investment*	Annual Income	June 30, Last Year Purchase Price	June 30, This Year Market Price
Money Fund	$ 6,500	$100,000	$100,000
11% T-bonds	$11,000	$100,000	$140,000
S&P Index Fund	$ 6,000	$100,000	$160,000
Computer Stock Fund	$ 3,000	$100,000	$ 85,000

*There have been <u>no</u> capital gains distributions.

10. During the 12 months from June 30, last year, through June 30, this year, the portfolio earned, in annual yield and before-tax appreciation, respectively:

    A. 5.5% and 17.5%
    B. 5.5% and 21.3%
    C. 6.6% and 17.5%
    D. 6.6% and 21.3%

11. On June 30, the current year, your client sells all the S&P Index fund shares and uses the proceeds, after paying a 15% capital gains tax, to buy T-bonds at par yielding the same current yield as the above referenced 11% T-bonds. The annual after-tax income on the newly purchased bonds, based on the client's 24% tax bracket, will be:

    A. $9,020
    B. $11,869
    C. $11,959
    D. $16,610

******

12. (Published question released January, 1999; updated)

Your client is single and his federal marginal tax rate is 35%. His state marginal rate is 8%. The client does not itemize deductions on his federal return and is considering investing in a municipal bond issued in his state of residence which yields 5%. What is the taxable-equivalent yield?

    A. 2.85%
    B. 3.25%
    C. 7.69%
    D. 8.77%
    E. 9.39%

******

13. (Published question released January, 1999)

Bond A has a 6% annual coupon and is due in 2 years. Its value in today's market is $900.

Bond B has a 10% annual coupon and is due in 4 years. It is priced to yield 12%.

Bond C is a 9% zero-coupon bond, priced to yield 11% in 8 years.

The yield to maturity of Bond A is closest to:

A. 9.90%
B. 10.40%
C. 10.90%
D. 11.40%
E. 11.90%

14. On June 1, Sam Clover (who is single and has taxable income of $230,000) bought $50,000 face value of municipal bonds at 94, paying $47,000. He also bought 500 shares of Merck at $50 per share, paying $25,000. He received bond interest of $2,100 and dividends on the stock of $400. December 20, Sam sold the bonds for 98 and the stock for $58 per share. Sam is in the 35% income tax bracket. What is his after-tax holding period return?

A. 8.5%
B. 8.8%
C. 9.7%
D. 11.8%

15. Dan Oaks files his taxes jointly with his spouse. They have an AGI of $205,000 and are taxed at the 24%% federal income tax rate. He has moved to the city of Philadelphia, where the city income tax is 4%, and the state income tax is 3%. If Dan buys U.S. Treasury bonds bearing an interest rate of 5.5%, what is his after-tax yield?

A. 3.79%
B. 4.18%
C. 5.11%
D. 5.33%

16. An 8.5% corporate bond is selling for $1,100. The bond can be called with a payment of 6 months' interest. Which of the following statements concerning this bond is correct?

A. The current yield exceeds the nominal yield.
B. The current yield exceeds the yield to maturity.
C. The yield to call exceeds the yield to maturity.
D. The yield to maturity exceeds the nominal yield.

17. Which of the following is the geometric average of this set of rates of return: 14%, 17%, 22%, and 23%?

A. 17.94
B. 18.94
C. 19.00
D. 19.19

18. The Reward-to-Variability Ratio (Sharpe Ratio):

    A. Makes use of beta in its measurement of risk
    B. Does not include the risk-free rate in its calculation
    C. Calculates that a portfolio has diversified away unsystematic risk
    D. Does not encompass total risk
    E. Is the preferred risk measure when measuring only one security

19. A client has inquired about a growth stock mutual fund recommended by a friend. Research discloses the following information on the fund:

Alpha	Beta	R^2	Return	Stan. Dev.
−1.32	.74	.88	15%	14.6%

How should you respond to the client?

    A. The client should not buy the fund because the beta is high.
    B. The client should buy the fund because the Sharpe Ratio is over 1.
    C. The client should buy the fund because the return is above the S & P 500 average.
    D. The client should not buy the fund because the alpha is negative.

20. Which of the following is the benchmark line for use in a graphic display of the Treynor Index?

    A. Capital market line (CML)
    B. Efficient frontier
    C. Characteristic line (CL)
    D. Security market line (SML)

21. The following information is available on Funds 1 and 2:

	Fund 1	Fund 2	Mkt. Index
Return Realized	16%	19%	17%
Beta	.75	1.25	1
Stan. Dev.	3.3	5.5	4.2
R^2	85	80	100

The T-bill rate is 4.5%.

Which of the following statements concerning Funds 1 and 2 is correct?

    A. The investor should purchase Fund 1 because the Sharpe Index is lower than for Fund 2.
    B. The investor should purchase Fund 2 because the Treynor Index is higher than for Fund 1.
    C. The investor should purchase Fund 2 because the realized return is higher than for Fund 1.
    D. The investor should purchase Fund 1 because the alpha is higher than for Fund 2.

22. (Published question released November, 1994)

The Performance Fund had returns of 19% over the evaluation period, and the benchmark portfolio yielded a return of 17% over the same period. Over the evaluation period, the standard deviation of returns from the Fund was 23%, and the standard deviation of returns from the benchmark portfolio was 21%. Assuming a risk-free rate of return of 8%, which of the following is the calculation of the Sharpe Index of performance for the fund over the calculation period?

    A. .3913
    B. .4286
    C. .4783
    D. .5238
    E. .5870

23. (Published question released November, 1994)

In computing portfolio performance, the Sharpe Index uses _____, while the Treynor Index uses _____ for the risk measure.

    (1) Standard deviation
    (2) Variance
    (3) Correlation coefficient
    (4) Coefficient of variation
    (5) Beta

      A. (5); (1)
      B. (1); (3)
      C. (1); (4)
      D. (1); (5)
      E. (2); (5)

24. (Published question released January, 1999)

Given the following diversified mutual fund performance data, which fund had the best risk-adjusted performance if the risk-free rate of return is 5.7%?

Fund	Average Annual Return	Standard Deviation of Annual Return	Beta
A	.0782	.0760	0.950
B	.1287	.1575	1.250
C	.1034	.1874	0.857
D	.0750	.0810	0.300

    A. Fund B because the annual return is the highest
    B. Fund A because the standard deviation is the lowest
    C. Fund C because the Sharpe Ratio is the lowest
    D. Fund D because the Treynor Ratio is the highest
    E. Fund A because the Treynor Ratio is the lowest

25. Which one of the following three funds should be recommended to a client?

	Fund R	Fund S	Fund T
Beta	1.9	1.8	1.4
R^2	35	42	32
Treynor	4.15	3.4	3.8
Sharpe	7.85	9.72	4.10

    A. Fund S because it has the highest Sharpe Index
    B. Fund T because it has the lowest beta
    C. Fund R because it has the highest Treynor Index
    D. Fund S because it has the highest R^2

26. A measure that quantifies the expected return on a given portfolio is called which of the following?

    A. Portfolio beta coefficient
    B. Portfolio average expected return
    C. Coefficient of return
    D. Weighted-average expected return

27. Assume that an investor has the following portfolio, with the current market values and expected returns shown for each component:

Asset	Current Market Value	Expected Return
200 Shs. DuPont Common Stock	$9,000	12%
100 Shs. AT&T Common Stock	3,700	10%
200 Shs. Continental Corp. Common Stock	5,800	12%
Treasury Bonds	10,000	8.5%
Money Market Fund	9,000	6.5%

The weighted-average expected return for this portfolio is closest to:

    A. 9.6%   D. 11.0%
    B. 10.0%   E. 11.5%
    C. 10.5%

Use the following table for Questions 28-31:

Security	Beta	Expected Return	Amount Invested
Stock X	1.4	15%	$10,000
Stock Y	1.2	12%	$15,000
Stock Z	0.9	9%	$11,000

28. What is the weighted-average expected return on this portfolio?

    A. 10%   C. 12%
    B. 11%   D. 13%

29. What is the weighted beta coefficient of this portfolio?

    A. 1.00   C. 1.30
    B. 1.17   D. 3.5

30. A client seeking to increase his or her expected return and willing to increase risk would logically do which of the following?

    A. Increase the amount of Stock X and decrease the amount of Stock Z.
    B. Increase the amount of Stock Y and decrease the amount of Stock X.
    C. Increase the amount of Stock Z and decrease the amount of Stock Y.
    D. None of the above.

31. A client planning to decrease risk but unwilling to reduce his or her expected return would logically do which of the following?

    (1) Increase the amount of Stock X and decrease the amount of Stock Z.
    (2) Increase the amount of Stock Y and decrease the amount of Stock Z.
    (3) Increase the amount of Stock Z and decrease the amount of Stock X.

    A. (1) only
    B. (1) and (2) only
    C. (1) and (3) only
    D. (2) and (3) only
    E. None of the above

******

32. Portfolio X has a weighted beta coefficient of 1.5, and Portfolio Y has a weighted beta coefficient of .8. Both portfolios are expected to earn the same weighted-average expected return. With these assumptions, which of the following statements is correct?

    A. An investor should choose Portfolio X because of its higher beta.

    B. An investor should choose Portfolio Y because it carries less risk for the given expected return.

    C. An investor may be indifferent between the two since the expected return is the same.

    D. The information given is not helpful in making a choice.

******

Use the following information to answer Questions 33-34:

An investor owns three investments in his or her portfolio. Stock FG has a current market value of $14,500, a beta of .85, and an expected return of 10.5%. Mutual Fund PR has a current market value of $8,600, a beta of .92, and an expected return of 11.7%. Mutual Fund SK has a current market value of $19,800, a beta of 1.25, and an expected return of 9.8%.

33. What is the weighted-average expected return on the portfolio?

    A. 8.5%   C. 10.42%
    B. 10.17%   D. 10.50%

34. What is the weighted beta coefficient on the portfolio?

    A. 1.02   C. 1.08
    B. 1.05   D. 1.13

******

Use the following information to answer Questions 35-36:

An investor owns four investments in his or her portfolio. Stock EF has a current market value of $10,200, a beta of 1.0, and an expected return of 7.2%. Stock ZZ has a current market value of $12,600, a beta of .91, and an expected return of 9.5%. Mutual Fund YY has a current market value of $6,900, a beta of 1.10, and an expected return of 11.0. Mutual Fund MN has a current market value of $13,500, a beta of 1.02, and an expected return of 9.8%.

35. What is the weighted-average expected return on the portfolio?

    A. 7.3%   C. 9.1%
    B. 8.5%   D. 9.3%

36. What is the weighted beta coefficient on the portfolio?

    A. 9.3   C. 1.02
    B. 1.0   D. 1.15

******

37. Which of the following statements concerning measures of return is (are) correct?

(1) Using a simple average of the returns of each security included in a portfolio as a measure of the return generated by the portfolio assumes equal amounts are invested in each of the securities.

(2) A holding period return would not be a proper measure of return over a period longer than one year.

(3) A geometric mean is a more useful measure of return over periods of time of more than one year than a simple average of annual returns.

A. (2) only
B. (1) and (2) only
C. (1) and (3) only
D. (2) and (3) only
E. (1), (2), and (3)

38. Assume the value of a portfolio grew from an initial $10,000 investment to $20,000 over six years. Further assume that dividends were reinvested over the six-year time span, no other funds were added to the portfolio, and no withdrawals were made from the portfolio. Which of the following statements concerning the average return and geometric mean return for the portfolio is correct?

A. The average return is 100%, and the geometric mean return is 115.44%.
B. The average return is 16.67%, and the geometric mean return is 115.44%.
C. The average return is less than 15%, and the geometric mean return is more than 15%.
D. The average return is greater than 16%, and the geometric mean return is greater than 100%.
E. The average return is greater than 16%, and the geometric mean return is less than 12.5%.

39. All the following investments may have their returns calculated by the TVM method, EXCEPT:

A. An investment in common stock where dividend payments vary from year to year
B. An investment in a zero-coupon bond
C. A dollar-cost averaging plan to purchase annuities
D. A savings account with all interest to be reinvested

40. Nine years ago, your client purchased an 1804 silver dollar for $100,000. Yesterday, this very rare coin (only one of 15 ever minted) was sold for $950,000. What IRR did your client earn from this investment?

A. 57.03%
B. 28.42%
C. 94.99%
D. 82.24%

41. Mrs. S. Avelot used dollar-cost averaging to purchase common stock of the Plunkton Lake Corporation. She invested $10,000 initially and $2,000 at the end of each year for seven years. The market value of this stock was $40,000 at the end of seven years. What IRR did Mrs. S. Avelot earn on her investment?

A. 14.27%
B. 11.08%
C. 10.83%
D. 8.28%

42. In 1975, Mr. Junque Collector paid $50 for a World War II clock salvaged from a submarine's bulkhead. Mr. Collector regards 14% to be a fair rate of return on his investment. What selling price should Mr. Collector ask for when he sells this item 42 years after the purchase?

A. $688   C. $5,504
B. $1,376   D. $12,274

43. Bob Waters sold a family "pass-me-down" telegrapher's key for $1,000. The original price was clearly marked as $3.00, and Bob thought it earned an internal rate of return of 10%. Based on the above facts, how many years ago had the key been purchased?

A. Approximately 61 years ago
B. Approximately 54 years ago
C. Approximately 45 years ago
D. Approximately 36 years ago

44. Seven years ago, Mark Victor invested $13,000 in the Go-Go Growth Mutual Fund, with all dividends and distributions to be reinvested. Seven years later, Mark liquidated the entire account and received a check for $24,000. What was the internal rate of return on this investment?

A. 6.28%   C. 10.24%
B. 9.15%   D. 12.00%

45. Fred Showme is offered a $1,000 bond that matures in nine years, has a 10.7% coupon with interest paid semiannually, and is priced at $902. What is the bond's IRR (or its yield to maturity)?

A. 11.70%   C. 13.46%
B. 12.55%   D. 14.21%

46. Bob Young wants to know the price to pay for a bond that has 10.7% coupon interest payable semiannually, matures in nine years, and has a maturity value of $1,000. Bonds with similar risk and maturity yield 13.5%. What is a fair price for Bob Young to pay for this bond?

A. $856.60 C. $898.80
B. $885.60 D. $1,000.00

47. Bob Young asks you to price a zero-coupon bond that matures in nine years for $1,000. Bonds with similar risk and maturity yield 13.5%. What is a fair price for Bob Young to pay for this bond?

A. $300 C. $306
B. $303 D. $309

48. Mrs. Penny Pinch has been using dollar-cost averaging to buy a mutual fund by paying $1,000 at the beginning of each year for nine years. Her mutual fund account at the end of the ninth year is $18,000. What is the IRR she has earned?

A. 10.17% C. 18.09%
B. 13.64% D. 100.00%

49. Mrs. Carole Careful purchased a real estate investment property for $100,000 and sold it seven years later for $200,000. In the intervening years, she made improvements and collected rents. Mrs. Careful received rent income in Year 1 of $10,000; her expenses exceeded her income by $3,000 in Year 2; for Year 3 she had income of $12,000; expenses exceeded income by $1,000 in Year 4; and she had positive income for Years 5, 6, and 7 of $12,000, $13,000, and $14,000, respectively. What was Mrs. Careful's IRR for this investment?

A. 15.05% C. 17.07%
B. 16.06% D. 18.08%

50. Paul recently purchased a bond for $950. It matures in 3 years and has a coupon rate of 9.5% paid semiannually. What is the internal rate of return (YTM) on this bond?

A. 5.24% C. 11.52%
B. 10.48% D. 11.75%

51. Larry recently purchased a bond for $780. It matures in 12 years and has a coupon rate of 7% paid semiannually. What is the internal rate of return (YTM) on this bond?

A. 4.37% C. 7.42%
B. 5.22% D. 10.22%

52. Greta recently purchased a zero-coupon bond for $520. It matures in 17 years. What is the annual compound rate of return (YTM) on this bond?

A. 1.94% C. 5.73%
B. 3.88% D. 7.98%

53. An investor purchased a stock mutual fund 3 years ago for $25,000 and then utilized a dollar-cost averaging strategy by investing $7,000 at the end of each of the next 3 years. The market value at the end of the third year was $52,500. What is the IRR (or average annual compound rate of return) on this investment?

A. 3.21%   C. 7.25%
B. 6.41%   D. 12.83%

54. An investor invested $570 at the beginning of each quarter for four years in a stock mutual fund. The value of the fund at the end of the fourth year was $11,300. What is the average annual compound rate of return on this investment?

A. 2.48%   C. 9.91%
B. 2.79%   D. 11.16%

55. An investor owns a 14% coupon bond that matures in 11 years. Comparable bonds (similar quality and maturity) are yielding 8.5%. What is the approximate intrinsic value (present value) of this bond?

A. $795   C. $1,100
B. $1,000   D. $1,388

56. A man purchased a mutual fund for $10,700 three years ago. Subsequently, he made the following purchases each year: $20,000, $18,000, and $13,700. At the end of the third year, the value of the investment was $68,000. What is the IRR on this investment?

A. 6.0%   C. 7.0%
B. 6.5%   D. 7.2%

57. Assume that an investor is planning to buy a $1,000 corporate bond today for $975. The bond will pay $80 of interest at the end of each of the next three years, at which time it will mature for its face amount. If the investor's required rate of return is 8.2%, what will be the net present value (NPV) of this investment?

A. –$11.04   C. +$9.11
B. –$8.23   D. +$19.86

58. A $10,000 zero-coupon bond is issued for a 25-year term and has a present market price of $2,775. The annual rate of return on this bond is which of the following?

A. 5.19%
B. 5.26%
C. 2.63%
D. Cannot be determined given the fact pattern presented.

59. Jim Edwards can purchase either a taxable corporate bond yielding 10% annually or a tax-exempt municipal bond. Jim's combined federal and state marginal tax bracket is 31%. What municipal bond yield would be comparable to the yield on the taxable bond (assume Jim's AGI is below $200,000 and that the bond is issued in his state of residence)?

A. 7.3%   C. 9.1%
B. 6.2%   D. 6.9%

60. An investor bought a bond at par that matures in 6 years. The bond has a coupon rate of 9%, paid annually, and the reinvestment rate is 11%. What is the realized compound yield of this bond?

    A. 9.0%   C. 10.3%
    B. 9.4%   D. 11.0%

61. An investor bought a bond at par that matures in 6 years. The bond has a coupon rate of 9%, paid annually. What is the realized compound yield of the bond if the reinvestment rate is 7%?

    A. 5.3%   C. 7.2%
    B. 6.5%   D. 8.6%

62. An investor bought a bond at par that matures in 15 years. The bond has a coupon rate of 13% (paid annually), and the reinvestment rate is 9%. What is the realized compound yield of this bond?

    A. 11.05%   C. 13.00%
    B. 12.55%   D. 14.10%

63. An investor bought a bond at par that matures in 15 years. The bond has a coupon rate of 13% (paid annually). What is the realized compound yield of the bond if the reinvestment rate is 15%?

    A. 10.25%   C. 14.05%
    B. 12.25%   D. 16.05%

64. An investor bought a bond for $1,000 that is callable in 8 years at $1,100. The bond matures in 15 years and has a 9% coupon rate, paid semiannually. What is the yield to call on this bond?

    A. 4.9%   C. 9.2%
    B. 6.3%   D. 9.8%

65. Gary recently bought a bond for $900 that is callable in 7 years at $1,200. The bond matures in 20 years and has an 11.5% coupon, paid semiannually. What is the yield to call on the bond?

    A. 7.79%   C. 13.77%
    B. 12.91%   D. 15.57%

66. Sally owns a bond with a 9% coupon payment that matures in 5 years. Comparable bonds of similar quality and maturity are yielding 12%. Under these conditions, the current market price of Sally's bond would logically be which of the following?

    A. $1,000.00   C. $765.00
    B. $889.60   D. $110.40

67. Mike owns a bond with a 14% coupon payment that matures in 7 years. Comparable bonds of similar quality and maturity are yielding 8%. Under these conditions, the current market price of Mike's bond would logically be which of the following?

    A. $1,316.89   C. $1,000.00
    B. $1,104.15   D. $888.81

68. Inez is offered a $1,000 bond that matures in eleven years, pays 8.8% coupon interest semiannually, and is priced at $960. What is the bond's IRR (or its yield to maturity)?

   A. 8.80%   C. 11.61%
   B. 9.39%   D. 12.03%

69. Jeff wants to know how much to pay for a bond that has 8.4% coupon interest, payable semiannually, matures in four years, and has a maturity value of $1,000. Bonds with similar risk and maturity yield 9%. What is a fair price for Jeff to pay for this bond?

   A. $980.21   C. $1,000.00
   B. $989.06   D. $1,007.33

70. Bill asks you to price a zero-coupon bond that matures in seven years for $1,000. Bonds with similar risk and maturity yield 10.5%. What is a fair price for Bill to pay for this bond?

   A. $473   C. $489
   B. $481   D. $497

71. Paula recently purchased a bond for $725. It matures in 3 years and has a coupon rate of 5%, paid semiannually. What is the internal rate of return (YTM) on this bond?

   A. 8.5%   C. 17%
   B. 12%   D. 19.5%

72. Lisa recently purchased a bond for $850. It matures in 10 years and has a coupon rate of 8%, paid semiannually. What is the internal rate of return (YTM) on this bond?

   A. 4.37%   C. 7.42%
   B. 5.23%   D. 10.45%

73. Graham recently purchased a zero-coupon bond for $650. It matures in 15 years. What is the annual compound rate of return (YTM) on this bond?

   A. 1.45%   C. 4.33%
   B. 2.89%   D. 5.83%

74. An investor owns a 10% coupon bond that matures in 7 years. Comparable bonds (with similar quality and maturity) are yielding 9%. What is the intrinsic value (present value) of this bond?

   A. $975   C. $1,025
   B. $1,000   D. $1,050

75. Sam, who is 64, will retire next year, and he wants to invest his entire savings of $175,000. Sam's only income will be a pension of $950 per month plus his investment income. Sam is considering two mutual funds. He does not want to take above-average risk, but he is concerned about loss of purchasing power in the years ahead.

Fund 1: Corporate bond fund yielding 10.2% currently and showing capital appreciation of 5.7% annually over the past five years; its beta is .56, and it invests in highly-rated corporate bonds.

Fund 2: Tax-exempt bond fund yielding 6.0% currently and showing capital appreciation of 3.5% annually over the past five years; its beta is .51, and it invests in high-grade municipal bonds.

Which fund is more appropriate for Sam?

A. Fund 2 because the income is tax-free, and it has a lower beta.
B. Fund 1 because it has had a higher capital appreciation rate over the past five years.
C. Fund 1 because it has a higher current yield.
D. Fund 2 because it has a better risk-return relationship.

76. Which of the following statements concerning the current yield and the yield to maturity are correct?

(1) Current yield and yield to maturity are equal when bonds sell at par.
(2) Current yield is less than yield to maturity when bonds sell at a premium.
(3) Yield to maturity is greater than current yield when bonds sell at a discount.
(4) Yield to maturity is greater than current yield when bonds sell at par.

A. (1) and (4) only
B. (1) and (3) only
C. (2) and (3) only
D (2) and (4) only

77. Jelly Bean International's $1,000 par value debenture bonds have a 9% coupon with interest payable annually. Each bond has four years to run and is convertible into 20 shares of Jelly Bean common, currently selling for $51 per share. If a discount rate of 8% reflects the degree of riskiness of the bonds, what is the minimum price at which they should be selling?

A. $1,000
B. $1,020
C. $1,033
D. $1,060
E. $1,085

For practice answering case questions related to Topic 36, please answer the following questions in the cases included in the Appendix at the back of this textbook.

Case	Questions
Donaldson	7, 8, 9, 10, and 11
Hilbert Stores, Inc.	
Maxwell	4, 6, and 7
Beals	4 and 5
Mocsin	1, 2, and 3
Eldridge	2
Young	2 and 3
Johnson	9, 10, 11, 12, 13, and 14
Thomas	12, 13, 14, and 15
Jim and Brenda Quinn	19, 20, 21, 22, 23, 24, 25, and 26

Asset Allocation and Portfolio Diversification (Topic 37)

CFP Board Student-Centered Learning Objectives

(a) Construct an optimal client portfolio by the allocation of wealth amongst risky assets and the risk free security.

(b) Develop and communicate to a client a portfolio rebalancing strategy.

(c) Recommend an asset allocation strategy consistent with a client's risk tolerance.

Asset Allocation and Portfolio Diversification
- A. *Strategic asset allocation*
  - 1) *Application of client lifecycle analysis*
  - 2) *Client risk tolerance measurement and application*
  - 3) *Asset class definition and correlation*
- B. *Rebalancing*
- C. *Tactical asset allocation*
- D. *Control of volatility*
- E. *Strategies for dealing with concentrated portfolios*
- F. *Efficient market hypothesis (EMH)*
  - 1) *Strong form*
  - 2) *Semi-strong form*
  - 3) *Weak form*
  - 4) *Anomalies*
- G. *Behavioral finance*

Strategic Asset Allocation

Asset allocation is a strategy wherein assets are combined in a manner designed to produce superior results with minimum risk. Brinson, Hood, and Beebower presented a major study on this concept in 1986 with the publication of *Determination of Portfolio Performance*. In it, the performance of 91 pension funds was studied in an attempt to explain the differences in their performance. **On average, 94% of the variance among total returns was related to how the funds allocated their assets.** Security selection and market timing were given very little weight. These findings helped set the stage for the use of asset allocation techniques in the management of assets.

The findings of the BHB study were supported in a 2000 study conducted by Ibbotson and Kaplan; *Does Asset Allocation Policy Explain 40, 90, or 100 Percent of Performance?* The percentages varied somewhat, but the findings were similar. The final decision as to which classes of assets are used and how (stocks, bonds, cash, and alternative investments) is a function of the investor's risk tolerance, investment objectives, time horizon, and age, among other factors. The following explains the various approaches to this important investment strategy:

Application of Client Life Cycle Analysis

The age of an investor should influence asset allocation decisions. Conservative vs. aggressive allocation decisions will depend largely upon the goals and objectives of individuals. Younger investors can make asset allocations with higher risk to seek higher rewards. Persons approaching retirement years are thought to be more risk averse. They are in the distribution phase of the life cycle and may need strategic allocations that reduce risk by including more fixed-income securities.

The life cycle phases may be broadly categorized as:

- The accumulation phase – generally younger investors, may have substantial debt, moderate but rising income, modest amount of wealth. Once emergency funds have been established, these clients are generally assumed to have a higher capacity and propensity for more aggressive asset allocations due to the long-term nature of many goals such as retirement and due to the ability to adjust choices regarding whether to work and how long to continue working.
- The consolidation phase – middle age, approaching retirement, moderate to high income, moderate to high wealth. The asset allocation may begin moving to a more moderate risk level due to the expectation of retirement in the near future.
- The distribution (spending) phase – older, in retirement, little debt, high wealth, focus on spending during retirement and transfer of wealth through gifts during lifetime or inheritances upon death. The asset allocation will be focused on providing tax-efficient income as well as some growth in an attempt to produce income that can increase to keep up with inflation and that will last throughout the retirement period. Fixed immediate annuities or deferred longevity annuities may be added to the asset mix to overcome the risk involved with superannuation (living a very long life).

Client Risk Tolerance: Measurement and Application

Modern portfolio theory assumes a rational investor and further assumes that investors are moderately risk averse, so adequate compensation for the risk taker is what needs to be measured. This is a task not easily undertaken. While preferring certainty to uncertainty, the investor almost always "feels" the pain of a loss more severely than the satisfaction from a gain of equal measure.

There are opportunity costs to minimizing risky positions, namely, lower overall returns. The expected risk-return trade-off is one that differs for each individual. Applying an optimal mix of asset classes according to the risk position assumed by the investor is a complex task in the decision process.

Risk Tolerance Versus Risk Capacity

Risk capacity is a measurement of the amount of risk a client can afford to take. A client will have greater capacity for risk if the client is able to adjust goals, has reliable sources of income, and is able to absorb losses in the investment portfolio without a detrimental impact on their standard of living. For example, if a client needs retirement income of $40,000 per year and if a pension and Social Security provide $40,000 per year of income, the client would have unlimited capacity for risk in the investment portfolio. Similarly, if the client would like to have $55,000 per year to live the desired lifestyle in retirement but is willing to travel less or do consulting work for extra income and if the $40,000 of income from pension and Social Security covers the essential expenses, the client would have a great amount of risk capacity in the investment portfolio. Younger clients may have a greater capacity for risk than older clients due to the length of time before income will be needed from the portfolio.

A client's risk propensity, or risk tolerance, doesn't always align with his or her capacity. Risk propensity is the amount of risk a client is actually willing to take. It is a psychological element based upon the client's comfort level with taking risk and can be difficult to measure objectively.

In investments, tolerance for risk is often measured on a scale from aggressive (high tolerance for risk) to conservative (low tolerance for risk), and people in the middle are described as moderate.

Return Required to Reach Goals

Determining the client's risk tolerance and capacity to take on risk is only one step in the process of determining asset allocation. If a client has a high level of risk tolerance, there is no rule or requirement that his portfolio be invested aggressively. There is no reason for the client to incur a high level of risk if the client's goals can be reached with less risk. The planner must determine the rate of return that will be necessary in order to provide the highest probability of attaining the client's goals. If the required return is consistent with a less aggressive portfolio, then the client can take less risk. Recall the discussion of portfolio theory in Topic 35 in which the rational investor will choose the lowest risk for any given level of return.

Risk-return combinations plotted on the CML (capital market line) can depict various asset allocation points between a risk-free asset and a risky portfolio.

The appropriate choice of asset allocation must also consider whether the goal of the portfolio is to produce income, to grow over time, or a combination of both. The choice of allocation should also factor in the income tax efficiency of various types of investments.

Asset Class Definition and Correlation

Correlation can measure the relationship between asset classes, whether they are positive or negative (ranging from [+1] to [–1]). **Correlation in returns among assets and the asset allocation scheme will determine the degree of diversification.**

T-bills are classified generally as representative of the risk-free asset class, and returns have very low correlation with corporate bonds (fixed-income). T-bill returns are opposite in correlation with returns from common stocks, small stocks, international stocks, and equity REITS.

EXHIBIT 37 – 1
Correlation in Returns

	Corporate Bonds	Common Stocks	Small Stocks	International Stocks	International Bonds	Equity REITs
Treasury Bills	Very Low	Opposite	Opposite	Opposite	Opposite	Opposite
Corporate Bonds	–	Mod. Low	Low	Low	Mod. Low	Moderate
Common Stocks	Mod. Low	–	High	Moderate	Low	Moderate
Small Stocks	Low	High	–	Moderate	Very Low	Moderate
International Stocks	Low	Moderate	Moderate	–	Mod. High	Mod. High
International Bonds	Mod. Low	Low	Very Low	Mod. High	–	Mod. Low

---

Rebalancing

The strategic allocation and fixed-mix strategy requires an investor to rebalance his or her portfolio periodically to restore the different asset classes to their originally weighted percentages or asset mix.

- **Strategic allocation** is predicated upon an investment policy that determines a suitable asset mix and establishes a range of values for the portfolio (for example, 55% large growth stocks, 30% intermediate bonds, 15% cash). It is closely aligned with the fundamentals behind modern portfolio theory in that it aims to create efficient portfolios from different asset classes. Although it may appear to resemble a passive buy-and-hold strategy, its implementation requires continuous portfolio monitoring. Rebalancing will be needed in order to restore the different asset classes to their originally weighted percentages in the portfolio.

- A **fixed-mix strategy** is based upon the belief that a preset mix of different asset classes over time can achieve the optimal portfolio. Over time, it is believed that an efficient market will reward a portfolio that contains different types and classes of assets. Many assets in this type of portfolio will remain for a number of years, so the strategy is a kind of buy-and-hold. As part of the ongoing monitoring process, asset classes may be rebalanced as changes in return predictions are made.

Tactical Asset Allocation

Tactical allocation uses security selection and market timing as its main approach to portfolio building. At certain periods, securities may appear overvalued or undervalued, and market forecasting is designed to improve performance. The logic behind this allocation theory is that the successful asset class may now be overvalued, while the least successful has become undervalued. From various market timing techniques employing technical analysis to sector rotation (for example, moving from health care stocks to technology stocks), the process is a continuous attempt to increase portfolio exposure to asset classes likely to outperform.

Control of Volatility

Volatility refers to the fluctuations around the market mean or average, which is measured by beta. The asset allocation method that looks to market changes for direction as to when to change the asset mix is called **dynamic asset allocation** or the dynamic hedging strategy. Under this allocation method, more risky assets might be sold in order to buy less risky assets and vice versa, depending upon the value of each mix. Portfolio allocations change as the market conditions and fortunes of some asset classes change. Primarily large, institutional investors utilize this approach, with technical analysis being an integral part of its underpinnings.

Practice Question

A balanced fund has specified that it will invest 60% in common stocks and 40% in bonds. Which asset allocation strategy is most similar to this fund's investment approach?

A. Strategic allocation
B. Tactical allocation
C. Dynamic asset allocation
D. Fixed-mix strategy

Answer:
The specification of investments 60% in common stock and 40% in bonds is similar to a fixed-mix strategy. The fund will not vary its mix as would occur in a strategic or dynamic asset allocation. *The answer is D.*

Strategies for Dealing with Concentrated Portfolios

Concentrated portfolios are usually characterized by overweighted positions in sectors. An overview of the entire financial position of a client is necessary. For example, a particular portfolio might seem concentrated in the technology sector, but a "total portfolio" view of the client's accumulated wealth might suggest not making any significant changes. Should, however, a client's portfolio comprise the bulk of his or her holdings, then appropriate selling of overweighted sectors is justified. If selling a large piece of the concentrated holding in a single year is undesirable from a tax perspective, put options or collar strategies can be used to protect the portfolio while the position is sold over several tax years.

Efficient Market Hypothesis (EMH)

The efficient market hypothesis (EMH) states the proposition that **investors are unable to outperform the market on a consistent basis**. The hypothesis contends that security pricing reflects all known information, which is obtained quickly and enables a company's stock price to adjust rapidly. In addition, it is believed that the daily fluctuation in price is a result of a random walk pattern. When price moves in this manner, any activist strategy is thought to add no value to the process since additional transaction costs must be incurred. Consequently, investors who believe in a passive investment strategy favor this theory.

While opposing any activist strategy, such as technical analysis, **EMH seems to lend some support to investors doing fundamental analysis**. By performing appropriate economic, industrial, and company analysis, the market may be kept more efficient, as the pricing of securities reflects the fundamental analysis performed upon security values.

EXHIBIT 37 – 2
Efficient Market Hypothesis

	Security Prices Reflect?	Does Hypothesis Support Technical Analysis?	Does Hypothesis Support Fundamental Analysis?
Strong form	Public and insider knowledge	No	No
Semi-strong form	Public knowledge	No	No
Weak form	Price and volume data	No	Yes

Strong Form

The strong form version of EMH holds that **all public and private information** is already reflected in the prices of securities. Neither technical nor fundamental analysis can improve upon the efficiency of the market to determine prices. Even inside traders should not be able to take advantage of private information to outperform the market on a consistent basis.

Semi-Strong Form

The semi-strong form version of EMH holds that security prices are reflected not only from **historical data, but also from data analysis of the economy, industry, and company financial statements**. This version includes the weak form since the data gathered are an integral part of the larger body of widely held information.

Even in the case of initial public offerings (IPOs) that may seem to disproportionately reward investors at commencement, empirical evidence seems to demonstrate that the market quickly adjusts the pricing of these instruments. Some small gain may be made by traders who illegally trade on inside information.

Weak Form

The weak form version of EMH holds that security prices reflect all **price and volume data**. It is in direct contradiction with technical analysis, which attempts to predict future pricing based upon the study of past pricing and volume patterns.

The weak form version sees no relationship between past and future pricing of securities. Fundamental analysis may have some value in identifying companies whose share values may increase.

If the client is a believer in strong or semi-strong form EMH, the appropriate recommendation will include index funds rather than actively managed portfolios. If the clients do not believe it is possible to outperform the market, they will not be willing to pay a portfolio manager to attempt to do so. Clients who believe in the weak form of EMH, however, are willing to pay a manager to attempt to outperform the market.

Anomalies

An anomaly occurs when an investment strategy appears to have positive results, cannot be explained away, and is in apparent contradiction with the efficient market hypothesis. It is important to remember that any testing of these strategies may not replicate actual stock trading activities that investors might utilize. Also, it is important to observe how fast prices may adjust to this information in attempting to take advantage of any apparent inefficiency in market pricing.

Efficient Market Anomalies

Researchers have identified the following anomalies:

- *The P/E effect* – Equities with smaller price-earning ratios appear to outperform those with high P/E numbers. Companies trading at lower price-to-earnings multiples appear, on average, to produce superior returns.

- *The small firm effect* – These firms have total capitalization in the lowest quintile (bottom 20%) of all stocks. This anomaly is also referred to as the "neglected firm" or "size" effect and suggests that few analysts are following these stocks. Consequently, many of them may not be efficiently priced. Value-oriented investors see this as an opportunity to outperform the market.

- *The January effect* – There is a tendency for stocks to decline in value during December, followed by a rebound in January, especially during the first week of trading. Some believe that tax-related sales might be a contributing factor, but no one cause has yet been found for this anomaly.

- *The Value Line effect* – Stocks that are rated "1" in Value Line's Investment Survey of 1,700 stocks ("5" being the lowest rated) for timeliness have a tendency to outperform the market over time.

🔑 **KEY SUMMARY 37 – 1** **Market Anomalies**	
P/E effect	Low P/E stocks outperform.
Small firm effect	Small company stocks outperform.
January effect	Stocks outperform during January.
Value Line effect	Value Line recommendations outperform.

Behavioral Finance

Both the modern portfolio theory and the efficient market hypothesis assume the investor always acts rationally. However, this hypothesis is subject to considerable doubt. Behavioral finance looks at how social, cognitive, and emotional factors impact investment decisions with the realization that there are boundaries as to how rational a person can be. Studies done in the 1970's by psychologists Daniel Kahneman and Amos Tversky led the way for understanding cognitive biases for common human errors. An example of an irrational financial decision is an investor who stays away from technology stocks if he or she lost a large sum of money during the tech.com bust in the early 2000s. On the flip side, an investor may continue to hold stock in the company he or she works for even though the financial data indicates the investor should sell the stock.

In some cases, a client's mental accounting will interfere with rational decision-making. People have a tendency to separate their accounts into "buckets" in their minds (based on various subjective criteria, but often based on the source of the funds), and the rules for each of these mental accounts may be viewed differently. For example, a client may view money that she has worked for as money that must be spent wisely and invested appropriately toward goals. But money received as an inheritance might be viewed as money to gamble with or to be used to go on vacation, rather than to be used toward paying down debt or saved toward goals in an asset allocation that is appropriate for the client's risk tolerance. The client's mental accounting may impact decisions regarding asset allocation and decisions regarding whether dividend distributions should be reinvested or used for current consumption. Mental accounting may also impact the client's reaction to fluctuations in the value of the portfolio.

Behavioral Finance Biases

Anchoring: A tendency to rely too much on a specific piece of information, often what was first learned about the subject.

Overconfidence: Overestimating one's ability to perform a specific task, such as picking stocks. This bias may lead to over-trading and/or taking undue risks.

Recency: Giving too much weight to recent observations or stimuli; for example, focusing on short-term past performance.

Hindsight: The belief that a past event was predictable, when in fact it could not have been predicted.

Illusion of Control: The tendency to overestimate one's ability to control events.

Confirmation Bias: The tendency to selectively filter information to confirm a preconceived opinion. For example, if a client's father recommended a particular stock, the client may do research on that company and pay attention only to the information that confirms the stock as a good pick, giving less credence to information that would imply the stock is a poor investment.

Overreaction: The tendency to overreact to new information. If efficient market hypothesis is correct, all new relevant information is instantaneously reflected in the price of a security. Investors who proceed to react to the new information would then be causing a temporary undue over- or under-pricing of the security.

Determining the Appropriate Asset Allocation

An asset allocation of 60% stocks and 40% bonds is generally accepted as a moderately risky portfolio. This allocation may serve as a good starting point in making asset allocation decisions, and then the allocation can be adjusted based on the factors discussed in this Topic. For example, if the time horizon is shorter, the allocation may be adjusted with a lower percentage in stocks and a higher percentage in bonds or cash. Or if the investor has a high tolerance for risk, the stock allocation may be adjusted upward.

Once the generally accepted allocation is determined, details regarding the specific assets can be added. For example, it may be determined that municipal bonds are more favorable than corporate bonds due to the tax treatment. The planner will need to ensure that, ultimately, an appropriately diversified portfolio is recommended, while also considering factors such as goals and objective, risk tolerance and capacity, tax efficiency, liquidity, and other factors.

KEY SUMMARY 37 – 2
Key Factors Affecting Asset Allocation Choices

Time horizon
Risk tolerance
Risk capacity
Return required to reach goals
Whether the goal is to produce income, growth, or both
Asset class correlations
Tax efficiency
Client's belief in whether markets are efficient or whether a
        manager can outperform the market

TOPIC 37 – APPLICATION QUESTIONS

1. The thinking behind much of the use of asset allocation is that:

A. It is secondary, but nevertheless important, to security selection in a portfolio.
B. The strategy has still not been fully tested.
C. It is responsible for much of the return performance in portfolios.
D. Distinct timing models can significantly mitigate the overall effectiveness of an asset allocation strategy.
E. Approximately 75% of the variance of returns can be explained by an asset allocation theory.

2. Larry is an investor who increases his stock allocation at times when the market appears to be rising and increases cash positions when anticipating market declines. This investment approach most resembles:

A. Expectation theory
B. Portfolio optimization
C. Strategic asset allocation
D. Tactical asset allocation
E. Life-cycle investing

3. Mary read in a section of *Investors Business Daily* a piece that stated, "Institutions favor an approach to investing where more risky assets are sold in order to buy riskless assets and vice versa, depending upon the mix." This strategy best describes:

A. Strategic asset allocation
B. Institutional cycle investing
C. Tactical asset allocation
D. A fixed mix strategy
E. Dynamic hedging strategy

4. When one is considering the life-cycle approach to investing, the highest risk tolerance level can be assumed to be:

A. In the consolidation phase
B. In the accumulation phase
C. In the consolidation phase and the spending phase
D. In the consolidation phase and the accumulation phase
E. In the accumulation and spending phase

5. Technical analysis is supported by which form of the efficient market theory?

A. Weak form
B. Semi-strong form
C. Strong form
D. None of the above

6. An investor who uses index funds is most likely to subscribe to which form of the efficient market theory?

A. Weak form
B. Semi-strong form
C. Strong form
D. None of the above

7. An investor who analyses the information contained in the annual reports for a company can be expected to achieve superior returns under which form(s) of the efficient market theory?

(1) Weak form
(2) Semi-strong form
(3) Strong form

    A. (1), (2), and (3)
    B. (1) only
    C. (1) and (2) only
    D. (2) and (3) only

8. Which of the following methods of investing is least likely to produce superior returns?

    A. Buying stocks in January
    B. Buying low P/E stocks
    C. Buying index funds
    D. Buying neglected stocks

9. The Value Line effect is consistent with which form of the efficient market theory?

    A. Weak form
    B. Semi-strong form
    C. Strong form
    D. None of the above

10. Jacob Mallory is a small business owner who consistently reinvests his profits back into his business to help it grow so that he can sell the business ten years from now in order to fund his retirement. During a recent discussion with Jacob, he expressed concern that his son was investing all of his retirement money in the stock of the company that he works for and exposing himself to a large amount of risk by doing so. When you suggested that Jacob was doing the same thing, he responded that "it is different for me because I am in control of my business". Jacob's attitude is an example of which type of behavioral finance bias?

    A. Confirmation bias
    B. Overconfidence bias
    C. Illusion of Control bias
    D. Anchoring

11. Darrell and Olivia Jameson are working with a financial planner to help them prepare for retirement and for assistance with education funding goals for their grandchildren. They would like to retire in 8 years to spend time travelling and visiting with their children and grandchildren who live in other states. They have provided the planner with information regarding their current retirement account balances and asset allocations, as well as their income and expenses, ongoing savings, and information regarding the education funding goals. During the information-gathering session, the planner also assessed the Jameson's risk tolerance. While analyzing the Jamesons current financial situation, the planner has determined that they cannot reach all of their goals using their current strategy, but with a slightly more aggressive asset allocation, the probability of the Jamesons reaching their goals is greatly increased. Which of the following is the most appropriate for the planner to present to the clients during their next meeting?

A. Present various scenarios in which the Jamesons travel less and work part time in retirement.
B. Present a plan in which the Jamesons reduce their retirement income goals, and use the purchase of life insurance to provide a death benefit to grandchildren who can use it to pay off education loans.
C. Present various scenarios illustrating the likelihood of reaching goals following several different asset allocation strategies.
D. Present scenarios utilizing various inflation rates to illustrate adjustments that may need to be made depending upon the actual economic conditions throughout their retirement years.

12. (Published question released December, 1996)

Which of the following would result in the largest increase in the price of a diversified common stock mutual fund?

A. Unexpected inflation
B. Expected dividend increases
C. Unexpected corporate earnings growth
D. Expected increase in the prime interest rate

13. All the following statements concerning the weak form of the efficient market hypothesis (EMH) are correct, EXCEPT:

A. Historical price series will not offer useful information for purposes of predicting future price changes.
B. Successive price changes are independent of past prices.
C. Technical analysis based on past price data is not likely to help an investor outperform the market.
D. All public and private information concerning a stock is fully reflected in its current price.

14. If security prices fluctuate in a random manner:

    A. Investors can outperform the market by selecting securities in a random manner.

    B. Investors who react to new public information will outperform the market.

    C. Investors who chart past security prices as a basis for stock selection will not be able to outperform the market.

    D. Investors can use historical price data to predict future prices.

15. Which of the following correctly states an implication of the efficient market hypothesis?

    A. Security prices adjust slowly to new information.

    B. The strong form asserts that technical analysis can produce superior performance.

    C. An investor will earn a risk-adjusted return consistent with the market.

    D. It is difficult to produce superior performance in nonfinancial markets.

16. A couple in a high marginal income tax bracket wants to invest in a mutual fund to provide a college fund for their children, ages 10 and 8. They are moderately conservative investors. Which of the following funds would be the most appropriate for this couple?

    A. An aggressive growth fund
    B. A sector fund
    C. A global fund
    D. A gold fund

17. Sheri and Dan are conservative investors who want to open a money market fund by investing a lump sum now and making additional investments every few months over the next three years, until retirement. They are considering the following two money market funds:

Fund A has a diversified portfolio of commercial paper, certificates of deposit, and Treasury bills, with an average maturity of 60 days.

Fund B has a portfolio of Treasury and federal agency securities, with an average maturity of 59 days.

Which money market fund is more appropriate for Sheri and Dan?

    A. Fund A because the average maturity is longer.

    B. Fund B because the underlying securities are less risky.

    C. Fund A because the underlying securities are more risky.

    D. Fund B because the average maturity is shorter.

18. All of the following statements concerning the correlation of international and domestic stocks and bonds are correct, EXCEPT:

    A. International bonds and domestic corporate bonds have a moderately low degree of correlation.

    B. There is a moderate degree of correlation between U.S. and Canadian stocks.

    C. International stocks have a moderately high correlation with Equity REITs.

    D. Risk reduction through diversification cannot occur if the international stocks and bonds have a higher standard deviation.

For practice answering case questions related to Topic 37, please answer the following questions in the cases included in the Appendix at the back of this textbook.

Case	Questions
Donaldson	
Hilbert Stores, Inc.	
Maxwell	
Beals	6
Mocsin	4
Eldridge	3 and 4
Young	4
Johnson	15, 16, and 17
Thomas	16, 17, 18, and 19
Jim and Brenda Quinn	27, 28, 29, 30, and 31

Bond and Stock Valuation Concepts (Topic 38)

CFP Board Student-Centered Learning Objectives

(a) Value a bond using discounted cash flow and explain how interest rates affect bond values.

(b) Estimate the value of a stock using discounted cash flow, the CAPM, and price multiples.

(c) Differentiate between fundamental and technical analysis.

Bond and Stock Valuation Concepts
- A. Bond duration
- B. Capitalized earnings
- C. Dividend growth models
- D. Ratio analysis
  - 1) Price/earnings
  - 2) Price/free cash flow
  - 3) Price/sales
  - 4) Price/earnings + growth (PEG)
- E. Book value
- F. Fundamental analysis
  - 1) Top-down analysis
  - 2) Bottom-up analysis
  - 3) Ratio analysis
    - a) Liquidity ratios
    - b) Activity ratios
    - c) Profitability ratios
    - d) Debt ratios
- G. Technical analysis
  - 1) Charting
  - 2) Sentiment indicators
  - 3) Flow of funds indicators
  - 4) Market structure indicators
- H. Options valuation models
  - 1) Black-Scholes option valuation model
  - 2) Binomial option pricing

Bond Duration

Interest rate risk has two facets: (1) its impact on the price of the security, and (2) its impact on the reinvestment opportunity for interest payments. These two effects move in opposite directions. If interest rates rise, the price of the security falls, but the yield from reinvesting rises. If interest rates fall, the reverse is true. Either type of change in interest rates, therefore, will cause the actual or realized return from an investment to differ from the expected return.

Investment theory concerning the intrinsic value of a security (discussed later) can be used to demonstrate that bonds with long maturities are more volatile in price and reinvestment rate than those with short maturities. Also, investment theory demonstrates that bonds with low coupon interest rates are more volatile than bonds with high coupon rates. Consequently, if an investor expects interest rates to rise, he or she should buy high-coupon, short-maturity bonds. If the investor expects interest rates to fall, he or she should buy low-coupon, long-maturity bonds.

How, though, can an investor decide which has a higher interest rate risk – a high-coupon, long-maturity bond or a low-coupon, short-maturity bond? Duration analysis gives the answer by combining the two elements of interest rate risk.

A bond's duration is the weighted-average number of years it takes for the investor to receive the present value of all of the bond's future cash inflows. The weights used are the number of years the investor must wait for each of those cash inflows.

To illustrate, assume that an investor buys a bond for $906.93 because comparable bonds are yielding 11%. The bond has a $1,000 face, or par, value; an 8% coupon payable annually; and 4 years to run before it matures. What is this bond's duration? The methodology for the calculation is as follows:

A	B	C = A x B	PV of C
Year #	Cash Inflow	Weighted Value	PV @ 11%
1	$ 80	$ 80	$ 72.07
2	80	160	129.86
3	80	240	175.49
4	1,080	4,320	2,845.72
		Total	$3,223.14

$3,223.14 ÷ $906.93 = 3.55 years duration

Note: The keystrokes for the column under "PV of C" above on an HP-12C are as follows:

Year 1: 1, n, 11, I, 0, PMT, 80, FV, and PV (answer = $72.07)
Year 2: 2, n, 11, I, 0, PMT, 160, FV, and PV (answer = $129.86)
Year 3: 3, n, 11, I, 0, PMT, 240, FV, and PV (answer = $175.49)
Year 4: 4, n, 11, I, 0, PMT, 4320, FV, and PV (answer = $2,845.72)

Alternatively, you can input the numbers in the Weighted Value column into the cash flow keys as a shortcut. The keystrokes on an HP-12C are as follows:

0, blue g, CFo
80, blue g, CFj
160, blue g, CFj
240, blue g, CFj
4320, blue g, CFj
11, i,
yellow f, NPV

This gives the answer of $3,223.14.

If you use the HP-10B II, the keystrokes are as follows:

0, CFj
80, CFj
160, CFj
240, CFj
4320, CFj
11, I/YR
Orange shift, NPV

This gives the answer of $3,223.14.

If you use the HP-17B II+, use the calculator's CFLO (cash flow) menu as follows:

0, INPUT (this is FLOW(0))
80, INPUT, INPUT
160, INPUT, INPUT
240, INPUT, INPUT
4320, INPUT, INPUT
EXIT, CALC
11, I% menu key
NPV

This gives the answer of $3,223.14.

If you use the TI BAII Plus, access the calculator's cash flow menu by pressing CF and then the following:

0, ENTER (this is CFo), ↓
80, ENTER, ↓, ↓
160, ENTER, ↓, ↓
240, ENTER, ↓, ↓

4320, ENTER
NPV (I = will appear on the screen)
11, ENTER, ↓ (NPV = will appear on the screen)
CPT

This gives the answer of $3,223.14.

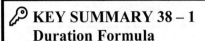 **KEY SUMMARY 38 – 1**
Duration Formula

$$\text{Duration} = \frac{\sum PV(C) \times t}{P}$$

Where:

PV(C) = Present value of the cash inflow C for each year
t = Year for which each cash inflow is received
P = Bond price

Editor's Note: This is a simplified version of the duration formula provided on the formula sheet.

A bond's duration will always be less than its years to maturity, except for zero-coupon bonds, where duration and maturity are equal. Also, the duration for short maturities is less than for long maturities and less for high coupons than for low coupons. The lower the duration, the lower is the susceptibility to the two combined effects of interest rate risk.

 KEY SUMMARY 38 – 2
Duration

(1) For zero-coupon bonds, time to maturity equals the duration.
(2) For coupon bonds, the duration is always less than the time to maturity.
(3) The longer the maturity of a bond, the greater the duration and the greater the price volatility.
(4) The smaller the coupon for a bond, the greater the duration and the greater the price volatility.
(5) The greater the duration for a bond, the greater the interest rate risk.

Duration analysis can also be used to "immunize" a portfolio from interest rate risk by choosing bonds with a duration that matches the time horizon for the goal. Immunization is discussed in more detail in Topic 40.

Modified Duration

The concept of modified duration is used to measure the effect of interest rate changes on a bond's price. Given the duration of a bond, one can use the formula for modified duration to estimate the effect on the bond's price of a small change in interest rates. The formula given on the test is as follows:

🔑 **KEY SUMMARY 38 – 3**
Modified Duration

$$\frac{\Delta P}{P} = -D\left[\frac{\Delta y}{1 + y}\right]$$

Where:

$\underline{\Delta P}$ = Change in the bond price
P

D = Duration of the bond
y = Interest rate yield on the bond
Δy = Change in the interest rate

Example:

An investor has purchased bonds that have a yield to maturity of 6.5%; the duration for the bonds is 11.6 years. The investor wants to invest $40,000 in the bonds. If interest rates rise by one-half of a percent, the change in price for the bonds is estimated by the formula as follows:

$$\frac{\Delta P}{P} = -D\left[\frac{\Delta y}{1 + y}\right]$$

$$= -11.6\left[\frac{.005}{1 + .065}\right]$$

$$= -(11.6) \times (.0047)$$

$$= -0.0545, \text{ or } -5.45\%$$

The change will mean a drop in the bonds' price of 5.45%, or a loss of (0.0545) ($40,000) = $2,180.

Practice Question

Corporate bonds can be purchased with a yield to maturity of 8% and a duration of 8.5 years. If an investor invests $10,000 in the bonds, what is the price change that should occur from a 1% increase in interest rates?

A. -$787
B. -$100
C. $100
D. $787

Answer:

$$\frac{\Delta P}{P} = -D \left[\frac{\Delta y}{1 + y} \right]$$

$$= -8.5 \left[\frac{.01}{1 + .08} \right]$$

$$= -8.5 \ \times \ (.009259) = -.0787$$

The price change will be $10,000 x −.0787 = −$787.
The answer is A.

Capitalized Earnings

The capitalized earnings approach to valuation of a security, also called the present-value approach, involves estimating the security's intrinsic value. **The intrinsic value of any investment is the present value of the net cash inflows it is expected to generate for the investor.** Hence, the method requires the investor to take the following three steps:

(1) Select an appropriate required rate of return to use in calculating the present value, based on the riskiness of the investment.

(2) Estimate the amount and timing of each net cash inflow from the investment.

(3) Compare the resulting value of the security with its current market price to see if it is overvalued, undervalued, or fairly valued.

To illustrate, assume that a preferred stock, a perpetuity, is expected to pay a dividend of $3.25 each year. If the investor decides that

12% is an appropriate discount or capitalization rate, the intrinsic value of the stock is:

$3.25 ÷ .12 = $27.08

Or, consider a security that is not a perpetuity, such as a bond. Assume that a $1,000 face amount bond with five years until maturity is now selling for $1,080. The bond has a 6% coupon rate, with interest payable semiannually, and the next interest payment will occur six months from today. If an investor believes that a 5½% interest rate accurately reflects the riskiness of this bond, is it fairly priced?

On a financial calculator, enter:

$1,000	FV
10	n
2.75	I/YR
$30	PMT (end-of-period)

Solve for PV, which is $1,022. Thus, the investor would conclude that the bond is overvalued at present since it is selling for $1,080.

Or, take the case of a zero-coupon $1,000 face amount bond that will mature in nine years. If 11% is an appropriate discount rate, the intrinsic value is found as follows:

$1,000	FV
18	n
5.5	I/YR

Solve for PV, which is $381.

Rental real estate properties can also be valued using the capitalization of earnings calculation. In this case the annual net operating income is divided by the appropriate discount rate. For example, if gross rents are $1,500 per month and fixed and variable expenses are $200 per month, the net operating income is $1,300 per month x 12 = $15,600. If the appropriate discount rate is 11%, then the investor is willing to pay $15,600/.11 = $141,818 for the property.

Dividend Growth Models

Often, the task of determining intrinsic value is complicated because the future net cash inflows are not as readily determinable as in the preceding illustrations involving a preferred stock or a bond. It is nevertheless possible to estimate the intrinsic value of the security, usually a share of common stock, by estimating the future growth rate(s) of the security's dividends. Three illustrative cases are presented below.

Zero-Dividend Growth Rate Model

The security with a zero-dividend growth rate is treated as a perpetuity, like preferred stock. Simply divide the present dividend, which presumably is the same as all future dividends, by the appropriate discount or capitalization rate to produce the intrinsic value.

Example:

A stock pays a dividend of $.50 per share, and no growth is expected. If a capitalization rate of 15% is selected, based on the riskiness involved, the intrinsic value is:

$$V = \frac{d}{k}$$

Where: V = Intrinsic value
d = Constant annual dividend
k = Discount rate

$$V = \$.50 \div .15 = \$3.33$$

🔑 **KEY SUMMARY 38 – 4**
Zero-Growth Rate Model (Preferred Stock)

$$V = \frac{d}{k}$$

Where: V = Intrinsic value
d = Constant annual dividend
k = Discount rate

Constant Dividend Growth Rate Model

Securities with a constant growth rate of dividends should be valued using a formula to calculate the present value of a stream of future dividends that are expected to grow by a constant percentage per year into infinity. The formula is:

$$V = \frac{D_1}{r - g}$$

Where:

D_1 = Next (not the present) annual dividend

r = Investor's required rate of return, based on the risk

g = Expected annual growth rate in the dividends

🔑 **KEY SUMMARY 38 – 5**
Constant Dividend Growth Model

$$V = \frac{D_1}{r - g}$$

Where:

D_1 = Next (not the present) annual dividend
r = Investor's required rate of return, based on the risk
g = Expected annual growth rate in the dividends

Example:

The most recent dividend on a stock was $4.00, and it is expected to grow by 10% per year for the foreseeable future. If the investor has a 20% required rate of return, the intrinsic value of this stock is:

$$\frac{\$4.00 \times 1.10}{.20 - .10} = \frac{\$4.40}{.10} = \$44.00$$

Notice that if the expected growth rate were higher and/or if the investor's required rate of return were lower, the gap $(r - g)$ would shrink, producing a higher intrinsic value for the stock.

Expected Rate of Return using Constant Dividend Growth Model

The constant dividend growth model formula can be rearranged as follows to solve for the client's expected rate of return:

$$r = \frac{D_1}{P} + g$$

Where:

r = Investor's expected rate of return
D_1 = Next (not the present) annual dividend
P = Price of the stock
g = Expected annual growth rate in the stock

Example:

The most recent dividend on a stock was $2.00, and the stock is expected to grow by 5% per year for the foreseeable future. If the intrinsic value of this stock is $25, the client's expected rate of return is:

= [($2.00 x 1.05)/$25] + 0.05

= 0.084 + 0.05

= 0.134, or 13.4%

Multiple Growth Rates

With multiple growth rates of dividends, we are talking about a stock whose dividends are expected to grow at one rate for an initial period, followed by a different growth rate or rates thereafter. In this case, the procedure is to separately discount each set of dividends at its expected growth rate and total the results to determine the stock's intrinsic value. To avoid undue complexity, we will use an example involving only two growth rates:

Example:

A stock's most recent annual dividend was $3.00, and it is expected to grow by 5% for the next two years, after which it is expected to grow at a 6% annual rate. If the investor's required rate of return is 8%, what is this stock's intrinsic value?

First, compute the present value of the first two expected dividends:

End of Yr.	Amt.	Disc. Rate	PV
1	$3.15	8%	$2.92
2	$3.31	8%	2.84
Total			$5.76

Next, compute the present value of the third and subsequent dividends, using the constant growth formula described earlier:

$$\frac{\$3.51}{.08 - .06} = \frac{\$3.51}{.02} = \$175.50$$

Note: $3.51 dividend is the $3.31 dividend grown by 6% ($3.31 x 1.06 = $3.51)

Since $175.50 represents the present value of expected dividends as of the start of Year 3 (or the end of Year 2), we next discount it back to the present:

$$
\begin{array}{ll}
175.50 & \text{FV} \\
8 & \text{I/YR} \\
2 & \text{n}
\end{array}
$$

Solve for PV, which is $150.46 today.

Combine today's present value of the two sets of dividends to produce the stock's intrinsic value:

$$\$5.76 + \$150.46 = \$156.22$$

Ratio Analysis – Valuation Ratios

Price/Earnings Valuation

An alternative to the dividend growth method of determining a stock's intrinsic value is the price/earnings ratio method. The P/E ratio is the ratio of market price to earnings per share. The P/E method can be used to value a stock when no dividend is paid. The formula for the P/E ratio is:

$$P/E = \frac{\text{Price per share}}{\text{Earnings per share}}$$

The earnings per share may be for the past year or for the next year. If future earnings are used, the ratio should be referred to as the future P/E ratio.

The P/E ratio for a company can change greatly, based on how the market views the company's prospects for growth. Nevertheless, an investor valuing a stock can make his or her own selection of a reasonable P/E for the company, determine the company's projected earnings, and then use the formula to arrive at a price per share. The investor can calculate a price per share by multiplying the P/E ratio by the earnings per share.

Example:

Beta Alpha Corporation pays no dividend. An investor has determined that a reasonable P/E ratio for the company's stock is 15. The earnings per share for the company is projected at $2 per share. A reasonable price for the stock, therefore, is 15 x $2 = $30.

Justified P/E Multiplier

Another method applies a "justified" P/E multiplier, rather than the present actual P/E multiplier. This method allows an investor to determine what the market price (intrinsic value) should be rather than what it is. The "justified" P/E multiplier is based on the following three factors:

- The investor's estimate of the stock's dividend payout ratio, or percentage of earnings that will be paid out as dividends (e.g., if a dividend of 10 cents per share is paid on earnings of 75 cents per share, the payout ratio is .10/.75 = .1333). The higher this ratio is, the higher will be the intrinsic value.

- The investor's expected dividend growth rate. The higher this rate is, the higher the intrinsic value will be.

- The investor's required rate of return. The higher this rate, the lower the intrinsic value.

The justified P/E multiplier is found by the following formula:

$$\text{JP/EM} = \frac{\text{Est. div. payout ratio}}{r - g}$$

Where:

r = Investor's required rate of return
g = Investor's estimate of the growth rate in dividends

For example, if an investor expects the firm to pay out 75% of its earnings per share in dividends, and if dividends are expected to grow by 10% per year, and if the investor's required rate of return is 12%, then:

$$\text{JP/EM} = \frac{.75}{.12 - .10} = \frac{.75}{.02} = 37.5$$

Therefore, if the estimated earnings per share for next year are $4.16, the intrinsic value of the stock for this investor is $4.16 x 37.5 = $156 per share. If the stock is presently selling for $132, it is undervalued and the investor should buy it.

Price/Free Cash Flow

Cash flow tracks what dollars are actually moving into and out of the company. The ratio of price to free cash flow uses operating cash flow which is net of any new investment or cash remaining after satisfying capital expenditures.

Price/Sales
Companies having no earnings to report may rely heavily upon this ratio tool (stock price/annual sales per share). The P/S ratio can vary greatly among different industries, as can profit margins. The use of this ratio for performance measurement has increased in recent years as a result of new start-up companies working to grow fast while in the beginning stages of development.

Price/Earnings/Growth (PEG)
PEG is calculated by dividing the P/E ratio by the sum of the estimated earnings growth rate and dividend yield. It indicates what price the market has placed on earnings expectations. A stock's dividend yield is added to EPS growth rate in the denominator of the equation. It is necessary to have realistic earnings growth and company sales growth percentages available. Stocks exhibiting below-average P/E ratios in combination with reasonable EPS growth rates may indicate a value-based equity.

Book Value
Book value is the value of each stock share per the books and based upon historical cost.

$$BV = \frac{\text{Total stockholder equity} - \text{Liquidation value of preferred stock}}{\text{Outstanding common shares}}$$

If the market price per share exceeds the book value by a sizeable amount, it may mean that the market may look favorably on the stock. Value investors, however, may search for stocks whose price is below book value, with the expectation that buying now may lead to substantial gains over the long term.

Fundamental Analysis
Fundamental analysis is evaluating a stock's price through discovery of its intrinsic value (estimated value of the security) by considering the assets, earnings, sales, management, and similar facts about the company.

Top-Down Analysis
In the top-down approach to fundamental analysis, there are three stages, starting with general factors and moving logically to specific factors:

1. First, **economic analysis** considers the state of economic affairs in order to learn what might be the future direction of prices. Interest rates and business cycle patterns are two important elements of this analysis. Determining whether rapid periods of growth or contraction are taking place within the economy will have a major influence on security prices. In analyzing the intrinsic value of different classifications of stocks, such as cyclical (most influenced by the economy, for example, autos) and defensive (mainly unaffected by economic change, for

example, beverages), fundamental analysis attempts to learn the direction of the market and what securities may be undervalued or overvalued.

2. **Industry analysis** attempts to determine the most opportune time for security selection. Industries can respond in significantly different ways over their life cycle. Rising and declining growth rates during the cycle are characterized by either product saturation by the industry or a consolidation and maturation stage. In the latter, industry leaders that are well capitalized usually gather more market share from smaller companies and begin to dominate the industry. Finally, a maturity stage arrives, characterized by both failing firms and market leaders, which now absorb market share. Market growth may continue, but at a much more modest rate.

Other factors that affect industry analysis include foreign market competition, financial requirements, and government regulations.

3. **Company analysis** is most important because much security analyst reporting is organized by industry. The analyst will look to a company's earnings and dividends paid. Dividends are paid out of earnings, so these two components are important ingredients in the fundamental evaluation process. Also, earnings per share and stock prices are highly correlated, and valuation techniques using present-value models (dividend discount model or P/E ratio) are key components of any forecasting of security prices.

🔑 **KEY SUMMARY 38 – 6**
   Stages of Fundamental Analysis

1. Economic analysis
2. Industry analysis
3. Company analysis

Bottom-Up Analysis

Bottom-up analysis begins with company analysis and seeks to identify companies with appealing valuation and solid financial characteristics. This company analysis will focus on financial statements, including ratio analysis. The bottom-up analysis will then compare the company to its industry and, finally, may conduct an economic analysis as the last step.

Ratio Analysis

Ratio analysis is a frequently used tool of financial analysts and is performed in two different ways.

1. Time-series analysis involves analyzing a company over a specific period of time, usually from one year to the next. Company performance is scrutinized, looking for any significant and recurring trends or patterns.

2. Cross-sectional analysis involves comparing companies in the same industry during a certain period. These analyses can be based upon the company's asset base, revenue stream, etc.

Financial Ratios

Financial statement analysis based on financial ratios is used to look at a company's or industry's liquidity, activity, profitability, or the degree to which debt financing is employed.

Liquidity Ratios

Liquidity ratios measure the degree to which assets are convertible into cash with relatively little or no price change. A company's creditors look to this number for guidance as to how likely they are to be repaid on a timely basis. The current ratio divides current assets (cash, marketable securities, accounts receivable, and inventory) by current liabilities, while the acid-test, or quick ratio, is calculated in the same manner but subtracts inventory from current assets. This quick ratio measures the degree to which the company can satisfy its debts with highly liquid assets.

🔑 KEY SUMMARY 38 –7
Liquidity Ratios

$$\text{Current ratio} = \frac{\text{Current assets}}{\text{Current liabilities}}$$

$$\text{Quick ratio (Acid-test)} = \frac{\text{Current assets} - \text{Inventory}}{\text{Current liabilities}}$$

Practice Question

Which of the following items are treated as a current asset for liquidity ratios?

(1) Preferred stock
(2) Accounts receivable
(3) Line of credit
(4) Patent

    A. (1) and (2) only
    B. (3) and (4) only
    C. (2) and (3) only
    D. (1), (2), and (3) only

Answer:
Current assets include cash, marketable securities, accounts receivable, and inventory. Assuming that the company owns another corporation's preferred stock, the preferred stock would be classified as a marketable security. A line of credit is a short-term debt financing arrangement, not a current asset. A patent is an intangible fixed asset and is not easily marketed.
The answer is A.

Activity Ratios

Activity ratios measure the rate at which assets are flowing through a company. The inventory turnover ratio indicates at what rate inventory is sold. It is expressed as cost of goods sold divided by average inventory. A ratio of 10.9, for example, would indicate that cost of goods sold are almost 11 times the average level of inventory, or that inventory turns over about every five weeks. Similarly, the receivables turnover ratio (credit sales ÷ accounts receivable) indicates how long receivables are outstanding, on the average.

 KEY SUMMARY 38 – 8
Activity Ratios

Inventory turnover ratio $= \dfrac{\text{Cost of goods sold}}{\text{Average inventory}}$

Receivables turnover ratio $= \dfrac{\text{Credit sales}}{\text{Accounts receivable}}$

Profitability Ratios

Profitability ratios measure performance. The earnings that a company produces are either distributed as dividends or retained as additional investments in the corporation. Return on assets (ROA), which is earnings after taxes divided by total assets, and return on equity (ROE), which is earnings after taxes divided by equity, are two of the more common profitability ratios utilized by analysts.

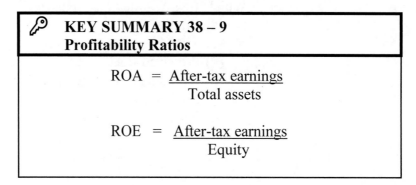

KEY SUMMARY 38 – 9
Profitability Ratios

$$ROA = \frac{\text{After-tax earnings}}{\text{Total assets}}$$

$$ROE = \frac{\text{After-tax earnings}}{\text{Equity}}$$

Debt Ratios

Debt ratios, sometimes referred to as capitalization or leverage ratios, measure the use of debt financing by a company. Depending upon the company's earnings, debt financing can magnify its shareholder returns or its losses. The ratio is expressed as debt divided by equity or total assets. No differentiation is made between short-term and long-term debt. A debt-to-total-assets ratio of 34% would indicate that 34% of the company's assets were debt-financed, while a debt-to-equity ratio of 1.4 would indicate that there was $1.40 in debt financing for every $1.00 of company stock.

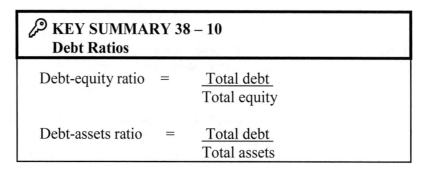

KEY SUMMARY 38 – 10
Debt Ratios

$$\text{Debt-equity ratio} = \frac{\text{Total debt}}{\text{Total equity}}$$

$$\text{Debt-assets ratio} = \frac{\text{Total debt}}{\text{Total assets}}$$

Technical Analysis

Technical analysis is the process used by financial analysts who believe that the study of past movements, trends, and patterns of a company's securities can assist in predicting future security prices. While fundamental analysis looks to the financial statements of companies, technical analysts look for the opportune time to buy or sell, utilizing specific data derived from charts, price and volume data, and the market's own record.

While many forms of technical analysis are widely used in practice, it is worth noting that some aspects of technical analysis cause it to be viewed with skepticism by many academics and financial planners. For example, several interpretations of each technical tool and chart pattern are not only possible, but are typical. In addition, a technical rule that proves to be correct is likely to become increasingly less effective as more investors use it. Finally, testing of many technical approaches has failed to confirm the value of those techniques.

Myriad approaches can be employed using technical analysis. We will discuss the two most common categories. One is concerned with the general market directions and patterns, while the other concentrates on analyzing buy/sell signals of particular securities. Within each of these categories, the technical analysis will focus on one or more of the following:

- Charting
- Investor sentiment towards the market
- The flow of funds in and out of the market
- The overall structure of the market

General Market Directions

Dow Theory

The Dow Theory is a technique based upon the Dow Jones Transportation and Dow Jones Industrial Averages. It is not concerned with the movement of individual securities, but with that of the broader market. The theory is predicated upon three types of price movements: primary (broad market swings), secondary (swing moves that are considered temporary but may last months), and tertiary (random daily price movements having no significance). The analyst looks for the Transportation Average to confirm the Industrials. Any divergence may suggest a downward trend in the market.

Barron's Confidence Index

The Barron's Confidence Index is an index that attempts to predict future security price movements by analyzing the spread between high-grade and intermediate-grade corporate bonds. During good times, investors will take on more risk, sell quality bonds, and purchase more speculative instruments. When sentiment is bearish, the opposite occurs, with investors selling lower-grade debt and buying high-quality bonds. Thus, the yield spread increases.

The index is constructed using Barron's index of yields on high- and intermediate-grade corporate bonds. The premise is that prices will rise when the yield spread is small (high-grade yields are near intermediate-grade yields). When the yield spread widens, this is interpreted to mean prices will decline. As with other types of technical indicators, there is no conclusive evidence that this approach can predict when a bear or bull market will occur.

Odd-Lot Theory

Contrarian investing is a strategy of buying and selling opposite to the decisions of most investors in the market at a given time. The odd-lot theory is a contrarian strategy based on the belief that most small investors (those buying fewer than 100 shares) generally make wrong investment decisions. Technicians believe that when there is an increased amount of short selling among small investors and they are bearish, the market will begin to show bullish, not bearish, indications since technicians think these small investors act upon incorrect information. Technicians generally rate a ratio of odd-lot purchases to odd-lot sales of 1.4 to .6 as average. When it approaches 1.4, small investors are buying more stock, a bearish signal. When the ratio approaches the .6 figure, odd-lot sales exceed purchases, a bullish signal.

Practice Question

What are the indices used by the Dow Theory to predict the direction of the market?

    (1) Dow Jones Industrial
    (2) Dow Jones Utility
    (3) Dow Jones Transportation
    (4) Dow Jones Composite

        A. (1) and (2) only
        B. (1) and (3) only
        C. (3) and (4) only
        D. (1), (2), (3), and (4)

Answer:
The Dow Theory uses the Dow Transportation and Dow Jones Industrial Averages. Analysts look for the Transportation Average to confirm the movement in the Industrials Average.
The answer is B.

Specific Security Indicators

Trends and Patterns

Trends and patterns detected through the use of charts and graphs are key tools used by technical analysts. Signals such as support and resistance levels are supply and demand forces helping to predict future stock patterns and prices. A support level is a price at which it is thought the security cannot go below, suggesting a price range that may indicate increased demand for stock. Resistance levels are a price at which the security cannot go above, suggesting a price range that may indicate a major increase in the supply of stock as existing owners sell once this price point is reached.

Charting	The bar chart depicts daily high and low prices, with a small horizontal tick designating the closing price. The vertical axis represents price, and the horizontal axis represents time. The height of the bar represents, at either end, the stock's high and low price for the day.
	The point-and-figure chart depicts equity prices that demonstrate significant price changes. No volume pattern is shown; X shows price increases, while 0 shows declining price movements. A congestion area (numerous price changes appear) may signify a breakout to either the upside or the downside.
Moving Averages	Moving averages are used to identify major trends in both the overall market and individual securities. An average price is determined, after which a new average is calculated by dropping the earliest observation and adding the latest one. The process is repeated and depends upon the time period measured, for example 200 days, 50 weeks, etc. When the average is compared to current market prices, a buy (prices moving up through the average line) or sell (prices decline through the average line) signal results.
Relative Strength	Usually depicted in graphic form, relative strength is the ratio of a stock price to a market or industry index. The objective here is to observe pricing trends and study how they might be affected by some significant event that could alter market direction. Ratios are calculated, and forecasts are made as to stock direction. Caution should be used with this technique, as a falling stock could display strong relative strength against a market that is declining by a much faster percentage.
Breadth Indicator (Advance-Decline Line)	The advance-decline line measures on a cumulative daily basis the net difference between advancing and declining stock prices. Any divergence between the line and the average suggests to technicians that a trend may soon change.
Short-Interest Ratio	Short-interest ratio is the ratio of total shares sold short to the average daily volume. Investors sell short when they expect a price decline.
Mutual Fund Liquidity	Mutual fund liquidity is a contrarian strategy similar to the odd-lot premise. When funds hold large cash positions, contrarian strategists believe that managers are bearish, which is a bullish sign. Conversely, small cash positions suggest that managers are bullish; this becomes a bearish signal for the contrarian.
Put/Call Ratio	Put/call ratio is another contrarian strategy wherein a higher number indicates pessimism but is a buy signal to the contrarian. Investors

buying options are looked upon as speculators who lose more than they gain.

For example, assume that the put/call ratio is .5. This signals to the contrarian that there are only 5 puts bought for every 10 call positions. A rise in this ratio would indicate pessimism on the investor's part, but it would be a bullish signal to contrarians, who believe the speculators are moving against market forces that indicate a buy opportunity.

KEY SUMMARY 38 – 11
Technical Analysis

General Directions

Dow Theory	The Dow Transportation Index confirms change in direction of the Dow Industrial Index.
Barron's Confidence Index	Prices will rise when the spread between high-grade and intermediate-grade corporate bonds is small.
Odd-Lot Theory	Increased odd-lot selling is bullish, and odd-lot buying is bearish for this contrarian strategy.

Specific Security Indicators

Charts	Prices for securities are drawn on charts to reveal direction.
Moving Averages	Price trends are graphed for the overall market and specific securities, and a price moving up through an average indicates a buy.
Relative Strength	Price trends are graphed using a ratio of stock price to a market or industry index.
Breadth Indicator	The daily difference between advancing and declining stock prices is compared with the average.
Short-Interest Ratio	A comparison is made of the ratios of total shares sold short to the average daily volume.
Mutual Fund Liquidity	Large cash positions by mutual funds are bullish for this contrarian strategy.
Put/Call Ratio	A high ratio is a buy signal for this contrarian strategy.

Options Valuation Models

Black-Scholes Option Valuation Model

The first option pricing model was developed by Fisher Black and Myron Scholes in 1973. Its purpose is to help determine the value of a call option of a non-dividend-paying stock. Five variables are part of this calculation:

- The current market price – Call premium is higher for higher priced stocks.

- The strike price of the option – Call premium will be higher for lower strike prices.

- The more volatile the stock, the greater the premium since the underlying stock's price may increase. This is the only variable not directly observable in the market.

- The premium will increase as the time to expiration increases.

- As the risk-free rate rises, so does the call premium.

The influence on both call and put options as they relate to these different variables can be termed positive or negative. With each variable, the remaining ones are assumed to remain fixed.

	Calls	Puts
Market Price	POS	NEG
Strike Price	NEG	POS
Expiration Time	POS	POS
Stock Volatility	POS	POS
Risk-Free Rate	POS	NEG

The Black-Scholes Option Pricing Model assumes that option prices are being fairly valued by the market and that there is continuous stock pricing. The model also assumes that the call option is a European (exercisable only on expiration date), not an American (exercisable at any time before expiration) style, option.

Other Models

There are two other models that were largely developed from the use of the Black-Scholes Option Pricing Model. They are the Put-Call Parity Model (the steady relationship between a put and a call on the same security) and the Hedge Ratio Model (the relationship of call options written to shares of stock as part of a riskless portfolio). A hedge ratio of less than one signifies that values in options prices are less volatile than price changes in the underlying stock.

Binomial Option Pricing

Another approach to option valuation is binomial option pricing. A model of this pricing is based upon the assumption that equity prices move to only two values over a small time period. This is another method of option valuation and is used often as a model that can help explain more complicated valuation procedures.

It is a simplistic model that has as its basic assumption the following: A stock from its current value will either increase to a set higher price or fall to a set lower price. By predicting option pricing using this assumption, a relationship between, for instance, call option value and the purchase of stock only can be established.

TOPIC 38 – APPLICATION QUESTIONS

1. (Published question released November, 1994)

The current annual dividend of ABC Corporation is $2.00 per share. Five years ago the dividend was $1.36 per share. The firm expects dividends to grow in the future at the same compound annual rate as they grew during the past five years. The required rate of return on the firm's common stock is 12%. The expected return on the market portfolio is 14%. What is the value of a share of common stock of ABC Corporation, using the constant dividend growth model? (Round to the nearest dollar.)

A. $11
B. $17
C. $25
D. $36
E. $54

2. (Published question released December, 1996)

Company ABC is currently trading at $35 and pays a dividend of $2.30. Analysts project a dividend growth rate of 4%. Your client Tom requires a rate of 9% to meet his stated goal. Tom wants to know if he should purchase stock in Company ABC.

A. Yes, the stock is undervalued.
B. No, the stock is overvalued.
C. No, the required rate is higher than the projected growth rate.
D. Yes, the required rate is higher than the expected rate.
E. No, the required rate is lower than the expected rate.

3. QRS Corp.'s common stock is currently selling for $9 per share. Bill expects that the company will earn $.85 per share in the next 12 months and will pay a dividend of $.17 per share. He expects that dividends will grow at a rate of about 10% per year for the foreseeable future. Bill requires a rate of return of at least 15% before he will invest in QRS. Which of the following should be elements of your advice to Bill as his financial planner?

(1) This stock has a justified P/E multiple of four-to-one.
(2) This stock would be worth more if it had a higher dividend payout ratio.
(3) This stock appears to be a very wise purchase for Bill at $9.

A. (1) and (2) only
B. (1) and (3) only
C. (2) and (3) only
D. (1), (2), and (3)
E. Neither (1), (2), nor (3)

4. Gene Allen recently bought a 6% coupon, $1,000 par value bond for $900.53. The bond was priced to yield 10%. The bond pays interest annually and will mature in 3 years. What is Gene's bond's duration?

A. 2.31 years
B. 2.67 years
C. 2.74 years
D. 2.82 years
E. 3.21 years

5. Which of the following statements concerning a bond's duration is not correct?

    A. If a bond has a high coupon, its duration will be lower than a similar one with a low coupon.

    B. If a bond has a long maturity, its duration will be lower than a similar one with a short maturity.

    C. The duration of a zero-coupon bond is equal to its years to maturity.

    D. For most bonds, duration is less than their years to maturity.

    E. A bond with a low duration has a lower susceptibility to interest rate risk than a similar bond with a high duration.

6. For which of the following investments can the duration be determined without a calculation?

    A. A 15-year bond whose call date is only four years away

    B. A custodial account with a mixture of equities and bond funds

    C. A bond fund that minimizes portfolio turnover and is tax-efficient

    D. A zero-coupon bond that matures in eight years

    E. A series of bonds with no call date provisions

7. (Published question released January, 1999)

Bond A has a 6% annual coupon and is due in 2 years. Its value in today's market is $900.

Bond B has a 10% annual coupon and is due in 4 years. It is priced to yield 12%.

Bond C is a 9% zero-coupon bond priced to yield 11% in 8 years.

Assuming that the duration of Bond A is 1.94 years, which of the following statements about the effect of a 1% decline in interest rates is true?

    A. Bond C, having a longer duration than Bond A, would have a larger percent increase in price than Bond A.

    B. The percent change in price of a bond is independent of the duration of a bond.

    C. It is not possible to determine the percent change in price of Bond A versus Bond C because the duration of Bond C is not given.

    D. Bond A would have a greater percent change in price than Bond C because it has a shorter duration.

    E. The percent change in the price of Bonds A and C is equal since it is not affected by duration.

8. (Published question released January, 1999)

The following set of newly issued debt instruments was purchased for a portfolio:

Treasury bond
Zero-coupon bond
Corporate bond
Municipal bond

The respective maturities of these investments are approximately equivalent.

Which one of the investments in the preceding set would be subject to the greatest relative amount of price volatility if interest rates were to change quickly?

A. Treasury bond
B. Zero-coupon bond
C. Corporate bond
D. Municipal bond

9. (Published question released January, 1999)

The duration of a bond is a function of its:

(1) Current price
(2) Time to maturity
(3) Yield to maturity
(4) Coupon rate

    A. (1) and (3) only
    B. (2) and (3) only
    C. (2) and (4) only
    D. (1), (2), and (3) only
    E. (1), (2), (3), and (4)

******

(Three published questions released January, 1999; updated)

You are faced with the following alternative fixed-income investments.

A. A U.S. Treasury bond with an 11.625% coupon, due in four years, with a price of $142.50 and a yield to maturity of 6.3%
B. A U.S. Treasury strip bond (zero-coupon) due in four years, with a price of $46.75 and a yield to maturity of 6.25%
C. A corporate B-rated bond with a 9.75% coupon, due in four years, with a price of $104.75 and a yield to maturity of 8.79%

10. _____ Which of these bonds has the greatest reinvestment rate risk?

11. _____ Which of these bonds has the greatest interest rate risk?

12. _____ Which of these bonds has the longest duration?

13. Sarah Dunham has invested $30,000 in a bond that has a coupon of 8% and yield to maturity of 7%. The bond's duration is 12.8 years. What price change can Sarah expect from an increase of 1% in interest rates?

A. +11.96%
B. +11.85%
C. −11.85%
D. −11.96 %

14. Which of the following factors will be least likely to affect the duration of a bond?

  A. Quality
  B. Coupon
  C. Time to maturity
  D. Yield to maturity

15. Which of the following statements concerning duration is correct?

  A. If interest rates increase, duration for an investor's bond portfolio will increase.
  B. If interest rates are expected to rise, an investor should shorten duration of a bond portfolio.
  C. A zero-coupon bond will not match duration and maturity in future years.
  D. If the coupon for a bond to be purchased is increased, the duration will increase.

16. Which of the following statements concerning duration is (are) correct?

  (1) An 8% coupon bond that has 5 years to run till maturity has a duration of more than 5 years.
  (2) A bond's duration is a weighted-average length of time a bondholder must wait before receiving the present value of all the payments from a bond.
  (3) A bond portfolio is immunized if its duration matches the duration of the investor's cash needs.

  A. (3) only
  B. (1) and (2) only
  C. (1) and (3) only
  D. (2) and (3) only
  E. (1), (2), and (3)

17. (Published question released November, 1994)

According to fundamental analysis, which phrase best defines the intrinsic value of a share of common stock?

  A. The par value of the common stock
  B. The book value of the common stock
  C. The liquidating value of the firm on a per share basis
  D. The stock's current price in an inefficient market
  E. The discounted value of all future dividends

18. A support level price indicator suggests the:

  A. Price range at which neither an increase nor decrease is expected
  B. Price range indicating increased demand for a stock
  C. Price at which a security cannot go above
  D. Price range where there is an expected increase in stock supply

19. What is the most familiar tool of technical analysis, that predicts market movement by using movement in one average to confirm another average?

  A. Dow Theory
  B. Barron's Confidence Index
  C. Relative Strength Line
  D. Moving Average Line
  E. Odd-Lot Theory

20. A contrarian may look to which of the following for guidance?

(1) Investment advisory sources
(2) The put/call ratio
(3) Relative strength ratio
(4) Mutual fund cash positions

   A. (1) and (3) only
   B. (1) and (2) only
   C. (1), (2), and (4) only
   D. (1), (3), and (4) only
   E. (2), (3), and (4) only

21. The top-down approach to fundamental analysis is a three-stage process, with the first being:

   A. Security analysis
   B. Economic analysis
   C. Industry analysis
   D. Company or firm analysis
   E. None of the above

22. A small horizontal tick displayed on a bar chart represents:

   A. The average of daily price ranges
   B. The intrinsic value of the security
   C. The closing price
   D. The moving average price of the stock

23. Fundamental and technical analysts tend to agree on which of the following?

(1) Past price movements are predictive of future price movements.
(2) Technical analysis can only apply to general market, and not individual security, prices.
(3) A minimum of 6 – 12 months is necessary in order to validate either process.

   A. (1) and (2) only
   B. (3) only
   C. (2) only
   D. (1), (2), and (3)
   E. None of the above

24. Barron's Confidence Index is a technical indicator that:

   A. Attempts to demonstrate how the Transportation and Industrial Averages must confirm each other
   B. Reveals how investors will take on more risk when sentiment is bearish
   C. Is predicated upon primary, secondary, and tertiary movements
   D. Suggests that the index ratio rises when high-grade yields are near intermediate-grade yields
   E. Suggests that the index ratio rises when intermediate-grade bonds are apart from high-grade yields

25. A high position in mutual fund liquidity suggests to the contrarian:

   A. A market buying opportunity
   B. A peak in the market cycle
   C. A resistance level soon being attained
   D. A trough in the market cycle
   E. An equilibrium point being attained between buyers and sellers

26. A ratio that measures the degree to which a company has utilized debt obligations is called a(n):

   A. Activity ratio
   B. Price/earnings (P/E) ratio
   C. Leverage ratio
   D. Liquidity ratio
   E. Profitability ratio

27. A client advises you that the latest financial report on the news networks suggests that the debt ratios of firms in a certain industry have increased. In explaining the concept, you should advise her that:

   A. Concern about debt ratio commentary from the financial media should be minimized.
   B. Increasing debt positions of firms within the industry may have a positive influence upon the bottom line.
   C. A sharp distinction is drawn between short-term and long-term debt in the ratio's calculation.
   D. A debt-to-asset position of less than 50% suggests that the industry is using leverage to its best advantage.

28. The best measure by which to evaluate a company's ability to satisfy debts with highly liquid assets is the:

   A. Acid-test ratio
   B. Current ratio
   C. Relative strength ratio
   D. Capitalization ratio
   E. Profitability ratio

29. If the current ratio for a firm is high, but the quick ratio is low, which of the following statements is most likely true for this firm?

   A. The firm has inadequate levels of inventory for its sales activity.
   B. The firm has excessive inventory in relation to its assets.
   C. The firm has a good level of inventory and sales.
   D. The firm is growing rapidly and has adequate liquidity for its growth.

30. (Published question released January, 1999)

In analyzing the financial statements of a client's business, you notice that the collection period for accounts receivable has been increasing. What does this increase suggest about the firm's credit policy?

   A. The firm's current ratio is also increasing.
   B. The collection period has <u>no</u> relationship to a firm's credit policy.
   C. The firm is losing qualified customers.
   D. The credit policy is too lenient.

31. The Option Pricing Model includes all the following variables in its calculations, EXCEPT:

    A. The volatility of the underlying stock
    B. The strike price of the option – call premium will be higher for lower strike price
    C. The interest rate for a risk-free asset
    D. The variance and covariance premiums
    E. The length of the option

32. According to the Black-Scholes Model:

    A. A call option expires worthless.
    B. Synthetic options are the key to effective portfolio insurance strategies.
    C. As volatility decreases, a call option's value increases.
    D. A call option's value increases as its time to maturity increases.
    E. None of the above statements regarding this price model are correct.

33. According to the Black-Scholes option valuation model, the value of a call option depends on which of the following factors?

    (1) The option's strike price
    (2) The current market price of the stock
    (3) The length of time until the option's expiration
    (4) The correlation coefficient between the stock's price and average stock prices
    (5) The risk-free rate of interest

    A. (1) and (2) only
    B. (1), (2), and (3) only
    C. (3), (4), and (5) only
    D. (1), (2), (3), and (5) only
    E. (2), (3), (4), and (5) only

34. A call option is trading in the market at $5 but under the Black-Scholes Model is valued at $4. What is the most likely explanation for the difference in price?

    A. The company has just announced higher than expected earnings
    B. A decreasing beta of the underlying stock
    C. A decrease in the price of the T-bill
    D. An increasing standard deviation of the underlying stock

35. Which of the following statements concerning the expected rate of return formula are correct?

(1) It is used for calculating the expected rate of return that an investment will provide.
(2) In the formula, P refers to the current stock price.
(3) If the expected rate of return exceeds the investor's required rate of return, then the stock is undervalued.
(4) In the formula, D_1 refers to the discount rate necessary to translate future values to present values.

    A. (1) and (3) only
    B. (2) and (4) only
    C. (1), (2), and (3) only
    D. (1), (3), and (4) only

36. Mr. Wood has a 17% required rate of return. He is contemplating investing in SDF Corporation, which is selling for $120 per share and now pays a dividend of $4.40 annually. He expects the dividends and earnings to increase at an annual rate of 12%. What is the expected rate of return for SDF? Is the stock overvalued or undervalued?

    A. 15.3%; overvalued
    B. 16.1%; overvalued
    C. 17.4%; undervalued
    D. 18.1%; undervalued

37. Based on the data from Question 36, what is the intrinsic value of a share of SDF Corporation stock?

    A. $98.56
    B. $104.19
    C. $111.61
    D. Cannot be determined from the information provided.

38. Which of the following statements concerning the constant dividend growth model formula are correct?

(1) It is used for calculating a stock's intrinsic value if dividends grow at a fixed rate.
(2) In the formula, V refers to the expected rate of return.
(3) In the formula, D_1 refers to the dividend expected to be received next year.
(4) In the formula, g refers to the fixed rate at which dividends are expected to grow.

    A. (1), (2), and (3) only
    B. (1), (2), and (4) only
    C. (1), (3), and (4) only
    D. (2), (3), and (4) only

39. Michelle has a 20% required rate of return. She is considering an investment in AMP, Inc., which currently pays an annual dividend of $.64 and is projected to increase its dividends and earnings by 17% annually. The current market price is $36.50. What is the expected rate of return from AMP stock, and is it overvalued or undervalued, given Michelle's requirements?

    A. 15.0%; overvalued
    B. 18.2%; overvalued
    C. 19.1%; overvalued
    D. 21.4%; undervalued

40. Based on the data from Question 39, what is the intrinsic value of AMP, Inc. stock per share?

   A. $24.96   C. $30.00
   B. $28.62   D. $36.50

41. Steve is a young bachelor who is looking for stocks to purchase to diversify his portfolio. He requires a 13% rate of return and is considering the purchase of one of the following two common stocks:

Stock 1: Dividends are currently $.35 annually and are expected to increase 10% annually; market price is $10.

Stock 2: Dividends are currently $1.10 annually and are expected to increase 8% annually; market price is $62.

Which stock would be more appropriate for Steve to purchase, based on the dividend growth model?

   A. Stock 1 because it is undervalued
   B. Stock 1 because the expected rate of return is less than Steve's required rate of return
   C. Stock 2 because it is overvalued
   D. Stock 2 because the expected rate of return is greater than Steve's required rate of return

42. Martha requires a 16% rate of return on her investment. She is considering the purchase of one of the following two common stocks:

Stock 1: Dividends are currently $1.35 annually and are expected to increase 12% annually; market price is $45.

Stock 2: Dividends are currently $.75 annually and are expected to increase 9% annually; market price is $10.50.

Which stock would be more appropriate for Martha to purchase, based on the dividend valuation method formula?

   A. Stock 1 because it is overvalued
   B. Stock 1 because the expected rate of return is greater than Martha's required rate of return
   C. Stock 2 because it is undervalued
   D. Stock 2 because the expected rate of return is less than Martha's required rate of return

43. Assume that the ABC Corporation is expected to pay a perpetual dividend on its common stock of $5 a year. If an investor's required return is 12%, the value of a share of this stock would be nearest to which of the following?

   A. $12   D. $60
   B. $42   E. $120
   C. $50

44. The intrinsic value of a stock can best be defined as which of the following?

A. Market value of the stock
B. Book value of the stock
C. Investment value of the stock based on estimated future cash flows, generated by an investment in the stock
D. Market value of the corporation's assets less capital consumption allowances
E. The owners' equity of the corporation, as shown in the balance sheet, divided by the number of common shares outstanding

45. Which of the following statements concerning intrinsic value and required return is (are) correct?

(1) The more risky an asset, the higher the discount rate should be for valuation purposes.
(2) Risk and required return are unrelated.
(3) Intrinsic value will tend to increase with increases in the discount rate.

A. (1) only
B. (1) and (2) only
C. (1) and (3) only
D. (2) and (3) only
E. (1), (2), and (3)

46. In general, the riskier an asset is perceived to be, the _____ the rate used to discount its _____, and the _____ its market value.

A. Lower, expected income stream, higher
B. Higher, historical income stream, lower
C. Lower, expected income stream, lower
D. Higher, expected income stream, lower

47. Assume that Corporation X is expected to pay a dividend of $1 at the end of the first year of holding the stock, $2.10 at the end of the second year, $3 at the end of the third year, and $3.50 at the end of the fourth year. Further assume that the dividend is then expected to grow at a 6% compound annual rate from the end of the fourth year to infinity and that an investor requires a return of 13% for the level of risk represented. The intrinsic value of this stock to that investor would be closest to:

A. $40   D. $65
B. $50   E. $70
C. $60

******

Use the following information to answer Questions 48-49, below. Assume that a stock sells for $50 per share and pays an annual dividend of $3.50, and dividends are expected to grow at 7% per year into perpetuity. The stock has a beta of 1.2. The market rate of return is 16%, and the risk-free rate of return is 9%.

48. The intrinsic value of this stock, based on the constant growth dividend valuation model, is _____.

A. $36.01
B. $38.89
C. $41.61
D. $50.00

49. The expected return on this stock is _____.

A. 7.00%
B. 14.49%
C. 17.40%
D. 19.20%

******

50. Assume that the market believes a firm has high growth prospects. It is likely that the firm would have a high:

A. Earnings per share
B. Price-earnings ratio
C. Debt-to-equity ratio
D. Beta for the stock

51. Which of the following is the correct definition of a stock's P/E ratio?

A. The ratio of the firm's stock price to earnings per share
B. The ratio of the firm's stock price to dividends per share
C. The ratio of the firm's earnings per share to its stock price
D. The ratio of the firm's dividends to earnings per share

52. Which of the following statements correctly describes duration?

A. There is a positive relationship between the coupon rate and duration.
B. There is an inverse relationship between the yield to maturity and duration.
C. Bonds with shorter durations are more volatile.
D. There is an inverse relationship between maturity and duration.

Editor's Note: For purposes of simplicity, in Questions 53-56, below, assume that the interest payments are made once per year. Therefore, make all discounting calculations on an annual basis.

53. An investor owns a bond with a coupon rate of 7% and 3 years to maturity. Comparable bonds are yielding 10%. What is the duration of this bond?

    A. 2.34 years   C. 4.08 years
    B. 2.80 years   D. 4.63 years

54. What is the duration of the bond in Question 53 if comparable bonds are yielding 5%?

    A. 2.33 years   C. 2.81 years
    B. 2.71 years   D. 3.88 years

55. An investor owns a bond with an annual coupon rate of 12% and 3 years to maturity. Comparable bonds are yielding 14%. What is the duration of this bond?

    A. 1.91 years   C. 2.68 years
    B. 2.46 years   D. 3.29 years

56. What is the duration of the bond in Question 55 if comparable bonds are yielding 9%?

    A. 2.70 years   C. 4.11 years
    B. 2.93 years   D. 4.62 years

57. An investor owns a preferred stock issue that pays an annual dividend of $4.80. The comparable yield on preferred stock of similar quality is 9%. The common stock is priced at $35. What is the intrinsic value of the preferred stock?

    A. $48.00   C. $53.33
    B. $51.72   D. $55.83

58. An investor owns a preferred stock issue that pays an annual dividend of $1.50. The comparable yield on preferred stock of similar quality is 16%. What is the intrinsic value of the preferred stock?

    A. $8.85   C. $10.25
    B. $9.38   D. $11.23

59. If a bond's duration, calculated on the basis of a 10% discount rate, is 4.17 years, by what percentage is the bond's price likely to change if interest rates rise to 10.2%?

    A. $-.24\%$ D. -2.11%
    B. $-.76\%$ E. $+.03\%$
    C. -1.38%

60. Which of the following statements correctly identifies factors affecting the value of a call option?

    A. The standard deviation of the stock market
    B. The price of a put option with the same underlying stock
    C. The exercise price of the call option
    D. The spread between the federal funds rate and the Treasury bonds rate

61. Which of the following correctly describes the relationship between the factors affecting the value of a call option and the value of that option?

A. A decrease in the stock price increases the value of the call option.
B. An increase in the strike price increases the value of a call option.
C. An increase in the time to expiration decreases the value of an option.
D. An increase in interest rates increases the value of an option.

62. The top-down approach to traditional security analysis begins with which of the following?

A. Examination of blue-chip securities
B. Examination of stock trading volume
C. Overall analysis of the economy
D. Industry analysis
E. Study of the extent of short selling activity

63. Which of the following matches a financial ratio to its definition?

A. Operating profit margin – ratio of net income to sales
B. Quick ratio – ratio of current assets to current liabilities
C. Gross profit margin – ratio of pretax income to sales
D. Payout ratio – ratio of dividends to earnings

64. Which of the following matches a financial ratio to its definition?

A. Current ratio – ratio of current assets to working capital
B. Operating profit margin – ratio of net income to sales
C. Return on equity – ratio of net income to retained earnings
D. Return on assets – ratio of net income to total assets

65. Which of the following are the ingredients that investors should logically study in following the fundamental analysis approach to stock selection?

(1) The price history of the company's common stock
(2) Economic conditions, such as the level of employment and economic growth
(3) Financial conditions, such as the level of and direction of changes in interest rates
(4) The firm's earning capacity and its growth potential

A. (1), (2), and (3) only
B. (1), (2), and (4) only
C. (1), (3), and (4) only
D. (2), (3), and (4) only

66. Which of the following is the correct definition of the return-on-assets ratio?

A. The ratio of earnings before interest and taxes to total assets
B. The ratio of net income to total assets
C. The ratio of earnings before interest and taxes to fixed assets
D. The ratio of net income to fixed assets

67. Which of the following statements concerning a moving average is correct?

   A. It indicates changes in the primary movement of the market.
   B. It indicates the basic trend of stock prices.
   C. It is obtained by comparing the stock's price to an index.
   D. It is obtained by comparing varying quality bond yields.

68. Which of the following statements concerning an index of relative strength is correct?

   A. It indicates changes in the primary movement of the market.
   B. It indicates the basic trend of stock prices.
   C. It is obtained by comparing the stock's price to an index.
   D. It is obtained by comparing varying quality bond yields.

69. Which of the following does a technical analyst believe indicates a strong bear market?

   A. Odd lot purchases are increasing.
   B. Short interest ratio is low.
   C. Stock prices are increasing on high volume.
   D. Spreads between high- and low-quality bonds are narrow.

70. Which of the following statements concerning the advance-decline line is correct?

   A. It is often referred to as indicating the relative strength of the market.
   B. It is compared to high- and low-quality bonds.
   C. It is measured on a cumulative basis.
   D. It indicates a strong market when net advances decline.

For practice answering case questions related to Topic 38, please answer the following questions in the cases included in the Appendix at the back of this textbook.

Case	Questions
Donaldson	12 and 13
Hilbert Stores, Inc.	4, 5, 6, 7, 8, 9, 10, 11, 12, 13, and 14
Maxwell	
Beals	
Mocsin	5
Eldridge	
Young	
Johnson	2, 18, 19, 20, 21, and 22
Thomas	19, 20, and 21
Jim and Brenda Quinn	32, 33, 34, 35, and 36

Portfolio Development and Analysis (Topic 39)

CFP Board Student-Centered Learning Objectives

(a) Assist a client in identifying his/her investment objectives, time horizons, and risk tolerances.

(b) Select an appropriate benchmark for assessing the value of portfolio management services.

(c) Develop and communicate an appropriate Investment Policy Statement (IPS) for a client.

(d) Apply duration and convexity in construction of fixed income portfolios.

(e) Construct a tax-efficient diversified portfolio meeting the goals, risk preferences and time horizon of a client.

(f) Measure and communicate a client's portfolio performance using different risk and return measures. [See Topic 36]

Portfolio Development and Analysis

A. *Investment policy statements*
B. *Bond duration and convexity*
C. *Appropriate benchmarks*
D. *Tax efficiency*
    1) *Turnover*
    2) *Timing of capital gains and losses*
    3) *Wash sale rule*
    4) *Qualified dividends*
    5) *Tax-free income*

Investment Policy Statements

An investment policy statement establishes the foundation for how the investor's goals and preferences will be reflected in the asset allocation as well as in selection of investment assets within each allocation category.

The IPS typically contains the following components:

- Purpose – Lists the objective(s) of the portfolio.
- Authorization – Identifies the portfolio managers and/or others who may be involved in management of the portfolio.
- Limitations/Restrictions – Describes the general types of investments that should be considered for the portfolio.

May set restrictions on quality of bonds that may be purchased, or may set limitations on the percentage that may be invested in illiquid assets.
- Monitoring and rebalancing guidelines

The investment policy statement may place restrictions on the relative amount of any particular security to be included in the portfolio, and procedures to follow when the maximum has been exceeded. It may also define a range of percentages considered an appropriate asset allocation. The portfolio's composition should be designed to minimize its systematic risk to a level commensurate with the investor's risk tolerance.

The investment policy statement will outline the broad boundaries for managing a portfolio. This is where the policy statement can make long-term assumptions about inflation and its impact upon risk-adjusted returns. Guidelines as to the beta coefficients of stocks or the durations of individual bonds reflect the policy's built-in restraints and investor preferences. Generally, the investment policy statement should not list specific securities to be bought for the portfolio, but may list specific securities or types of securities that are undesirable based upon the investor's social conscience.

The investment policy statement should also outline rebalancing guidelines as well as monitoring criteria and frequency. Determination of the appropriate frequency of monitoring investment selections should take into account factors such as:

(1) prevailing general economic conditions,
(2) the investment strategies being utilized,
(3) the investment objectives, and
(4) the volatility of the investments selected

Construction of Fixed Income Portfolios – Duration and Convexity

Duration is important for managing a portfolio of bonds. If interest rates are expected to rise, the manager will seek to shorten duration. In this situation, the manager will try to buy bonds with larger coupons and shorter maturities. If interest rates are expected to fall, the manager will seek to lengthen duration. In this case, the manager will try to buy bonds with smaller coupons and longer maturities.

The duration of a bond portfolio is a weighted average of the durations for the individual bonds. Thus, if a portfolio is invested 1/3 in Bond S, with a duration of 7.2 years, and 2/3 in Bond T, with a duration of 7.8 years, the portfolio will have a duration of:

$$D = 1/3(7.2) + 2/3(7.8) = 2.4 + 5.2 = 7.6 \text{ years}$$

Convexity

In its most simple terms, convexity measures all of a bond's price sensitivity to interest rates that is not measured by duration. It is the nonlinear relationship exhibited when a bond's price and yield depart from a straight-line relationship. While duration appears adequate for measuring interest rate sensitivity for small changes in bond yields, convexity measurement is necessary to obtain price-yield relationships that are larger. Prices of bonds with high convexity increase more when yields decrease and decline less when yields increase.

Figure 39-1

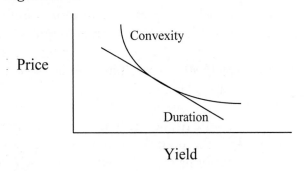

Appropriate Benchmarks

Those securities held as a unit in an alternative portfolio that are representative of a particular industry sector or asset class are called benchmark portfolios. The benchmark portfolio provides a performance measurement gauge against which other portfolios can make relative comparisons regarding risk, total returns, and the objectives of a portfolio manager. Thus, a fund's investment style may be better evaluated by contrasting its performance to a benchmark or index-type fund that is representative of the securities contained within the fund itself.

Performance measurement of a portfolio may be from the perspective of the entire portfolio's composition or simply from segments or classes of a portfolio's makeup. Therefore, while it may be appropriate, for example, to measure the performance of a large-cap growth fund against that of the S&P 500 Index, that index would be an inappropriate measurement standard for a small-cap value fund. Measuring the performance of the total portfolio may require the use of a blended benchmark.

Some common benchmarks used for various portfolio styles include:

- U.S. large-cap stocks – S&P 500 index
- U.S. small-cap stocks – Russell 2000 index
- U.S. broad market – Wilshire 5000 index

- Global stocks – MSCI EAFE index
- World developed markets – MSCI World index
- U.S. bonds – Barclay Capital U.S. Aggregate Bond index

When considering a portfolio's performance against that of a suitable benchmark portfolio, it is important to consider that a return in excess of the benchmark must make allowances for a measurement known as tracking error. This is a statistical tool that can support the conclusion that a portfolio's performance results are correctly "tracking" the benchmark portfolio's behavior.

Benchmark portfolios must be carefully evaluated when looking to match a portfolio with an appropriate benchmark. The underlying securities that make up a portfolio and the performance achieved by them can result in different style categories when compared to a particular index.

The portfolio method of analysis looks to the securities that make up the portfolio and is a direct way of looking at a portfolio's performance. The returns method (factor analysis) is more indirect and looks to the returns of a manager as a more reliable way to judge performance against an index. It is important that the composition of the benchmark index be understood in order that the appropriate choice of a benchmark portfolio is made.

Tax Efficiency

The performance of stocks in a portfolio must ultimately be measured in terms of what return is achieved after taxes. Unexpected increases in corporate earnings would raise the price of a stock. Issues that might need to be managed include stocks with hefty dividend payouts and stocks that do not pay dividends but have embedded capital gains, resulting from price appreciation.

Tax Loss Harvesting

Capital losses from the sale of securities can be used to offset capital gains from the sale of other securities within the same tax year. If the result of netting capital gains and losses is a net loss, a maximum of $3,000 of that loss can be used to offset the taxpayer's ordinary income. Losses above that amount are carried forward to the following tax year.

Experienced investors may utilize a tax strategy that manages the tax implication of having both securities that may be currently sold at gain and securities that may be sold at a loss. Through prudent time management, these investors can sell their losing securities, realizing a tax loss, while keeping their moneymakers. In this strategy, securities with losses are sold and securities with an equal amount of gains are sold so that the losses offset the gains. The securities with gains can immediately be repurchased, creating a higher cost basis in those securities. Using this strategy does not cause a problem under the wash sale rule (discussed below) since the wash sale rule only applies to securities sold at a loss.

Turnover

A portfolio's turnover rate measures the level of buying and selling of investments. High turnover can lead to higher expenses. The implication for tax-efficiency depends upon the investor's ability to pair gains and losses. However, all things being equal, **a higher turnover rate usually means more stock sales and taxes on those sales.**

Timing of Capital Gains and Losses

The tax rate on a capital gain will depend on whether the investor held the stock for up to one year or longer than one year.

Short-term gains are realized when securities held 1 year or less are sold. Those gains are treated as ordinary income and taxed according to the individual's tax bracket.

Long-term gains are realized when securities held longer than 1 year are sold. Those gains will be taxed at 15% for most taxpayers. The Tax Cuts and Jobs Act (TCJA) of 2017 changed the way long term capital gains are taxed. Instead of matching the rate to the tax bracket, TCJA matches the rate to taxable income (TI).

In 2018, long-term capital gains will be taxed at:

- 0% for taxable income up to:
  - $38,600 for single taxpayers
  - $77,200 for married filing jointly
  - $51,700 for head of household
- 15% for taxable income up to:
  - $425,800 for single taxpayers
  - $479,000 for married filing jointly
  - $452,400 for head of household
- 20% for taxable income over the maximum 15% thresholds

Note: Beginning in 2013, the Patient Protection and Affordable Care Act (PPACA) imposes an additional 3.8% Medicare tax on net investment income for single taxpayers with AGI over $200,000 ($250,000 MFJ, $125,000 MFS). This additional tax creates an effective tax rate on capital gains and qualified dividends of 18.8% or 23.8% for taxpayers with AGI over the threshold amount.

Capital losses can be used to offset capital gains. If an investor has a net overall capital loss for the year, the investor can only deduct up to an additional $3,000 capital loss against ordinary income. Any additional capital losses are carried forward to the next year.

Unrealized capital gains (losses) reflect the price appreciation (depreciation) in securities not yet sold. No taxable event occurs until such time as the asset is sold.

Index funds are thought to be very tax-efficient, as imbedded long-term gains usually accumulate for long periods of time. Usually, when a security is replaced, any gain is treated as long-term and is fully taxable at the long-term capital gains rate (again, either 20%, 15%, or 0% under current rates).

Exhibit 39-1 Taxation of Capital Gains	
Short-term (held for 1 year or less)	Taxed at the rates for ordinary income

Long-term (held for longer than 1 year)	Taxed at:
	• 0% for taxable income up to:
	  ▪ $38,600 for single taxpayers
	  ▪ $77,200 for MFJ
	  ▪ $51,700 for head of household
	• 15% for taxable income up to:
	  ▪ $425,800 for single taxpayers
	  ▪ $479,000 for MFJ
	  ▪ $452,400 for head of household
	• 20% for taxable income over the 15% thresholds

Unrealized (not sold)	Not a taxable event
Index funds	Most gains are long-term (taxed at 0%, 15%, or 20% depending on taxable income)

Identifying the Cost Basis of Stocks and Bonds

The cost basis of stocks and bonds is generally the purchase price plus commissions and fees. The basis will be adjusted when there is a stock split, which results in the existing basis being allocated among the new total number of shares.

When stocks or bonds are sold, the broker is required to report the sale proceeds on Form 1099-B. The broker will also report the cost basis for stocks and ETFs purchased after January 1, 2011, and for fixed-rate bonds purchased after January 1, 2014. For securities purchased prior to those dates, accurate record-keeping from the client must generally be relied upon in order to establish cost basis. If no records have been kept, the cost basis is assumed to be zero.

If shares of the same stock (or bond) were purchased in multiple transactions over a period of time, the broker will typically assume that the shares are sold on a first in, first out (FIFO) basis. This will result in the longest holding period, but does not allow for control over the amount of gain that is reported (for example the cost basis for one lot of shares may be much lower than the basis for a different lot of shares, resulting in a higher realized gain). When the specific lot of shares can be adequately identified, the IRS allows the taxpayer to elect the specific shares that are to be sold (called specific identification, or a versus purchase order). For example, the client may specify that 100 shares of IBM are to be sold, versus the purchase on January 3, 2010.

Mutual fund shareholders are also permitted to use an average cost basis for all shares purchased (of the same fund), as an alternative to FIFO or specific identification. Using an average cost basis for mutual funds may be the easiest way to track basis since mutual funds are often purchased by investing a small dollar amount each month. In addition, reinvested dividends and capital gains are taxed in the year they are declared (even when reinvested), and this also results in the creation of cost basis. If a mutual fund (or other regulated investment company) or real estate investment trust (REIT) declares a dividend or capital gain distribution in October, November, or December, payable to shareholders of record on a date in one of those months, but actually pays the dividend during January of the next calendar year, it is considered to have been received on December 31st. Therefore, the dividend is taxed in the year it was declared.

Securities received as a gift will have a carryover holding period and carryover cost basis from the donor. In other words, the donee retains the donor's cost basis and holding period. Securities received as an inheritance will receive a step-up or step-down in cost basis to the value of the securities on the date of death. The ability for the beneficiary to receive a step-up in cost basis can greatly reduce, or eliminate, the income tax on the gain. However, investments held in tax qualified accounts, such as traditional and Roth IRAs and qualified retirement plans, do not receive the step-up in basis.

Wash Sale Rules

If an investor sells securities at a loss and buys substantially identical securities within 30 days before or after the sale, the losses cannot be deducted on the tax return. However, the disallowed loss amount can be added to the cost basis for the securities purchased. When the securities are eventually sold, the taxable gain or loss will include any loss incurred on the original shares.

Obviously, selling and then buying the same stock is "substantially identical". Substantially identical securities may also include call options on the same stock that was sold for a loss or convertible bonds that can be converted into the same stock that was sold for a loss.

For bonds to avoid being treated as substantially identical, they must have different issuers, or different maturity dates, or different coupon rates.

Also be aware that selling at a loss in a taxable account and then purchasing the same security in an IRA or Roth IRA will still trigger a wash sale, as will selling in one spouse's account and buying in the other spouse's account.

Qualified Dividends

Qualified dividends received are investment income taxed similarly to long-term capital gains, as described on page 39.5.

In order to qualify for this favorable dividend tax rate, the taxpayer must have owned the stock for at least 60 days, but the 60 days of ownership must be in a 120-day period that starts 60 days before the stock goes ex-dividend. Mutual fund dividends that are distributions of interest or short-term capital gains are not eligible for this reduced rate. Dividends from money market funds, REITs, and S corporations are also ineligible for the dividend tax rate.

 K Study Tip – **The maximum tax rate for long-term capital gains and qualified dividends is 15% for most taxpayers. It is 0% for individuals with taxable income under $38,600 (Single) and $77,200 (MFJ), and is 20% for taxpayers with taxable income over $425,800 (Single) and $479,000 (MFJ). The additional 3.8% Medicare tax on net investment income applies to taxpayers with AGI above the threshold amount ($200,000 single, $250,000 MFJ).**

Tax-Free Income

The higher an investor's tax bracket, the more attractive are tax-free bond instruments.

Interest from municipal bonds issued in the taxpayer's home state are generally exempt from state and local income taxes, as well as federal income tax. For high-income investors in states with high state income taxes, these triple tax-free municipal bonds become very attractive. Note that it is only the interest on these bonds that is federally tax-free. Capital gains from buying and selling bonds are taxable.

U.S. Treasury securities are subject to federal income tax but are exempt from state and local taxes.

Taxable-Equivalent Yield

Because municipal bonds are exempt from federal income taxes, they require a lower yield than a corporate bond, which is taxable. To calculate the *taxable-equivalent yield (TEY)* for a municipal bond, use the following formula:

EXHIBIT 39 – 2
Taxable-Equivalent Yield

$$TEY = \frac{\text{Tax-exempt municipal yield}}{1 - \text{Marginal tax rate}}$$

Example:

An investor in the 25% combined federal and state tax bracket who invests in a 4% municipal bond issued in their state of residence would have to earn 5.33% on a comparable taxable bond.

$$TEY = \frac{\text{Tax-exempt yield}}{1 - \text{Marginal tax rate}} = \frac{.04}{1 - .25} = 5.33$$

Single investors with AGI above $200,000, or married taxpayers with AGI above $250,000 are subject to an additional 3.8% Unearned Income Medicare Contribution Tax on net investment income. The 3.8% tax is assessed on the lesser of: (1) Net investment income, or (2) the amount by which modified adjusted gross income (MAGI) exceeds the threshold. For most individuals MAGI will be their adjusted gross income (AGI) unless they are living abroad and have foreign earned income. **For taxpayers who are subject to this additional tax, the taxable-equivalent yield should also be adjusted to reflect this additional tax.**

Combining Accounts

Clients with multiple taxable brokerage accounts may seek to combine those accounts to a single account over which the planner will provide investment management services. Rather than liquidating holdings in those accounts and causing taxation on gains, the planner can use an ACAT (Automated Customer Account Transfer Service) transaction initiation form (TIF) to transfer securities in-kind from one broker-dealer to another without triggering taxation on the holdings.

Appropriate Assets for Tax-Advantaged vs. Taxable Accounts

When constructing portfolios, planners must also consider the type of account that is most advantageous to the client from a tax standpoint. Traditional IRA contributions may be tax deductible, and earnings grow tax-deferred. When a distribution is made from a traditional deductible IRA after the participant reaches age 59½, it is taxed as ordinary income, regardless of whether the earnings were from long-term capital gains, qualified dividends, or interest income. Traditional IRAs also require minimum distributions beginning at age 70½, which will necessitate appropriate management of assets to ensure that sales of securities are not required at inopportune times in order to meet this liquidity need.

Roth IRA contributions are not tax deductible, and earnings in the account are tax-deferred and can be distributed tax-free if the distribution is at least 5 years after the first contribution and the participant is at least age 59½. (Editor's Note: Additional rules apply to traditional and Roth IRAs, but are beyond the scope of this textbook. See Keir's Retirement Income and Distribution Planning textbook for additional details.)

A planner should not recommend using tax-advantaged retirement accounts to buy investments that provide tax-exempt income, e.g., municipal bonds. The income is generally lower than on corporate or U.S. Treasury bonds, and retirement distributions of the tax-exempt income will be taxed as ordinary income anyway.

When an individual has investments both in tax-advantaged and taxable accounts, investments for growth and capital gains should be allocated to the taxable accounts, and investments that generate interest income should be allocated to the tax-advantaged accounts. Interest income will be taxable at ordinary income tax rates, and holding the interest-bearing investments in retirement accounts takes full advantage of the tax deferral offered by the retirement plans. The growth investments will take advantage of the lower capital gain rates only if they are held outside retirement plans. Distributions of capital gains from retirement plans are taxed as ordinary income, so the benefit of lower capital gains rates is lost in the retirement plan.

EXHIBIT 39 – 3 **Appropriate Assets for Tax-Advantaged and Taxable Accounts**	
Tax-Advantaged Accounts	Taxable Accounts

• Should hold
   – Corporate bonds
   – Zero coupon bonds
   – TIPS
 	
• Should not hold
   – Municipal bonds
   – Investments that would be taxed at LTCG or qualified dividend rates if not held in a tax-advantaged account
   – Investments that violate rules against self-dealing in an IRA
 	
• Exception:
   – Roth IRAs may hold growth securities (which would be taxed at LTCG rates in a taxable account) to take advantage of tax-free earnings potential over a long period of time
	• Should hold
	   – Investments normally taxed at LTCG or qualified dividend rates
	   – Municipal bonds

TOPIC 39 – APPLICATION QUESTIONS

1. In evaluating the performance of a portfolio, an investor should <u>not</u>:

A. Consider past performance returns of the manager
B. Compare different style funds to one standard benchmark
C. Account for different risk levels
D. Periodically monitor the portfolio

2. An investment policy statement:

A. Should include the client's opinion on bull/bear market projections
B. Should not include any statement dealing with the minimization of risk
C. Should establish a broad foundation for investor preferences regarding asset selection
D. Should include the specific securities to be included in any investment portfolio

3. Which of the following statements is true concerning the tax treatment of stock mutual funds?

A. Index fund distributions are taxed as ordinary income.
B. Qualified dividends are taxed at 20%, 15%, or 0%.
C. Short-term capital gains are taxed at 20%, 15%, or 0%.
D. Long-term capital gains are taxed as ordinary income.

4. An investor who is single with AGI below $200,000 and in the 32% tax bracket who invests in a 5% municipal bond would have to earn what percent on a comparable taxable bond?

A. 3.40%
B. 6.65%
C. 7.35%
D. 7.78%

5. Three years ago, an investor bought 200 shares of IBM stock at $100 per share and 200 shares of GE stock at $30 per share. On December 15 of last year, the investor sold 100 shares of IBM at $75 per share and 100 shares of GE at $35 per share. On January 10, the investor bought 100 Shares of IBM at $77 per share and 100 shares of GE at $32 per share. What are the income tax consequences the investor must report from these transactions?

A. A long-term capital gain of $500
B. A long-term capital loss of $2,500
C. A net long-term capital loss of $2,000
D. No capital gain or loss

6. An investor has a portfolio of $100,000 worth of bonds with duration of 7.75 years. The investor would like to lengthen the duration to 8 years and has $25,000 to purchase additional bonds. What should the duration be for the bonds purchased?

A. 8.25 years
B. 8.50 years
C. 8.75 years
D. 9.0 years

7. Factoring in the principle of _____ can improve upon the accuracy of a linear approximation for price sensitivity to interest rate changes and their effect on bond yields.

   A. Duration
   B. Immunization
   C. Convexity
   D. Dedication strategy

8. Two years ago Clyde paid $144,000 for 4,000 shares PLT stock. The market value of PLT has been fluctuating wildly and is expected to continue to do so for the next several months. Clyde has heard about tax loss harvesting and he would like to sell the PLT shares in December to take a loss that can offset other gains, and then purchase the PLT shares back sometime in January. Which of the following will yield the greatest amount of tax savings for Clyde this year?

   A. Sell at $125,000 on December 10th and buy them back on January 9th
   B. Sell at $130,000 on December 10th and buy them back on January 9th
   C. Sell at $125,000 on December 10th and buy them back on January 18th
   D. Sell at $135,000 on December 10th and buy them back on January 18th

9. Capital losses may be used to offset which of the following?

   (1) Ordinary income in excess of $3,000
   (2) Capital gains

   A. (1) only
   B. (2) only
   C. Both (1) and (2)
   D. Neither (1) nor (2)

10. Your client purchased the T. Rowe Price Emerging Markets Stock Fund on January 1st, at a net asset value of $12 per share. Exactly one year later, the net asset value of this Emerging Markets Stock Fund was $13.44 per share. There had been no splits or stock dividends during the year. Which of the following statements best evaluates the performance of your client's Emerging Markets Stock Fund?

   A. The Emerging Markets Stock Fund gained 12%, but it underperformed the appropriate benchmark, the MSCI Emerging Markets Index.
   B. The Emerging Markets Stock Fund gained 12% and outperformed the appropriate benchmark, the S&P 500.
   C. The Emerging Markets Stock Fund gained 13% and outperformed the appropriate benchmark, the MSCI World Index.
   D. The Emerging Markets Stock Fund gained 13% and just matched the appropriate benchmark, the Wilshire 5000.

11. A mutual fund company is said to be operating a "tax-efficient" fund when:

   A. It elects to no longer act as a conduit for income to flow through to investors.
   B. It attempts to match portfolio gains with losses at the time it distributes income to its clients.
   C. It files with the SEC to distribute only 80% of all income from security transactions.
   D. It operates as a nondiversified mutual fund company.

12. All the following are important tax considerations which pertain to the management of investment portfolios, EXCEPT:

    A. Excessive portfolio turnover
    B. Unrealized capital appreciation in portfolio
    C. Timing of capital gains in an IRA
    D. Designation of shares sold

13. In evaluating the risk-adjusted return of a portfolio, it is important to consider certain factors. Which of the following factors is (are) relevant?

    (1) The dispersion of returns around the mean average
    (2) The appropriateness of the benchmark index selected
    (3) The appropriateness of the proxy for r_f (risk-free rate)
    (4) The sufficiency of the length of the performance period being measured

    A. (2), (3), and (4) only
    B. (1) and (3) only
    C. (1) and (4) only
    D. (1) only
    E. (1), (2), (3), and (4)

14. Ralph, who is 55, is an aggressive investor, interested in capital gains. Ralph is in the top marginal income tax bracket and dislikes paying any income taxes. Ralph believes that interest rates are falling, and he does not like the idea of investing his money abroad. Which of the following mutual funds would be the most appropriate for Ralph?

    A. A high-yield municipal bond fund
    B. A global stock fund
    C. A government securities fund
    D. An index fund

For practice answering case questions related to Topic 39, please answer the following questions in the cases included in the Appendix at the back of this textbook.

Case	Questions
Donaldson	
Hilbert Stores, Inc.	
Maxwell	8
Beals	
Mocsin	
Eldridge	
Young	2
Johnson	11
Thomas	18 and 22
Jim and Brenda Quinn	37, 38, 39, 40, and 41

Investment Strategies (Topic 40)

CFP Board Student-Centered Learning Objectives

(a) Explain and apply investment strategies such as buy-and-hold, immunization, core and satellite, passive (indexed) and active management techniques such as tactical allocation, market timing, and sector rotation.

(b) Evaluate the use of options and futures for investment risk management purposes.

Investment Strategies
- *A. Market timing*
- *B. Passive investing (indexing)*
- *C. Buy and hold*
- *D. Portfolio immunization*
- *E. Swaps and collars*
- *F. Formula investing*
  - *1) Dollar-cost averaging*
  - *2) Dividend reinvestment plans (DRIPS)*
  - *3) Bond ladders, bullets, and barbells*
- *G. Riding the yield curve*
- *H. Use of leverage (margin)*
- *I. Short selling*
- *J. Hedging and option strategies*

Market Timing

Market timing is an active strategy in which individuals attempt to anticipate the movement of equities and earn returns in excess of the market. Technical analysis is the principal underpinning behind this activity, which seeks to analyze price movements and patterns by observing moving average lines and graphical trend patterns so as to buy low and sell high. Market timers must always be cognizant of the effect that taxes and brokerage commissions have on the overall portfolio's bottom line.

Many consider the biggest risk in this type of activity to be the lack of exposure to the market at times when equities have achieved double-digit gains. Less-than-perfect timing may have proponents out of the market and missing the positive, upward bias of the market over longer periods of time. Nevertheless, advocates of this active strategy continue to believe that the market is less than efficient and that there are multiple opportunities to employ timing techniques that exploit market inefficiencies.

Sector Rotation

Sector rotation is an active strategy in which economic data is utilized to predict where the economic cycle is headed in the future, and position the portfolio in the appropriate industry sector in an attempt to outperform the market. For example, gas and utility stocks tend to perform well in the beginning of an economic contraction. Since the stock market tends to be a leading indicator of the economy, the portfolio manager must transition into the appropriate industry sector well in advance of the actual change in the economic cycle. This strategy can be implemented quite easily through the use of sector-based ETFs or mutual funds.

Passive Investing (Indexing)

Index funds may be selected based upon the investor's preference for diversification across investment styles. Here, the selection process favors owning mutual funds consisting of stocks or bonds designed to match an equity or fixed-income index. Selection of index funds assumes that this portion of the portfolio is not looking to forecast market movements based upon any fundamental or technical analysis of undervalued or overvalued securities. Index funds may make up a "core" portion of the portfolio (passive strategy), with additional securities selected for a value-added component (active strategy).

Core and Satellite

The core and satellite method of portfolio construction combines passive and active strategies. The core of the portfolio is invested in passive vehicles, such as index funds or ETFs that track major market indices. The satellite is comprised of actively managed assets which could be individual securities or actively managed funds. The goal is to achieve on part of the portfolio the benefits of passive investing, obtaining average returns with low costs and low taxes; then on the satellite portion, the investor will seek to benefit from the skills of active managers who can add returns that will exceed the benchmarks. Satellite investments may also provide opportunities to reduce volatility or risk if the portfolio is invested in assets that have a low correlation with core assets.

Indexed Portfolio

An indexed portfolio is a passive strategy that has as its foundation the belief that capital markets are efficient and fully reflect all information in securities prices. Market timing and the search for undervalued securities is an activity viewed as unlikely to outperform the market.

Indexed portfolios are investment vehicles meant to replicate the total market or a subsection of the market (equity or bond). Most indexed instruments designed to track the entire equity market construct portfolios through the use of what are called representative sampling techniques. This technique allows the manager to lower transactions costs in the purchase and sale of securities when indexes alter their underlying securities.

Mutual fund companies have popularized this strategy, and underlying portfolios of funds have been constructed so as to match the performance of the corresponding market or bond index. Examples of indices that have indexed portfolios constructed around them by popular families of mutual funds include the following:

Domestic Market	S&P 500 Index
	Russell 3000
Bond Market	Merrill Lynch High Yield 100
	Barclays Capital U.S. Aggregate Bond Index (the BarCap Aggregate)
International	MSCI EAFE Index

It should be noted that the replication of a very broad bond index is not practical due to the continual removal of instruments because of differing maturities. Otherwise, a constant rebalancing would need to occur, which leads to expense ratio increases. Here, sampling is the preferred method of managers seeking to match the performance of their fund with the index.

Practice Question

A passive management strategy is characterized by:

    A. Investors not attempting to outperform the market
    B. A bear market period
    C. Increased portfolio evaluation
    D. The careful monitoring of interest rate changes

Answer:
This characterization of passive strategies as not attempting to outperform the market is one way to look at these strategies and is the best choice among those offered. B is not a responsive answer because passive investing may be used in bear or bull market periods. C and D are not correct. Passive investing means reduced portfolio evaluation and little attention to interest rate changes.
The answer is A.

Buy and Hold

A buy/hold strategy is a passive strategy utilized in both bond and stock portfolios in a belief that efficient markets cannot be surpassed on a risk-adjusted basis.

Bonds: A portfolio of fixed-income instruments is held, rather than attempting to actively engage in their purchase or sale. This strategy, however, does not negate the necessity of making selections based upon some knowledge of bond markets and interest rates. The use of bond index funds can be an alternative approach.

Stocks: A buy/hold strategy here involves purchasing stocks for the long term and avoiding the necessity to trade in and out of a position. Here, too, the initial selection of stocks must be based upon research and the risk tolerance and objectives of the investor. Tax considerations, as well as the composition of the portfolio after many years, may require some action on the investor's part. A dividend reinvestment plan (DRIP) may be part of this strategy.

It is important to note that a buy/hold strategy, unlike immunization, will subject itself to interest rate risk since there is no matching of cash flow needs with the length of time the portfolio is held.

Portfolio Immunization

Immunization is a mostly passive investment strategy that has as its objective safeguarding a bond portfolio from both reinvestment rate risk and interest rate volatility. **By matching the bond portfolio's duration (the weighted-average time necessary to fully recover principal and interest payments) with the desired time horizon, a balance is achieved between return and price changes.** The immunization process is successful when, despite interest rate volatility, a stable compound rate of return is earned that is equivalent to the yield to maturity that should have been calculated at the portfolio's inception. As a result, interest rate risk has been successfully neutralized. Remember that the components of interest rate risk move inversely as follows:

- When interest rates fall, reinvestment rates, including income, fall. However, the bond price rises.

- When interest rates rise, reinvestment rates, including income, rise. However, the bond price falls.

Although categorized as a largely passive investment strategy, the immunization process requires that the manager constantly match the duration of the portfolio to the time horizon established. Duration cannot be matched to the time horizon of the portfolio initially and then be forgotten. A constant rebalancing of the portfolio must occur.

The following is an illustration of the immunization process:

- After the investment goal of a client is learned, a time h[orizon] that matches this goal is set, such as 15 years.

- Bonds with different maturities are bought, with some being more than 15 years, and others being less than 15 years. It is most important that the weighted-average duration of these bonds be equal to the 15-year time horizon goal.

- The bond portfolio is rebalanced semiannually or annually (this is the active portion of this strategy) so that after six months, the portfolio duration should equal 14.5 years.

- This immunization process continues until such time as the time horizon is reached.

Immunization is sometimes referred to as a hybrid strategy because of the very nature of the process. Although it may be classified as being passive in its objective to match an investor's time horizon with duration, the strategy's implementation certainly requires continuous rebalancing of portfolio components as time progresses.

KEY SUMMARY 40 – 1
Active vs. Passive Investing

Active Strategy	Passive Strategy
Market timing	Buy-and-hold
Security selection	Indexing
Bond swaps	Immunization

Swaps

A bond swap is an active strategy in which fixed-income instruments are bought and sold for numerous purposes, such as increasing yields, reducing taxes, or reducing risk. Proponents attempt to take advantage of changing environments wherein bonds may be mispriced. There are a number of different types of bond swaps that managers of bond portfolios may employ. Among them are the following:

- A substitution swap involves the exchange of bonds with identical or nearly identical characteristics (maturity, quality, call feature, coupon payments, etc.) that sell for different prices and, therefore, different yields to maturity. The price difference may be viewed as an arbitrage opportunity to make a simultaneous purchase and sale. If successful, a swap is made into the higher-yielding bond and as the bond's yield declines in relation to the other bond, affords a capital gains profit. There are risks in this strategy, such as profits being substantially reduced by transaction costs, the fact that bonds may not be good proxies for each other, and the length of time it may take for bond prices to equal each other.

- A pure-yield pickup swap involves the sale of a lower-yielding bond and the purchase of a higher-yielding bond. Unlike the substitution swap, this activity does not require any significant expectation that the market will change direction. The sole purpose is to make a bond exchange that obtains a higher yield. In order to achieve the higher yield, the swap should be made for a bond with lower quality or a longer term to maturity.

- An intermarket spread (sector) swap attempts to identify differences in bond yields that appear excessive. The swap involves the exchange of like-type bonds with different coupon payments. Any perceived misalignment in yield spread is seen as an opportunity to capitalize upon the difference. The strategist will look to see if the yield spread is significant enough, compared to the historic spread, to yield a profit.

- A rate anticipation swap involves a forecast being made on the likely movement of interest rates. When rates are expected to rise, bonds with longer maturities should be swapped for short-term bonds. The price of long-term bonds, sensitive to interest rates, will decline. Likewise, when interest rates are anticipated to fall, long-term bonds are purchased to take advantage of price increases in them.

- A tax swap attempts to take advantage of current tax laws. An individual might take a capital loss on a bond purchased for $1,000 and now selling for $750. The proceeds are available for investment and provide a $250 capital loss, which may be used to offset a capital gain in the same year. If the investor has no capital gains for the year, up to $3,000 of losses may be taken against ordinary income. At the same time, the $750 may be used to repurchase a similar bond (but with a different issuer, coupon, or maturity, to avoid a wash sale transaction).

- An interest rate swap is a strategy usually confined to large, global institutions. It is a contract between two parties that exchange a series of different cash flows based on fixed-income securities. No physical exchange of securities is made, however.

  An institution might look for the opportunity to pay a fixed interest rate in exchange for a series of payments from a short-term, floating-rate bond instrument. No physical securities are traded, as the institution is "swapping" the cash flow from the fixed-interest rate fund amount for the cash flows produced by the short-term floating-rate bond.

Interest rate swaps are used for hedging portfolios and may involve institutions anticipating changing conditions in the bond market. These transactions usually involve a major bank acting as dealer for the swap, and the difference between the funds received and what the dealer paid constitutes the spread or income.

Formula Investing

There are several different formulas an investor can follow when purchasing assets, including dollar-cost averaging; dividend reinvestment plans; and bond ladders, bullets, and barbells.

Dollar-Cost Averaging

Dollar-cost averaging is buying a fixed-dollar amount of an asset on a periodic basis (for example, monthly, bimonthly, or quarterly). By committing funds systematically to an investment purchase, the investor is assured of achieving an average cost that will be lower than the asset's average price.

The following example shows how dollar-cost averaging works. Column A displays a volatile fund's net asset value at the end of each month over a six-month period and its average price below it. Column B demonstrates how systematically investing $100 at the end of each month enables an investor to purchase more shares when the price is lower and fewer shares when the price is much higher. This method lowers the average cost of the fund over the term.

Column A	Column B		
Average Price	Cost	Purchase Amt.	Shares Obtained
$ 5.00	$ 5	$100	20.00
$ 7.00	$ 7	$100	14.29
$12.00	$12	$100	8.33
$15.00	$15	$100	6.67
$ 8.00	$ 8	$100	12.50
$ 5.00	$ 5	$100	20.00
$52.00		$600	81.79

Average price from Column A:

$52.00 ÷ 6 = $8.67 per share

Dollar-cost averaging method from Column B:

$600 ÷ 81.79 = $7.34 average cost per share

By dividing the total amount invested, $600, by the number of shares purchased over the six-month period, 81.79, one finds that the average cost is $7.34 (rounded), an average cost per share savings of $1.33 when compared to the average price per share of $8.67 in Column A.

This occurs because the investor purchases more shares when the price is lower and fewer of them when the price is higher. Consequently, a commitment to buy an asset that experiences high price volatility can actually work to help minimize losses in a down market. Dollar-cost averaging does not assure a profit, nor does it protect a portfolio from losses when the market experiences negative returns. Therefore, dollar-cost averaging works best in conjunction with an overall investment plan suitable to a long-term investment horizon.

🔑 **KEY SUMMARY 40 – 2**
Dollar-Cost Averaging

Characteristics:
- Investor buys fixed dollar value at regular intervals.

Advantages:
- Average costs are reduced in a fluctuating market.
- The investor avoids timing the market; timing risk is reduced.
- An investor buys more shares when the price is low and fewer shares when the price is high.

Risks:
- The strategy will not protect an investor from losses in a down market.
- Investors have difficulty continuing the strategy in a down cycle.

Dividend Reinvestment Plans (DRIPs)

Dividend reinvestment is an investment strategy commonly referred to by the acronym DRIPs (Dividend Reinvestment Plans). This is a strategy whereby shareholders participate in a company plan that reinvests dividends in additional stock shares, usually at no additional cost. Many companies now sell shares directly to investors, as well as making them available through traditional brokerage firm outlets. By participating in the reinvestment of dividends, the investor is participating in a form of dollar-cost averaging because more shares are purchased at lower stock prices, and fewer shares are purchased when prices rise. It is important to note that shareholders are considered to be in constructive receipt of these dividends, and, as such, dividend reinvestment is a taxable event. Companies also benefit not only by fostering goodwill among their shareholders, but also by raising additional capital at minimal expense.

Bond Ladders

A laddered portfolio (staggered) holds bonds purchased with an array of maturity dates. For example, $50,000 worth of bonds would be purchased, with maturities ranging from one to ten years, in a total portfolio of $500,000. The bonds with much shorter maturities would be subject to less price sensitivity and serve to reduce exposure to interest rate risk.

This type of portfolio offers liquidity since a bond is maturing each year. The cash may be used for other purposes or to purchase another bond with a ten-year maturity. This helps reduce interest rate risk and helps maintain the original staggered maturity portfolio. However, if for some reason the portfolio needs to be restructured, all the bonds in it will need to be liquidated.

Share Averaging

Share averaging is purchasing the same number of shares, without consideration to market price volatility. Unlike dollar-cost averaging, the average cost and the average price are one and the same. It is calculated by adding up each price and dividing by the total number in the series.

Value Averaging

Value averaging is generally a more complex strategy than dollar-cost averaging. The basic rule here is to target the value of a portfolio to rise by some predetermined amount (for example, $1,000 every month). The focus is on the resulting value more than the investment cost. A good example of this is when a portfolio rises by more than the predetermined amount, which would necessitate the selling off of some assets.

Bullets

A bullet bond is a bond that may not be called prior to maturity. Due to the eliminated call risk, the bond will have a lower coupon rate compared to similar callable bonds. A bullet bond is also sometimes called a virgin bond.

Investors using the buy-and-hold strategy might select bullet bonds to avoid having a bond called prior to the maturity date.

Barbells

A barbell (dumbbell) strategy is an investment in short-term and long-term bonds that requires the periodic rebalancing of the portfolio. For example, in a $400,000 portfolio of bonds, $200,000 would be invested in short-term bonds and the remainder in long-term bonds. If the portfolio needs to be restructured due to a change in interest rates, only one group of bonds need be sold. This is an active strategy requiring that maturing short-term bonds be reinvested. The maturity of long-term bonds is also being reduced, which requires a rebalancing of the portfolio.

Riding the Yield Curve

Riding the yield curve is a strategy in which bonds with maturities longer than the investor's time horizon are purchased and are sold at the end of the time horizon. Assuming a stable, and steep upward-sloping yield curve, holding period returns may exceed those of a simple strategy of buying bonds with maturities equal to the time horizon. Note however, that buying longer-term maturities increases interest rate risk (due to the higher duration of longer-term securities); therefore, a substantial rise in interest rates may cause a loss.

The rational (unbiased) expectations hypothesis of the term structure of interest rates holds that the shape of the yield curve is a function of expectations concerning future interest rate movements. If the rational expectations hypothesis is correct, the long-term rate of interest will tend to equal the average of expected short-term rates for the time period. For example, purchasing a bond with a 5-year maturity should provide the same holding period return as purchasing a series of 1-year maturity bonds for 5 consecutive years. Similarly, the holding period return for purchasing a bond with a 2-year maturity to match a 2-year time horizon should provide the same holding period return as purchasing a 5-year bond and selling it after 2 years. If the rational expectations hypothesis holds true, then riding the yield curve should not produce superior results.

Unbiased Expectations Theory – Calculating the Expected Spot Rate on an N-Years to Maturity Bond

The expectations theory is based on the concept that the shape of the yield curve is determined by the expectation of where rates are headed in the future: that today's long-term rates reflect expectations about future 1-year spot rates and that there is no risk-premium demanded for longer term maturities. In other words, as described above, you should end up with the same holding period return whether you purchase a 5-year bond today or you purchase 5 consecutive 1-year bonds. Likewise, you should end up with the same holding period return if you buy a 1-year bond, or if you buy a 5-year bond and sell it after 1 year. If today's 5-year rate were not in equilibrium with the expected 1-year rates for the next 5 years, an arbitrage opportunity would exist.

The formula used to calculate the expected spot (current) rate on an n-years to maturity bond is provided on the formula sheet as follows:

$$_1R_N = [(1+_1R_1)\ (1+E(_2r_1))...(1+E(_Nr_1))]^{1/N}-1$$

The subscripts in this formula are identifying timing. The subscript before r is the number of each successive year. The subscript after r is the term to maturity of the bond in that year. Notice that the second subscript is 1 in the formula, so, conceptually, you are looking at the current spot rate of a 1-year bond, the expected spot rate return $[E(r)]$ of a one-year bond one year from today, two years from today, three years from today, and so on for as many number of years (N) as you want to look at.

For example, given the following information:

	Current 1-year rate	Next year's expected 1-year rate	Expected 1-year rate two years from now	Expected 1-year rate three years from now	Expected 1-year rate four years from now
T-bills	3.15%	4.20%	5.97%	7.25%	8.31%

The current rate on a 5-year maturity T-note should be:

$$[(1.0315)(1.0420)(1.0597)(1.0725)(1.0831)]^{1/5} - 1 = .0576 = 5.76\%$$

Based on the information provided above, we can also calculate that the current rate on a 2-year maturity T-note should be:

$$[(1.0315)(1.0420)]^{1/2} - 1 = .0367 = 3.67\%$$

And the current rate on a 3-year maturity T-note should be:

$$[(1.0315)(1.0420)(1.0597)]^{1/3} - 1 = .0443 = 4.43\%$$

Note that taking the results inside the brackets to the 1/n power is similar to taking the nth root, as used in the formula for geometric mean return:

$$= \sqrt[3]{(1+R_1)(1+R_2)(1+R_3)\ldots} - 1$$

Like the GMR, the unbiased expectations formula can be easily solved using the TVM functions on a financial calculator:

The current rate on a 5-year maturity T-note should be:

PV = -1
FV = (1.0315)(1.0420)(1.0597)(1.0725)(1.0831) = 1.3231
N = 5
Solve for I = 5.76%

Similarly, the current rate on a 2-year maturity T-note can be calculated as:

PV = -1
FV = (1.0315)(1.0420) = 1.07482
N = 2
Solve for I = 3.67%

Use of Leverage (Margin)

The term "leverage" refers to an investor's use of borrowed money to increase earnings. While leverage can enhance returns, it also adds to the investor's financial risk. From purchasing stocks on margin (short-term borrowing) to securing a residential mortgage (long-term borrowing), leverage is a way to magnify gains or losses. In corporate finance, leverage is most often associated with the corporation's borrowing through the sale of bonds or preferred stock to obtain capital that can be used to increase its return on investment (ROI) or return on equity (ROE). Financial leverage is sometimes referred to as trading on the equity. The amount of leverage desirable is mainly a function of investor objectives and stability of earnings.

Margin Account

A margin account is an account opened at a brokerage house, requiring either cash or marginable securities as collateral. The New York Stock Exchange (NYSE) mandates that member firms require an initial cash deposit of $2,000 or the equivalent in securities, although firms can request a higher amount. When money is borrowed and interest charged, the investor pays a margin interest rate (which can be comparable to a bank's prime interest rate) to the brokerage firm. When the latter borrows money from a bank to lend money to its customers, the firm is charged the broker call rate. These accounts can be accessed for everything from providing overdraft protection in amounts up to the loan value to the further buying of equities through the use of leverage.

Margin itself refers to the amount the investor initially pays to start up the brokerage account. This amount may not be borrowed.

Initial Margin – 50%

The Board of Governors of the Federal Reserve sets the requirement for the initial margin for a securities transaction, currently 50% (Regulation T). For example, if the initial margin requirement is 50% on a $25,000 transaction (250 shares @ $100 per share), the investor must deposit $12,500 (which may be

$12,500 in cash or $25,000 in marginable securities), while borrowing $12,500 from the broker.

Maintenance Margin

Margin accounts are marked-to-market (updated based on current value) on a daily basis. These changes in value may require that additional funds or securities be deposited into the account to maintain a certain minimum amount of equity.

The stock exchanges and brokerage houses establish the maintenance margin requirement, which can differ, depending upon the exchange or brokerage. The NYSE and FINRA have set the minimum maintenance margin at 25%. The brokerage firms can set their minimum maintenance margin at a higher level, and many firms set their rates at 35%. The maintenance margin acts as a floor below which the actual margin cannot fall.

As the price of the stock fluctuates, so does the investor's equity position. The equity is calculated according to the formula:

Equity = MV – L
MV = Market value of account
L = Borrowed funds

If at any time the equity position falls below the minimum maintenance margin, the brokerage firm will make a margin call, requiring the investor to add cash or marginable securities to the account.

Calculating Margin Calls

To calculate the price at which a margin call will be made, the initial percent borrowed (1 – initial margin) is divided by one minus the maintenance margin percentage, and then the result is multiplied by the original purchase price of one share of stock. The formula is:

EXHIBIT 40 – 1
Maintenance Call Price Formula

$$\text{Maintenance call price} = \frac{(1 - IM)}{(1 - MM)} \times \text{Share price}$$

Where:

IM = Initial margin %
MM = Maintenance margin %

Example:

An investor buys 250 shares of ABC company stock on margin at $100 per share. The investor must deposit $12,500 in the margin account to satisfy the initial margin requirement. The brokerage firm requires a 30% maintenance margin. The price at which a margin call will occur is calculated as follows:

$$\text{Margin call price} = \frac{(1 - .50)}{(1 - .30)} \times \$100 = \$71.43$$

Margin Call

If the price of the stock declines to $65, with the maintenance margin requirement at 30%, then the equity required is $4,875, that is, 250 x $65 x .3, but the actual equity is $3,750, that is, 250 x $65 – $12,500. The broker will make a margin call requiring the investor to deposit $1,125 in additional cash or marginable securities. Maintenance calls must be met within three business days.

Calculating ROI for Securities Purchased Using Margin

Because the investor purchases the stock by paying less than the full value out-of-pocket, the ROI of securities purchased on margin will be exponential. To calculate the ROI, the first step is to determine the total cost of the investment. This includes the interest paid on the margin account and any brokerage fees. The second step is to calculate the net profit by subtracting the total costs from the sales proceeds and adding in any dividends received. The third step is to divide the net profit by the total out-of-pocket investment.

$$\frac{(\text{End value} - \text{begin value}) - \text{interest} - \text{fees} + \text{dividends}}{\text{out-of-pocket investment}} = \text{ROI}$$

Example:

Joe buys 100 shares of JVZ stock on margin when the initial margin rate is 50% and the stock is trading for $50 per share. Interest on the margin account is 7% per year and brokerage fees total $80. If Joe sells the stock at $57 per share one year later, what is Joe's ROI on the margined stock?

Step 1: total cost of the investment = $5,000 price of the stock + $175 interest (amount borrowed is $2,500 x .07 = $175) + $80 in brokerage fees = $5,255

Step 2: Sales proceeds are $5,700 minus total costs of $5,255 = net profit of $445

Step 3: Net profit divided by total out-of-pocket investment = $445/$2,500 = 17.8% ROI

Using the formula:

$$\frac{(5,700 - 5,000) - 175 - 80}{2,500} = 17.8\% \text{ ROI}$$

Short Selling

The use of short sales is a strategy that involves the sale of borrowed stock, in the expectation that it can be repurchased for delivery at a lower price. Short sales are book-entry transactions that do not involve the purchase or sale of actual stock certificates. The process is as follows:

- An investor borrows stock from a broker. An initial margin is required of the investor in order to assure the broker that any losses will be satisfied.

- The borrowed stock is obtained by the broker from street-name margin accounts for loan to the short seller, who, in turn, sells the borrowed stock.

- The short seller instructs the broker to repurchase the stock in the open market.

- The borrowed stock is now replaced.

If the price of the stock has declined, the seller has profited from the difference between the borrowed stock that was sold and the recently repurchased stock. Conversely, a loss will be sustained if the seller has to replace the borrowed stock at a price higher than when it was sold. The usual buy-sell procedure has been "flipped." The normally "buy low and sell high" advice is reversed; the successful short seller is selling high first, then buying low to replace the borrowed shares.

Uptick Rule

The uptick rule has been repealed. Prior to July 6, 2007, the uptick rule required that the stock that was to be part of a short sale must first trace an uptick or increase. For example, if a series of stock prices read (30, 29.875, 29.625, 28.25, 28.375), a short sale could not be transacted until the share price moved from 28.25 to 28.375.

Rules of Short Selling

Important considerations:

- Dividends on stock sold short must be paid by the seller to the owner of record. The stock has been borrowed, and the terms of the loan obligate the seller to cover the declared dividend amount.

- The broker, not the seller, keeps the proceeds from the short sale. The margin account is marked-to-the-market each day, so that if the stock price has fallen, the short seller can receive the difference between the sale price and the current share price. If the stock price has risen, the short seller will have to supply additional funds.

- There is no time limit on a short sale transaction, but short selling in a thinly traded market might cause problems due to the lack of outstanding shares from which to borrow.

Hedging

Hedging is a strategy that relies upon the use of derivative instruments (a financial contract whose value is dependent upon some underlying asset or assets). Hedge positions are taken in order to reduce the risk associated with exposure to an underlying asset or assets. In attempting to reduce the risk associated with commodity prices, investors will take different positions.

Short Hedge and Long Hedge

- Short hedge – A farmer who raises wheat, in effect, takes a long position in wheat production and may wish to reduce risk by taking a short position to reduce exposure to price volatility. The farmer does this by selling a futures contract in wheat. If wheat prices increase, the long position is positive; if its price falls, the value of the short position increases.

- Long hedge – In this instance, assume that a producer of charcoal processes wood into charcoal, so the producer is exposed to the risk of price increases for wood. Any price increase for wood will make his costs higher and cut his profits. The producer is in need of wood, so in effect the producer is short the commodity of wood. The short position means the producer will profit from a decline in the price for wood. In order to reduce the risk to future price increases, the producer will hedge the exposure by taking a long position in wood, which means buying a futures contract for wood. The futures contract gives the producer the ability to buy cords of wood at a fixed price such as $210. If the current market price is $200, the futures contract will limit the future increase to $210, and it will limit the producer's loss to a known and predetermined amount.

Using Options as a Hedge

When an option and an underlying stock are combined, a hedge position is formed for the purpose of having the stock protect the option against a loss, or the option protect the stock against a loss. When combined with an underlying stock, long options provide protection (short options positions in combination with a stock are used to add income to the portfolio). If the underlying stock position is a long position (the investor owns the stock), a long put will insure against a loss by allowing the holder of the option to exercise and sell at the strike price. When the underlying stock position is a short position (the investor borrowed the shares to sell in anticipation that the price would drop), the risk to the investor is that the price will rise, giving the short position an unlimited loss potential. In order to protect that position, the investor should purchase a call option allowing him to exercise at the strike price, thereby limiting his potential loss.

Collar

An investor creates a collar by selling a call and buying a put. The collar strategy is typically used when a stock has climbed rapidly and is not expected to continue much higher. The investor locks in a gain with the purchase of a put and gains premium income by selling the call. The collar locks in a sales price within a given range. This strategy may be particularly useful when a client holds a concentrated position and wishes to spread the sale of the position over multiple tax years while minimizing the risk of price fluctuations.

Example:

100 shares of ABC stock were bought at $50 per share. Today's price is $80 per share. The owner writes a covered call with an expiration in January of the following year at an exercise price of $85. At the same time, the investor buys a put option with an expiration in January of the following year and an exercise price of $75. If the stock price rises above $85 at the end of the term, the holder of the call option will exercise and the investor will sell the shares at $85. If the stock price falls below $75 at the end of the term, the investor will exercise the put and sell for $75. The sale price has been "collared" between $75 and $85 per share when sold in the January of the following year, allowing the gains to be recognized in a different tax year while protecting the sale price within a certain range. The trade-off for the ability to collar the sale price is that the investor forfeits the additional upside potential above $85.

Covered Calls

A covered call is an option that is sold by an investor who also owns shares in the same stock that will be deliverable upon the call's exercise. The position in the stock is long, while the position in the call is short. The writer of the call is covered since he or she owns the stock and can make good on delivery if the call is exercised. The strategy allows for the writer of the call to sell the stock at a fixed price and collect a call premium. Should the stock rise, the writer has limited the gain in the stock in the event it is called away.

However, the writer's losses are absorbed by the call premium collected when the stock price declines.

Example:

100 shares of ABC stock were bought six months ago at $50 per share. Today's price is $60 per share. The owner writes a covered six-month call at an exercise price of $62 and receives a call premium of $5. If the stock price rises to $61 at the end of the term, the option will expire worthless. The owner has retained the stock and the $5 premium per share.

Naked Call

When an investor writes a call without owning the underlying stock, the option is a naked call. With a naked call, the investor does not have the protection of owning the underlying stock that must be delivered in the event the call is exercised. The investor's risk is unlimited because the stock could go up by any amount, and the investor would need to buy the stock to make delivery.

Covered Put

A covered put describes the combination of a sale of a put option on a stock and the short sale of the same stock. If the put is exercised, the writer must buy the stock, but the writer has the offsetting position of the short sale of the same stock. The stock purchase will close out the short sale position.

Protective Put

A protective put is the purchase of a put option when an investor holds a long position in the underlying stock. In effect, the owner has a long position in both the underlying stock and the put, and these two positions guarantee a floor price at which the stock may be sold. This strategy serves to provide protection to the stockowner from major losses, thus reducing his or her exposure to risk.

Example:

The same 100 shares of ABC stock were bought for $50 per share. However, the situation now involves a protective put strategy. The owner, not wanting to suffer any major losses, buys a put with a strike price of $50 at a premium of $2.75, while maintaining the original stock position. Should ABC stock fall $10, to $40 per share, the put's intrinsic value rises by $10 ($50 – $40), while the stock's value has lost $10 ($50 – $40). The result is that, on a per-share basis, the owner has limited his or her loss to the cost of the put's premium of $2.75 ($7.25 put profit – $10 loss per share).

TOPIC 40 – APPLICATION QUESTIONS

1. A client asks a certified financial planner to invest $10 million in two different fixed-income instruments with durations of 5.5 years and 7.4 years, respectively. The client will need all the cash from this investment in six years. In order to properly immunize this portfolio, the planner must:

A. Anticipate the interest rate environment at the time of the portfolio's maturity.

B. Factor in the reinvestment income from coupon payments.

C. Calculate the weighted average of both bonds' durations to match the client's time horizon.

D. Purchase additional bonds with coupons equal to or slightly greater than six years.

E. Calculate the standard deviation of each bond.

2. An investor who engages in market timing and refrains from any type of buy/hold strategy:

A. Is highly concerned about interest rate risk

B. May sacrifice returns when not invested in the market

C. Will disregard technical analysis

D. Minimizes tax and commission costs over the long term

E. Still believes in the basic efficiency of market forces

3. (Published question released November, 1994)

Which combination of the following statements about bond swaps is (are) true?

(1) A substitution swap is designed to take advantage of a perceived yield differential between bonds that are similar with respect to coupons, ratings, maturities, and industry.

(2) Rate anticipation swaps are based on forecasts of general interest rate changes.

(3) The yield pickup swap is designed to change the cash flow of the portfolio by exchanging similar bonds that have different coupon rates.

(4) The tax swap is made in order to substitute capital gains for current yield.

A. (1), (2), and (3) only
B. (1) and (3) only
C. (2) and (4) only
D. (4) only
E. (1), (2), (3), and (4)

4. (Published question released December, 1996)

A client has a cash need at the end of seven years. Which of the following investments might initially immunize the portfolio?

(1) A 9-year maturity coupon bond
(2) A 7-year maturity coupon Treasury-note
(3) A series of Treasury bills

    A. (1), (2), and (3)
    B. (1) only
    C. (2) and (3) only
    D. (2) only
    E. (1) and (2) only

5. (Published question released January, 1999)

To immunize a bond portfolio over a specific investment horizon, an investor would do which of the following?

    A. Match the maturity of each bond to the investment horizon.
    B. Match the duration of each bond to the investment horizon.
    C. Match the average-weighted maturity of the portfolio to the investment horizon.
    D. Match the average-weighted duration of the bond portfolio to the investment horizon.

6. One characteristic of a company dividend reinvestment plan (DRIP) is:

    A. The above-average cost of implementing the plan
    B. The popularity it has gained among investors who time the market
    C. The IRS exemption for investors from the "constructive receipt" rule
    D. The minimal cost to the company in raising capital
    E. The discount companies must offer to shareholders with large holdings

7. A new client relates that his last financial adviser was against employing any bond investment strategies. He currently has $400,000 and would like to invest in individual bonds. You have already performed a risk profile analysis and an asset allocation review and believe that a bond investment of this amount is appropriate. The client wants liquidity and protection from interest rate risk but wants to change the portfolio's structure after three or four years. You should advise him that:

    A. A significant contribution to equities must follow this large an investment in bonds.
    B. A barbell strategy can be employed with no requirement that short-term bonds be reinvested.
    C. A staggered bond portfolio might meet this objective, but only if his time horizon extends beyond the three- or four-year time horizon.
    D. A dedicated portfolio of four $100,000 high-yield bonds should be invested over a three-year period.
    E. This strategy may involve interest rate swaps after the first year.

8. A fixed amount of dollars regularly invested for the long term into a volatile mutual fund:

    A. Will achieve a lower average fund price as compared to its average cost
    B. Lowers the average cost to the investor
    C. Is a classic example of following the value average strategy
    D. Guarantees a profit if held over the long term
    E. Is superior to any buy/hold strategy

9. (Published question released December, 1996)

Which combination of the following statements are true regarding the investment strategy known as "dollar-cost averaging"?

    (1) Invests the same dollar amount each month over a period of time
    (2) Purchases the same number of shares each month over a period of time
    (3) Lowers average cost per share over a period of time (assuming share price fluctuations)
    (4) Invests the same dollar amount each month to protect the investment from loss of capital

    A. (1) and (2) only
    B. (1) and (3) only
    C. (2) and (3) only
    D. (2) and (4) only
    E. (1), (2), (3), and (4)

10. Valerie wishes to open a margin account next Monday in the amount of $30,000. In order for her to do so, which of the following statements is (are) correct?

    (1) The initial margin requirement of at least $15,000 must be deposited into the account.
    (2) The initial margin must be in cash.
    (3) The initial margin may be $15,000 in either cash or marginable securities.
    (4) Maintenance margin requirements may differ among different exchanges or brokerage houses.

    A. (1) and (2) only
    B. (1) and (4) only
    C. (1) and (3) only
    D. (2) and (4) only
    E. (2) only

11. Stewart purchases 200 shares of a stock at a price of $130 per share and a margin of 50%. The broker's maintenance margin is 35%. Which of the following is the stock price below which a margin call will be made?

    A. $125.00
    B. $84.50
    C. $100.00
    D. $105.65
    E. None of the above

12. Julie's stock in her margin account has dropped 33% since the purchase price of $60 per share on June 1, 2017. The initial margin was 50%, and the maintenance margin is .30. If she originally purchased 200 shares, how much will she be required to deposit when the margin call is made?

    A. $400.00
    B. $650.00
    C. $372.00
    D. $428.57
    E. $520.00

13. Your client is considering purchasing shares of IBM common stock and asks you about the wisdom of buying the stock on margin. (Assume that the current initial margin requirement is 60%.) Show the client the rate of profit he or she would realize, ignoring all transactions costs, if 100 shares of the stock are bought at 86 and sold at 92 with margin vs. without margin.

    A. 6.7% vs. 9.9%
    B. 8.9% vs. 5.6%
    C. 11.6% vs. 7.0%
    D. 11.4% vs. 9.9%

14. If John wants to be able to sell a stock short, he must realize that:

(1) The maintenance margin requirement is set by the Federal Reserve Board of Governors.
(2) The NYSE determined the initial margin requirement.
(3) Dividends cannot be ignored in the transaction.
(4) All short sellers must have a margin account.

    A. (1) only
    B. (2), (3), and (4) only
    C. (3) and (4) only
    D. (1), (3), and (4) only
    E. (2) and (4) only

15. Ralph and Ed are two speculators who believe that they can profit in the next 3 to 6 months by going "short." This means:

    A. Both expect prices to rise.
    B. Buying stock index futures is their only real alternative.
    C. A straddle position will be taken.
    D. Long positions will be sold off in steady increments over the next 3 to 6 months.
    E. Both expect prices to decline.

16. 100 shares of MNO stock were purchased six months ago for $50 per share. Today's price is $60 per share. The owner writes a six-month covered call at an exercise price of $62 and receives a call premium of $5. If the price of the stock rises to $61 by term's end:

    A. The option has maintained its intrinsic value.
    B. The option has expired worthless.
    C. The owner forfeits the $5 call premium.
    D. The option is at the money.

17. If Sally decides upon a protective put strategy, a possible result of such an activity is:

    A. Her long position could be called away.
    B. Her loss could be limited to the cost of the put premium.
    C. Her exposure to risk must increase.
    D. The creation of a naked put will result.
    E. The loss of a floor price at which the stock may be sold.

18. Regarding the short sale process, which of the following considerations must be remembered?

    (1) The seller must deposit additional amounts if the price of the stock rises.
    (2) The seller must cover any declared dividend amount of stock sold short.
    (3) Margin accounts are marked-to-the-market on a weekly basis.

    A. (1) and (2) only
    B. (1) only
    C. (2) and (3) only
    D. (1), (2), and (3)
    E. Neither (1), (2), nor (3)

19. Fred wants to make a short sale of 100 shares of Disney common stock, currently trading at 108 per share. Immediately after Fred places his market order, the following are the prices at which the Disney stock trades: 107, 106, 103, 104, 101. If Fred later repurchases the Disney stock at 102, what will be his profit?

    A. $0
    B. $200
    C. $500
    D. $600

20. (Published question released January, 1999)

Jasmine has a large paper profit in her Amalgamated Corporation shares, currently at 46. She is happy with the stock but realizes that a good thing <u>cannot</u> go on forever. If she is willing to sell at 50, what strategy could you recommend to her?

    A. Buy $50 call options.
    B. Sell $50 call options.
    C. Buy $50 put options.
    D. Sell $50 put options.

21. Morgan is the owner of a well-diversified portfolio of common stocks, but Morgan is concerned that the market may decline soon. He has been advised to buy a put on a market index such as the S&P 500. In this situation, which of the following statements is correct?

    A. Morgan has been given bad advice because if the market declines, the value of his option will decline.

    B. Morgan has been given bad advice because if the market declines, the value of his option will be zero.

    C. Morgan has been given good advice because if the market declines, the value of his option will rise.

    D. Morgan has been given good advice because if the market rises, the value of his option will rise.

22. (Published question released November, 1994)

A client with a well diversified common stock portfolio expresses concern about a possible market decline. However, he/she does not want to incur the cost of selling a portion of his or her holdings nor the risk of mistiming the market. A possible strategy for this client would be:

    A. Buy an index call option.

    B. Sell an index call option.

    C. Buy an index put option.

    D. Sell an index put option.

    E. The client cannot protect against the decline with these options.

23. (Published question released December, 1996)

Jennifer is optimistic about the long-term growth of her Widget stock. However, the stock, currently priced at $58, has made a sharp advance in the last week, and she wants to lock in a minimum price in case the shares drop. What might Jennifer do?

    A. Buy $55 call options

    B. Sell $55 call options

    C. Buy $55 put options

    D. Sell $55 put options

24. Which of the following are advantages of dividend reinvestment plans?

    (1) The reinvested dividends receive special tax treatment, which differs from the tax treatment of cash dividends.

    (2) The sources of the new common shares issued could be previously existing shares or newly issued shares.

    (3) The investor may pay less in brokerage commissions.

    (4) These plans may result in a major source of new capital for the firm.

    A. (1), (2), and (3) only

    B. (1), (2), and (4) only

    C. (1), (3), and (4) only

    D. (2), (3), and (4) only

25. Which of the following statements concerning the writing of a covered call option are correct?

(1) Any loss on the long position in the stock will be reduced by the dollars received for the sale of the call.

(2) If the market price of the stock increases to one-half of a point above the strike price, the writer would have been better off not selling the call.

(3) The writer reduces his or her downside risk but gives up possible upside opportunity.

(4) The premium received is considered a return of capital.

A. (1) and (2) only
B. (1) and (3) only
C. (2) and (4) only
D. (3) and (4) only

26. Which of the following are logical reasons for buying a call?

(1) To profit when stock prices increase
(2) To utilize leverage
(3) To generate income in a flat market.
(4) To hedge against an existing short stock position.

A. (1) and (2) only
B. (1) and (3) only
C. (1), (2), and (4) only
D. (2), (3), and (4) only

27. Which of the following are logical reasons for writing a covered call?

(1) To profit when stock prices increase
(2) To utilize leverage
(3) To provide additional income in a flat market.
(4) To provide additional gain while disposing of a long stock position.

A. (1) only
B. (1) and (3) only
C. (1), (2), and (4) only
D. (3) and (4) only

28. Which of the following are logical reasons for buying a put?

(1) To profit when stock prices decrease
(2) To utilize leverage
(3) To benefit from the income payable periodically
(4) To hedge against an existing portfolio

A. (1) and (3) only
B. (1) and (4) only
C. (1), (2), and (4) only
D. (2), (3), and (4) only

29. Which of the following correctly describes a covered put?

    A. A combination of a put and a call on the same stock with different expiration dates and exercise prices

    B. A combination of a put and a call on the same stock with the same expiration dates and exercise prices

    C. Sale of a stock short and sale of a put

    D. Purchase of a stock (long) and a put (short)

30. Which of the following correctly describes a protective put?

    A. A combination of a put and a call on the same stock with different expiration dates and exercise prices

    B. A combination of a put and a call on the same stock with the same expiration dates and exercise prices

    C. Sale of a stock short and sale of a put

    D. Purchase of a stock and a put

31. Which of the following correctly indicates a difference between puts and short sales?

    A. Puts are profitable when stock prices decrease; short sales are profitable when stock prices increase.

    B. Puts provide a greater amount of leverage than short sales.

    C. Short sales have a shorter time frame than puts.

    D. Puts provide more potential for capital loss than short sales.

32. Hank and his wife Hortence both decided to make periodic deposits to purchase shares of LDK mutual fund. Hank decided to spend $200 each month, while Hortence decided to buy 50 shares each time. What is the average cost per share for Hank and Hortence if the price per share for each purchase was $25, $20, $15, and $10?

    A. Hank: $13.50; Hortence: $14.32

    B. Hank: $14.32; Hortence: $15.58

    C. Hank: $15.59; Hortence: $17.50

    D. Hank: $17.50; Hortence: $17.50

33. Jim began purchasing shares of the ERT stock mutual fund several years ago. He has followed a dollar-cost averaging approach by investing $700 each year for four years. The following data depict Jim's purchases:

Year	Fund Price
1	$10.25
2	$20.15
3	$15.60
4	$17.35

What is Jim's average cost per share for this fund?

    A. $14.87   C. $35.17

    B. $15.23   D. $44.20

For practice answering case questions related to Topic 40, please answer the following questions in the cases included in the Appendix at the back of this textbook.

Case	Questions
Donaldson	
Hilbert Stores, Inc.	
Maxwell	9, 10 and 11
Beals	7
Mocsin	
Eldridge	
Young	
Johnson	23 and 24
Thomas	17, 23, and 24
Jim and Brenda Quinn	42, 43, 44, 45, and 46

Alternative Investments (Topic 41)

CFP Board Student-Centered Learning Objectives

(a) Define and describe what qualifies as an alternative investment.

    i. Explain asset class and describe the basic differences between the traditional asset classes and alternative asset classes

    ii. Explain the primary rationale and uses for alternative asset classes

    iii. Explain the primary differences between traditional investment strategies and alternative investment strategies including the potential advantages and disadvantages of utilizing alternative investment strategies

    iv. Explain how the incorporation of alternative asset classes in a traditional asset portfolio structure can potentially improve both absolute and risk-adjusted portfolio returns

---

Alternative Investments

    A.   *Introduction to alternative investments*
        1.   *Examples of alternative investments*
        2.   *Reasons to include alternative investments in the portfolio*
            a.   *Diversification*
        3.   *Common characteristics of alternative investments*
            a.   *Illiquidity and lack of transparency*
            b.   *Inefficiency*
            c.   *Non-normal returns*
            d.   *Inconsistent correlations*
            e.   *Larger minimum purchases required and high fees*
            f.   *Benchmarking*
        4.   *Suitability*
        5.   *Taxation*
    B.   *Regulation of alternative investments and private placements*
        1.   *Private placements*
        2.   *Liquid alternative funds*
    C.   *Real Estate Investments*
        1.   *Direct investment in real estate*
        2.   *Evaluating a direct real estate investment*
            a.   *Net operating income*
            b.   *Taxation, cash flows, and appreciation*
                 1.)   *Taxation of directly-owned real estate investments*
            c.   *Borrowing funds for direct ownership of real estate investments*
        3.   *Forms of ownership for real estate investments*

---

    4.   *Real estate investment trusts (REITs)*
        a.   *REIT investment considerations*
        b.   *Non-traded REITs*
    5.   *Real estate mortgage investment conduits (REMICs)*
    6.   *Real estate limited partnerships (RELPs)*

D.   *Limited Partnership Interests*
    1.   *Non-publicly traded limited partnership interests*
    2.   *Master limited partnerships (MLPs)*
        a.   *Taxation of MLPs*

E.   *Collateralized Debt Obligations (CDOs)*
    1.   *Mortgage-backed securities*
        a.   *Collateralized mortgage obligations (CMOs)*

F.   *Hedge Funds*
    1.   *Hedge fund alternatives*

G.   *Managed futures*

H.   *Private equity funds*

I.   *Bank loan funds*

J.   *Tangible Assets*
    1.   *Collectibles*
    2.   *Natural resources*
    3.   *Precious metals*

INTRODUCTION TO ALTERNATIVE INVESTMENTS

Investment asset classes are generally thought of as cash, equities, and bonds. Any asset that is not one of the three traditional asset classes can be considered an alternative investment.

According to the Morningstar-Barron's Alternative Investment 2015 Survey, alternative investment strategies have hit the mainstream with nearly $200 billion flowing into alternative fund categories from the start of 2009 through 2013. The survey found that many large institutional funds now allocate a small portion (typically less than 10%) of their portfolios to alternative investments. For example, pensions and private endowments are adding hedge funds to their portfolios. The annual survey tracked a growing interest among institutions and advisors in liquid alternatives (such as mutual funds and ETFs investing in alternative assets).

Examples of Alternative Investments

The list of alternative investments is broad, and includes real estate-backed securities, limited partnership interests, Collateralized Debt Obligations (CDOs), hedge funds, private equity, collectibles, natural resources, and precious metals.

Alternative investments also include derivative securities, such as options and futures, discussed in earlier topics in this textbook.

Practice Question

Which of the following are classified as the client's alternative investments?

(1) Limited partnership interests
(2) High yield bonds
(3) Gold bullion

    A. (3) only
    B. (1) and (2) only
    C. (1) and (3) only
    D. (1), (2), and (3)

Answer:
High yield bonds are speculative grade bonds, but they are still in the traditional asset class of bonds and are not considered alternative assets.
The answer is C.

Reasons to Include Alternative Investments in the Portfolio

Investors select alternative investments primarily as a way to reduce overall investment risk through additional asset diversification and to cushion their portfolios against extreme market conditions.

Diversification

Alternative investments can play an important role in the construction of a diversified portfolio. Returns on most financial assets tend to be positively correlated. In contrast, returns of many alternative investments have low correlations to financial assets, and the returns of some physical assets, such as precious metals, can even be negatively correlated.

Alternative investments are expected to have a low correlation with equities and bonds. When stocks decline, alternative investments with low correlation will not decline as much as the market and may even increase, thus reducing the overall risk of the portfolio. Alternative investments follow the rule that the addition of an asset or class of assets that are not perfectly positively correlated (+1.0) to the other assets in the portfolio will reduce the portfolio's standard deviation, resulting in lower total risk.

Alternative investments are sometimes referred to as absolute return products because they are generally analyzed on an absolute basis rather than in relation to the returns on traditional investments. Absolute return strategies seek returns independent of traditional benchmark indices and are measured against their own return goals. An absolute return strategy is intended to provide positive absolute returns in various market environments while reducing market volatility. In addition, absolute return strategies remove constraints on portfolio managers by allowing them to pursue more asset classes and more varieties of investments.[1]

Common Characteristics of Alternative Investments

Typically, alternative investments are actively managed, use leverage to enhance their returns, invest in illiquid assets, and have no or very limited liquidity and transparency.

Illiquidity and Lack of Transparency

Liquidity may be limited or nonexistent with alternative investments because they trade infrequently or with very low volumes. The majority of alternative investments generate little or no current income. There is no secondary market for many alternative investments. If the fund redeems investments, advance notice is typically required, and funds are redeemed at specified times (such as quarterly or year-end) at the discretion of the fund manager. Investment in these assets should be limited to funds that can be committed for an extensive period of time.

In addition, numerous investment strategies employed by managers are proprietary and not disclosed by the asset manager, reducing the amount of transparency.

Inefficiency

As discussed in prior topics in this textbook, the efficient market hypothesis assumes that market prices reflect all available known information, eliminating the ability to achieve superior risk-adjusted returns. Alternative assets are likely to trade at inefficient prices because all relevant information may not be readily available.

Non-normal Returns

To this point, we have looked at returns as displaying the characteristics of a normal, bell-shaped distribution. Alternative assets, however, are likely to exhibit non-normality in the distribution of long-term returns, making approximations with a normal bell-shaped curve inaccurate. For many types of alternative investments, the curve will be asymmetric.

---

[1] See also, *Absolute Return Strategies Offer Modern Diversification,* Putnam Investments, February 2015.

Inconsistent Correlations

The correlation between asset classes is not constant. A state of flux is normal. As an alternative investment becomes popular and available, it is not unusual for its correlation to stocks and bonds to increase and returns to decline. The success of a particular alternative investment may be its undoing. Correlations may not be sustainable under certain market conditions. During the extreme markets of 2008 and 2009, most asset classes declined and expected correlations did not materialize for many alternative investments.

Larger Minimum Purchases Required and High Fees

Alternative investments may require large minimum purchases. For alternative investments such as hedge funds, venture capital, and private equity funds, fees are generally 1% – 2% of assets under management and 10% – 20% of the gains.

Benchmarking

Because alternative investments are such a broad asset class, it is difficult to evaluate them as a class or to find the right benchmark to measure their investment performance. Alternative funds use diverse strategies that do not conform to typical approaches of portfolio construction, adding to the benchmarking difficulty.

Some strategies perform well during one market cycle and then under-perform during the next cycle. Each strategy should be evaluated on its own merits during several market cycles to determine whether it produces the desired risk-adjusted performance after adjusting for fees, illiquidity, and volatility.

Suitability

Many alternative investments are not suitable for the general public. Due to their complexity, limited regulatory oversight, lack of liquidity, and high minimum purchase requirements, most alternative investments are purchased by institutional investors or accredited high-net-worth individuals.

Alternative investments may reduce total portfolio risk, but investors need to consider in the overall analysis the additional facts of their limited liquidity, complex structure, possible failure to react as expected during major market moves, and high fees. The attractiveness of alternative assets is not necessarily their returns but the possibility of risk reduction. They are typically used to reduce total portfolio risk by the addition of assets that have low correlation coefficients with other portfolio assets. As noted, these correlation relationships generally change over time and may not perform as expected during all market conditions.

Alternative investments are not considered compatible with a truly conservative investment strategy. Many investors have a substantial percentage of their net worth in alternative investments in the form of their personal residence and vacation property. Due to their risk and illiquidity, alternative investments should generally comprise a minimal percentage of an investor's total portfolio.

Taxation

Alternative investments are subject to varying tax rules depending on the asset. For example, collectibles and precious metals are subject to a maximum 28% long-term capital gain rate, and most REIT dividends are taxed as non-qualifying ordinary income. It is important to understand the tax treatment of the alternative asset before investing.

🔑 **KEY SUMMARY 41 – 1**
Alternative Investments – Advantages and Disadvantages

<u>Advantages</u>	<u>Disadvantages</u>
• Diversification (low correlation with traditional asset classes) • Use of varied investment strategies • Inefficiency (potential ability to outperform with active management)	• Illiquid • Lack of transparency • High minimum investment • Potentially high fees • Potential for increased risk due to use of leverage in many alternative investment strategies • Many types of alternative investments are largely unregulated

---

Practice Question

Alice, a 45-year-old senior executive, is a high net worth client with ample current income. She has asked your advice in developing a diversified investment portfolio. Which of the following portfolios would you recommend?

A. 80% total US equity index fund, 20% hedge funds
B. 50% S&P 500 ETF, 10% International fund, 10% REIT, 10% private equity, 10% managed futures, 10% hedge fund
C. 45% Wilshire 5000 ETF, 15% Total International index fund, 30% bond index fund, 5% mix of several alternative investments, 5% cash
D. 60% S&P 500 ETF and 40% bond fund

Answer:

Answer A has no fixed income or international allocation, no cash, and too much allocated to non-liquid risky alternative investments. Answer B has no fixed income or cash allocation and is overly weighted in a variety of alternative investments. Answer D is the classic equity-fixed income allocation but lacks the asset allocation diversity of answer C. The client asked for a diversified investment allocation recommendation. Answer C is the best answer because it has a more balanced and diversified portfolio.

The answer is C.

REGULATION OF ALTERNATIVE INVESTMENTS AND PRIVATE PLACEMENTS

Most alternative investments have less regulatory scrutiny than public offerings, and some are not regulated at all by the SEC.

Private Placements

The term "private placement" refers to the offer and sale of any security not involving a public offering. Most private placements are offered under Regulation D, which provides an exemption allowing companies to sell their securities without registering them with the SEC. It is estimated that approximately one-third of corporate debt issues are placed privately.

Private placements can be sold to any number of accredited investors, plus up to 35 non-accredited investors. Accredited investors include natural persons with a net worth over $1 million (excluding the value of their primary residence), or with income over $200,000 ($300,000 joint with spouse) in each of the two most recent years with a reasonable expectation of the same income in the current year.

Private placements are usually sold to large banks, mutual funds, insurance companies, and pension funds. The private placement market is information-intensive. Decisions to commit funds to bonds or other debt instruments issued by borrowers in the private placement market are made on the basis of assessments of the credit quality of the issuer and negotiated covenants (negotiated terms of the bond indenture, for example restrictions on the issuance of new debt or restrictions on certain activities). Privately placed bonds are particularly attractive to insurance companies who wish to match their long-term liabilities with long-term assets. The issuer saves the time and expense of registering the issue with the SEC, the costs of a prospectus, flotation costs (costs incurred in the issuance of new securities, such as underwriting fees and registration fees) if the issue is placed directly without the assistance of an investment firm, and the advantage that the issue will not be immediately resold by the purchaser. The purchaser can negotiate the maturity and terms of the issue to meet its particular requirements. The purchaser may obtain a higher interest rate than would be available in a public offering due to the lack of liquidity. The higher interest rate is offset in part by the lack of underwriting costs. The terms of the issue are separately negotiated and may be tailored to meet both the issuer's and purchaser's requirements.

Investors purchasing private placements should be aware of restrictions, which make them highly illiquid. Individual investors should realize that the lack of disclosure of material risk factors normally required in a prospectus make private placements risky to potential investors.

Private placements are only suitable for high net worth investors who have the knowledge and/or financial resources to evaluate the risk factors of the issue, are not concerned about the illiquidity of the investment, and have a high-risk tolerance.

Liquid Alternative Funds

Investors not meeting the requirements of an accredited investor or who want to commit a small amount to alternative investments can invest in a number of mutual funds and ETFs known as "liquid alternative funds." These funds attempt to mimic the strategies of hedge funds. They are priced daily, have lower minimums for purchase, provide liquidity, and offer transparency at lower costs. While liquid alternative funds provide more liquidity, they may experience dramatic price declines during periods of market stress.

REAL ESTATE INVESTMENTS

One of the most common types of investments that may fall into the category of alternative investments is real estate.

There are basically four major types of real estate: land, residential real estate, commercial real estate, and industrial real estate.

- Raw land may be classified as improved or unimproved. Improved land has certain improvements, such as curbs, gutters, and sewers, whereas unimproved land does not have such improvements. Unimproved land has the disadvantage that it does not generate cash flow nor depreciation charges, yet it is still taxed and assessed. It can, however, appreciate (or depreciate). Improved land may have disadvantageous zoning and land-use restrictions.
- Residential real estate includes single family dwellings and multiple family dwellings, such as apartments, hotels, and motels.
- Commercial real estate includes office buildings, retail stores, shopping centers, and specialty buildings, such as banks, movie theaters, and bowling alleys.
- Industrial real estate includes factories, warehouses, industrial parks, and utility facilities.

Investment in real estate can be by direct ownership of property, by buying shares of a Real Estate Investment Trust (REIT), by acquiring an interest in a Real Estate Limited Partnership (RELP), or through a Real Estate Mortgage Investment Conduit (REMIC).

Direct Investment in Real Estate

Direct investment in real estate may include residential rental properties, commercial properties, or industrial properties. An investor can buy an interest in a piece of real estate individually or as part of a group of individual investors.

Direct investing in real estate can provide the advantages of a flow of income from rents, a tax shelter for rental income, inflation protection from appreciation of the property, leverage through the use of borrowed funds, and capital gains from potential appreciation.

Direct investing in real estate has the disadvantages of requiring a sizeable dollar investment, usually some indebtedness, a need for active management, high transaction costs (including commission costs of 5% – 7%), lack of liquidity, and potential legal liability.

A number of factors must be considered before entering into a direct investment in real estate. These factors include, but are not limited to, the following:

1) Location (most important)
2) Cost of purchasing the property (including closing costs and the cost to borrow funds/interest rates)
3) Annual expenses for real estate taxes, liability insurance, and maintenance of the property (mowing, trash removal, posting)
4) Design and construction of the property
5) Projections as to expected return on the investment
6) Length of time to sell, and possibility of loss on the sale

Additional considerations when purchasing raw land include:

1) Land may be held for its potential capital appreciation; and when sold, land is taxed at capital gain rates for investors and as ordinary income for professional land dealers.
2) Land is not depreciable for tax purposes. It can, however, appreciate (or depreciate) in value. Land is subject to a number of risks: it may not be possible to obtain the desired zoning; the property may be subject to rezoning, which may not be favorable; the property may be annexed by the local municipality with increased real estate taxes and with new zoning and land-use restrictions; it may not be possible to get necessary building permits; the anticipated population or development of adjacent properties may not materialize; or the land may not appreciate.
3) An investor in raw land needs to be prepared for negative cash flow for a projected period of time and have a long-term investment horizon.

Evaluating a Direct Real Estate Investment

Net Operating Income

A piece of real estate to be purchased for investment purposes can be valued by dividing its net operating income (NOI) by an appropriate capitalization rate.

NOI can be calculated using the following steps:

Gross rental receipts
+ Other income (such as vending machine, laundry, parking receipts)
= Gross potential income
– Vacancy and collection losses
= Gross income before expenses
– Operating expenses (excluding interest & depreciation)
= Net Operating Income NOI

Only cash expenses, excluding interest and depreciation, comprise operating expenses. Depreciation is not a cash expense, but a tax adjustment. Interest expenses associated with financing the purchase of the property are not included since they are expenses of the investor, not of the property.

NOI should be calculated as an average over several years. Once NOI has been calculated, divide NOI by an estimated capitalization or discount rate to obtain the property's intrinsic value. The choice of a capitalization rate is subjective (the seller will prefer a low rate and the buyer a high one), but should be equal to the investor's required rate of return to invest in the property. As an example, if an investor requires a 10% rate of return, divide NOI by .10 to obtain the maximum amount the investor is willing to pay for the property.

Example:

An investor is considering the purchase of a rental property. The property rents for $1,200 a month, garage parking spaces rent for $100 a month, the property is expected to be rented 95% of the year, and collection losses are estimated at 5%. Real estate taxes are $2,000 a year, liability insurance is $150 a month, depreciation is $3,800 a year, and interest expense on the property loan is $5,120 a year. What is the intrinsic value of the property if the investor has a 10% required rate of return?

$14,400	Gross rental receipts ($1,200 x 12)
+1,200	+ other income (parking receipts) (12 x $100)
$15,600	= Gross potential income
–1,560	– Vacancy and collection losses (5% + 5%) x $15,600
$14,040	Gross income before expenses ($2,000 + $1,800 (12 x $150)
–3,800	– Operating expenses (excluding interest & depreciation)
$10,240	= Net Operating Income NOI
$10,240	divided by .10 capitalization rate equals $102,400 intrinsic value

Note that the depreciation and interest expense is not included in the NOI calculation.

NOI divided by the required rate of return or appropriate capitalization rate determines the intrinsic value of the investment itself without consideration of the cash flow and tax benefits to the investor.

Taxation, Cash Flows, and Appreciation

In evaluating a real estate investment, three benefits should be analyzed: the original tax benefit, the reinvestment of the cash flow that the property generates, and the price appreciation of the property.

While net income generated by the property (rental income less expenses) is important to the intrinsic value of the property, after-tax cash flow is more important to the investor. After-tax cash flow is net after-tax earnings plus depreciation (which is deductible for tax purposes but does not require current cash out flow) minus principal repayment (which is a cash out flow but is not tax deductible). Cash flow is considered more important because it is a source of funds, which can be reinvested or used to pay down debt.

Investors in real estate need to do a cash flow projection before investing, realizing that many of the projected factors are subject to change. Important factors are the cost of the investment, rental income, maintenance costs, depreciation, taxes, interest, principal repayments, and rates of reinvestment of the positive cash flow. Other aspects to consider are the property's location, the appropriateness of design, the soundness of construction, and the cost of capital.

Taxation of Directly-Owned Real Estate Investments

Real estate investors report rents as ordinary income, and they deduct expenses for mortgage payments, taxes, insurance, maintenance, utilities, and depreciation.

While depreciation improves the after-tax cash flow, investors need to remember that at the sale of the property a special tax rate of 25% applies to the amount of unrecaptured depreciation under Section 1250 of the tax code. Any additional long-term capital gains above the amount of depreciation are subject to the maximum rate for capital gains of 15% for most taxpayers (20% for taxpayers with taxable income above $425,800 (Single) or $479,000 (MFJ), and 0% for taxpayers with taxable income less than $38,600 (Single) or $77,200 (MFJ)).

Deduction of Rental Income from Pass-Through Entity – Sec. 199A

The Tax Cuts and Jobs Act of 2017 created a new deduction under Section 199A for "Qualified Business Income" of pass-through entities (sole proprietorships, partnerships, LLCs, and S-corporations), for tax years 2018 – 2025. For purposes of Section 199A, some rental real estate investments reported on Schedule E of the investor's Form 1040 income tax return are included in the definition of pass-through entities. Additional details regarding the Sec. 199A deduction are provided below.

Passive Loss Limitations

For investors who are not professional dealers in real estate, rental income is passive income (passive activity loss rules), and losses from rental properties are passive losses. These passive losses may only be used to offset passive gains. Losses are further limited to the amount an investor has at risk (under the at-risk rules). If the property produces a loss, the loss cannot be used to offset earned income or investment income. The loss is suspended and carried forward to offset future passive gains or is used when the property is sold to decrease the realized gain on the property. A real estate professional must report any gain on the sale of rental property as ordinary income.

There is an exception for the small investor who actively participates in the management of the rental property. A small investor is a single or married individual with modified adjusted gross income (AGI) of $100,000 or less. Under the tax code, a small investor may use up to $25,000 of annual rental losses to offset active or portfolio income. The deduction is phased out at a rate of $1 for every $2 of modified AGI over $100,000 and is completely phased-out for modified AGI over $150,000.

Borrowing Funds for Direct Ownership of Real Estate Investments

Investment in real estate usually entails obtaining some type of mortgage or a pledge of the property as collateral to secure the debt.

- Conventional mortgage – the lender offers a standard loan with no government insurance or subsidy; the property is the collateral; the loan extends over several years and is repaid in installments consisting of a gradually decreasing amount of interest and a gradually increasing amount of principal.

- FHA or VA mortgages – these loans are similar to conventional mortgages, but they are available only to certain audiences; in case of default, the FHA or Department of Veterans Affairs repays the loan.

- Fixed-rate mortgage – interest, and so payments, are unchanged throughout the duration of the loan.

- Variable-rate mortgage – interest rate, and so payments, vary with market rates of interest, usually within limits.

A factor to consider in taking out a new or replacement mortgage is the "points" charged. A point is a onetime up-front charge by the lender. A point is one percent of the mortgage loan amount. Points are frequently paid by the borrower to obtain a lower mortgage rate.

Taxpayers who itemize deductions are permitted to deduct the interest paid on up to $1 million (for mortgage debt incurred before Dec. 15, 2017; $750,000 for mortgage debt incurred after Dec. 14, 2017) of acquisition debt for a mortgage *secured by their personal residence*. This deduction limit applies to both first and second home acquisition indebtedness combined. Home equity loan interest is deductible only if the debt is used to improve the property and is included in the above limits. Points paid on a new home mortgage are deductible in the year paid. However, points paid to refinance a mortgage must be amortized over the life of the loan.

Interest actually paid or incurred during the year on mortgages taken out *on investment property* is generally deductible against the rental income generated from the property. This interest is not an itemized deduction but is subtracted from the investor's rental income and from other income in computing adjusted gross income, as discussed earlier.

Forms of Ownership for Real Estate Investments

Real estate may be held in outright ownership (fee simple deed), a general partnership or joint venture, a limited partnership, a C corporation, an S corporation, or a real estate investment trust (REIT).

The forms of ownership differ with respect to the personal liability incurred, the management effort required, the income tax consequences, the transferability of the investment, and the continuity of the ownership entity, that is, the consequences of the death of one of the investors. When real estate is owned outright, the investor has full personal liability. This liability includes the financial responsibility for negligent acts and for debts incurred. All of the costs as well as all of the tax benefits accrue to the individual owner.

A general partnership is an organization in which two or more people invest together. Liability for the acts of the partnership and partners is shared among the partners. The partnership is not taxed as a separate entity, and the partnership files only an information return Form 1065 with IRS. Income and deductions are passed through to the individual partners on Schedule K-1 to be reported on their individual tax returns (Form 1040). Usually, the death of one of the partners terminates the partnership.

Another form of ownership is a condominium, which means joint ownership and control of a project. In a condominium, each apartment or unit is owned separately, but the common areas of the building, for example, the lobby, are jointly owned. Individuals pay their own property taxes in addition to a condominium fee to pay for the maintenance of the common areas.

A cooperative is yet another form of ownership in real estate. An individual buys shares in a corporation, the cooperative. The cooperative is the single owner of the apartment building and is run by a board of directors. Each share in the cooperative has the right to lease and use a designated apartment. Each owner pays monthly assessments that include property taxes.

Practice Question

All of the following statements concerning investing in real estate are correct, EXCEPT:

A. Raw land has negative cash flow, is illiquid, and is subject to zoning risks.
B. Residential real estate income may be offset by expenses and depreciation in calculating income taxes.
C. Real estate investing is a form of tax shelter that can use leverage to enhance returns and may serve as an inflation hedge.
D. NOI (net operating income) for a real estate investment is the rental income less expenses, depreciation, and interest expense on the loan.

Answer:
Answer choice D is incorrect because depreciation and interest expenses are not considered in the calculation of NOI.
The answer is D.

Real Estate Investment Trusts (REITs)

As an alternative to direct investment in real estate, the principal vehicle for investing indirectly in real estate is the real estate investment trust (REIT). A REIT is a publicly traded closed-end investment company that invests in a diversified portfolio of real estate, real estate mortgage loans, and/or construction loans. A REIT cannot act as a real estate developer, because REITs are prohibited from holding real estate primarily for sale to customers in the ordinary course of business.

REITs enable even a small investor to obtain a diversified, professionally managed real estate portfolio that is traded in the secondary market (providing reasonable liquidity). REITs also offer the benefits of allowing investors to invest in real estate with only limited liability and with lower transfer costs than direct investments in real estate.

When considering investing in a REIT, the investor should consider the types of assets in which the REIT will invest, the extent to which the REIT will rely on debt financing (leverage), the extent to which the REIT will diversify, and whether the REIT will focus on current income or capital appreciation.

There are three types of REITs:

> Equity REIT
> Mortgage REIT
> Hybrid REIT

Equity REITs invest in properties, such as apartments and shopping centers, and seek appreciation of the properties acquired or a combination of rental income and property appreciation. Equity REITs provide moderate income and the potential for an increasing cash flow and capital appreciation.

Mortgage REITS invest primarily in mortgages and construction loans and, in some cases, in mortgage-backed securities, such as GNMAs, with a focus on generating income. Mortgage REITs function essentially as lenders on real estate and tend to be highly leveraged. Mortgage REITs provide high income but less potential for growth and appreciation.

Hybrid REITs use the strategies of both the equity REIT and the mortgage REIT.

Investors who want to participate in the potential appreciation of real estate will select an equity REIT. Investors desirous of current income will choose a mortgage REIT. Mortgage REITs are more sensitive to changes in general interest rates.

A REIT is a pass-thru entity that must invest at least 75% of its assets in real estate, government securities, or cash. A REIT must receive at least 75% of its income from real estate and must distribute 90% of its income annually. The REIT itself is not taxed on income distributed to shareholders.

REITs pay income to investors in the form of dividends; however, the majority of **REIT dividends are non-qualifying dividends, so they are taxed as ordinary income**. The expenses and losses of the REIT are not passed through to investors as they are with limited partnerships. Many individuals purchase REITs for their dividend yield, and should consider the tax rules that apply to REIT income. As a result of the new Section 199A "qualified business income" deduction created by the Tax Cuts and Jobs Act of 2017, REITs may become more attractive for investors who qualify, because some REIT dividends will qualify for the deduction. See below for details regarding the Sec. 199A deduction.

REITs may be appropriate for conservative investors seeking current income, such as that which is needed for retirement income, and diversified real estate exposure. REITs are preferably held in a tax deferred vehicle, such as a 401(k) or IRA, due to the non-qualifying nature of their dividends.

REIT Investment Considerations

Questions to be considered when determining whether the management philosophy of a particular REIT is suitable for a particular investor include:

1) In what kinds of assets will the REIT invest?

2) What, if any, limits does the REIT place on debt and the use of leverage?

3) Will the REIT diversify investments or concentrate in a particular type or sector?

4) Will the REIT diversify geographically?

5) Does the REIT have limits on the amount of its assets that can be placed in any one project?

6) Will the REIT focus on income or capital growth?

7) What is the typical vacancy rate of the REIT?

8) How have the REIT's dividends grown historically?

9) What track record does the management of the REIT have as measured by their decisions? Are they conservative or risk takers with their decision?

10) What are the REIT's current and historical expense ratios?

REITS are not easy to value using the traditional stock valuation model because it is very difficult to select the appropriate discount factor. Also, it is difficult to predict future dividends and earnings for REITS. To evaluate REIT management, the investor should look at past performance based upon expense ratios, vacancy rates, and the dividend payout record.

🔑 **KEY SUMMARY 41 – 2**
Types of REITs

- **Equity REITs** invest primarily for appreciation of the properties acquired
- **Mortgage REITs** invest primarily for income
- **Hybrid REITs** are a combination of equity and mortgage REITS

Non-Traded REITs

A non-traded REIT is a form of real estate investment trust that does not trade on a securities exchange and is generally illiquid, often for periods of eight years or more. The entity that creates the REIT is the sponsor who generally has a subsidiary that markets and sells shares to investors. As much as 15% of the initial investment is paid in commissions and marketing expenses. The offering period is generally three years long. Shares are sold directly to small investors via networks of financial advisers and broker-dealers. Early redemption of a non-traded REIT can result in high fees. The trusts usually seek to return their cash to investors within three to five years by selling their portfolios or by listing their shares on a stock exchange. Non-traded REITs must see big increases in value or in operating income in order to compensate for up-front fees charged by brokers. If property prices don't appreciate enough, the trusts can't return money to shareholders. Some trusts have been criticized for aggressive sales tactics, high fees, and concentration in a small number of investments, and trusts have also been criticized for paying distributions to shareholders out of capital raised from other people who later put money into the funds. Non-traded REITs are subject to the same IRS requirements as traded REITs, which include returning at least 90% of taxable income to shareholders.

The non-traded REIT is a risky, illiquid, high fee investment that should only be considered by the most knowledgeable investor after extensive due diligence. They are not appropriate for the conservative, moderate net worth investor. Due to the abuses of several funds, FINRA has issued a Public Non-Traded REIT Tip Sheet available on their web site.

The following bullet points are from FINRA's Public Non-Traded REIT Tip Sheet (August 15, 2012) (https://www.finra.org/investors/public-non-traded-reit-tip-sheet). These tips can help avoid some common pitfalls and misconceptions surrounding public non-traded REIT investing:

> Do not put all your investments in one basket: Avoid putting too much of your nest egg in a single REIT or in multiple REITs of the same family. Older investors should be particularly cautious about investing large portions of their retirement income in non-traded REITs.
> Your initial investment in a non-traded REIT is not guaranteed and may increase or decrease in value.
> Do not invest solely based on distributions the non-traded REIT may currently be generating. Distributions can be suspended for a period of time or halted altogether. Unlike interest from a CD or bond, REIT distributions may be funded in part or entirely by cash from investor capital or borrowings – leveraged money that does not come from income generated by the real estate itself.
> Redemption policies can change, making it extremely difficult to get money out of the non-traded REIT when you need it.
> Think hard before deciding to reinvest any distributions, especially if you think you might need the money in the near future. Reinvested distributions are generally subject to the same redemption policies as other investments, which means they may be illiquid for significant periods of time.
> Be wary of claims that a non-traded REIT "is about to go public." The public offering process is often lengthy and may never come to fruition; and if it does, the REIT may trade at a price that is lower than its current valuation.

Your best source of information about a non-traded REIT's path to liquidity will be SEC filings made by the REIT itself, found on the SEC's <u>EDGAR database</u>.

➢ Decisions about distributions, redemptions, and "liquidity events," such as going public or selling property, are made by the REIT that owns the actual real estate. Most non-public REITs have an investor relations department that can help answer questions about a REIT's business operations, including a REIT's redemption program. <u>Contact the SEC</u> if you have concerns about the REIT itself.

Practice Question

Which of the following statements about REITs (Real Estate Investment Trusts) is correct?

A. REITs are required to invest 90% of their assets in real estate and to distribute at least 75% of their income.
B. The majority of REIT dividends are qualifying dividends taxed at the taxpayer's capital gain rate.
C. An investor interested in current income would purchase an Equity REIT.
D. Mortgage REITs are more sensitive to interest rate changes than Equity REITs.

Answer:
A is incorrect. By law REITs are required to invest at least 75% of their assets in real estate and to distribute at least 90% of their income annually.

B is incorrect. The majority of REIT dividends are non-qualifying dividends taxed to the taxpayer as ordinary income.

C is incorrect. An investor seeking current income should purchase a Mortgage REIT.
The answer is D.

Real Estate Mortgage Investment Conduits (REMICs)

Real estate mortgage investment conduits (REMICs) are flow-through entities that hold pools of residential and commercial mortgages and issue securities to investors.

Unlike a traditional pass-through entity that distributes income and principal pro rata, REMICs separate interest and principal payments into separately traded securities. New securities are created that have different classes from A to Z, called tranches, they may have different interest-rate payments, maturities, and stipulations for prepayment. The Z-class REMIC pays no cash to the investor until other classes are paid off. The variety of investment options enables these securities to meet the needs of different investors. The REMIC is a type of collateralized mortgage obligation (CMO) (CMOs are discussed later in this topic).

Real Estate Limited Partnerships (RELPs)

Real estate limited partnerships (RELPs) are another way real estate may be held for investment purposes. A limited partnership provides limited liability to the limited partners. The partnership has at least one general partner, who is responsible for managing the property and any number of limited partners who have contributed capital. Limited partners are not active participants in the activities of the real estate firm, but are considered passive investors. All of the partners share in the rental income and in any appreciation when the property is sold.

RELPs were a very popular tax shelter in the 1980s due to the depreciation deductions on the buildings. However, the active-participation and passive-activity rules instituted in the 1986 Tax Reform Act limited the tax saving advantages. Income from RELPs is deemed to be passive income for the limited partners.

LIMITED PARTNERSHIP INTERESTS

A limited partnership is a business owned by general and limited partners. The general partners are responsible for managing the business and are considered active owners, while the limited partners are not permitted to participate in management and are considered passive investors. General partners have unlimited liability for debts and obligations of the firm, but the liability of limited partners extends only to the amount of their investment.

The limited partnership, like other partnerships, is not a tax-paying entity, so income is passed through to the partners. Limited partners receive passive income according to their share of investment in the firm, and general partners receive active income.

Non-publicly Traded Limited Partnership Interests

Non-publicly traded or privately offered limited partnership interests are not suitable for the average investor since they are usually illiquid, invest in riskier investments, do not permit limited partners to participate in management, and may restrict the sale of partnership interests.

Losses from non-publicly traded limited partnerships may only be used to offset income from another non-publicly traded limited partnership.

Non-publicly traded limited partnerships are not appropriate for the general investor. Only the risk-tolerant, aggressive, high net worth, high income tax bracket investor who can tolerate the illiquid nature of the investment should consider them.

Master Limited Partnerships (MLPs)

Master limited partnerships (MLPs) have been formed to make limited partnership interests more liquid and marketable. They acquire or merge limited partnerships and make units available to trade in the secondary market similar to stocks. Many MLPs are traded on the major stock exchanges. These units of master limited partnerships are usually organized for natural resources (such as oil and gas) or real estate holdings due to regulations requiring that, in order to be taxed as a flow-through entity, the MLP must derive at least 90% of gross income from activities related to exploration, development, and mining or production of minerals and natural resources, from real property income, or from gain from commodities (IRC Section 7704).

Distributions by limited partnerships usually occur on a quarterly basis, but MLPs may make distributions to unitholders whenever management considers it appropriate. The primary reason to purchase an MLP is cash flow, and the MLP will typically trade based on a multiple of cash flow (as opposed to net income).

While studies comparing the performance of MLPs and the stock market have not been conclusive, MLPs have not been found to outperform the stock market in the long term, and the stock market outperforms MLPs in some periods.

Taxation of MLPs

The tax treatment of MLPs and limited partnerships is generally the same, with income and gains or losses passed through to the investors. Some of the income generated from MLPs may be considered "portfolio" income and some income considered "passive", as shown on the Schedule K-1 received by the unitholder each year.

Losses from MLPs cannot be used to offset income from non-publicly traded or other publicly traded limited partnerships, and such losses can only be used to offset income from the same MLP. For tax purposes, distributions from MLPs are a return of capital and reduce the investor's cost basis, but the distributions are not subject to income tax. The investor is taxed when the

MLP is sold. Thus, MLPs allow investors to defer much of their personal income tax liability for years into the future or, in many cases, indefinitely.

Unlike regular corporations, a master limited partnership doesn't pay traditional corporate-level tax. Instead, these partnerships pass through the majority of their income to investors in the form of regular quarterly distributions that are treated as a return of capital (reducing basis). It is often said that 80 to 90 percent of the distribution received from most MLPs is tax-deferred until the MLP is sold or liquidated. This is because each unitholder's share of earned income each year will increase basis, and each distribution made will decrease basis. The quarterly distributions from an MLP are typically based on free cash flow, rather than earnings, and will most often be treated as a return of capital. Once basis has been reduced to zero, any additional distributions will be taxable gains.

At the time of sale of the MLP interest, the gain will be the difference between the sale price and the adjusted basis (which has been reduced by the quarterly distributions but increased by earnings each year). When the unit holder sells his or her units, some of the gain may be taxed as ordinary income (under recapture rules) and some of the gain may be capital gain. **MLPs should not be held in a tax-deferred account, such as an IRA. IRAs are subject to the "unrelated business taxable income" (UBTI) rule which may result in a tax on IRA holders for these investments.**

The MLP tax-advantaged yields and recession-resistant growth potential is best suited for a risk averse, high net worth, high tax bracket investor, **and held in a taxable account.**

🔑 KEY SUMMARY 41 – 3
Limited Partnerships and Master Limited Partnerships

- Non-publicly traded limited partnership interests are illiquid and have low marketability.
- Losses from non-publicly traded limited partnerships may only be used to offset income from another non-publicly traded limited partnership.
- Master limited partnerships (MLP) are more liquid and marketable than non-publicly traded limited partnerships. MLPs trade in the secondary market similar to stocks.

Sec. 199A Deduction for Qualified Business Income

The Tax Cuts and Jobs Act of 2017 created a new deduction under Section 199A for "Qualified Business Income" of pass-through entities (sole proprietorships, partnerships, LLCs, and S-corporations), for tax years 2018 – 2025. For purposes of Section 199A, some rental real estate investments reported on Schedule E are included in the definition of pass-through entities (watch for additional IRS guidance regarding which rental real estate activities qualify). Business income from these entities flows through to the owners and is taxed at the owner's marginal rate. C-Corporations, which are taxed at the entity level rather than as a tax flow-through, do not qualify.

The deduction is a below-the-line deduction on the investor's Form 1040, which reduces taxable income but does not reduce adjusted gross income. Taxpayers who qualify for the deduction are permitted to take the deduction, regardless of whether the standard deduction or itemized deductions are selected.

The deduction is generally 20% of the taxpayer's Qualified Business Income (QBI). The net result is to reduce the tax rate on the business income by 20%. For example, for a taxpayer in the highest marginal bracket (37% in 2018), the tax on the business income is effectively reduced to 29.60% (37% x (1 − .20) = 29.60%).

The deduction is actually based on the taxpayer's "combined qualified business income", which can generally be described as a combination of the QBI from each flow-through business plus **qualified REIT dividends and qualified publicly traded partnership income**.

The deduction is also limited to 20% of the taxpayer's taxable income (after reducing by any capital gains) from all sources, including the spouse's income if married filing jointly. If the taxpayer's taxable income from all sources (without regard to the Sec. 199A deduction; and including the spouse's income if MFJ) is over $157,500 (single, $315,000 MFJ), additional restrictions apply.

If the net combined QBI from all businesses results in a loss for the year, no deduction is permitted and the net combined QBI loss is carried forward to apply against combined QBI in the following year.

Additional details regarding the deduction are beyond the scope of this textbook but can be found in Keir's Income Tax Planning textbook. Also **note that as of the time of printing this textbook, additional IRS guidance is pending regarding the details of the various limitations of this deduction.**

COLLATERALIZED DEBT OBLIGATIONS (CDOs)

Collateralized debt obligations (CDOs) are a type of structured security product that is created to display specific risk, return, or tax attributes. This is frequently accomplished by separating the cash flows of the underlying investments into unique portfolios, called tranches These tranches may have various levels of seniority and different maturity dates.

Mortgage-Backed Securities

A conventional mortgage consists of monthly payments of interest and principal. As long as the mortgage is current and has not been repaid, these payments are known. However, if the borrower sells the home or refinances the loan the principal is repaid, and the investor is subject to reinvestment rate risk. The uncertainty of the timing of mortgage payments can affect the valuation of the mortgage as an investment. The collateralized mortgage obligation (CMO) was developed as a means of reducing the reinvestment rate risk of receiving principal payments before the maturity of the mortgage, and possibly forcing reinvestment of the principal at lower rates.

Collateralized Mortgage Obligations (CMOs)

Collateralized mortgage obligations (CMOs) are debt obligations supported by mortgages and are sold in a series to reduce the prepayment risk associated with mortgage-backed securities, such as Ginnie Maes, Freddie Macs, and Fannie Maes. Homeowners may, for many reasons, decide to pay off their existing mortgages early. The prepayments are passed through to the investors and expose them to reinvestment risk, that is, the risk of reinvestment at lower interest rates.

Investors uncomfortable with such prepayment uncertainty can turn to CMOs. CMOs are backed by a pool of mortgages but are grouped into a series of bonds that have stated maturities of 3, 5, 10, 20, and 30 years. CMOs can have up to 12 classes, or "tranches." If principal is repaid, the cash flow is used to repay the CMO tranches with the shortest term first. Thus, the 3-year tranche will be retired first, then the 5-year, and so on until the entire CMO is repaid. CMOs have been said to control prepayment risk, but not to eliminate it.

CMOs may be guaranteed by government or U.S. government agencies or may be backed by those individual mortgages that are not guaranteed by government agencies. The latter type, called "private label" CMOs, generally sell at higher yields than agency-backed CMOs because of the higher risks. CMOs are very difficult to compare on a risk-return basis as a result of the prepayment uncertainty.

CMOs may provide monthly or quarterly payments to investors, and the amount paid as interest or principal will vary by tranche. While the CMO tranche will often have a stated maturity, it is possible that the tranche will mature sooner if borrowers pay off the underlying mortgages sooner than anticipated. The yield to the investor in a CMO will usually be higher than comparable Treasury securities, but lower than the interest rates on the underlying mortgage loans.

With a very basic tranche structure, a CMO would divide principal and interest payments such that the first tranche would receive all principal payments initially and would be the only tranche receiving principal until it had been fully paid (matured) and retired, then principal would move to the second tranche, and so on. In the meantime, higher tranches that are not currently receiving principal payments are receiving interest payments. A simplified example is illustrated in the chart below:

	Years 1 – 5	Years 6 – 10	Years 11 – 15
Tranche 1	Interest + principal	retired	retired
Tranche 2	Interest only	Interest + principal	retired
Tranche 3	Interest only	Interest only	Interest + principal

In this chart, the investors in Tranche 1 receive payments of principal and interest for the first five years, and then that tranche is fully paid and retired. Investors in Tranche 2 receive interest only in the first five years, receive interest and principal in years six through ten, and then that tranche is fully paid and retired. Investors in Tranche 3 receive interest only in the first 10 years and then receive interest and principal in years 11 through 15.

CMO interest payments are taxed as ordinary income at the federal, state, and local levels.

The minimum investment in a CMO may be as small as $1,000. CMOs trade in the over-the-counter market, but are not as liquid as other types of securities such as Treasuries. The actual degree of liquidity for each individual CMO can vary widely.

HEDGE FUNDS

Hedge funds are alternative investments that use pools of money to acquire a variety of assets and employ a wide range of investment strategies. Hedge funds may be aggressively managed, make use of derivatives, create short positions, use leverage, and invest in both domestic and international markets with the goal of generating high returns (either in an absolute sense or over a specified market benchmark). The fund's general manager has virtually complete discretion as to how funds are invested. The strategies employed are proprietary and may not be disclosed in any detail. Long short, global-macro, market-neutral, and merger- arbitrage funds are several of the more popular strategies.

Investopedia describes hedge funds as typically being organized as offshore limited partnerships open to a limited number of accredited investors and requiring a large initial minimum investment. Investments in hedge funds are illiquid and typically require investors to keep their money in the fund for at least one year, a time known as the lock-up period. There is usually a withdrawal policy that specifies that withdrawals are limited to certain intervals such as quarterly or bi-annually, require advance notification to the fund, and are at the discretion of the fund manager.

(http://www.investopedia.com/terms/h/hedgefund.asp#ixzz3ZHy 1DaV0)

Since hedge funds are private they are not subject to the normal disclosure and regulatory requirements of publicly traded securities. There is no secondary market for the fund. Hedge funds self-report their returns. Hedge funds typically charge 1% to 2% for assets under management (AUM) and 10% to 20% of gains. Compensating managers via a distribution of a percentage of profits is referred to as **"carried interest"**. If the profits are produced from the sale of investments held longer than three years (the Tax Cuts and Jobs Act of 2017 increased the carried interest holding period requirement from one year to three years), the carried interest is taxed as a long-term capital gain, making it an attractive method of compensation. This method of compensation is thought to align the interests of the managers with the interests of the investors.

Given the lack of liquidity, risks, high fees, and availability to only accredited investors, hedge funds are not suitable or available for the general investing public.

Hedge Fund Alternatives

There are two hedge-fund-like alternatives available to the non-accredited investor: fund of funds and liquid alternative funds.

A fund of funds is a mutual fund that invests in hedge funds and offers diversification, liquidity, and availability to non-accredited investors. However, there are now two management fees, the hedge funds fees and the fund of funds fees. Given the high fees it is difficult for the investment to produce gains for any investor.

Liquid alternative funds are mutual funds that attempt to mimic the strategies of hedge funds. They are priced daily, have lower minimums for purchase, provide liquidity, and offer transparency at lower costs. This is a relatively new concept available to the general non-accredited investing public, and it is not known how the concept will perform under stressful market conditions.

Hedge funds, funds of funds, and liquid alternative funds are not generally appropriate for conservative investors, investors that require current income, need liquidity, have low or moderate risk tolerance, or have only moderate net worth.

MANAGED FUTURES

Managed futures are an alternative investment class consisting of futures contracts managed by professional money managers, known as "commodity trading advisors" (CTAs). CTAs manage their clients' assets using proprietary trading systems that may be long or short futures contracts in various precious metal, commodities, foreign currency, stock indexes, or interest rate contracts. Management fees are typically 2% of AUM plus 20% of gains. The advertised benefits of managed futures are diversification and low or negative correlation with equities. There are no expected returns, uncertain correlation benefits, unproven history as a portfolio investment, opaque, limited access, and extremely high cost. Managed futures are not recommended for the general investor.

PRIVATE EQUITY FUNDS

Private equity funds are pools of money that make focused investments in other companies. They have high minimum investment requirements and no liquidity. Private equity funds typically take the legal form of a limited partnership designed to liquidate after about 10 years. Buyout funds and venture capital funds are two of the primary types of private equity funds.

Buyout funds acquire other companies, attempt to improve operations at the acquired companies by taking an active role in management, and then sell the companies. These funds typically employ a high degree of debt financing and are also known as "leveraged buyout funds". They may take a company private or acquire a privately held company.

Venture capital funds typically provide start-up capital or expansion capital for entrepreneurs. If the business venture is successful, the investors may profit significantly from an initial public offering (IPO) of the previously privately held business, or the company may be sold to another company.

Private equity funds typically charge an asset management fee of 2%, and other types of fees are also common, including incentive fees based on the performance of the fund. Private equity funds are often structured as limited partnerships with the fund manager serving as the general partner who is responsible for investment decisions. Although the general partners may not contribute capital, they are compensated through distributions of profits (often 20% or more of profits). This method of compensation is referred to as "**carried interest**", as described for hedge fund managers earlier in this topic. This method of compensation is thought to align the interests of the managers with the interests of the investors.

Private equity funds are not recommended for the general investor due to their high minimum investment requirements, lack of liquidity, and risk. They are not designed to be traded and typically provide no liquidity.

Private equity funds should be considered only by high net worth individual investors who can manage to have their investment tied up for 10 years or more, do not need current income from the investment, have an aggressive risk tolerance, and are making an investment that represents only a small portion of their investment portfolio.

BANK LOAN FUNDS

Bank loan funds are mutual funds that invest in loans that banks make to corporations. The corporations are often below investment grade BBB- by S&P and typically pay a floating interest rate reset every 30, 60, or 90 days, with the lending banks receiving premiums over a chosen benchmark, usually LIBOR. These loans have seniority in the event of default or bankruptcy, and they take precedence over all other claims except those initiated by the IRS, but default risk must still be considered.

There are a few open-end mutual funds in the sector, but most have expensive sales loads, and a few, due to the nature of the asset class, limit withdrawals to once quarterly. Closed-end funds, which often trade at a discount to their net asset values (NAV) and pay above average dividends, may be more attractive but are riskier due to leverage.

Bank loan funds have less interest rate risk in a rising rate environment since they have a floating rate, which will adjust upward. However, due to the below investment grade credit quality, bank loan funds are subject to price declines in a stock market decline. If many investors decide to sell their bank loan fund at the same time, the fund may not actually have the cash to pay for those redemptions. This could cause the price of bank-loan funds to decline even further.

While bank loan funds appeal to investors seeking income, they are vulnerable to defaults, suffer from a lack of liquidity, and should be treated as aggressive investments not appropriate for conservative investors without high net worth and high-risk tolerance.

TANGIBLE ASSETS

Unlike financial assets, tangible assets have a physical existence. Examples of tangible assets are real estate, gold, and collectibles. The market for tangible assets is somewhat different from the market for financial assets. The market for financial assets is well organized, especially for exchange-traded securities, while the market for tangible assets is quite informal, with no organized center. For this reason, price quotations are not readily available, and the volume of transactions is not usually recorded. Therefore, the market for physical assets is not nearly as efficient as the market for financial assets. Also, in most cases, there is no government regulation to prevent fraud.

Still, tangible assets have a place in many portfolios because they provide diversification. The returns on most financial assets tend to move in the same direction, but the returns on physical assets may have a negative correlation with the returns on financial assets. Prices of tangible assets tend to do better in times of inflation than will prices of financial assets. Thus, physical assets should complement, not replace, financial assets.

There are some risks that are unique to investments in tangible assets. Not only is there a risk of market fluctuation, but there is the risk that consumer taste may change, for example, in the art market. Also, there is the risk of not keeping pace with inflation, as well as the risk of theft and fraud. There is also a liquidity risk since physical assets are not as liquid or marketable as financial assets.

As with most illiquid markets, there is a big difference between the bid and the ask price. In addition, selling physical assets may involve sales commissions. Many physical assets will have to be insured as well.

Collectibles

Collectibles, such as baseball cards, antiques, or fine art, do not have a highly organized secondary market, nor is there much government regulation. Consequently, liquidity risk and possibilities for fraud are high. Collectibles are generally less marketable and may have higher commissions than financial assets. Prices of collectibles tend to rise with inflation, though they are subject to loss due to changes in consumer tastes. The value of collectibles is directly related to their scarcity and physical condition. Collectibles can be added to a portfolio for diversification since there is a low correlation between collectibles and financial assets.

Collectibles are assets such as art, antiques, and oriental rugs. Most collectibles are purchased through dealers who make a market in these items. This means they both buy and sell items. When dealers sell items on consignment, the commission can be quite large. While an individual can seek to sell an asset privately, the dealers and auction houses can usually obtain better prices.

The scarcity factor enhances the value of all collectibles. The condition and quality of the objects affect value, as does the reputation of the artist. Collectibles also have value to the investor in terms of the enjoyment which they provide the owner. Therefore, the value of collectibles is very subjective. Investors in collectibles should attempt to become as knowledgeable as possible in a specific area, rather than trying to diversify into many areas.

Net long-term gains from sales of collectibles are taxed at the lesser of the taxpayer's ordinary income rate or 28%.

Natural Resources

Investments in natural resources like timber or oil can be made directly or by buying shares in companies with large holdings of these resources. The supply of these resources is highly inelastic (cannot be increased very quickly). Therefore, any increase in the demand for them causes their value to rise significantly. Conversely, if the demand decreases, the value of the resource will drop precipitously.

An investment in land might be made because of the natural resources the land contains. Oil and timber are examples of natural resources in which one may invest. The investor may invest in the resource itself, in the stock of companies with large holdings of natural resources, in specialized limited partnerships, or in natural resource mutual funds.

Precious Metals

Investors wanting to invest in precious metals, such as gold or silver, can either purchase the actual metal, a futures contract, or an exchange-traded fund. There are several companies that specialize in precious metals, including Monex, which can assist clients in the different investment options.

An inflation hedge protects the investor from the devastating effects of inflation. An inflation hedge is effective when the real return on the underlying asset (or return adjusted for inflation) increases as inflation increases. By comparison, the real return on most investments declines as inflation increases. Gold and real estate have long been considered inflation hedges.

The essential difference between gold and other real assets is that gold is more liquid than real estate, gems, art, and antiques. Further, it is easier to discern the true value of gold since it is extensively traded, and transaction prices are widely published.

There are several different ways to invest in gold, including gold bullion, gold bars, numismatic coins, stocks in companies that mine gold, and gold ETFs.

Gold mutual funds, as the name implies, are funds which specialize in gold investments. As with other types of mutual funds, the funds provide diversification for the investor and provide professional management otherwise unavailable to the small investor.

Gold futures and options provide the investor with organized and regulated markets, which means greater liquidity. The futures market provides significant leverage, which implies a huge potential for gains as well as losses. The U.S. government, as well as foreign governments, have a significant influence on the price of gold which may be hard for the investor to predict, and wrong guesses are hugely magnified in the futures market.

Gold options and commodities offer the potential for significant leverage. Losses are limited in the options market to the price of the option.

TOPIC 41 – APPLICATION QUESTIONS

1. Which of the following statements concerning REITS is correct?

   A. Dividends paid to individuals by REITs generally qualify for long term capital gains rates.
   B. Shares in one REIT can provide an investor with a diversified real estate portfolio.
   C. Shares of a REIT are redeemed with the fund and do not trade on an exchange.
   D. A REIT is a nontaxable entity like a limited partnership and passes income and losses through to shareholders.

2. All of the following statements correctly describe drawbacks of direct real estate investment, EXCEPT:

   A. The investment is not liquid.
   B. The market for real estate is local, and mortgage payments are relatively fixed over the term of the loan.
   C. The asset cannot be moved when the investor moves away, and changing or adapting the property is difficult.
   D. Investors are unlikely to be able to benefit from use of leverage.

3. Which of the following statements concerning outright ownership of real estate by an individual investor is (are) correct?

   (1) The investor will have full personal liability for negligent acts arising out of the ownership and use of the property.
   (2) Tax benefits are not passed through to the extent that they are for investors in limited partnerships.
   (3) The investor is restricted in his or her ability to convey title to portions of the property.

   A. (1) only
   B. (1) and (2) only
   C. (2) and (3) only
   D. (1), (2), and (3)

4. Which of the following statements concerning the requirements for a real estate investment trust (REIT) is (are) correct?

   (1) A REIT must be at least 75% invested in real estate, government securities, or cash.
   (2) A REIT must distribute at least 90% of its annual taxable income.
   (3) A REIT may not be a real estate developer.
   (4) An investor's interest in a REIT must be fully transferable.

   A. (1) only
   B. (2) and (4) only
   C. (1), (2), and (4) only
   D. (1), (2), (3), and (4)

5. Which of the following statements could a financial planner appropriately make to a client concerning investing in real estate?

(1) Direct ownership of real estate is an excellent investment for short- or long-term investors.
(2) For a long-term hedge against inflation, an equity REIT is preferable to a mortgage REIT.
(3) For diversification and liquidity, a REIT is preferable to direct ownership of residential real estate.
(4) Studies have amply shown that master limited partnerships will outperform the stock market in the long term.

    A. (1) and (3) only
    B. (2) and (3) only
    C. (1), (2), and (4) only
    D. (1), (2), (3), and (4)

6. All of the following are disadvantages of investing in a non-traded REIT, EXCEPT:

    A. The commissions are generally high, and the non-traded REIT may be illiquid.
    B. The initial investment in the non-traded REIT may not be guaranteed.
    C. Non-traded REITs are not required to distribute 90% of taxable income to investors.
    D. Distributions from a non-traded REIT may be suspended for a period of time.

7. Which of the following statements concerning investments in REITs in correct?

    A. An investor who seeks income and appreciation should invest in a mortgage REIT.
    B. The dividends from hybrid REITs are taxed at the same rate as long term capital gains.
    C. The dividends from equity REITs are taxed as ordinary income.
    D. An investor who seeks high levels of income without much appreciation should invest in an equity REIT.

8. Which of the following questions would be important for a financial planner to consider in determining whether the philosophy of a REIT is suitable for a client?

(1) What limits does the REIT place on leverage?
(2) Will the REIT focus on income or capital growth?
(3) May the client invest small amounts and add to the investment?

    A. (1) and (2) only
    B. (2) and (3) only
    C. (1) and (3) only
    D. (1), (2), and (3)

9. Which of the following statements concerning the advantages of investing in a real estate limited partnership (RELPs) is (are) correct?

    (1) Income, deductions, and credits flow through to the limited partners.
    (2) Limited partnerships have greater liquidity and diversification than other real estate investments.
    (3) Limited partners are only liable for the original amount of their investment.

    A. (1) only
    B. (1) and (3) only
    C. (2) and (3) only
    D. (1), (2), and (3)

10. Which of the following statements correctly identify(ies) differences between master limited partnerships and other limited partnerships?

    (1) MLPs are traded on the major stock exchanges; limited partnerships are not.
    (2) Some income distributions from MLPs are portfolio income; income distributions from limited partnerships are passive income.
    (3) MLPs are more liquid and often more diversified than limited partnerships.

    A. (1) only
    B. (1) and (2) only
    C. (2) and (3) only
    D. (1), (2), and (3)

11. Which of the following real estate investments would be recommended for a conservative investor seeking current income for retirement?

    A. A master limited partnership
    B. A mortgage REIT
    C. An S corporation investing in commercial real estate
    D. Outright ownership of subdivided building lots

12. Which of the following risks are associated with investing in physical assets?

    (1) Market risk
    (2) Theft risk
    (3) Fraud risk
    (4) Liquidity risk

    A. (1) and (4) only
    B. (2) and (3) only
    C. (2), (3), and (4)
    D. (1), (2), (3), and (4)

13. All of the following are factors in the valuation of collectibles, EXCEPT:

    A. Scarcity value
    B. Published prices in tables in the financial pages
    C. Consumer tastes
    D. Physical condition

14. Which of the following factors should be considered when valuing a real estate investment?

(1) After-tax cash flow, calculated as net after-tax earnings, plus depreciation minus principal repayment
(2) Net operating income divided by an appropriate capitalization rate
(3) The cost of the investment, which is calculated by adding maintenance costs, depreciation, and taxes to rentals

    A. (1) only
    B. (1) and (2) only
    C. (1) and (3) only
    D. (1), (2), and (3)

15. All of the following statements about alternative investments are correct, EXCEPT:

A. Alternative investments are assets that do not fall in the traditional asset classes of cash, equities, or bonds
B. Alternative investments are purchased for their high correlation to equities and bonds and are available only to accredited investors
C. Alternative investments typically are actively managed, use leverage to enhance returns, have limited or no liquidity, and high fees
D. Liquid alternative investments refer to mutual funds and ETFs that mimic the investment strategies of hedge funds and are available to non-accredited investors

16. Which of the following lists of characteristics best describe alternative investments?

A. Illiquid, high fees, high returns, high risks, use leverage, high correlation with stocks, passive management, moderately regulated
B. Only available to institutional and accredited individual investors, passive management, illiquid, high fees, not for conservative investors
C. Highly regulated, low fees and risk, complex structure, available to the general public, active management, good way for a conservative investor to gain diversification
D. Illiquid, high fees and risk, use leverage, low correlation with equities and bonds, little or no regulation, active management, must be an institutional or accredited individual investor, not recommended for conservative investors

17. Which of the following is the best reason(s) to invest in alternative investments?

A. To achieve additional risk reduction through the addition of a low correlation asset
B. To improve current income and achieve a higher rate of investment return
C. To add a high return, liquid asset to the portfolio
D. To increase the diversification of the portfolio with a low cost asset that is appropriate for the average investor

18. Which of the following statements best describes private placements?

  A. Private placements are purchased by individuals for their increased return and liquidity
  B. Private placements are available to the general public and can be purchased through most brokerage firms
  C. Private placements are exempt from SEC registration under Regulation D
  D. Individuals are the primary purchasers of private placements

19. All of the following statements concerning partnership interests are correct, EXCEPT:

  A. A Real Estate Limited Partnership (RELP) is a passive investment; an individual may use any losses to offset passive income
  B. A REMIC (Real Estate Mortgage Investment Conduit) separates interest and principal payments into separately traded securities referred to as tranches that may have different interest-rate payments, maturities, and stipulations for prepayment
  C. Non-publicly traded or privately offered limited partnership interests are not suitable for the average investor since they are usually illiquid, invest in riskier investments, do not permit limited partners to participate in management, and may restrict the sale of the partnership
  D. Losses from MLPs can be used to offset income from non-publicly traded or other publicly traded limited partnerships and can allow investors to defer much of their personal income tax liability for years into the future

20. Bob, a moderate risk tolerance investor, is 50, married, with current family taxable income of $150,000, a net worth of $1,500,000, exclusive of equity in his home, all in nonqualified investment accounts. He plans to retire at age 66. Bob needs current income to pay for his daughter's college expenses. Which of the following investment portfolios is most appropriate for Bob?

  A. 30% S&P index fund, 15% international index fund, 20% mortgage REIT, 20% medium-term corporate bond fund, 5% money market fund, and 10% hedge fund
  B. 30% money market fund, 20% large cap stock mutual fund, 15% international index fund, 25% MLP, 10% private equity fund
  C. 5% money market fund, 45% US Total Market index fund, 15% international index fund, 35% medium-term municipal bond fund
  D. 60% S&P 500 Index fund, 20% international fund, and 20% managed futures fund

21. All of the following are characteristics of collateralized mortgage obligations (CMOs), EXCEPT:

  A. CMOs are backed by pools of mortgages.
  B. CMOs pay principal back monthly in the early years for all classes.
  C. CMOs are grouped into series that have stated maturities.
  D. CMOs may offer 10 to 12 classes, called "tranches."

22. All of the following are characteristics of collateralized mortgage obligations (CMOs), EXCEPT:

   A. CMOs pay a fixed rate of interest.
   B. Cash flows from CMOs are used to pay back principal one tranche at a time.
   C. CMOs control prepayment risk but do not eliminate it.
   D. CMOs are designed to minimize the otherwise very high default risk associated with the underlying mortgages.

23. Which of the following is a characteristic of collateralized mortgage obligations (CMOs)?

   A. Automatic reinvestment of principal as each obligation matures.
   B. Good for matching a specific investment horizon.
   C. Payment of equal amounts of principal and interest to all investors.
   D. Writing of options on securities by the security issuer.

24. Which of the following statements concerning the disadvantages of a direct investment in real estate is (are) correct?

   (1) Real estate requires extensive management effort.
   (2) The substantial leverage required is usually a disadvantage for investors during an inflationary period.
   (3) Commercial real estate typically requires a large commitment of funds over a long period of time.

   A. (1) only
   B. (1) and (3) only
   C. (2) and (3) only
   D. (1), (2), and (3)

25. Which of the following statements concerning the advantages of an investment in a REIT is (are) correct?

   (1) The trustee provides centralized management.
   (2) Investors have limited liability like stockholders in a corporation.
   (3) REIT expenses pass through as deductions to the owners' individual tax returns.

   A. (1) only
   B. (1) and (2) only
   C. (2) and (3) only
   D. (1), (2), and (3)

26. Which of the following statements concerning the advantages of a direct investment in real estate is (are) correct?

    (1) Residential real estate has relatively high liquidity.
    (2) Real estate has tax-shelter potential.
    (3) Real estate is a hedge against inflation.

    A. (1) only
    B. (1) and (2) only
    C. (2) and (3) only
    D. (1), (2), and (3)

27. All of the following are critical factors in assessing the quality of management for a REIT, EXCEPT:

    A. Dividend payout record
    B. Expense ratios
    C. Vacancy rates
    D. Comparison to small-cap index

28. A cash flow valuation of an income-producing property takes into account which of the following variables?

    (1) Taxes
    (2) Projected rental income
    (3) Projected reinvestment rates

    A. (1) only
    B. (1) and (2) only
    C. (2) and (3) only
    D. (1), (2), and (3)

29. Which of the following statements concerning an investment in land is (are) correct?

    (1) Gain on the sale of land is taxed at capital gains rates for investors but at ordinary income rates for professional real estate agents.
    (2) Land is typically held for capital appreciation but often contains zoning risks.
    (3) Location is one of the most important variables to consider when evaluating a possible purchase of land.

    A. (1) and (2) only
    B. (2) and (3) only
    C. (1) and (3) only
    D. (1), (2), and (3)

30. All of the following statements concerning alternative investments are correct, EXCEPT:

    A. Hedge funds have high expense charges, are illiquid, lack transparency, are only available to accredited investors, typically use leverage, are highly regulated, and self-report their returns
    B. Funds of funds and liquid alternative funds are alternatives to direct hedge fund investing and are available to non-accredited investors
    C. Private equity funds charge high fees, have no liquidity, typically have a 10 year life, and take the form of either venture capital funds or buy-out funds
    D. Bank loan funds are mutual funds that invest in loans banks make to corporations, have a floating rate, are subject to credit risk, and may lose value during stock market declines

For practice answering case questions related to Topic 41, please answer the following questions in the cases included in the Appendix at the back of the textbook.

Case	Questions
Donaldson	14, 15, 16, 17, and 18
Hilbert Stores, Inc.	
Maxwell	
Beals	
Mocsin	
Eldridge	
Young	
Johnson	
Thomas	25
Jim and Brenda Quinn	29, 31, 47, 48, 49, 50, and 51

APPENDIX

DONALDSON CASE

Joe and Mary Donaldson, both in their late forties, have one child, Matthew, age 15. Matthew probably will be attending the local state university as a commuting student beginning in three years. The annual cost of tuition, books, and fees there this year is about $8,500, a total that the Donaldson's expect to grow at about an 8 percent compound annual rate in each of the next several years.

Joe and Mary view themselves as shrewd investors. Over the years they have accumulated the following diverse list of securities designed to help pay for Matthew's college education:

- 100 shares of Alpha Corp. common stock, traded in the over-the-counter market; current market price is about $30 per share, the same as a year ago; current annual dividend is $1.00 per share and is expected to grow at a rate of about 5 percent per year for the next several years.

- Three tax-exempt municipal bonds issued by the government of the city where the Donaldson's live; each bond has a $1,000 face amount, is selling for about $980 currently, the same price as a year ago, has a 6 percent annual coupon rate, and is scheduled to mature 4 years from now.

- Five recently acquired zero-coupon bonds issued by Beta Corp. several years ago and scheduled to mature in 5 years at a face value of $1,000 each; current market price of each bond is $920.

- Two bonds issued by Gamma Corp. several years ago; each bond has a $1,000 face amount, a 9 percent annual coupon rate, and a call price equal to the face amount plus one year's interest; the bonds are currently selling at $1,020 each, the same price as a year ago, and may be called at any time prior to their maturity date, which is 6 years from now; the coupon interest payments are made once per year.

- 100 shares of Delta Corp. common stock that is listed on an organized securities exchange; historically, this stock has exhibited a beta of about 1.3; the stock currently is selling for about $7.00 per share and pays no dividend.

DONALDSON CASE
APPLICATION QUESTIONS

1. If the Donaldsons' municipal bonds could be sold for $1,020, which of the following statements is correct?

(Topic 33)

A. The Donaldsons will receive $1,020 for each bond at the time the bonds mature.
B. The Donaldsons can sell the bonds and owe no federal income tax for the year on the bonds.
C. The Donaldsons can sell the bonds and pay only capital gains on the increase in price of the bonds.
D. If the Donaldsons sell the bonds, they will owe federal capital gains tax on the price appreciation and federal income tax on the interest.

2. Which of the following statements concerning the Gamma Corp. bonds are correct?

(Topic 33)

(1) The bonds are now selling at a premium.
(2) The bonds have a current yield that is higher than their coupon rate.
(3) The bonds' call feature is of no value to Gamma Corp. at the present time.

    A. (1) and (2) only
    B. (1) and (3) only
    C. (2) and (3) only
    D. (1), (2), and (3)
    E. (1) only

3. Which of the following statements correctly describes the federal income tax treatment of the Donaldsons' Beta Corp. zero-coupon bonds?

(Topic 33)

A. The difference between $1,000 per bond and $920 per bond will be taxed as a capital gain in the year in which the bonds mature.
B. The annual appreciation in the value of each bond will be taxed as ordinary income in each of the next five years.
C. There is no federal income tax on zero-coupon bonds because such bonds provide no annual cash flow to the investor.
D. The difference between $1,000 per bond and $920 per bond will be taxed as ordinary income in the year in which the bonds mature.
E. The annual appreciation in the value of each bond will be taxed as a capital gain in each of the next five years.

4. Which of the following would be likely to lead to an exercise of the call privilege by the Gamma Corp.?

(Topics 34 and 33)

(1) A sharp increase in the general level of interest rates in the economy
(2) The passage of 5 years
(3) An increase in the size of the call premium

    A. (1) only
    B. (2) only
    C. (1) and (2) only
    D. (1), (2), and (3)
    E. Neither (1), nor (2), nor (3)

5. If the risk-free interest rate is now 3% and the market interest rate is 9%, what would be the Donaldsons' required rate of return, according to the capital asset pricing model, on the Delta Corp. common stock?

(Topic 35)

A. 9.9%   D. 11.7%

B. 10.3%   E. 12.1%

C. 10.8%

6. Are the Donaldsons actually earning more than the CAPM required rate of return on the Delta Corp. stock?

(Topic 35)

A. No, because they are not earning any rate of return on the Delta Corp. stock.

B. Yes, because the stock is selling at a very low price of $7.00 per share.

C. No, because the beta of 1.3 indicates that the Delta Corp. stocks price is more volatile than that of an average stock.

D. Yes, because the beta of 1.3 is greater than 1.0.

E. The answer cannot be determined from the information provided.

7. If the Donaldsons are in a combined (federal, state, and local) marginal income tax bracket of 35% and their AGI is below $250,000, what is the taxable-equivalent current yield they are realizing on their municipal bonds?

(Topic 36)

A. 2.10%   D. 9.42%

B. 3.90%   E. 9.96%

C. 6.12%

8. Which of the following will be the compound annual rate of return the Beta Corp. zero-coupon bonds will provide if the Donaldsons hold the bonds until they mature?

(Topic 36)

A. 1.68%   D. 8.70%

B. 1.74%   E. 16.00%

C. 2.37%

9. If the Gamma Corp. bonds are called three years from now, which of the following would be the yield to call for the Donaldsons from today until the time of the call?

(Topic 36)

A. 2.91%   D. 11.68%

B. 8.22%   E. 12.34%

C. 10.88%

10. The Donaldsons are considering liquidating the present portfolio and investing the proceeds elsewhere at a higher rate of return. They estimate that the liquidation would produce a cash fund of about $12,500 after selling costs. If so, what after-tax rate of return would the Donaldsons have to earn on the fund during the next three years in order to have about $17,750 available at the start of Matthew's freshman year?

(Topic 36)

A. 9.6%   D. 13.3%

B. 10.1%   E. 13.8%

C. 12.4%

11. Which of the following is the Donaldsons' current yield on the Alpha Corp. common stock?

(Topic 36)

A. 3.3%
B. 3.5%
C. 5.0%
D. 33%
E. Cannot be determined from the information provided.

12. What should happen to the intrinsic value of the Alpha Corp. common stock if Joe and Mary now decide that the stock is much riskier than they have previously been thinking?

(Topic 38)

A. The intrinsic value of the stock should fall because Joe and Mary should adopt a higher required rate of return on the stock.
B. The intrinsic value of the stock should fall because many investors will begin selling the stock, thus lowering its market price.
C. The intrinsic value of the stock should not change because a stock's intrinsic value is not affected by its riskiness.
D. The intrinsic value of the stock should rise because its increased riskiness will cause speculators to bid up its market price.
E. The intrinsic value of the stock should rise because the issuer will have to increase the dividend.

13. If Joe and Mary's required rate of return on the Alpha Corp. common stock is 10% per year, according to the constant-dividend-growth formula, Alpha's stock has an intrinsic value of about

(Topic 38)

A. $5.00 per share
B. $10.50 per share
C. $21.00 per share
D. $30.00 per share
E. $31.50 per share

******

The Donaldsons have received advice from two sources as to how to invest the $12,500 of sales proceeds from the present portfolio during the next 3-7 years in order to meet the costs of Matthew's college education. One person has suggested buying a small piece of unimproved real estate. The other has suggested investing in a real estate investment trust (REIT).

Matching Questions: Match the type of real estate investment (A or B) with each of the investment characteristics below (14-18).

A. Purchase of a piece of unimproved real estate
B. Investment in a REIT

14. Lower degree of liquidity _____

(Topic 41 and 33)

15. Higher transfer costs _____

(Topic 41 and 33)

16. Higher degree of diversification _____

(Topic 41 and 33)

17. Lower opportunity for dollar cost averaging _____

(Topic 41 and 33)

18. Lower degree of potential legal liability

_____

(Topic 41 and 33)

HILBERT STORES, INC. CASE

Presented below is a simplified balance sheet, as well as certain supplementary information, for Hilbert Stores, Inc., a chain of retail department stores located in several states in the southeastern portion of the U.S.

Assets

Cash & marketable securities	$ 75,000
Inventory (average)	700,000
Accounts receivable	225,000
Fixed assets, net of depreciation	1,000,000
Total assets	$2,000,000

Liabilities

Miscellaneous accruals	$ 50,000
Accounts payable	300,000
First mortgage bonds, $1,000 par,	
7% coupon rate	100,000
Debenture bonds, $1,000 par,	
8% coupon rate	200,000
Total liabilities	$ 650,000

Owners Equity

Preferred stock, $5 par,	
10% dividend rate	$ 50,000
Common stock, $1 par	200,000
Retained earnings	1,100,000
Total owners equity	$1,350,000
Total liabilities & owners equity	$2,000,000

Supplementary Information

The company's sales, all on credit, totaled $3,200,000 and its net income after all expenses and taxes and after the payment of preferred dividends in the year just ended was $160,000. Of this, $40,000 was paid to the common stockholders as cash dividends. The company's common stock is traded over the counter and has a current market price of about $12 per share.

HILBERT STORES, INC. CASE
APPLICATION QUESTIONS

1. Which of the following statements concerning Hilbert Stores, Inc.'s preferred stock are correct?

(Topic 33)

(1) It pays an annual dividend of $.50 per share.
(2) The preferred dividend must be paid if the company has sufficient earnings to do so.
(3) The preferred dividend must be paid before any dividend can be paid to the common stockholders.

    A. (1) and (2) only
    B. (1) and (3) only
    C. (2) and (3) only
    D. (1), (2), and (3)
    E. (3) only

2. The main difference between debenture bonds and first mortgage bonds such as those issued by Hilbert Stores, Inc. is that debenture bonds typically

(Topic 33)

    A. have lower coupon rates of interest than first mortgage bonds.
    B. are riskier for an investor than first mortgage bonds.
    C. have shorter maturities than first mortgage bonds.
    D. are more heavily collateralized than first mortgage bonds.
    E. have higher priority on assets in time of liquidation.

3. A financial analyst recently referred to the bonds of Hilbert Stores, Inc. as junk bonds. By using this term, the analyst was pointing out that the bonds

(Topic 33)

    A. are in default.
    B. are of investment quality.
    C. are not recommended for purchase.
    D. are rated below investment quality by the rating services.
    E. are issued by manufacturing concerns in the rust-belt region of the country.

4. What is the payout ratio for Hilbert Stores, Inc.?

(Topic 38)

    A. 5%   D. 25%
    B. 15%   E. 33%
    C. 20%

5. Retained earnings are net income not distributed to shareholders. How much was added to the retained earnings balance of Hilbert Stores, Inc. as a result of the most recent year's results?

(Topic 38)

    A. $120,000   D. $3,200,000
    B. $160,000   E. $3,350,000
    C. $2,000,000

6. Which of the following is the current ratio for Hilbert Stores, Inc.?

(Topic 38)

    A. .86 to 1   D. 3.08 to 1
    B. 1.54 to 1   E. 4.31 to 1
    C. 2.86 to 1

7. Which of the following is the acid-test or quick ratio for Hilbert Stores, Inc.?

(Topic 38)

A. .21 to 1   D. 3.7 to 1
B. .86 to 1   E. 3.9 to 1
C. 2.2 to 1

8. Which of the following is the inventory turnover ratio for Hilbert Stores, Inc.?

(Topic 38)

A. .23 to 1   D. 4.57 to 1
B. 2.86 to 1   E. 5.06 to 1
C. 3.72 to 1

9. Which of the following is the receivables turnover ratio for Hilbert Stores, Inc.?

(Topic 38)

A. 1.6 to 1   D. 14.22 to 1
B. 3.44 to 1   E. 15.11 to 1
C. 8.89 to 1

10. Which of the following is the average collection period on the receivables of Hilbert Stores, Inc.?

(Topic 38)

A. 8.89 days   D. 34.41 days
B. 25.32 days   E. 38.09 days
C. 30.00 days

11. What were the earnings per share of Hilbert Stores, Inc. in the most recent year?

(Topic 38)

A. $.80   D. $16.00
B. $1.71   E. $18.00
C. $10.00

12. What is the price/earnings (P/E) ratio of the common stock of Hilbert Stores, Inc.?

(Topic 38)

A. 8 to 1   D. 25 to 1
B. 15 to 1   E. 28 to 1
C. 18 to 1

13. What is the return on assets for Hilbert Stores, Inc.?

(Topic 38)

A. 2%   D. 27%
B. 8%   E. 31%
C. 16%

14. What is the turnover of total assets for Hilbert Stores, Inc.?

(Topic 38)

A. 1.6 to 1   D. 4.8 to 1
B. 2.3 to 1   E. 5.9 to 1
C. 3.3 to 1

MAXWELL CASE

Clint Maxwell, a financial planner specializing in the field of investments, has made a variety of recommendations to some of his clients in recent weeks, as follows:

- Recommended to client Mrs. Evans that she sell at year end certain of her stock in which she has a capital loss, and repurchase the same stock immediately after the first of the year.

- Recommended to client Mr. Foster that he dispose of his holdings of long-term bonds because of the substantial interest rate risk the bonds represent, and replace the bonds with shares in a money market mutual fund.

- Recommended to client Ms. Grant that she commence an investment program utilizing dollar cost averaging.

- Recommended to client Dr. Hanover that Dr. Hanover purchase shares in a promising new company. Maxwell believes the shares have a 10% chance of yielding 5% per year, a 25% chance of yielding 20% per year, a 50% chance of yielding 30% per year, and a 15% chance of yielding 50% per year.

- Recommended to client Mrs. Ingram that she purchase certain convertible bonds with $1,000 face amounts. The bonds are convertible at $50 per share into stock currently selling for $48 per share. Each bond pays $80 interest once a year and matures in nine years. Nonconvertible debt of similar riskiness currently is yielding about 12%.

- Recommended to client Mr. Jefferson that he purchase for $500,000 a piece of commercial real estate that can be expected to provide net cash flows of $40,000 at the end of year 1, $60,000 at the end of years 2 through 8, and $75,000 at the end of year 9, at which time the property can also be sold for $600,000.

MAXWELL CASE
APPLICATION QUESTIONS

1. With respect to the recommendation to Mr. Foster, which of the following statements concerning money market mutual funds are correct?

(Topic 33)

(1) They tend to invest mostly in short-term securities.
(2) Among the investments in which they concentrate are U.S. Treasury bills, commercial paper, and real estate mortgages.
(3) They are characterized by a high degree of safety and of liquidity.

A. (1) and (2) only
B. (1) and (3) only
C. (2) and (3) only
D. (1) only
E. (1), (2), and (3)

2. If Mrs. Ingram buys the convertible bonds recommended by Maxwell, how many shares of stock will she receive if at some point she exercises the conversion privilege?

(Topic 33)

A. 20
B. 50
C. 100
D. 500
E. 1,000

3. With respect to Maxwell's recommendation to Mrs. Ingram, what is the present conversion value of each of the bonds *as stock*?

(Topic 33)

A. Zero
B. $960
C. $1,000
D. $1,960
E. $2,180

4. With respect to the recommendation to Mrs. Ingram, what is the investment value of each of the convertible bonds *as debt*?

(Topics 33 and 36)

A. Zero
B. $100
C. $787
D. $1,720
E. Answer cannot be determined from the information provided.

5. With respect to Maxwell's recommendation to Mr. Foster, what is the meaning of the term interest rate risk?

(Topic 34)

A. The possibility that the price of the bonds will fall because interest rates in the economy fall
B. The possibility that the issuing corporation will default on the interest payment on the bonds
C. The possibility that the fixed amount of interest paid on the bonds to the investor will lose purchasing power due to inflation
D. The possibility that the price of the bonds will fall because interest rates in the economy rise
E. The possibility that the coupon interest rate on the bonds will fall

6. If Maxwell's assessment of the shares he has recommended to Dr. Hanover is correct, which of the following is the weighted average expected return on the stock?

(Topic 36)

A. 26.5%
B. 27.5%
C. 28.0%
D. 30.0%
E. 31.7%

7. With respect to the recommendation to Mr. Jefferson, what will be the internal rate of return on this investment if all of the cash flows materialize as expected?

(Topic 36)

A. 9.13%   D. 14.06%
B. 12.82%   E. 15.11%
C. 13.11%

8. Which of the following statements concerning Maxwell's recommendation to Mrs. Evans is (are) correct?

(Topic 39)

(1) What Maxwell is recommending is called a wash sale.
(2) If Mrs. Evans follows Maxwell's advice, she will be allowed to take the capital loss at year end as an offset against some of her capital gains.

A. (1) only
B. (2) only
C. Both (1) and (2)
D. Neither (1) nor (2)

9. With respect to Maxwell's recommendation to Ms. Grant, which of the following is (are) among the advantages of dollar cost averaging?

(Topic 40)

(1) Dollar cost averaging produces a lower average cost per share.
(2) Dollar cost averaging produces a semi-compulsory form of investing.
(3) Dollar cost averaging produces time diversification.

A. (1) only
B. (2) only
C. (1) and (3) only
D. (2) and (3) only
E. (1), (2), and (3)

10. Assume that Ms. Grant follows Maxwell's advice and invests $500 each month in shares that have the following prices:

Month 1	$10	Month 4	$13
Month 2	$11	Month 5	$14
Month 3	$12	Month 6	$15

What will be Ms. Grant's average cost per share?

(Topic 40)

A. $11.41   D. $13.80
B. $12.26   E. $13.92
C. $12.50

11. If Ms. Grant does not follow Maxwell's advice to engage in dollar cost averaging but, instead, buys 40 shares of the stock each month at the prices shown in the preceding question, what will be her average cost per share?

(Topic 40)

A. $12.00
B. $12.50
C. $13.00
D. $13.50
E. Answer cannot be determined from the information provided.

BEALS CASE

James and Anne Beals had been married for 24 years and are now separated. James, who is 55 years of age, is a funeral director and is the owner of two funeral parlors. Anne is 51 years of age and owns and operates a graphics design business. The couple has two children: Ronald age 16 and Christine age 13. All of the Beals are in good health. James and Anne have simple wills leaving their entire estates to each other.

Anne Beals started her graphics design business about 8 years ago. The business is called Beals Designs, and Anne is the sole owner. In order to expand her business, Anne took out a loan about five years ago from the Bank of New York-Mellon in the amount of $50,000, and James Beals cosigned the loan. Anne has paid back $5,000 of the original loan amount, leaving a balance of $45,000. Anne makes monthly payments on the loan. The business has done well, and Anne nets about $72,000 annually after paying her expenses.

Anne has three employees. She has adopted a profit-sharing Keogh plan for herself and her employees. Although the plan offers several different investment options, Anne has her account balance invested through the plan in guaranteed investment contracts (GICs). In addition, she has invested IRA money in a balanced mutual fund. She describes herself as a conservative investor. Anne has named James as the beneficiary of her profit-sharing plan and of her IRA.

James Beals has moved out of the home that he owns with Anne as tenants by the entirety. He is currently renting an apartment for $800 per month. Since Anne and James have agreed that she will keep the house in her name, Anne makes the monthly mortgage payment. James and Anne bought the house for $180,000 and have spent $40,000 on capital improvements. The current fair market value of the house is $325,000.

The children will remain with Anne and spend vacations with their father. Anne is currently receiving child support and alimony from James. James earns approximately $120,000 annually from his business. He is also the owner of two buildings that are rented to the Beals Funeral Home, Inc. One building was purchased 22 years ago for $175,000, and the other was built 12 years ago for a cost of $350,000. Each building is now worth approximately $500,000. James is the sole stockholder and President of the Beals Funeral Home, Inc., which is an S corporation.

Beals Funeral Home, Inc. has a 401(k) plan that matches employee contributions at a rate of 50 cents for each dollar contributed by an employee on up to 6% of each employee's compensation. The company has eight employees in addition to James. The 401(k) plan offers different investment options, and James has invested his 401(k) plan contributions in a balanced mutual fund. James describes himself as a conservative investor. James has named Anne the beneficiary of his 401(k) plan account balance and of his IRA account assets.

James Beals owns a whole life insurance policy with a face amount of $200,000 and term life insurance in the amount of $300,000. Anne Beals owns a universal life insurance policy with a face amount of $200,000. James and Anne have named each other as beneficiaries of these policies. James has a disability income insurance policy that will pay him $1,000 monthly if he is disabled.

Since James Beals is a funeral director, he would like to have a lavish funeral. The costs of his funeral will be in the range of $40,000. Assuming he dies today, the administrative expenses for his estate are expected to be $30,000.

JAMES BEALS

Personal Balance Sheet

Assets

Invested Assets

Cash/Cash equivalents	$ 14,500
Marketable Securities	250,000
Business Interest	800,000
Life Ins. Cash Value	35,000
	$1,099,500

Use Assets

Business real estate	$1,000,000
Personal Property	45,000
Automobiles	30,000
	$1,075,000

Retirement Plan Assets

IRA	$ 25,000
401(k)	175,000
	$ 200,000

Total Assets	$2,374,500

Liabilities

Auto Loan	$ 7,000
Mortgage *	200,000
Lawyers fees	8,000
	$ 215,000

Net Worth	$2,159,500

Total Liabilities and Net Worth	$2,374,500

---

* Business real estate: 15 years at 9 %.

ANNE BEALS

<u>Personal Balance Sheet</u>

Assets

Invested Assets

Cash/Cash equivalents	$ 2,500
Marketable Securities	150,000
Business Interest	300,000
Life Ins. Cash Value	30,000
	$482,500

Use Assets

Primary Residence	$325,000
Personal Property	52,500
Automobiles	25,000
	$402,500

Retirement Plan Assets

IRA	$ 24,500
Profit-sharing plan	75,000
	$ 99,500

Total Assets	$984,500

Liabilities

Auto Loan	$ 7,500
Lawyers fees	7,000
Business loan	45,000
Mortgage *	50,000
	$109,500

Net Worth	$875,000
Total Liabilities and Net Worth	$984,500

---

* Principal residence: originally 30 years @ 8%.

JAMES BEALS
Projected Monthly Cash Flow Statement

Cash Inflows

Salary – S Corporation	$ 8,000
Distribution – S Corporation	2,000
Net rental income	5,000
Interest income (tax-exempt)	400
Dividend income	250
Interest income (taxable)	200

Outflows

Rent	800
Food	150
Utilities	125
Transportation (gas, oil, maintenance)	150
Car payment	400
Clothing	250
Entertainment	400
Travel	500
Life insurance	200
Disability insurance	100
Auto insurance	150
Family gifts	500
Charitable gifts	300
Mortgage (business property: PITI)	2,250
Federal income tax	2,800
State income tax	600
Social Security and Medicare taxes	600
401(k) contribution	700
Savings and Investment	
Miscellaneous	100
Alimony	700
Child Support	500

ANNE BEALS
Projected Monthly Cash Flow Statement

Cash Inflows

Business income	$6,000
Interest income (tax-exempt)	500
Dividend income	50
Interest income (taxable)	100
Alimony *	700
Child Support	500

* Payments cease upon Anne's death or remarriage.

Outflows

Mortgage	1,500
Food	550
Utilities	175
Transportation (gas, oil, maintenance)	230
Car payment	300
Clothing	350
Entertainment	250
Travel	250
Life insurance	150
Auto insurance	150
Family gifts	300
Charitable gifts	100
Federal income tax	900
State income tax	200
Social Security and Medicare taxes	700
Savings and Investment	
Miscellaneous	300

JAMES BEALS – Investment Portfolio

Common Stock	Fair Market Value
Disney	$ 15,000
DuPont	10,200
Exxon	20,000
Intel	41,400
AT&T	16,200
PepsiCo	12,800
Verizon	11,200
Beals Funeral Home, Inc.	800,000
Common stock mutual fund	13,200
Balanced fund (401(k))	175,000
Municipal Bonds	
Dreyfus General Municipal Bond Fund	$ 70,000
Bonds	
Vanguard High Yield Corporate Bond Fund	$ 40,000
Income Fund (IRA)	25,000
Cash and Equivalents	
Cash	$ 4,500
Cash equivalents, incl. Money Markets	10,000
TOTAL	$1,264,500

ANNE BEALS – Investment Portfolio

Common Stocks	Fair Market Value
Cisco Systems	$ 40,000
Common stock mutual fund	10,000
Balanced fund (IRA)	24,500
Municipal Bonds	
Merrill Lynch	
Long Term Municipal Bond Fund	$ 90,000
Bonds	
Deutsche High Yield Bond Fund	$ 10,000
Cash and Equivalents	
Cash	$ 2,500
GICs – Profit-sharing plan	75,000
TOTAL	$252,000

BEALS CASE
APPLICATION QUESTIONS

1. Assume that for retirement planning purposes Anne Beals has only the investments in her profit-sharing plan and IRAs to provide for her retirement needs. What changes, if any, should be recommended to her for the investment of this retirement fund?

(Topic 33)

A. She should increase her investment in growth stocks and municipal bonds and reduce the holdings of GICs.

B. She should increase her investment in growth stocks and corporate bonds and reduce the holdings of GICs.

C. She should increase her investment in Treasury bills and corporate bonds and reduce the investment in the balanced mutual fund.

D. She should allocate all of her retirement investments to aggressive growth stocks.

E. She should maintain her existing allocation of investments.

2. Both James Beals and Anne Beals have in their investment portfolio shares of a high-yield corporate bond fund. Which of the following statements concerning this type of fund is (are) correct?

(Topic 33)

(1) It will tend to invest mainly in junk bonds.

(2) It will tend to invest in bonds that have low default risk.

(3) It will tend to invest in bonds rated lower than BBB by Standard & Poors.

A. (1) only
B. (2) only
C. (3) only
D. (1) and (2) only
E. (1) and (3) only

3. Which of the following assets in James Beals' investment portfolio probably has the lowest degree of liquidity?

(Topic 34)

A. Disney common stock
B. Vanguard bond fund
C. Beals Funeral Home, Inc. common stock
D. Cash equivalents
E. Common stock mutual fund

4. Anne Beals' common stock mutual fund was purchased two years ago for $8,000. Since then it has paid dividends at the end of each quarter as follows:

Qtr. #1 – $250	Qtr. #5 – $350
Qtr. #2 – $250	Qtr. #6 – $350
Qtr. #3 – $300	Qtr. #7 – $350
Qtr. #4 – $300	Qtr. #8 – $400

All dividends have been taken in cash. If Anne were to sell the shares today for their fair market value, what would be her approximate annual internal rate of return from this investment?

(Topic 36)

A. 14%
B. 19%
C. 26%
D. 31%
E. 33%

5. Use the same facts as in the previous question but assume that all dividends had been reinvested in the fund and thus were included in the current market value of Anne's shares, calculate Anne's approximate internal rate of return on this investment.

(Topic 36)

    A. 12%
    B. 14%
    C. 16%
    D. 18%
    E. 20%

6. If after her divorce Anne Beals altered her investment risk profile so that she became a moderately aggressive investor, which of the following changes in her investment portfolio should be recommended?

(Topic 37)

(1) A reduction in her holdings of cash
(2) An increase in her holdings of the Merrill Lynch Long-Term Municipal Bond Fund
(3) A withdrawal of the money in the GICs to invest in the common stock fund she holds outside the retirement plan
(4) A shift of investments from the Deutsche High Yield Bond Fund to a Long-Term Treasury Fund

    A. (1) only
    B. (4) only
    C. (2) and (4) only
    D. (1), (2), (3), and (4)
    E. None of the above

7. Assume that James Beals has taken a short position with respect to the Verizon common stock in his investment portfolio. Which of the following statements is correct?

(Topic 40)

(1) James can be short and long for the Verizon stock at the same time.
(2) James expects the Verizon stock to appreciate substantially soon.
(3) If a dividend is declared and paid while James is short the stock, he must provide funds to cover the declared dividend amount.

    A. (1) and (2) only
    B. (1) and (3) only
    C. (2) and (3) only
    D. (1), (2), and (3)
    E. None of the statements are correct

MOCSIN CASE

PERSONAL INFORMATION

Richard Mocsin is 46 years old and his wife Gloria is 37 years old. Richard and Gloria were married 8 years ago; it was Richard's second marriage and Gloria's first marriage. Richard and Gloria have one child, Charles, who is 6 years of age. Richard has two children by his prior marriage: Laura who is 14 years of age and Elaine who is 12. All of the children attend public schools.

Richard is a biology professor at the university and is a partner in Wizard Research Associates, a biotechnology firm that Richard started with three of his associates from the university.

ASSET INFORMATION

The Mocsins own their personal residence in joint tenancy with right of survivorship, and it is valued currently at $250,000. They purchased the home seven years ago for $175,000. They have finished the basement and added a room and bathroom at a cost of $40,000. They have a mortgage balance of $150,000. The Mocsins household furnishings are valued at $70,000, and Gloria's jewelry and furs are valued at $30,000. Richard and Gloria live in a state that follows the common law forms of property ownership.

Richard and Gloria have a joint checking account that contains $7,000 and a joint savings account that contains $15,000. Interest income on the savings account last year was $450. The Mocsins also have $12,000 in money market mutual funds that paid dividends last year of $515. Richard owns shares in a growth stock mutual fund that he purchased three years ago for $5,000, is now worth $5,750, and paid dividends last year of $100. Dividends on these shares are expected to grow by 8% per year, and Richard believes that a 10% rate of return would be appropriate for these shares with their degree of risk. Gloria owns shares in a municipal bond fund purchased for $6,300, currently valued at $7,000, and yielding $400 per year tax-free. The Mocsins jointly purchased 500 shares in Power Station, Inc., a public utility company. These shares were acquired at a cost of $6,250, are currently valued at $8,000, and pay annual dividends of $480.

Richard's father died two years ago, and his mother died last year, leaving Richard an inheritance of $150,000 in U.S. Treasury securities paying 8% interest ($12,000 annually) and a one-half interest in common with his brother in a Florida condominium. The condominium was valued in his mother's estate at $120,000 and was purchased six years ago for $125,000. Real estate taxes on the condominium, half of which Richard includes among his itemized deductions for federal income tax purposes, total $1,000. Both of Gloria's parents are still living.

The Mocsins are also joint owners of a parcel of undeveloped land in the mountains where they plan to build a vacation home. The parcel of land cost them $75,000 and is currently valued at $70,000. They have a $30,000 mortgage on the property. Interest on the mortgage is $2,700 per year. Real estate taxes are $700.

Richard owns an apartment building near the university that he rents to students. The apartment building was purchased four years ago for $95,000 and is currently valued at $125,000. The annual gross rental income from the property is $11,000. Richard has a mortgage balance of $60,000, and his interest payments total $4,950. His real estate taxes and maintenance expenses are $3,000, and depreciation is $2,850.

The Mocsins are joint owners of two automobiles. The cars are valued at $25,000 and $17,500. Richard owns a sailboat which he bought for $35,000 and is valued now at $40,000.

Richard has a one-fourth interest in the partnership, Wizard Research Associates, which is engaged in research for genetic engineering of various plants. There are no employment contracts for the partners. In addition to the partners, the firm has eight employees, including four research assistants, two secretaries, and two maintenance/hot house workers. The research assistants are paid $30,000 each, the secretaries are paid $18,000 each, and the other workers are paid $20,000 each.

Richard and his partners believe that the value of Wizard Research Associates is approximately $1 million. There has been no objective valuation, however. The largest asset of the firm is its building and grounds where the firm has a laboratory, hot houses, and fields for growing experimental plants. The building and land were purchased for $250,000, and $150,000 was allocated to the building and $100,000 to the land. Additional buildings have been added at a cost of $75,000, and the current value is estimated to be $400,000. The firm has a mortgage balance on the building and land of $150,000. The partnership has been depreciating the building for tax purposes.

INCOME TAX INFORMATION

Richard earns $60,000 in annual salary from the university, and he reports another $48,000 of net taxable income from the biotechnology firm. Gloria earns $30,000 working in public relations for a hospital. She also receives $5,000 at the beginning of each year from a trust established by her grandfather with securities valued currently at $100,000. At Gloria's death, the trust income will be paid to Charles, or if Charles is over age 25, the corpus will be distributed to him. The Mocsins file joint tax returns.

Richard pays child support for his two daughters in the amount of $400 each per month, and these payments are probably 75% of their support annually. Richard's daughters are in the custody of their mother and live with her for approximately nine months of the year. Richard is required by his divorce decree to maintain a $100,000 life insurance policy to provide child support in the event of his death.

Several years ago, Richard established custodian accounts for Laura and Elaine. Laura's account generates annual income of $1,500 and Elaine's account has annual income of $1,000.

Richard and Gloria incur home mortgage interest costs of $12,000 per year. Real estate taxes on their home are $2,500. They will pay $4,500 in state income taxes this year and $150 in personal property taxes. Their contributions to charities totaled $2,000.

RETIREMENT INFORMATION

Gloria owns IRA accounts totaling $17,000. She is now an active participant in a defined contribution pension plan through the hospital where she works, and her vested account value is $35,000. Eight percent of Richard's gross salary at the university is deducted each year and contributed to a tax-deferred annuity. The university contributes an additional six percent dollar for dollar on a tax-deferred basis. The plan is projected to pay Richard $2,500 per month when he retires at age 65 or to Gloria at his death.

One of the partners in Wizard Research Associates is age 65 and about two years away from retirement, and two partners are age 55. The partners would like to prepare for the expected retirement of the age-65 partner as well as the unexpected death or disability of any partner. The partners are also contemplating a retirement program for the firm and would like advice concerning the design.

INSURANCE INFORMATION

The university provides disability income coverage for one-third of Richard's salary, group medical expense insurance covering Richard and his family through a Health Maintenance Organization, and group term life insurance for Richard with a death benefit of $50,000. Richard owns a whole life insurance policy that will pay a death benefit of $100,000 and has a cash value of $5,500, and he owns a universal life policy with a face value of $150,000 and a cash value of $3,000. The annual premium on the whole life policy is $2,000, and the annual premium on the universal life policy is $800. Gloria has group term life insurance through her employer in a face amount that is equal to her salary.

Property and liability insurance that insures the Mocsins house for its replacement cost has an annual premium of $1,200. The Mocsins cars are insured under a Personal Auto Policy providing limits for bodily injury of $100,000/$300,000, property damage of $25,000, uninsured motorist coverage of $10,000/$20,000, no-fault benefits, and a collision deductible of $250. Richard's sailboat is insured under a yacht policy.

ESTATE PLANNING INFORMATION

Richard's will leaves his entire estate to Gloria, but if Gloria predeceases Richard, the estate will be left in trust for Richard's three children equally. Gloria's will leaves her entire estate to Richard or, if he predeceases her, to Charles.

MOCSIN CASE
APPLICATION QUESTIONS

1. Which of the following was the compound annual rate of growth in the value of the Florida condominium from the date of its purchase for $125,000 until the date of its valuation in Richard's mother's estate six years later at $120,000?

(Topic 36)

A. –0.68% D. –4.00%

B. –3.33% E. +0.68%

C. –3.71%

2. Richard's investment in the apartment building has entailed the following cash flows since he bought it.

(Topic 36)

Beginning of year 1   ($95,000)
   Purchase price

End of years 1, 2, 3, and 4 $ 2,050
   Net rental income

If today, at the end of year 4, Richard were to sell the building for $125,000, minus a 6% realtor's commission and $2,000 in closing costs, what will have been his pre-tax annual internal rate of return on this investment?

A. 4.1% D. 7.0%

B. 5.3% E. 8.2%

C. 6.5%

3. Which of the following is the current yield on Richard and Gloria's $12,000 investment in the money market mutual fund?

(Topic 36)

A. $515

B. 4.3%

C. 6.1%

D. 6.8%

E. Answer cannot be determined from the information in the case.

4. Richard and Gloria believe that the assets set aside for an education fund for Charles should be invested for maximum capital appreciation and protection against inflation. Which of the following investment vehicles would be most appropriate for achieving these goals?

(Topics 37 and 33)

A. U.S. Treasury securities

B. Growth stocks

C. Municipal bonds

D. Money market mutual funds

E. High-yield corporate bond fund

5. Based on the constant-dividend-growth valuation model, which of the following is the intrinsic value of Richard's shares in the growth stock mutual fund whose most recent dividend was $100, whose dividends are expected to grow at an 8% annual rate, and for which Richard has a 10% required rate of return?

(Topic 38)

A. $5,000 D. $6,125

B. $5,400 E. $6,319

C. $5,750

ELDRIDGE CASE

PAT AND LIBBY ELDRIDGE

FAMILY INFORMATION

Pat Eldridge, age 59, is the national director of training for a chemical company. His wife, Libby, age 57, is the financial supervisor for a small dental practice. Their three children, Tom, Dick, and Mary, are ages 35, 34, and 31, respectively. Tom and Dick are married. Tom's children are ages 8 and 5, while Dick's children are ages 6 and 2. Mary is divorced and has one child, age 10.

INCOME TAX INFORMATION

Pat's salary is $100,000 per year. He also earns $27,000 per year as a freelance consultant to a company that produces training films. Libby's salary of $35,000 per year is her only source of income.

The Eldridges are in a 22% federal income tax bracket.

RETIREMENT INFORMATION

Pat is a participant in his employer's 401(k) profit-sharing plan, contributing the maximum allowable each year, matched dollar-for-dollar by the chemical company. Libby is a participant in the dental practice's qualified target-benefit pension plan. The target is to provide $5,000 of annual retirement income in today's dollars.

Pat and Libby both expect to receive Social Security benefits when Pat retires at age 65. Pat expects that he will be eligible to receive benefits of $15,000 per year. They expect to live 25 years beyond retirement age. They do not plan to sell their home when they retire. During retirement, they expect that they will be able to earn an investment return of 6.5% after tax.

ECONOMIC INFORMATION

The Eldridges expect that inflation will average 4.5% per year both before and after they retire. Both Pat and Libby expect their salaries will increase 5% annually.

Mortgage interest rates are currently 7.0% for 30 year mortgages and 6.5% for 15 year mortgages. The lender will require three "points" for settlement. In any refinancing of the home mortgage, the Eldridges would pay the settlement costs separately.

Pat and Libby Eldridge
Statement of Financial Position
December 31, 20XX

ASSETS

Cash and cash equivalents	
H - checking account	$ 4,000
Investments	
JT - Savings account	80,000
W - Money market mutual fund	38,000
JT - Growth mutual fund	414,000
H - Miscellaneous common stocks	333,000
H - 401(k) vested balance	530,000
W - Pension plan vested balance	27,000
Use assets	
JT - Home (replacement cost of dwelling)	155,000
JT - Personal property[1]	48,000
JT - Cars	38,000
Total Assets	**$1,667,000**

LIABILITIES AND NET WORTH

Credit card balances[2]	$ 19,000
Auto loans[3]	27,000
1st mortgage on home[4]	62,000
Home equity loan[5]	21,600
Total Liabilities	$129,600
Net Worth	$1,537,400
Total Liabilities and Net Worth	$1,667,000

---

[1] Includes jewelry valued at $12,000
[2] 19.8% APR
[3] 12.9% APR
[4] 8.5%, 25-year fixed rate mortgage; principal amount last year was $66,200
[5] 9.75%, 10-year fixed rate mortgage; principal amount last year was $23,300

H = Husband
W = Wife
JT = Joint tenancy

Pat and Libby Eldridge
Statement of Cash Flows
January 1 – December 31, 20XX

Annual Inflows

H - Salary	$ 100,000
H - Consulting income	27,000
W - Salary	35,000
H/W - Investment income	4,000
Total Inflows	$166,000

Annual Outflows

Contributions to 401(k)	$ 17,500
U.S. income and FICA taxes	44,800
1st mortgage payment (P&I)	9,600
Home equity loan (P&I)	3,900
Auto loans (P&I)	12,000
Credit cards (P&I)	19,500
Property taxes	2,000
Auto and homeowners insurance	4,400
Utilities and phone	3,100
Auto operating expenses	2,800
Food	4,800
Clothing/personal care	3,500
Entertainment and travel	4,700
Medical/dental (includes premium for spouse)	1,500
Charitable contributions	3,600
Miscellaneous	1,300
Total Outflows	$139,000

INSURANCE INFORMATION

- HO-3 on home; face amount $110,000 on dwelling, $50,000 liability limit.
- PAP on both autos; liability limits $50,000/$100,000/$25,000; collision and other-than-collision coverage subject to $100 deductible.
- Group term life insurance on Pat equal to five times his annual salary; reduces to 50% of final year's salary at age 65.
- Group comprehensive major medical expense insurance through Pat's employer, covering both Pat and Libby, subject to a $250 per year family deductible, and an 80% coinsurance clause.

INVESTMENT INFORMATION

- Savings account: insured by FDIC; current interest income is $4,000 per year, which is withdrawn in cash each year.
- Money market mutual fund: no-load fund yielding 5.5 percent per year, which is reinvested in the fund. The Eldridges have designated the money market fund as their emergency fund.
- Growth mutual fund: purchased for $300,000, the yield (both income and capital appreciation) was -3.6 percent in the most recent year; in the previous five years, it was 7 percent, 9 percent, 14 percent, -2.2 percent, and 11 percent. All income is reinvested in the fund.
- Miscellaneous common stocks: purchased for $26,000, these five highly speculative, small-cap, high-tech stocks were bought by Pat on hunches and pay no dividends and there is no near-term likelihood of their doing so. The expected return for the common stocks is 12% of which at least 11% will be capital gain.
- 401(k) vested balance: allocated 50 percent to a junk bond fund and 50 percent to a guaranteed investment contract (GIC) account; rate of return in past 10 years has been 5%, 9%, 8%, 13%, 4%, 4%, 11%, 12%, 8%, and 16%. The future expected return on the 401(k) assets is 7.5%.
- Target benefit pension plan vested balance: invested as part of a separate account of the insurance company that provides the pension plan; the separate account seeks a mix of income and long-term capital growth. The expected return on these assets is 7%. The contributions by Libby's employer are expected to average $2,500 annually.
- The Eldridges describe themselves as moderately conservative investors.

FINANCIAL OBJECTIVES

The Eldridges have decided that they both would like to retire in six years, when Pat will reach age 65. At that time, they would like to have an income of $110,000 per year in terms of today's purchasing power. Another objective is to develop an estate plan. They now have no estate plan, not even wills. The basic thrust of the estate plan would be that, following the deaths of both Pat and Libby, everything would go in equal shares to their five grandchildren, particularly to fund their college educations. They want to leave their personal property to their children. They also have as a high-priority objective the retirement of all of their debt by Pat's age 65.

ELDRIDGE CASE
APPLICATION QUESTIONS

1. What has been the approximate standard deviation of the rates of return on Pat's 401(k) plan in the past ten years?

(Topic 35)

A. 2   D. 5

B. 3   E. 6

C. 4

2. Which of the following is the time weighted return earned by the Eldridges on their growth mutual fund over the past six years?

(Topic 36)

A. 5.66%   D. 6.19%

B. 5.87%   E. 6.33%

C. 6.03%

3. Which of the following recommendations would be appropriate for the Eldridges' investments in view of their retirement objectives?

(Topic 37)

(1) They should change to a different growth stock mutual fund.

(2) They should change the investments in the 401(k) to equity investments.

(3) They should invest the savings account money in a high-yield bond fund.

(4) They should sell the common stocks and invest the money in a U.S. Treasury bond fund.

A. (1) and (2) only

B. (1) and (3) only

C. (2) and (3) only

D. (2) and (4) only

E. (3) and (4) only

4. Which of the following phrases most accurately describes the overall collection of the investments owned by Pat and Libby?

(Topic 37)

A. Highly conservative

B. Highly risky

C. Extremely inconsistent

D. Focused on income production

E. Diversified globally

YOUNG CASE

HAROLD AND MILDRED YOUNG

PERSONAL INFORMATION AND BACKGROUND

Mildred Young has come to consult with you in January of this year, because her husband Harold has recently died. Harold handled most of the family finances, and Mildred wants some help with arranging her affairs. Harold Young was 74 when he died and Mildred is currently 69. The Youngs were married just short of 50 years when Harold died. The marriage produced two children: Michael who is 49 years of age and Darlene who is 45.

Mildred worked for a gas company as a home economist until her first child was born. She stayed home to take care of the children until they left for college. She then worked with her husband in his business for 15 years. She stopped working at age 60 to devote herself to church work. She has remained very active in her church work and plans to continue it. Harold worked until his retirement last year.

<u>Family Information</u>

Mildred's son Michael is a lawyer and has two children ages 12 and 9. Her daughter Darlene is a public school teacher and has three children ages 17, 15, and 4. Darlene is recently divorced. Darlene's oldest child is planning to start at the state university in the fall of this year. Darlene lives in a community property state.

ECONOMIC ENVIRONMENT

- Mildred expects that inflation will average 4% per year.
- T-bills are currently yielding 2.5%. The 30-year Treasury bond is yielding 5.25%.
- Corporate bonds are yielding 8%. Junk bonds are yielding 9-10%.
- Certificates of deposit are earning 5.5%.
- The expected return on the S&P 500 Index is 10%.

    - The expected return on the Russell 2000 Index is 14%.
    - The expected return on growth stocks is 12%.
    - Mortgage rates are currently 7% on a 30-year mortgage and 6.5% on a 15-year mortgage. Closing costs are 3% of the mortgage amount.

MILDRED YOUNG'S OBJECTIVES

- Increase amount of current annual income
- Arrange estate plan to minimize transfer taxes and costs and maximize amounts passing to children and grandchildren
- Help Darlene and her family financially
- Determine long-term care insurance needs

- Determine best method for taking distributions from retirement plans
- Plan for charitable gifts to her church

INSURANCE INFORMATION

<u>Homeowners Insurance</u>

Primary Residence – Homeowners Policy Form HO-3

<u>Section I Coverages</u>

A - Dwelling	$275,000
B - Other Structures	$ 27,500
C - Personal Property Coverage	$137,500
D - Loss of Use	$ 55,000
Section I Deductible	$ 250

<u>Section II Coverages</u>

E - Personal Liability	$100,000
F - Medical Payments to Others	$ 1,000

Vacation Home – Homeowners Policy Form HO-3

<u>Section I Coverages</u>

A - Dwelling	$125,000
B - Other Structures	$ 12,500
C - Personal Property Coverage	$ 62,500
D - Loss of Use	$ 25,000
Section I Deductible	$ 250

<u>Section II Coverages</u>

E - Personal Liability	$100,000
F - Medical Payments to Others	$ 1,000

Rental Property – Dwelling Policy Form DP-2

<u>Section I Coverages</u>

A - Dwelling	$150,000
Fire	
Extended Coverage	
Landlord's Liability	

Appendix – Young Case

Automobile Insurance

Personal Auto Policy

Mercedes

Coverage A	
- Liability - Bodily Injury	$300,000 each occurrence
- Liability - Property Damage	$100,000 each occurrence

Coverage B	
- Medical Payments	$5,000 each person

Coverage C	
- Uninsured Motorists	$300,000 each occurrence
- Underinsured Motorists	$300,000 each occurrence

Coverage D	
- Other than collision	Actual cash value less $100
- Collision	Actual cash value less $100

SAAB

Coverage A	
- Liability - Bodily Injury	$300,000 each occurrence
- Liability - Property Damage	$100,000 each occurrence

Coverage B	
- Medical Payments	$5,000 each person

Coverage C	
- Uninsured Motorists	$300,000 each occurrence
- Underinsured Motorists	$300,000 each occurrence

Life Insurance

Insured	Harold Young
Face Amount	$100,000
Type	Whole Life
Cash Value	$ 72,000
Annual premium	$ 3,000
Beneficiary	Mildred Young
Contingent beneficiary	Michael and Darlene
Owner	Harold Young

Single Premium Deferred Annuity

Owner	Harold Young
Type of Annuity	Fixed
Current Value	$100,000
Purchase price	$ 50,000
Interest rate	7.5%
Issue Date	4/30/87
Beneficiary	Mildred Young

INCOME TAX INFORMATION

Mildred will file a joint income tax return for herself and Harold for this year. They have been in a 22% federal income tax bracket. There is no state income tax in the state where Mildred lives.

INVESTMENT INFORMATION

Mildred wants to have the same income that she has enjoyed with Harold, but she does not want to take on additional risk. She describes herself as a conservative investor. The Youngs have designated their money market fund as an emergency fund and felt that the $50,000 contained in that fund was sufficient.

The rental property was purchased 19 years ago for $100,000, of which $15,000 is attributable to the cost of the land.

RETIREMENT INFORMATION

Harold had a pension and profit-sharing plan through his employer. Harold retired in June of last year and had just begun receiving distributions from the company plan before his death. Harold named Mildred as his designated beneficiary.

OTHER DATA

- Mildred's will leaves everything to Harold. She would like to make a substantial gift to her church in the most tax effective way and in a way that will not reduce her income.
- Mildred inherited the vacation home from her mother. The vacation home is located in another state from where Mildred has her primary residence.
- Harold's estate is in probate. His will left $600,000 in a trust that will pay income to Mildred annually, and at her death the remaining assets in the trust will be divided between their two children. The trustee is a bank in the city near where Mildred lives. The remainder of the estate passes to Mildred.
- The Statement of Financial Position and Cash Flow Statement were prepared just before Harold died.

Harold and Mildred Young
Statement of Financial Position
December 31, 20XX

ASSETS

Cash/Cash Equivalents

JT	Checking account	$ 12,000
JT	Money market fund (Emergency fund)	50,000
H	Treasury T-Bills	300,000
JT	Certificate of deposit	150,000
	Total Cash/Cash Equivalents	$512,000

Invested Assets

JT	Marketable Securities[1]	$301,400
JT	Rental Property	175,000
H	Life Ins. Cash Value	72,000
H	Annuity[2]	100,000
		$648,400

Use Assets

JT	Principal Residence	$200,000
W	Vacation home	150,000
W	Personal property[3]	80,000
JT	Automobiles	42,000
		$472,000

Retirement Plan Assets

H	IRA	$ 75,000
W	IRA	40,000
H	Money Purchase Pension	300,000
H	Profit-sharing Plan	100,000
		$515,000

	Total Assets	$2,147,400

___

W = Wife; H = Husband; JT = Joint Tenancy WROS
[1]See Investment Portfolio Supplement.
[2]The single premium deferred annuity earns a fixed rate of 7.5%.
[3]Mildred's jewelry is valued at $40,000.
[4]Rental property: originally 30 years at 9.5%

Harold and Mildred Young
Statement of Financial Position
December 31, 20XX

LIABILITIES

Auto Loan	$	6,000
Credit cards		10,000
Mortgage[4]		75,600
Total Liabilities	$	91,600

NET WORTH $2,055,800

Total Liabilities and Net Worth $2,147,400

W = Wife; H = Husband; JT = Joint Tenancy WROS
[1]See Investment Portfolio Supplement.
[2]The single premium deferred annuity earns a fixed rate of 7.5%.
[3]Mildred's jewelry is valued at $40,000.
[4]Rental property: originally 30 years at 9.5%

Harold and Mildred Young
Statement of Cash Flows
January 1 – December 31, 20XX

Annual Inflows

Salary (Harold)	$ 75,000
Social Security (Harold)	22,000
Interest Income (taxable)	22,500
Interest Income (tax exempt)	4,000
Dividend Income	4,400
Rental Income	20,100
Pension and profit-sharing plans	12,000
IRA Distributions	5,000
Total Inflows	$165,000

Annual Outflows

Mortgage (rental: PI) (int. $7,227)	$ 8,100
Food	4,800
Car Payment	6,200
Utilities (residence)	3,600
Utilities (vacation home)	2,200
Utilities (rental)	1,000
Transportation (gas, oil, maintenance)	2,400
Clothing	3,700
Property taxes (residence)	2,600
Property taxes (vacation home)	2,000
Property taxes (rental)	1,900
Homeowners insurance (residence)	1,000
Homeowners insurance (vacation home)	800
Fire Insurance (Rental)	900
Auto Insurance	1,500
Life Insurance	3,000
Hospitalization (Medigap/Medicare)	1,200
Entertainment	8,000
Travel	6,600
Credit cards	18,000
Charitable contributions	7,600
Federal income tax	28,300
Investments	5,000
Miscellaneous	3,400
Total Outflows	$ 123,800

   800-795-5347

Harold and Mildred Young
Investment Portfolio

Mutual Funds	Fair Market Value
Growth fund	$ 30,000
Small cap growth fund	15,000
S&P 500 Index fund	25,000
Total	$ 70,000

Common Stocks

AT&T	$ 3,000
JP Morgan Chase & Co.	6,500
Chevron	8,000
Coca Cola	7,000
Dell Computer	6,800
Disney	6,500
General Electric	9,000
Verizon	6,500
Home Depot	5,000
IBM	16,500
Nokia	10,000
Qualcomm	5,800
AT&T	4,800
United Healthcare	6,000
Total	$ 111,400

Municipal Bonds

G.O. bonds due in 2023	$ 50,000
Revenue bonds due in 2022	20,000
Total	$ 70,000

Annuities and Insurance

Deferred Annuity	$ 100,000
Life Insurance cash value	72,000
Total	$ 172,000

Bonds

Treasury bonds	$ 50,000
Total	$ 473,400

YOUNG CASE
APPLICATION QUESTIONS

1. Which of the following characteristics of Mildred's CD make(s) it an ideal investment for her?

(Topic 33)

(1) Its complete safety, since it is insured by the FDIC
(2) Its generous yield, considering the tax-exempt status of the income it produces
(3) Its high degree of liquidity, since it can be redeemed at any time on short notice

    A. (1) only
    B. (2) only
    C. (3) only
    D. (1), (2), and (3)

2. What is the approximate federal taxable-equivalent rate of return Mildred will earn this year on her municipal bonds?

(Topics 36 and 39)

    A. 4.45%   D. 7.32%
    B. 5.71%   E. 8.50%
    C. 7.25%

3. Assume that Mildred decides to sell her small cap growth fund and reinvest the proceeds in General Electric debenture bonds with a $1,000 par value and a coupon rate of 7 percent, or $35 every six months. The bonds have nine years to run until they mature and are currently selling for $865 each. What will be Mildred's yield to maturity on these bonds?

(Topic 36)

    A. 6.37%   D. 8.84%
    B. 7.00%   E. 9.24%
    C. 8.00%

4. Which of the following reallocations of Mildred's funds should be recommended to her?

(Topic 37)

(1) Sell some of her Treasury bonds and reinvest the proceeds in high-grade corporate bonds.
(2) Sell her municipal bonds and reinvest the proceeds in junk bonds.
(3) Sell the portfolio of common stocks and reinvest the proceeds in T-bills.

    A. (1) only
    B. (2) only
    C. (2) and (3) only
    D. (3) only

JOHNSON CASE

PERSONAL INFORMATION AND BACKGROUND

Joel and Joanne Johnson live in Texas and have been married for 18 years. Joel, age 45, is a physician in a private practice. Joanne, age 47, is a director of a local private elementary school where she has worked for the last 10 years. They have three daughters named Emily, Casey, and Lindsay. The Johnsons live in a 6-bedroom home and own three cars. They also have a vacation home in South Carolina where Joanne and the girls spend the summer.

Name	Relationship	Age	Occupation	Health	Comments
Joel	Husband	45	Physician	Excellent	
Joanne	Wife	47	Elementary school director	Excellent	Wants to retire next year
Emily	Daughter	16	Student	Excellent	Plays on the varsity soccer team
Casey	Daughter	12	Student	Excellent	Plays on the volleyball team
Lindsay	Daughter	10	Student	Excellent	Cheers for the flag football team

Joanne's mother has been a widow for 30 years, and is comfortable living off of Social Security pension and CDs valued at approximately $200,000. Joanne is an only child.

Joel's parents live in South Carolina and are in good health. They decided to start a new florist business after their retirement from the medical field. They invested nearly all of their savings into the start up costs of the new business. Joel has three younger brothers, but he only sees them once a year for the holidays.

BUSINESS INFORMATION

Joel established his practice as a C corporation over 15 years ago. Joel owns the building in which his private practice is located. Since he currently does not utilize all of the space, Joel leases the extra space to another physician. Joel has four full time employees, including one physician, who has expressed an interest in a partnership.

INCOME TAX INFORMATION

Joel receives a salary and bonuses of $210,000 per year. Joanne's salary is $52,000 per year. The Johnson's are in the 24% federal tax bracket. Texas does not have an individual state income tax.

RETIREMENT INFORMATION

Joel would like to cut back on his schedule beginning in 10 years before he fully retires at age 65. Joanne is considering retiring next year to spend more time traveling to her kids' sporting events. They anticipate needing at least 80% of Joel's income for retirement, plus adjustments for rising healthcare costs. Their family has proven longevity, with many relatives living well into their 90's. As a result, they want to plan for their retirement funds to last through age 93 for both of them.

The Johnsons have a second home in South Carolina near Joel's parents. They would ultimately like to sell their home in Texas and retire to their home in South Carolina.

Joel has a 401(k) through his practice and he contributes $15,000 every year. Joanne has a SIMPLE IRA plan offered through her employer, and she contributes $10,000 annually. Joanne also has a beneficiary IRA which she recently received when her aunt passed away. Joanne elected to stretch the IRA over her life expectancy.

The Johnsons view themselves as having a moderate investor profile.

EDUCATION INFORMATION

All three of the Johnson children are expected to attend state college. Joel and Joanne would like to pay for 100% of their children's college education. They have started saving funds in a single 529 college savings account and plan to continue in the future. However, the Johnsons are still not confident that they will have enough money saved to meet the anticipated costs of $20,000 (in today's dollars) per year per child for state college. They anticipate having to take out loans and use current cash flow to cover the remaining costs while the kids are in school.

MEDICAL INFORMATION

The Johnsons have a high deductible health insurance policy and a health savings account (HSA) through Joel's practice.

Neither Joel's parents nor Joanne's mother have long-term care insurance. Joanne's mother has adequate funds for retirement, but as an only child, Joanne anticipates the need to provide assistance to her mother at some point in the future. Joel's parents do not have sufficient funds to pay for extended medical care, if necessary. Currently, annual nursing home costs in South Carolina average $60,000 and assisted living facilities average $36,000. The Johnsons anticipate these costs will increase 5% per year.

ESTATE INFORMATION

Joel and Joanne have not updated their wills since the birth of their first child. Their wills provide for all assets to go to the surviving spouse or to Emily if the surviving spouse has predeceased. They named Joanne's mother as the guardian for Emily. The Johnsons know they need to update their wills and address any estate planning issues, but they continue to avoid the conversation.

ECONOMIC INFORMATION

The Johnsons anticipate at least 3% annual inflation until retirement, at which point they expect inflation to rise to over 6% due to increased medical costs. Joel's salary has historically grown 10% annually. However, they expect this rate will likely slow as his practice reaches capacity and he begins to cut back on his hours.

The Johnsons believe the risk free rate is 2% and generally expect the S&P 500 Index, their proxy for "the market," to produce an average annual return of 10%. The standard deviation of such a market is 6%. They are also avid followers of international markets and believe the MSCI EAFE Index is the appropriate benchmark for their international investments. The MSCI EAFE Index has an average return of 16%.

The following table summarizes other key economic assumptions the Johnsons would like to assume:

Education inflation rate	7%
Current mortgage refinancing rates – 30-year loan	6.5%
Current mortgage refinancing rates – 5-year ARM	5.0%
Home Equity Line of Credit rates	7.0%

GOALS AND OBJECTIVES

The following are the Johnson's financial goals:

1. Pay for their children's college education.
2. Save for retirement.
3. Help Joanne's mother and Joel's parents with long-term care expenses, as necessary.
4. Buy a sailboat to keep at their home in South Carolina.

Statement of Financial Position
Joel and Joanne Johnson
as of December 31st Last Year

ASSETS[1]

Cash and Cash Equivalents	
Checking account[2]: JT	$ 20,000
Savings account[3]: JT	$ 75,000
CD[4]: W	$ 50,000
Total Cash and Cash Equivalents	$ 145,000
Invested Assets	
401(k)[5]: H	$ 82,000
SIMPLE IRA[6]: W	$ 34,000
Beneficiary IRA[7]: W	$ 80,000
Brokerage account: JT	$ 432,000
529 College Savings Account	$ 53,000
Commercial Building: H	$ 750,000
Total Invested Assets	$1,431,000
Personal-Use Assets	
Primary Residence[8]: JT	$ 400,000
Second Home[9]: JT	$ 450,000
Cars: JT	$ 50,000
Total Personal-Use Assets	$ 900,000
Total Assets	**$2,476,000**

LIABILITIES AND NET WORTH[10]

Current Liabilities	
Credit Cards[11]: JT	$ 43,000
Total Current Liabilities	$ 43,000
Long-Term Liabilities	
Mortgage – Primary Residence[12]: JT	$ 320,000
Mortgage – Second Home[13]: JT	$ 300,000
Mortgage Commercial Building[14]: H	$ 650,000
Equity Line of Credit[15]: JT	$ 89,000
Small Business Loan[16]: H	$ 69,000
Total Long-Term Liabilities	$1,428,000
Total Liabilities	**$1,471,000**
Net Worth	**$1,005,000**
Total Liabilities and Net Worth	**$2,476,000**

Notes to the Financial Statements

H = Husband
W = Wife
JT = Joint tenancy

[1] All assets are quoted at fair market value.
[2] The checking account earns 1.25% interest per year.
[3] The savings account earns 2.25% interest per year.
[4] CD has a 4% interest rate and matures two years from today.
[5] Joanne is named as the sole beneficiary.
[6] Joel is named as the sole beneficiary.
[7] Joel is named as the primary beneficiary with the three kids as the contingent beneficiaries.
[8] The land is worth $80,000. Their basis is $225,000.
[9] The land is worth $100,000. Their basis is $550,000.
[10] Liabilities are stated at principal only.
[11] They have 4 credit cards with interest rates ranging from 0% promotional rates for 6 months to fixed 9.99%.
[12] The 30-year loan has 28 years remaining at a fixed 6.5% interest rate.
[13] The 15-year loan has 10 years remaining at a fixed 7.3% interest rate.
[14] There are 5 years remaining on the loan at a fixed 10% interest rate.
[15] They have maxed out their line of credit. They have 15 years to repay the loan. The interest rate is prime + 1.0%.
[16] There are 3 years remaining on the loan at a fixed 9% interest rate.

Statement of Cash Flows
Joel and Joanne Johnson
January 1st – December 31st of this Year

Annual Inflows

Joel's Salary and Bonuses	$210,000
Joanne's Salary	$ 52,000
Distribution from Beneficiary IRA	$ 3,200
Rental Income	$ 49,800
Total Inflows	$315,000

Annual Outflows

Contribution to 401(k) plan	$ 15,000
Contribution to Simple IRA plan	$ 10,000
Contribution to 529 plan	$ 6,000
Federal Tax	$ 67,900
Mortgages – Primary	$ 20,800
Mortgage – Second Home	$ 22,500
Mortgage – Commercial	$ 56,700
Credit Cards (P&I)	$ 6,900
Property Taxes	$ 22,500
Auto & Homeowners Insurance	$ 7,000
Life Insurance	$ 2,000
Utilities, cable, & cell phones	$ 7,500
Auto Maintenance	$ 1,000
Food	$ 12,000
Clothing/Personal Care	$ 14,000
Entertainment & Travel	$ 5,000
Medical/Dental	$ 7,500
Charitable Contributions	$ 1,500
Total Outflows	$285,800
Discretionary Cash Flow	$ 29,200

Select investment information for the Johnsons:

Joel's 401(k)

Mutual Funds

Name	Shares	5-Year Avg. Return	Std. Deviation	FMV
Green Leaf	500	3.00%	3.00%	$30,000
Blue Sky	250	7.30%	4.00%	10,000
Yellow Lion	250	27.00%	17.00%	7,000
Purple Elephant	750	14.00%	12.00%	35,000
				$82,000

Joanne's Beneficiary IRA

Asset	5-Year Avg. Return	Weight	Beta	FMV
Tulip Corp. stock (large-cap)	10.00%	15%	1.00	$12,000
Bluebell Corp. stock (small-cap)	13.70%	10%	1.40	8,000
Goldenrod Corp. stock (Int'l stock)	22.30%	25%	1.20	20,000
Bonsai Fund (Int'l HY bonds)	9.20%	50%	1.35	40,000
				$80,000

Joanne's SIMPLE IRA

Year	Hot Pharma Stock Rate of Return	Hot Biotech Stock Rate of Return
1	3.4%	27.0%
2	−5.0%	24.0%
3	−12.0%	2.0%
4	22.0%	−34.0%
5	5.0%	−9.0%

529 College Savings Account

Mutual Funds

Name	Shares	5-Year Avg. Return	Std. Deviation	FMV
Very Aggressive Fund	1,000	15.50%	12.00%	$53,000

Joint Brokerage Account

The Johnsons hold all of their brokerage assets in a margin account. The initial margin requirement is 50%, and the maintenance requirement is 30%.

Among the investments in the account are:

- 200 shares of **Amarillo Fund**, an open-end international investment company. The Fund has a beta of 1.10, a standard deviation of 19%, and a coefficient of determination of 85.8%. The Johnsons purchased the fund for $19.80 per share.

- 200 shares of **Austin Corp**. common stock, a software company listed on the NASDAQ. The stock has a beta of 1.7, a standard deviation of 21%, a coefficient of determination of 70%, and a 5-year average rate of return of 22%. The stock has a P/E ratio of 19, cost basis of $30 per share, current market price of $44 per share, and an expected growth rate of 12% per year for the foreseeable future. The Johnsons wrote two contracts of $40 call options on this stock that expire today. The option premium was $0.50 per share.

- Five municipal bonds issued by **Beaufort County**, purchased yesterday, and maturing in 13 years. Each bond has a face value of $1,000, 3% coupon, and a current market price of $990.20.

- 500 shares of **Beaumont Corp.** preferred stock. Beaumont has a beta of 1.2, a standard deviation of 9%, a 5-year average return of 7.5%, a current price of $88, and pays an annual dividend of $2.50. The Johnsons determined they require a 6% return on this investment given the low associated risks.

- 250 shares of **Canyon Fund**, a closed-end investment company with a dividend yield of 11%.

- 200 shares of **Dumas Corp.** common stock, an international conglomerate that trades on the NYSE. With a current market price of $52 and P/E of 12, the company issued a dividend of $3.20 in the current year, and has announced that it plans to grow its dividend at 5% for the next several years. The stock has a beta of 0.9, a standard deviation of 8%, a coefficient of determination of 95%, and a 5-year average rate of return of 12%. The Johnsons determined they require a 10% rate of return on this stock given the associated risk.

- 10 zero coupon bonds issued by **Humble Corp.** with a 12-year maturity.

- 400 shares of an investment grade corporate bond fund that tracks the **Large Bank Aggregate Bond Index**. The bonds all mature within 5 to 10 years. The fund typically pays dividends ranging between $0 and $1 per share per year.

- An **Orange Corp.** 10-year, non-callable, 7.5% bond, purchased for $1,100 yesterday.

- **Pflugerville Corp.** Five non-callable, 5.0% bonds. They are currently trading at par with 5 years to maturity. The Johnsons purchased them 2 years ago for $4,700.

- 2,000 shares of **Plano Corp.** common stock, a penny technology stock listed on the NYSE MKT (AMEX). Plano Corp. does not issue a dividend, has a current price of $1.20, a standard deviation of 11%, a 5-year average rate of return of 15%, a P/E of 2.0, and a beta of 2.25. The Johnsons purchased the stock anticipating the same 15% rate of return over the next 5 years, given the risks associated with small technology companies.

- A **San Marcos Corp.** 5-year, 9% bond, purchased yesterday for $1,070.

- A 6-month **U.S. Treasury bill** purchased yesterday for $1,995.80 and a face value of $2,000.

- $5,000 face value of 5-year, **U.S. Treasury bond**, 4.0% coupon, trading at par, purchased 6 months ago.

- $15,000 face value of 10-year, **U.S. Treasury bond**, 4.5% coupon, trading at par, purchased 6 months ago.

- Twenty $1,000 convertible bonds of **Waco Corp.**, with 5-year maturities. They have a coupon rate of 6% and the bonds can be converted at $40 per share. Waco Corp. stock is currently trading at $42.50. Similar bonds are yielding 5.5%.

INSURANCE INFORMATION

Life Insurance

Insured	Owner	Beneficiary	Face Amount	Type	Cash Value	Annual Premium	Notes
Joel	Joel	Joanne	$250,000	Term		$2,000	Bought 15 years ago
Joanne	Joanne	Joel	$100,000	Term			Company-provided

Disability Insurance

Insured	Current Benefit Amount	Benefit Period	Inflation Rider	Premium	Notes
Joel	$5,000/month	5 years	None	$600/year	100% of premium paid by business
Joanne	$1,000/month	5 years	3% per year	$100/year	100% of premium paid by employer

Medical Insurance

Insured	Plan Type	Copayments	Coinsurance	Deductible	Premium
Joel	PPO	none	20%	$5,000	Paid by business

Long-Term Care Insurance

Insured	Current Benefit Amount	Benefit Period	Inflation Rider	Premium	Date of Issue
Joel	None				
Joanne	None				

Homeowners Insurance

Type	Dwelling Amount	Contents Coverage	Liability	Premium
HO-3 (Texas home)	$300,000	$150,000 ACV	$1,000,000	$2,000/year
HO-3 (South Carolina home)	$300,000	$150,000 ACV	$1,000,000	$2,000/year

Automobile Insurance

Vehicle	Type	Liability Limits	Collision	Comprehensive (other-than-collision)	Premium
Joel's Truck	Personal auto policy	50/100/25	$1,000 Broad Form Deductible	$1,000 deductible	$100/month
Joanne's Minivan	Personal auto policy	50/100/25	$1,000 Broad Form Deductible	$1,000 deductible	$75/month
Emily's Honda	Personal auto policy	50/100/25	$1,000 Broad Form Deductible	$1,000 deductible	$100/month

JOHNSON CASE
APPLICATION QUESTIONS

1. If the NAV of the Canyon Fund increases by 5%, what is the effect on Canyon's share price?

(Topic 33)

A. Increases by 5%
B. Decreases by 5%
C. Unchanged
D. Cannot be determined by the information given

2. Which of the following investments would be most affected by an increase in interest rates?

(Topics 33 and 38)

A. San Marcos Corp bond
B. Orange Corp bond
C. 5-year Treasury bond
D. Investment grade corporate bond fund

3. What would be the most likely result of the options the Johnsons have on the Austin Corp stock?

(Topic 33)

A. The options will expire worthless.
B. 200 shares will be called at $40.
C. 200 shares will be called at $44.
D. 2 shares of Austin Corp stock will be called at $40.

4. What will be the Johnson's profit percentage before taxes if the Austin Corp. options are exercised today?

(Topic 33)

A. 31%
B. 33%
C. 35%
D. 37%

5. Which of the following investments has the greatest reinvestment risk?

(Topic 34)

A. San Marcos Corp bond
B. Orange Corp bond
C. Humble Corp bond
D. Investment grade corporate bond fund

6. Which of the following investments has the greatest volatility?

(Topic 35)

A. Austin Corp.
B. Dumas Corp.
C. Plano Corp.
D. Beaumont Corp.

7. Which of the following investments provides the least variability risk?

(Topic 35)

A. Austin Corp.
B. Dumas Corp.
C. Plano Corp.
D. Beaumont Corp.

8. What is the required (or expected) return for the Amarillo Fund if it is calculated using the security market line?

(Topic 35)

A. 10.8%
B. 16.0%
C. 17.4%
D. 19.2%

9. What is the expected return of Joel's 401(k) plan for this year?

(Topic 36)

A. 11.76%
B. 12.83%
C. 10.27%
D. 10.48%

10. What was the yield to maturity for the Pflugerville Corp. bond when it was purchased?

(Topic 36)

A. 3.03%
B. 3.11%
C. 5.00%
D. 6.06%

11. What is the tax equivalent yield of the Beaufort municipal bonds?

(Topics 36 and 39)

A. 1.55%
B. 3.09%
C. 4.07%
D. 4.28%

12. What is the current price of a Waco Corp. bond?

(Topic 36)

A. $1,000.00
B. $1,021.60
C. $1,062.50
D. $1,105.00

13. What is the time-weighted return of Hot Pharma Stock?

(Topic 36)

A. 2.06%
B. 2.68%
C. 5.23%
D. 12.78%

14. Which of the following investment funds exhibits the most favorable Sharpe Ratio?

(Topic 36)

A. Green Leaf
B. Blue Sky
C. Yellow Lion
D. Purple Elephant

15. What is an appropriate alternative to the Amarillo Fund?

(Topic 37)

A. Large-cap equity fund
B. International ETF
C. Global company stock
D. Balanced fund

16. Which of the following should the Johnsons add to their portfolio to offset the purchase of additional shares of Amarillo Fund?

(Topic 37)

A. Corporate bond
B. International bond
C. Small company stock
D. REIT

17. Which of the following would be prudent advice for Joanne regarding her Beneficiary IRA?

(Topic 37)

A. Consider replacing a portion of her high yield international bond position with an international stock fund.
B. Consider replacing a portion of her high yield international bond position with a small cap index fund.
C. Consider replacing a portion of her high yield international bond position with an S&P 500 Index fund.
D. Consider replacing a portion of her high yield international bond position with an international REIT.

18. Which of the following is most likely to have an effect on Plano Corp. stock?

(Topic 38)

A. The P/E effect
B. The small-firm effect
C. The January effect
D. Both the P/E effect and the small-firm effect

19. What is the duration of the Humble Corp. bond?

(Topic 38)

A. 5
B. 6
C. 10
D. 12

20. What is the intrinsic value of Dumas Corp. stock?

(Topic 38)

A. $32
B. $52
C. $67
D. $70

21. Using the capitalized earnings approach, what is the intrinsic value of the Beaumont Corp. preferred stock?

(Topic 38)

A. $25.00
B. $41.67
C. $64.84
D. $88.00

22. Which of the following investments has the greatest duration?

(Topic 38)

A. Humble Corp. bonds
B. San Marcos Corp. bonds
C. Orange Corp. bonds
D. Pflugerville Corp. bonds

23. Which of the following strategies does it appear the Johnsons are using?

(Topic 40)

A. Security selection
B. Indexing
C. Swaps
D. Buy and hold

24. Which of the following strategies does Dr. Johnson employ with regard to his 401(k) investments?

(Topic 40)

A. Diversification
B. Dollar cost averaging
C. Market timing
D. Life cycle investing

THOMAS CASE

PERSONAL INFORMATION AND BACKGROUND

David and Kelly Thomas have been married for a little over 25 years. They currently live in Beaufort, South Carolina with their 10-year-old twins, Alex and Emily. David is a managing partner in a successful regionally-based accounting firm. He also moonlights as a business consultant. Kelly was recently hired as the nurse at her children's private school. Prior to this position, she worked part time in the local hospital to maintain her nursing skills.

Name	Relationship	Age	Occupation	Health
David	Husband	52	Accountant/Business Consultant	Good
Kelly	Wife	50	Nurse	Excellent
Alex	Son	10	Student	Excellent except for seasonal allergies
Emily	Daughter	10	Student	Excellent except for seasonal allergies

Several years ago, David and Kelly built their dream home with four bedrooms and three and half baths. They hope to stay in this home for at least 20 years. Both David and Kelly like to get new automobiles every three years. As a result, they are currently leasing a sedan and a minivan.

Kelly's parents are divorced, but both have remarried. Kelly's mom lives in North Carolina and her dad lives in Delaware. She does not anticipate needing to provide support for either parent in the future. Kelly's parents are both in their early 70s.

David's parents are also divorced; however, neither has remarried. David's parents both live in Beaufort, South Carolina to be close to their grandchildren. David anticipates that he and his sister, Casey Ford, will need to provide financial assistance to one or both of his parents in the future. David's parents are both in their late 70s and enjoy living alone.

Casey, age 50, has worked in the medical field for over 20 years. She is currently the manager of a local medical practice. Casey was divorced over 10 years ago and has one adopted son. Casey lives about an hour away from David and Kelly.

INCOME TAX INFORMATION

David receives a salary of $230,000 per year through the accounting firm. His earnings from the consulting practice vary year-to-year in the range of $100,000 to $125,000. Kelly's new salary is $15,000 plus a discount on her children's tuition at the school. The Thomas' marginal federal and state income tax brackets are 32% and 7%, respectively.

RETIREMENT INFORMATION

David anticipates selling his partnership interest in the accounting firm in 3 years and increasing the time spent in his consulting practice. Kelly intends to continue working part time as a nurse in the hospital after her children finish high school.

They plan to finance their retirement by selling one of the investment properties held in the LLC every five to ten years.

David participates in his company's 401(k) plan and has a defined benefit plan for his consulting income. Kelly has a rollover IRA from a previous employer. Kelly is not yet eligible to participate in her new employer's plan.

David and Kelly would like their retirement funds to last through age 85.

EDUCATION INFORMATION

David and Kelly are strong proponents of education and make annual contributions to custodial accounts for each of their two children. They intend to pay for college and graduate school. The local State College currently costs $15,000 per student per year including room and board. David and Kelly believe these costs will increase 5% annually. They expect each child will be in school for a total of seven years in order to finish an undergraduate and graduate degree.

MEDICAL INFORMATION

The twins currently receive weekly allergies shot to help keep their seasonal allergies under control. The only other medicine the family takes on a regular basis is a daily multi vitamin.

David's firm pays $500 per month towards their medical insurance premium. David pays the other $250 per month on a pretax basis.

David and Kelly purchased long-term care policies for themselves two years ago. See the Insurance Information section for policy information.

ESTATE INFORMATION

David and Kelly recently updated their wills and powers of attorney on the advice of their advisor. Their wills leave everything to the surviving spouse. If the spouse has predeceased, the assets will be split equally between Alex and Emily. The surviving spouse will be the executor of the estate. Casey will serve as the executor if the surviving spouse is unable to serve. Casey is also named as the guardian of Alex and Emily. Casey is also named after the spouses on the powers of attorney.

David and Kelly established an LLC about ten years ago to hold all of their real estate investments. They also established a revocable trust, but have not yet funded it.

ECONOMIC INFORMATION

David and Kelly anticipate an inflation rate of 2.4% for the foreseeable future. The current risk-free rate is 2.5%, and the expected market return is 8% with a standard deviation of 8%.

PERSONAL AND FINANCIAL GOALS

1. Pay for their children's college and graduate education.
2. Save for retirement.
3. Assist their parents with long-term care costs, as necessary.
4. Minimize income, gift and estate taxes
5. Buy or lease a new car every three years.
6. Take a two week Alaskan cruise for David's 55th birthday.

Statement of Financial Position
David and Kelly Thomas
as of December 31st Last Year

ASSETS[1]

Cash and Cash Equivalents

Checking account: JT[2]	$ 20,000
Savings account: JT[3]	75,000
Life insurance cash value: JT	95,000
Total Cash and Cash Equivalents	$ 190,000

Invested Assets

401(k): H	$ 469,000
DB Plan: H	54,000
Rollover IRA: W	67,000
Pinestraw Corp. Stock: H	250,000
Brokerage Account: JT	675,000
Custodial Acct: C1	44,000
Custodial Acct: C2	44,000
Investment Property: LLC[4]	1,500,000
Total Invested Assets	$3,103,000

Personal Use Assets

Primary Residence: JT	$800,000
Personal Assets: JT	50,000
Total Personal Use Assets	$850,000

Total Assets	**$4,143,000**

LIABILITIES AND NET WORTH[5]

Current Liabilities

Credit Cards: JT[6]	$9,000
Total Current Liabilities	$9,000

Long-Term Liabilities

Mortgage – Primary Residence: JT[7]	$ 720,000
Investment Property[8]	1,200,000
Equity Line of Credit: JT[9]	89,000
Total Long-Term Liabilities	$2,009,000

Total Liabilities	**$2,018,000**
Net Worth	**$2,125,000**
Total Liabilities and Net Worth	**$4,143,000**

Notes to the Financial Statements

H = Husband
W = Wife
JT = Joint tenancy
C1 = Alex
C2 = Emily
LLC = Limited Liability Corporation

[1] All assets are quoted at fair market value.

[2] The checking account earns 1.25% interest per year.

[3] The savings account earns 2.25% interest per year.

[4] Investment properties combined for purposes of financial statements.

[5] Liabilities are stated at principal only.

[6] Credit card balances represent current charges as of December 31st. They pay off their credit card balance every month. The interest rate on the card is 12.99%. The card gives them miles with their preferred airline.

[7] They refinanced their loan two years ago at fixed 6.7% for 30 years.

[8] The loans on the investment properties range from 15 years to 30 years. The interest rates also range from a 5.0% ARM (3 years remaining until the interest rate can change) to 8.2% fixed interest rate.

[9] The interest rate on the LOC is 7.3%. They currently only pay the monthly interest charge as they do not need to repay the balance for 10 years.

Statement of Cash Flows
David and Kelly Thomas
January 1st – December 31st of This Year

ANNUAL INFLOWS

David's Salary	$230,000
David's Consulting Income	100,000
Kelly's Salary	15,000
Rental Income	100,000
Total Inflows	$445,000

ANNUAL OUTFLOWS

Contributions to 401(k) and defined benefit plans	$ 40,000
Contribution to custodial accounts	20,000
Federal and state taxes	126,000
Mortgages – Primary	48,000
Mortgages – Investment property	75,000
Credit cards – Miscellaneous expenses	6,900
Property taxes	49,000
Auto and homeowners insurance	6,000
Life insurance	17,000
Utilities, cable & cell phones	7,500
Auto maintenance	1,200
Food	12,000
Clothing/personal care	15,000
Entertainment and travel	5,000
Medical and dental	7,500
Charitable contributions	1,000
Total Outflows	$437,100

Discretionary Cash Flow   **$ 7,900**

INVESTMENT INFORMATION

David and Kelly prefer a conservative investment strategy. They also believe in the semi-strong form of the Efficient Market Hypothesis.

David and Casey both have a sizeable amount of Pinestraw Corp. stock that was bequeathed to them by their grandmother several years ago. David's basis for his 2,750 shares is $50.50 per share. As indicated on the balance sheet, David's holding in Pinestraw Corp. was worth $250,000 at the end of last year.

The following tables provide select information on the Thomas' accounts.

David's
401(k)   Mutual Funds

Name	Shares	5-Year Avg. Return	Standard Deviation	Beta	FMV
Pine Cone Fund	100	12.30%	10.00%	1.50	$ 46,700
Palm Frond Fund	100	6.20%	4.20%	0.50	12,500
Tin Roof Fund	100	25.00%	17.00%	(0.20)	167,000
Green Leaf Fund	100	3.10%	6.00%	(1.50)	78,000
Brown Thumb Fund	100	9.90%	9.50%	0.27	89,500
Holly Berry Fund	100	7.90%	8.30%	1.25	43,000
Holly Berry Fund	100	6.90%	9.00%	1.09	32,300
					$469,000

Kelly's Rollover
IRA

Asset	5-Year Avg. Return	Weight	Standard Deviation	Beta	FMV
S&P 500 Index Fund	8.00%	50%	8.00%	1.00	$33,500
Financials Index Fund	22.00%	50%	14.20%	1.30	33,500
					$67,000

Custodial Account – Emily

Year	Cool Sports Stock Rate of Return	Big Shoes Stock Rate of Return
1	-2.5%	39.0%
2	-2.8%	17.9%
3	12.4%	12.4%
4	17.9%	-2.8%
5	39.0%	-2.5%

Appendix – Thomas Case

LLC Information

The LLC holds the following properties

Location	Adjusted Basis	Fair Market Value
Duck Puddle Pond, MA	$120,000	$200,000
Lake Tahoe, NV	$500,000	$750,000
Lake of the Pines, CA	$100,000	$175,000
Outer Banks, NC	$250,000	$375,000
Total	**$970,000**	**$1,500,000**

David purchased the Lake of the Pines property for $126,000 four years ago. The cash flow from the property has been as follows:

Year 1	1,200
Year 2	800
Year 3	(600)

David is thinking of selling the property as it generates such a small amount of income each year. David currently projects that the property will break even this year resulting in no cash flow. A realtor recently approached David with an offer from a perspective buyer who wants to close at the end of this year. The LLC would receive $150,000 after all expenses are paid.

The LLC carries adequate insurance on all properties in addition to liability coverage.

Thomas' Joint Investment Account

David and Kelly hold all of their brokerage assets in a margin account. The initial margin requirement is 50%, and the maintenance requirement is 30%.

Among the investments in the account are:

- 500 shares of **Big Blue Fund**, a closed-end investment company with a dividend yield of 7%, an NAV of $14.65, and market price of $14.00.
- Seven 10-year $1,000 **Freedom Corp. bonds**, 4.6% coupon, currently selling at $1,001.25, purchased six months ago.
- 500 shares of **Go Green Fund**, a closed-end investment company with a dividend yield of 9%, a current NAV of $22.20, a current market price of $17.50, and a beta of 1.0. They require an 8% return given the riskiness of this fund.
- Five 7-year, $1,000 **Greater Speed Corp bonds**, 4.7% coupon, currently selling at $1,002.50 purchased 2 years ago.
- Five **Hot Pink Corp.** 5 year 5% bonds, non-callable, interest paid semiannually purchased 2 years ago for $978.00, currently trading at par.
- 50 call option contracts on the **India Index**, purchased for $4.00 per share, expiring in 3 mos. with an exercise price of $100 per share.

- 450 shares of a high yield **international bond fund** currently trading at $28.32 per share.
- 10 municipal bonds issued by **Johnson County**, purchased yesterday, and maturing in 13 years. Each bond has a face value of $1,000, 3% coupon, and a current market price of $964.
- 1,000 shares of **Large Cap Index Fund**; a beta of 1.0, standard deviation of 8%, coefficient of determination of 95%, and a 5-year average rate of return of 8%.
- 550 shares of **Micro Corp.** common stock, a small company stock that trades over-the-counter. With a current market price of $15.45 and P/E of 35, the company does not issue a dividend. The stock has a beta of 1.6, a standard deviation of 15%, a coefficient of determination of 40%, and a 5-year average rate of return of 12%. Micro Corp has a large option market.
- 1,000 shares of **Ocean Hopper Corp. common stock**, a German-based high-end apparel company doing business around the globe. Ocean Hopper has a current price of $22.30, a standard deviation of 11%, a P/E of 17, and a beta of 1.2. Ocean Hopper issues an annual dividend of $0.90 per share. They recently announced plans to increase their dividend 3% annually. David and Kelly require a 12% return on this investment given its risk level.
- 700 shares of **Ocean Hopper Corp. preferred stock**, a German-based high-end apparel company doing business around the globe. Ocean Hopper recently issued an annual dividend of $2.90 per share, a 2% increase over prior year's dividend.
- 1,000 shares of **Quasi-Emerging Markets Index Fund**; an emerging markets index fund with a beta of -1.4, standard deviation of 19%, coefficient of determination of 55%, and a 5-year rate of return of 16.2%.
- 500 shares of **Red Tape Fund**, a unit investment trust with a dividend yield of 9%, a NAV of $22.50, a beta of 0.9, standard deviation of 4.9% and a 5-year rate of return of 8%.
- 20 put option contracts on the **S&P 500 Index** purchased for $1.20 per share, expiring in 6 mos. with an exercise price of $1,100 per share.
- Five $1,000 convertible bonds of **Sea Salt Corp.**, with 7-year maturities.
- A **Slate Gray Corp.** 10 year, non-callable, 7.5% bond, paid semiannually, purchased yesterday at the $1,000 face value.
- Five 20-year, $1,000 **Small Company bonds**, 4.5% coupon, trading at par, purchased yesterday.
- Two 6-month $1,000 **Treasury bills** purchased yesterday for $997.90.
- 200 shares **Union Jack Fund**, an open-end investment company with a focus on developed Europe. The Fund has a beta of 0.6, a standard deviation of 12%, and a coefficient of determination of 70%.
- Five 3-year, $1,000 **U.S. Treasury bonds**, 4.2% coupon, trading at par, purchased 6 months ago.
- 10 zero coupon bonds issued by **Yellow Corp.** with a 15-year maturity.

INSURANCE INFORMATION

Life Insurance

Insured	Owner	Beneficiary	Face Amount	Type	Cash Value	Annual Premium	Notes
David and Kelly	David and Kelly	Alex and Emily	$2,000,000	Whole Life Second to Die Policy	$95,000	$17,000	Bought 10 years ago

Disability Insurance

Insured	Current Benefit Amount	Benefit Period	Inflation Rider	Premium	Notes
David	$12,000/month	To age 65	3%	$4,000/year	100% of premium paid by David's firm

Medical Insurance

Insured	Plan Type	Copayments	Coinsurance	Deductible	Maximum Benefit	Premium
David, Kelly, Alex and Emily	PPO	None	20%	$3,000 family	Unlimited	$750 per month

Long-Term Care Insurance

Insured	Current Benefit Amount	Benefit Period	Inflation Rider	Premium	Date of Issue
David	$150/day	5 years	5% Simple	$750/year	2 years ago
Kelly	$150/day	5 years	5% Simple	$750/year	2 years ago

Homeowners Insurance

Type	Dwelling Amount	Contents Coverage	Liability	Premium
HO-3 - Residence	$650,000	$250,000 Replacement Cost	$500,000	$2,400/year

Automobile Insurance

Vehicle	Type	Liability Limits	Collision	Comprehensive (other-than-collision)	Premium
David's Sedan	Personal auto policy	100/500/100	$1,000 Broad Form Deductible	$500 deductible	$1,500/year
Kelly's Minivan	Personal auto policy	100/500/100	$1,000 Broad Form Deductible	$500 deductible	$1,200/year

THOMAS CASE
APPLICATION QUESTIONS

1. Which of the following investments are passively managed by the fund managers?

(Topic 33)

   A. Big Blue Fund
   B. Go Green Fund
   C. Red Tape Fund
   D. Union Jack Fund

2. If David and Kelly want to buy additional shares of a fund that can be traded on an exchange, which of the following investments should they purchase?

(Topic 33)

   A. Big Blue Fund
   B. Red Tape Fund
   C. Union Jack Fund
   D. Quasi-Emerging Markets Index Fund

3. An increase in which of the following would have a negative impact on the Thomas' S&P 500 index options?

(Topic 33)

   A. Expiration date
   B. Market price
   C. Stock volatility
   D. Strike price

4. What would be the total amount of the Thomas' profit if they exercise their India Index options when it is currently trading at $110?

(Topic 33)

   A. $300
   B. $600
   C. $30,000
   D. They would not exercise the option as they are out of the money.

5. Which of the following 401(k) investments has the greatest total risk per $100 investment?

(Topic 35)

   A. Brown Thumb Fund
   B. Green Leaf Fund
   C. Pine Cone Fund
   D. Tin Roof Fund

6. Which of the following investments in the Thomas' portfolio have the least systematic risk?

(Topic 35)

   A. Large-Cap Index Fund
   B. Micro Corp
   C. Quasi-Emerging Markets Index Fund
   D. Union Jack Fund

7. What percentage of movement of the Quasi-Emerging Markets Index Fund is due to unsystematic risk?

(Topic 35)

   A. 45%
   B. 50%
   C. 55%
   D. Cannot be determined from the information given

8. Which of the following investments possesses the most risk in a well diversified portfolio?

(Topic 35)

   A. Go Green Fund
   B. Micro Corp.
   C. Ocean Hopper Corp.
   D. Union Jack Fund

9. What percentage of the time should Kelly expect the S&P 500 Index Fund in her IRA to have a return equal to or greater than 0%?

(Topic 35)

A. 16%
B. 34%
C. 68%
D. 84%

10. What is the required rate of return for Green Leaf Fund in David's 401(k) plan using CML?

(Topic 35)

A. 4.1%
B. 6.6%
C. 8.0%
D. 10.5%

11. What is the expected return of the Large-Cap Index Fund using SML?

(Topic 35)

A. 2.5%
B. 5.5%
C. 8.0%
D. 10.5%

12. What is the dollar weighted return for the Lake of the Pines investment property if they accept the offer from the potential buyer?

(Topic 36)

A. 3.0%
B. 4.7%
C. 5.6%
D. 6.4%

13. What is the current yield of the Johnson County bonds?

(Topic 36)

A. 3.00%
B. 3.11%
C. 3.34%
D. 6.68%

14. What is the time weighted return of Big Shoes Stock?

(Topic 36)

A. 1.12%
B. 7.46%
C. 11.79%
D. 12.80%

15. What is the Sharpe ratio for the Quasi-Emerging Markets Index Fund?

(Topic 36)

A. 0.72
B. 0.85
C. 9.78
D. 11.57

16. Which of the following would you recommend David and Kelly purchase to provide diversification for the risk of their Lake of the Pines investment?

(Topic 37)

A. Equity REIT
B. Corporate bond
C. Small company stock
D. Treasury bill

17. Taking into consideration David and Kelly's investment strategy, which of the following best describes David's 401(k) portfolio?

(Topics 37 and 40)

- A. Appropriate
- B. Diversified
- C. Overly aggressive
- D. Strategically allocated

18. What is an appropriate alternative to the Ocean Hopper Corp. common stock?

(Topics 37 and 39)

- A. European closed-end fund
- B. Balanced fund
- C. Global open-end fund
- D. International ETF

19. Which of the following is the most significant indicator of David and Kelly's belief about the efficiency of the stock market?

(Topics 38 and 37)

- A. 20 day moving average
- B. Put/call ratio
- C. Relative strength
- D. None of the above

20. What is the current per share dividend amount for the Go Green Fund?

(Topic 38)

- A. $1.40
- B. $1.58
- C. $1.78
- D. $2.00

21. What is the intrinsic value of Ocean Hopper Corp. common stock?

(Topic 38)

- A. $7.50
- B. $7.72
- C. $10.30
- D. $22.30

22. Which of the following investments should David and Kelly be the most concerned about turnover within the investment?

(Topic 39)

- A. Large-Cap Index Fund
- B. Micro Corp.
- C. Sea Salt Corp.
- D. Union Jack Fund

23. Which of the following best describes the Thomas' current bond strategy?

(Topic 40)

- A. Barbell
- B. Bell
- C. Bullet
- D. Ladder

24. If David and Kelly are bearish about their investment in Ocean Hopper Corp common stock, which of the following strategies is the best one for them to execute?

(Topic 40)

- A. Buy $22 call options
- B. Sell $22 call options
- C. Buy $22 put options
- D. Sell $22 put options

25. Which of the Thomas' investments are alternative investments?

(Topic 41)

A. Micro Corp stock
B. LLC Investment Properties
C. Quasi-Emerging Markets Index Fund
D. Ocean Hopper Corp. preferred stock

JIM AND BRENDA QUINN CASE

PERSONAL INFORMATION AND BACKGROUND

Jim and Brenda Quinn live in North Carolina and have been married for 12 years. They have 10-year-old twin boys, both of whom attend a local public school. The Quinns own a five-bedroom home, lease two cars, and have adopted a special-needs greyhound.

Brenda's father was recently killed in a car accident. Brenda inherited $200,000 in cash and $100,000 in stock, which she deposited into a joint checking account and a joint brokerage account. Brenda's mother received $3 million dollars. She would like to invest $200,000 of the inheritance in an investment that will provide a favorable after-tax yield, that makes distributions of income on a quarterly basis, and that can be sold on an exchange when she no longer wishes to own it. Brenda's mother would like to separately invest $750,000 of her inheritance in a portfolio that will produce income for her to use as "fun money" to go on bus trips to the casino with her friends. She has a moderately aggressive tolerance for risk in the "fun money" account, does not plan to access the principal at any time, and would like the investments to be tax efficient. She has no other financial needs. Brenda's brother, Sam Moore, inherited $200,000 in cash, and $100,000 in stock, and his father's duck stamp collection valued at $70,000.

Jim's parents are newly retired and live on their pensions and Social Security checks, but they do not have any money saved.

Jim Quinn
Jim Quinn is 44 years old and is the general partner of Design This, LP, an architectural firm he started four years ago. Jim is the lead architect, and he has five full-time employees. Design This leases space in a local business complex.

Brenda Quinn
Brenda Quinn is 41 years old and has been employed for 10 years by A Home of One's Own, a local nonprofit organization. She was recently promoted from grant writer to the Development Director.

Sam Moore
Sam Moore is 39 years old and single. He is a yacht salesman and earns $230,000 per year. He is always looking for opportunities to make a huge return on investment. Sam is a limited partner in Design This. He is a very aggressive investor and a contrarian. He is also convinced that he can time the market.

INCOME TAX INFORMATION

Jim takes a salary of $150,000 per year and invests all the remaining profit back into Design This. Brenda's salary is $75,000 per year. The Quinns are in the 24% federal income tax bracket, and the state and local taxes for the Quinns are 9.8%. Sam Moore is in the 35% federal income tax bracket and the 9.8% state and local tax brackets.

RETIREMENT INFORMATION

The Quinns would like to retire at age 65. They anticipate needing 80% of their current income in retirement, plus adjustments for inflation. Many of the elders in Jim's and Brenda's families are still alive, and their already deceased family members lived well into their 80s. The Quinns realize that, traditionally, women live longer than men, but they want to plan for retirement to last through age 90 for both of them.

The Quinns would like to buy a second home in Florida right before Jim retires, in order to have a warm place to live during the winter. They will probably buy a house that is currently in the range of $400,000.

Jim recently started a SIMPLE IRA for Design This. He also has an IRA funded with a rollover of his 401(k) plan from his job before he started Design This. Brenda has been contributing to her company's 403(b) for eight years. She would like to contribute the maximum each year. Returns on the retirement accounts have varied, most recently declining from 12% to 6%.

The Quinns are risk averse and consider themselves to be conservative investors. They both believe the market is efficient, and they do believe fundamental analysis produces superior results.

EDUCATION INFORMATION

The Quinns would like the twins to attend Halverton College since this is where Jim and Brenda met in the dorms their freshman year. The Quinns are not sure how they are going to be able to afford the tuition once the twins start college, as the current tuition is $37,000 per student. They expect the tuition to increase 3% per year.

MEDICAL INFORMATION

The family is covered under a comprehensive PPO through Brenda's job. They have an annual deductible of $1,000 per person, with a maximum family deductible of $3,000 per year. The plan also requires the Quinns to pay 20% of all expenses above the deductible, up to a total out-of-pocket amount of $5,000 per year.

Jim and Brenda are concerned that Jim's parents do not have long-term care insurance or ample savings to pay for extended medical care. The Quinns would like to set aside money to be able to help Jim's parents, in the event they need long-term care. Nursing home costs currently average $56,000 per year, assisted living facilities average $22,500 per year, and home care averages $14,000 per year.

ESTATE INFORMATION

Jim and Brenda have never executed wills, as they are not concerned about estate taxes, given the applicable credit amount available today and the size of their estates.

ECONOMIC INFORMATION

The Quinns expect inflation to average 3% per year until they retire. They anticipate Jim's salary will increase 10% annually, and Brenda's will increase 3% annually.

The Quinn's believe the risk-free rate is 3%, and the expected return on the market is 10% with a standard deviation of 6%. The 5-year average return of the S&P500 is 10%.

PERSONAL AND FINANCIAL GOALS

These are the Quinns' financial goals, in order of priority:

1. Pay for the twins to attend Halverton College for four years.
2. Help Jim's parents with long-term care expenses.
3. Build a small house that will act as an office for Design This.
4. Save for retirement.
5. Buy a second home in Florida.

Statement of Financial Position
Jim and Brenda Quinn
December 31st of Last Year

ASSETS[1]

Cash and Cash Equivalents		
	Checking account[2]: JT	$20,000
	Savings account[3]: JT	15,000
	Total Cash and Cash Equivalents	$35,000
Invested Assets[4]		
	SIMPLE IRA: H	$ 8,000
	Rollover IRA: H	195,000
	403(b): W	80,000
	Brokerage account: JT	160,000
	Ownership of Design This: JT	30,000
	Total Investments	$473,000
Personal-Use Assets		
	House: JT	$485,000
	Jewelry: W	27,000
	Watch: H	11,000
	Furniture and household items: JT	40,000
	Total Personal-Use Assets	$563,000

Total Assets   **$1,071,000**

LIABILITIES[5] AND NET WORTH

Current Liabilities		
	Credit card: JT	$16,000
	Credit card: W	4,275
	Credit card: H	7,450
	Total Current Liabilities	$27,725
Long-Term Liabilities		
	Mortgage: JT	$227,100
	Total Long-Term Liabilities	$227,100

Total Liabilities   **$254,825**

Net Worth   **$816,175**

Total Liabilities and Net Worth   **$1,071,000**

Notes to Statement of Financial Position

H = Husband
W = Wife
JT = Joint tenancy

[1] All assets are stated at fair market value.
[2] The checking account is a non-interest-bearing account.
[3] The savings account earns 2% per year.
[4] See details for selected information on investment accounts.
[5] Liabilities are stated at principal only.

Statement of Cash Flows
Jim and Brenda Quinn
January 1st – December 31st This Year

Annual Inflows

Jim's partnership income	$150,000
Brenda's salary	75,000
Investment income	17,350
Inheritance: cash	200,000
Inheritance: stock	100,000
Total Inflows	**$542,350**

Annual Outflows

Contribution to 403(b) plan	$ 13,000
Contribution to SIMPLE IRA	10,000
Federal tax	66,000
State and local taxes	12,194
Federal and state payroll taxes	16,550
Mortgage	52,164
Auto leases	12,000
Credit cards (P&I)	6,000
Property taxes	4,950
Auto and homeowners insurance	2,222
Life insurance (term: Jim and Brenda)	2,100
Utilities, cable, and phones	4,200
Auto maintenance	1,362
Food	5,200
Clothing/personal care	7,000
Entertainment and travel	7,300
Medical/dental	2,357
Pet care	1,500
Charitable contributions	13,000
Miscellaneous	1,875
Total Outflows	**$240,974**
Discretionary Cash Flow	**$301,376**

THE QUINNS' SELECTED INVESTMENT INFORMATION

Brenda's 403(b) plan

Mutual Funds

Name	Shares	5-Year Avg. Return	Std. Deviation	FMV
Aries (small-cap)	200	9.6%	11%	$10,000
Leo (large value)	400	7%	9%	20,000
Scorpio (global)	200	2.9%	2%	10,000
Taurus (large-cap)	200	5.75%	5%	20,000
Gemini (small-cap int'l.)	400	8.25%	15%	20,000
				$80,000

Jim's SIMPLE IRA

Asset	5-Year Avg. Return	Weight	Beta	FMV
Calico Corp. stock (large-cap)	6.7%	20%	.75	$1,500
Minx Corp. stock (int'l. stock)	12.1%	10%	–1.25	1,250
Tabby Corp. stock (small-cap)	15.0%	20%	2.00	1,550
Dalmatian Fund (int'l. bonds)	7.9%	30%	2.50	2,000
King Charles Fund (corp. bonds)	4.6%	20%	–1.00	1,700
				$8,000

Jim's IRA

Year	Jetson Corp. Stock Rate of Return	Munster Corp. Stock Rate of Return
1	4.2	–2.1%
2	4.0	–1.7%
3	–6.9	8.9%
4	–3.6	17.1%
5	9.1	6.9%
6	5.8	–3.4%
7	3.1	–2.2%
8	20.0	15.0%

Joint Brokerage Account

The Quinns hold all of their stock in a margin account. The initial margin requirement is 50%, and the maintenance requirement is 30%.

Among the investments in the account are:

- A **$5,000, 6-month Treasury bill**. They purchased it yesterday for $4,950.50.
- A **10-year, $10,000 U.S. Treasury bond**, 5% coupon, trading at par, purchased three years ago.

- A **20-year, $5,000 U.S. Treasury bond**, 6% coupon, trading at par, purchased two years ago.

- Ten $1,000 convertible bonds of **Alpha Corp.**, with maturities of 10 years.

- 600 shares of **Beagle Fund**, a closed-end investment company, purchased seven years ago with a beta of 1.2, a standard deviation of 12%, a coefficient of determination of 92%, and a five-year average return of 5%. The funds pay a $6 annual dividend per share.

- 200 shares of **Berry Corp.** common stock, which is a technology company that trades over-the-counter. It has a beta of 1.6, a standard deviation of 15%, a coefficient of determination of 70%, a five-year average return of 12%, a current price of $50, and an annual dividend of $1.00 per share, which is expected to grow at 4% per year for at least the next several years. The Quinns purchased the stock yesterday, believing they would earn their required 6.5% annual return for a stock with similar risks.

- A **Brittany Corp.** 10-year, 5.5% bond, purchased for $1,010, which may not be called for three years, but can be called thereafter for $1,055.

- A **Citadel Corp.** 10-year, noncallable, 9% bond, paid semiannually, purchased at par, and the bond was issued yesterday.

- A **Clemson Corp.** five-year bond with a coupon rate of 8%, semiannual payments, and a face value of $1,000, purchased for $1,020.

- Five bonds issued by the engineering company, **Compass Corp.**, purchased at par. Each bond has a $1,000 face amount, an 8% annual coupon rate, and a call price of $1,080. The bonds are currently selling for $1,020 each, the same price as a year ago, and may be called any time prior to their maturity date, which is five years from now. The coupon interest payments are made once a year. They have a rating of B.

- 400 shares of **Crazy Corp.** preferred stock, which has a beta of .97, a standard deviation of 5%, a current price of $22 per share, a five-year average return of 6%, and pays an annual dividend of $2. The Quinns bought the stock last month with a goal of an 18% return, given the risks associated with the company.

- Five zero-coupon bonds issued by an oil company called **Dante Corp.** which are scheduled to mature in six years at a face value of $1,000 each; the current market price of each bond is $920. They bought the bonds one year ago for $750 each.

- 300 shares of **Indigo Fund, an open-end technology mutual fund**. The stock has historically exhibited a beta of 2.0, has a standard deviation of 22%, a coefficient of determination of 65%, and a five-year average return of 15%; it is currently selling for $78.00 per share and pays no dividend. It is expected to grow at 6% per year for the near future. The P/E ratio is 3.

- 1,000 shares of **Score Corp.** common stock, which is a software company listed on the NYSE MKT (formerly AMEX). It has a beta of .90, a standard deviation of 11%, a coefficient of determination of 30%, a five-year average return of 8%, and is currently selling for $68, pays no dividend, and is expected to grow at 5% per year. The P/E ratio is 2.40.

- Four tax-exempt municipal bonds issued by **Spring Lake**, the city in North Carolina where the Quinns live. Each bond has a $1,000 face amount, is selling for about $980 currently – the same price as a year ago when they bought them, has a 5% annual coupon rate, and is scheduled to mature four years from now.

- 300 shares of **Tanker Fund**, an open-end investment company, purchased six years ago, with a beta of 1.8, a standard deviation of 17%, a coefficient of determination of 61%, and a five-year average return of –5%. The fund pays a $3 annual dividend per share.

Brenda is considering investing in a 7% CD or a limited partnership that would generate the following cash flows at the end of Years 1-5:

Year	Cash Flow
1	$ 10,000
2	20,000
3	40,000
4	80,000
5	160,000

SAM'S BROKERAGE ACCOUNT

Asset	Type	Shares	Basis/Share	FMV/Share
Nano Systems stock (tech.)	Small-cap	300	$30.00	$110.00
SEMI Stock (tech.)	Int'l.	500	$12.00	$25.00
Interiors Software stock	Small-cap	1,500	$30.00	$18.00
Rydel Properties REIT	REIT	1,000	$22.00	$26.13
Stein & Cattle REIT Fund	REIT Fund	20,000	$15.00	$18.10

Sam acquired Nano Systems one year ago, SEMI two years ago, Interiors 18 months ago, Rydel six months ago, and Stein & Cattle three months ago. None of Sam's investments pay dividends.

JIM AND BRENDA QUINN CASE
APPLICATION QUESTIONS

1. What would be the most appropriate investment for the Quinns to replace the Compass Corp. bonds if they are called?

(Topic 33)

  A. A bond with a similar yield and the same credit quality

  B. A bond with a higher rating but slightly lower yield

  C. A growth stock with no dividend and a potential cure for cancer

  D. A high-yield bond mutual fund

2. If the Alpha Corp.'s business declines but remains viable, which of the following is most likely true?

(Topic 33)

  A. The probable return of the investment will be closer to that of a bond.

  B. The bond will increase along with the stock price of Alpha Corp.

  C. The bond will not pay interest.

  D. The bond will have a higher yield to maturity for the Quinns if the price declines.

3. What would be an appropriate alternative to the Quinns' shares of the Tanker Fund?

(Topic 33)

  A. Shares of an S&P 500 index fund

  B. Shares of the two best performing NASDAQ stocks last year

  C. Shares of Minisoft, which trades on the NASDAQ

  D. Shares in a leveraged, high-yield, closed-end bond fund

4. If the Quinns wish to increase their equity exposure, what might be the best alternative?

(Topic 33)

  A. A corporate bond fund

  B. An index call option

  C. An index fund

  D. A closed-end, high-yield bond fund

5. What is the difference in structure of the Tanker Fund and the Beagle Fund?

(Topic 33)

  A. The Beagle Fund has the ability to issue more shares to create more supply.

  B. The Tanker Fund always sells at its NAV after the exchanges close each day.

  C. The Tanker Fund can trade at a discount to its NAV.

  D. The Beagle Fund's capitalization is not fixed.

6. Under what circumstances would Sam profit the most if he bought an Interiors $20 put option?

(Topic 33)

  A. Interiors going to $16

  B. Interiors going to $17

  C. Interiors going to $22

  D. Interiors going to $23

7. Which of the following investments has the highest systematic risk?

(Topic 34)

  A. Berry Corp.

  B. Beagle Fund

  C. Indigo Fund

  D. Tanker Fund

8. Which of the Quinns' investments is most affected by inflation risk?

(Topic 34)

- A. Compass Corp.
- B. Berry Corp.
- C. Tanker Fund
- D. Beagle Fund

9. Which of the Quinns' investments has the highest reinvestment rate risk?

(Topic 34)

- A. Dante Corp.
- B. Berry Corp.
- C. Score Corp.
- D. Indigo Fund

10. Which of the following investments has the most total risk?

(Topic 34)

- A. Score Corp.
- B. Beagle Fund
- C. Tanker Fund
- D. Indigo Fund

11. Which of the following would help manage the unsystematic risk of the Quinns' brokerage account?

(Topic 34)

- A. A foreign stock fund
- B. A technology stock
- C. A convertible bond
- D. A stock listed on the Dow Jones

12. Which of the following of the Quinns' assets are moving most nearly to the same extent?

(Topic 35)

- A. Indigo Fund and Berry Corp.
- B. Indigo Fund and Score Corp.
- C. Score Corp. and Beagle Fund
- D. Score Corp. and Tanker Fund

13. The variation of which of the following assets can be attributed mostly to the movement of its index?

(Topic 35)

- A. Score Corp.
- B. Berry Corp.
- C. Tanker Fund
- D. Beagle Fund

14. For which of the following is the measure of unsystematic risk essentially 30%?

(Topic 35)

- A. Score Corp.
- B. Berry Corp.
- C. Tanker Fund
- D. Beagle Fund

15. Which of the following securities is most likely to deliver periodic returns closest to its expectation?

(Topic 35)

- A. Indigo Fund
- B. Berry Corp.
- C. Score Corp.
- D. Beagle Fund

16. Which of the following is correct if the Quinns create a portfolio composed of 50% Munster Corp. stock and 50% Flintstone stock, if Flintstone has an identical standard deviation around its rate of return as Munster?

(Topic 35)

A. If Munster Corp. and Flintstone Corp. are perfectly negatively correlated, the standard deviation of the portfolio will be twice that of Munster Corp. or Flintstone Corp.

B. If Munster Corp. and Flintstone Corp. are perfectly positively correlated, the standard deviation of the portfolio will be zero.

C. If Munster Corp. and Flintstone Corp. are perfectly positively correlated, the standard deviation of the portfolio will be twice that of either Munster Corp. or Flintstone Corp.

D. If Munster Corp. and Flintstone Corp. are perfectly negatively correlated, the standard deviation of the portfolio will be zero.

17. What is the required rate of return under the security market line (SML) for Tabby Corp.?

(Topic 35)

A. 7%

B. 10%

C. 14%

D. 17%

18. What is the required rate of return under the capital market line (CML) model for the Aries Fund?

(Topic 35)

A. 8.79%

B. 12.30%

C. 15.83%

D. 19.32%

19. If Sam were to sell his shares of the Nano Systems, what would be his total return?

(Topic 36)

A. 27%

B. 80%

C. 100%

D. 267%

20. Which of the following is the Quinns' current yield on Berry Corp. common stock?

(Topic 36)

A. 2.0%

B. 2.4%

C. 3.0%

D. 3.2%

21. What was the time-weighted return (TWR) of Munster Corp. stock for the first six years the Quinns held the stock?

(Topic 36)

A. 2%

B. 4%

C. 6%

D. 8%

22. What is the yield to maturity for the Clemson Corp. bond?

(Topic 36)

A. 3.76%

B. 3.99%

C. 7.52%

D. 7.98%

23. What is the yield to call, based on the earliest call, for the Brittany Corp. bond?

(Topic 36)

A. 3.0%

B. 3.4%

C. 6.0%

D. 6.8%

24. What is the Treynor index for the Dalmatian Fund?

(Topic 36)

    A. 1.96
    B. 2.40
    C. 3.76
    D. 5.44

25. During their annual review, the Quinns have inquired as to whether the Leo Fund has outperformed the market on a risk-adjusted basis. Which of the following is the best response for the financial planner to answer the Quinn's question if the Leo Fund is not diversified?

(Topic 36)

    A. A risk-adjusted return comparison of a mutual fund and the market cannot be made.
    B. The Leo Fund's Sharpe ratio of .44 indicates that it has outperformed the market on a risk-adjusted basis.
    C. Mutual funds should only be compared to other similar mutual funds and should not be compared to the market.
    D. The Leo Fund's risk-adjusted return over the last 5 years is well below that of the market.

26. What is the Jensen ratio for the Dalmatian Fund?

(Topic 36)

    A. −20.5
    B. −12.6
    C. 12.6
    D. 20.5

27. With which form of efficient market hypothesis would Sam be most likely to agree?

(Topic 37)

    A. Strong form
    B. Semi-strong form
    C. Weak form
    D. None. He would probably agree more with anomalies.

28. Which of the following would be the best advice for Sam?

(Topic 37)

    A. He should consider purchasing some bonds.
    B. He needs to rebalance his portfolio according to a more appropriate asset allocation plan.
    C. He needs to purchase some larger-cap stocks.
    D. He needs to rethink his percentage of real estate.

29. If Brenda's mother wants to make a gift of $100,000 to the Quinns to be invested for the twins' college education, which of the following is the most appropriate asset allocation for this account?

(Topics 37, 33, and 41)

A. 30% large cap stock fund, 10% mid-cap stock fund, 10% international stock fund, 20% emerging markets fund, 20% intermediate term bond fund, 10% high yield bond fund.

B. 30% aggressive growth fund, 25% international stock fund, 15% emerging markets fund, 10% municipal bond fund, 10% GNMA fund, 10% private equity.

C. 35% large cap value fund, 5% mid-cap stock fund, 5% international fund, 20% intermediate term bond fund, 20% municipal bond fund, 15% short-term U.S. government bond fund.

D. 10% large cap growth fund, 70% certificate of deposit with 5-year maturity, 20% money market.

30. If Brenda's mother wishes to invest $750,000 to provide additional retirement income, which of the following should the planner do first?

(Topic 37)

A. Assess her risk tolerance level.

B. Evaluate the impact of taxes on her portfolio income.

C. Analyze the need for inflation protection.

D. Evaluate risk-return trade-offs for various asset classes using the capital market line (CML).

31. Which of the following is the most appropriate asset allocation mix for Brenda's mother's "fun money"?

(Topics 37, 33, and 41)

A. 40% large cap growth fund, 10% mid-cap value fund, 10% emerging markets fund, 30% high yield bonds, 10% REITs.

B. 40% large cap value stocks, 10% international stock fund, 20% high yield bond fund, 10% intermediate term treasury fund, 20% REITS.

C. 30% S&P 500 index fund, 15% MSCI EAFE index ETF, 15% small-cap value fund, 5% emerging markets fund, 20% municipal bond fund, 10% REITs, 5% GNMA fund.

D. 50% blue chip stocks, 30% municipal bond fund, 10% REITs, 10% GNMA fund.

32. What is the intrinsic value of Berry Corp. common stock for Jim and Brenda?

(Topic 38)

A. $15.38
B. $33.20
C. $41.60
D. $50.00

33. Which stock, Indigo Fund or Score Corp., has a higher earnings per share?

(Topic 38)

A. Indigo Fund
B. Score Corp.
C. They are identical.
D. There is insufficient information to determine the answer.

34. Which bond should you recommend the Quinns buy to fund the twins' college education for their freshman year?

(Topic 38)

A. AA-rated, zero-coupon, 8-year maturity, selling for $575
B. AA-rated, 5-year maturity, 4.73 duration, 6.25% coupon, selling for $954
C. AAA-rated, 7-year maturity, 5.76 duration, 6.5% coupon, selling for $982
D. AAA-rated, 9-year maturity, 6.42 duration, 7% coupon, selling for $1,000

35. How much are the Quinns willing to pay for more shares of Crazy Corp.?

(Topic 38)

A. No more than $11.11
B. No more than $14.88
C. No more than $22.00
D. No more than $36.00

36. What is the intrinsic value of the Citadel Corp. bond?

(Topic 38)

A. $910
B. $955
C. $1,000
D. $1,026

37. If interest rates are expected to decline in the near future, a portfolio manager is most likely to increase which of the following holdings?

(Topic 39)

A. Clemson Corp. bonds
B. Dante Corp bonds
C. Spring Lake bonds
D. 20-year Treasury bonds

38. When developing an Investment Policy Statement (IPS) for Jim and Brenda Quinn, which of the following is least appropriate?

(Topic 39)

A. A listing of their current portfolio holdings.
B. A requirement that no more than 5% of the bond portfolio be invested in high yield bonds.
C. A guideline for asset allocation of 40% – 60% stocks, 25% – 50% fixed income, and 10% – 15% cash equivalents.
D. A guideline for monitoring of the portfolio on a semi-annual basis, with rebalancing according to the stated range of percentages for each asset class.

39. Which of the following benchmark indices is most appropriate for evaluating the performance of Sam's brokerage account?

(Topic 39)

A. S&P 500 index
B. MSCI EAFE index
C. Wilshire 5000 index
D. A blended benchmark that includes the Vanguard REIT index, the Russell 2000 index, and the MSCI EAFE index

40. What is the taxable equivalent of the coupon rate on the Quinns' Spring Lake bonds?

(Topic 39)

A. 6.57%
B. 7.55%
C. 8.01%
D. 9.73%

41. Which of the following pairs of assets would you recommend that Sam sell to minimize his federal income taxes?

(Topic 39)

A. Nano Systems and Interiors
B. Nano Systems and SEMI
C. Rydel and Stein & Cattle
D. SEMI and Stein & Cattle

42. The technique of dollar-cost averaging will likely be most beneficial for the Quinns when used with which of the following investments?

(Topic 40)

A. Leo Fund
B. Indigo Fund
C. Taurus Fund
D. Crazy Corp.

43. Which of the following is the closest to the Quinns' current bond strategy?

(Topic 40)

A. A ladder
B. A barbell
C. A bullet
D. There does not appear to be a discernible strategy.

44. What would you recommend to the Quinns as a strategy to immunize their joint brokerage account for their goal of buying a second home?

(Topic 40)

A. Purchase 20-year bonds.
B. Purchase 30-year bonds.
C. Purchase bonds to give the account a weighted-average duration of 20 years.
D. Purchase bonds to give the account a weighted-average duration of 30 years.

45. What price must the SEMI stock fall to in order for Brenda to receive a margin call if Brenda purchases 200 shares of SEMI at its current price? (Assume the SEMI stock is the only investment in the account.)

(Topic 40)

A. $17.86
B. $18.44
C. $18.93
D. $19.93

46. The Quinns are optimistic about the long-term growth of Berry Corp., which has had a 10% increase in share price in the last month. Which of the following would you recommend if they want to lock in a minimum price, in case the shares drop?

(Topic 40)

A. Buy $48 put options.
B. Buy $52 call options.
C. Sell $52 put options.
D. Sell $48 call options.

47. Which of the following might be an advantage of Brenda choosing the Limited Partnership Interest over the CD?

(Topic 41)

A. Increased liquidity
B. Diversification
C. High degree of marketability
D. Income taxed at capital gain rates

48. Which of the following alternative investments is most appropriate for Jim and Brenda Quinn?

(Topic 41)

A. REITs
B. Private equity
C. Hedge funds
D. Artwork

49. Brenda's mother would like a recommendation for the $200,000 investment for income. Which of the following is most likely to meet her objectives for this investment?

(Topic 41)

A. Private Placement
B. Limited Partnership Interest
C. Private Equity Fund
D. Master Limited Partnership (MLP)

50. The Quinns are considering adding REITs to one of their accounts. Which account should their planner recommend the REITs be held in?

(Topic 41)

A. The taxable brokerage account because their REIT dividends are taxed as qualified dividends.
B. The taxable brokerage account because their REIT dividends are taxed as ordinary income.
C. Jim's IRA because his REIT dividends are taxed as ordinary income.
D. Brenda's 403(b) because REIT dividends are taxed as qualified dividends.

51. If Sam Moore sells the duck stamp collection for $100,000, how will the gain be taxed?

(Topic 41)

A. At Sam's marginal tax rate
B. At 20% capital gain rate
C. At 28% capital gain rate plus 3.8%
D. At 0% because it was inherited property

2017 vs. 2018 Key Facts and Figures

Note: We highlighted the information that changed between 2017 and 2018 with a box.

* 2018 numbers are based on the Tax Cuts and Jobs Act (TCJA) of 2017. (Note: the formal name of H.R. 1 is "An Act to provide for reconciliation pursuant to titles II and V of the concurrent resolution on the budget for fiscal year 2018", however, we will refer to it by its former and more commonly used name, the "Tax Cuts and Jobs Act".)

Personal Exemption	**2017**	**2018**
Personal exemption amount per person	4,050	N/A
Phaseout of 2% for every $2,500 ($1,250 MFS) or fraction thereof that AGI exceeds the following amounts		
Single	$261,500	N/A
Married filing jointly or surviving spouse	$313,800	N/A
Married filing separately	$156,900	N/A
Head of household	$287,650	N/A

Standard Deductions	**2017**	**2018**
Single	6,350	12,000
Married filing jointly or surviving spouse	12,700	24,000
Married filing separately	6,350	12,000
Head of household	9,350	18,000

Additional standard deduction amount if age 65 or older or blind

	2017	2018
Married (per person)	1,250	1,300
Unmarried	1,550	1,600

Phaseout of Itemized Deductions	**2017**	**2018**
Phaseout of 3% of the amount by which AGI exceeds the threshold:		
Single	$261,500	N/A
Married filing jointly or surviving spouse	$313,800	N/A
Married filing separately	$156,900	N/A
Head of household	$287,650	N/A

Employment Taxes	2017	2018
Social Security tax rate		
Employer's portion	6.2%	6.2%
Employee's portion	6.2%	6.2%
Total for self-employed individual	12.4%	12.4%
Maximum amount of earnings subject to Social Security taxes	$127,200	$128,400
Medicare tax rate		
Employer's portion	1.45%	1.45%
Employee's portion (on all net self-employment income)	1.45%	1.45%
Total for self-employed individual (on all net self-employment income)	2.9%	2.9%
Employee's additional Medicare surtax on earnings above $200,000 ($250,000 MFJ, $125,000 MFS)	.9%	.9%
Maximum amount of earnings subject to Medicare taxes	Unlimited	Unlimited
Total employment taxes		
Employer's portion	7.65%	7.65%
Employee's portion	7.65%	7.65%
Total for self-employed individual	15.3%	15.3%
Percentage of self-employed earnings subject to SE taxes	92.35%	92.35%
Percentage of SE taxes deducted above-the-line	50%	50%

Kiddie Tax	2017	2018
Amount of unearned income not subject to tax due to standard deduction	1,050	TCJA is unclear regarding these thresholds. Waiting for IRS guidance.
Amount of unearned income taxed at child's rate	1,050	
Unearned income above these amounts taxed at	parents' marginal tax rate	
Earned income of a child under age 19 (24 if a student)		Taxed as single
Unearned income of a child under age 19 (24 if a student)		Taxed using Trust & Estate ordinary income rates and LTCG rate breakpoints

Child Tax Credit	2017	2018
Child tax credit per child under age 17	1,000	2,000
Tax credit per qualifying dependent, other than a child under age 17	N/A	500
Phaseout of $50 for every $1,000 or fraction thereof that AGI exceeds the following amounts (completely phased out if AGI exceeds threshold by $20,000 per child):		
Single	75,000	200,000
Married filing jointly or surviving spouse	110,000	400,000
Married filing separately	55,000	200,000
Head of household	75,000	200,000

Child or Dependent Care Credit	**2017**	**2018**
Maximum amount of qualifying expenses		
One child or dependent	3,000	3,000
Two or more children or dependents	6,000	6,000
AGI amount when credit reduced to 20% level	43,000	43,000
Maximum credit, assuming taxpayer's AGI at 20% level		
One child or dependent	600	600
Two or more children or dependents	1,200	1,200

American Opportunity Tax Credit	**2017**	**2018**
Credit percentage amounts		
First $2,000	100%	100%
Second $2,000	25%	25%
Maximum credit	$2,500	$2,500
Phaseout at the following AGI amounts:		
Single	80,000 – 90,000	80,000 – 90,000
Married filing jointly or surviving spouse	160,000 – 180,000	160,000 – 180,000
Married filing separately	0	0
Head of household	80,000 – 90,000	80,000 – 90,000

Lifetime Learning Credit	**2017**	**2018**
Credit percentage amounts		
First $10,000	20%	20%
Maximum credit	$2,000	$2,000
Phaseout at the following AGI amounts:		
Single	56,000 – 66,000	57,000 – 67,000
Married filing jointly or surviving spouse	112,000 – 132,000	114,000 – 134,000
Married filing separately	0	0
Head of household	56,000 – 66,000	57,000 – 67,000

Deduction for Education Loan Interest	2017	2018
Above-the-line deduction for educational loan interest payments	2,500	2,500

Phaseout of educational loan interest deduction at the following AGI amounts:

	2017	2018
Single	65,000 – 80,000	65,000 – 80,000
Married filing jointly or surviving spouse	135,000 – 165,000	135,000 – 165,000
Married filing separately	0	0
Head of household	65,000 – 80,000	65,000 – 80,000

Deduction for Tuition and Related Expenses	2017	2018
Above-the-line deduction for tuition and related expenses	expired	expired

AGI limitations to claim up to the full $4,000 above-the-line deduction

	2017	2018
Single	expired	expired
Married filing jointly or surviving spouse	expired	expired
Married filing separately	expired	expired
Head of household	expired	expired

AGI limitation to claim up to $2,000 above-the-line deduction if AGI exceeds the limits above for the $4,000 deduction

	2017	2018
Single	expired	expired
Married filing jointly or surviving spouse	expired	expired
Married filing separately	expired	expired
Head of household	expired	expired

Tax-Free Treatment on Series EE Bonds to Pay Qualified Education Expenses	2017	2018

Phaseout of tax-free treatment on Series EE bonds at the following AGI amounts:

	2017	2018
Single	78,150 – 93,150	79,700 – 94,700
Married filing jointly or surviving spouse	117,250 – 147,250	119,550 – 149,550
Married filing separately	78,150 – 93,150	79,700 – 94,700
Head of household	78,150 – 93,150	79,700 – 94,700

Coverdell Education Savings Accounts	2017	2018
Coverdell Education Savings Account (ESA) contribution limit	2,000	2,000

Phaseout of ESA contribution at the following AGI amounts:

	2017	2018
Single	95,000 – 110,000	95,000 – 110,000
Married filing jointly or surviving spouse	190,000 – 220,000	190,000 – 220,000
Married filing separately	95,000 – 110,000	95,000 – 110,000
Head of household	95,000 – 110,000	95,000 – 110,000

Section 179 Deduction	2017	2018
Section 179 deduction amount	510,000	1,000,000
Limit on property placed in service	2,030,000	2,500,000

Health Savings Accounts	2017	2018

High deductible health plan minimum deductible amounts

	2017	2018
Single	1,300	1,350
Family	2,600	2,700

Maximum out-of-pocket limits

	2017	2018
Single	6,550	6,650
Family	13,100	13,300

Contribution Maximums

	2017	2018
Single	3,400	3,450
Family	6,750	6,900
Catch-up contributions (age 55 or older)	1,000	1,000

Income Tax Rates		2017		2018

Marginal tax rate ends at the following income levels:

Single				
	10%	9,325	10%	9,525
	15%	37,950	12%	38,700
	25%	91,900	22%	82,500
	28%	191,650	24%	157,500
	33%	416,700	32%	200,000
	35%	418,400	35%	500,000
	39.6%	Unlimited	37%	Unlimited
Married filing jointly or surviving spouse				
	10%	18,650	10%	19,050
	15%	75,900	12%	77,400
	25%	153,100	22%	165,000
	28%	233,350	24%	315,000
	33%	416,700	32%	400,000
	35%	470,700	35%	600,000
	39.6%	Unlimited	37%	Unlimited
Married filing separately				
	10%	9,325	10%	9,525
	15%	37,950	12%	38,700
	25%	76,550	22%	82,500
	28%	116,675	24%	157,500
	33%	208,350	32%	200,000
	35%	235,350	35%	300,000
	39.6%	Unlimited	37%	Unlimited
Head of household				
	10%	13,350	10%	13,600
	15%	50,800	12%	51,800
	25%	131,200	22%	82,500
	28%	212,500	24%	157,500
	33%	416,700	32%	200,000
	35%	444,550	35%	500,000
	39.6%	Unlimited	37%	Unlimited

Income Tax Rates		2017		2018
Trusts, Estates; for 2018, Kiddie Tax on Unearned Income of a Child Under Age 19 (24 if a student)				
	15%	2,550	10%	2,550
	25%	6,000	24%	9,150
	28%	9,150	35%	12,500
	33%	12,500	37%	Unlimited
	39.6%	Unlimited		

Long-Term Capital Gain Rates	2017	2018
Tax rates for long-term capital gains and dividends		
Taxpayers in the 39.6% bracket	20%*	
Taxpayers in the 25%, 28%, 33%, and 35% tax brackets	15%*	
Taxpayers in the 10% or 15% tax bracket	0%	
Long-term capital gain and dividend tax rate ends at the following income levels:		
Single		
	0%	$ 38,600
	15%*	425,800
	20% *	Unlimited
Married filing jointly or surviving spouse		
	0%	$ 77,200
	15%*	479,000
	20%*	Unlimited
Married filing separately		
	0%	$ 38,600
	15%*	239,500
	20%*	Unlimited
Head of household		
	0%	$ 51,700
	15%*	452,400
	20%*	Unlimited
Trusts & Estates		
	0%	$ 2,600
	15%*	12,700
	20%*	Unlimited

Long-Term Capital Gain Rates (continued)	2017	2018
IRS Section 1250 depreciation recapture	25%	25%
Collectibles	28%	28%

*For single taxpayers with AGI over $200,000 ($250,000 MFJ; $125,000 MFS; $12,500 Estates & Trusts) an additional 3.8% Medicare Contribution tax will apply to capital gains to the extent that Net Investment Income exceeds the threshold level.

Alternative Minimum Taxes (AMT)	2017	2018
AMT exemption amounts		
Single	54,300	70,300
Married filing jointly or surviving spouse	84,500	109,400
Married filing separately	42,250	54,700
Head of household	54,300	70,300

Phaseout of AMT exemption of 25% of AMTI that exceeds the following amounts:

	2017	2018
Single	120,700	500,000
Married filing jointly or surviving spouse	160,900	1,000,000
Married filing separately	80,450	500,000
Head of household	120,700	500,000

Alternative Minimum Taxes (AMT)	2017	2018
AMT tax rates		
Single, married filing jointly, head of household, and estates and trusts		
26% on income up to	187,800	191,500
28% on income over	187,800	191,500
Married filing separately		
26% on income up to	93,900	95,750
28% on income over	93,900	95,750
Maximum tax rate on capital gains and dividends	20%**	20%**

**The maximum tax rates on capital gains and dividends used in computing the regular tax are used in computing the tentative minimum tax as well (15% for most taxpayers, 20% for high-income taxpayers)

Estate, Gift, and GST Taxes	**2017**	**2018**

Annual gift tax exclusions

Gifts to any person	14,000	15,000
Gifts to a U.S. citizen spouse	Unlimited	Unlimited
Gifts to a noncitizen spouse	149,000	152,000

Lifetime gifts

Applicable exclusion amount	5,490,000	11,200,000***
Applicable credit amount	2,141,800	4,425,800

Bequests at death

Applicable exclusion amount	5,490,000	11,200,000***
Applicable credit amount	2,141,800	4,425,800

*** The Tax Cuts and Jobs Act of 2017 doubled the base amount of the estate and gift tax exclusion, for years 2018 – 2025. The exact 2018 inflation-adjusted exclusion amount will be calculated and released by the IRS some time during 2018, but is expected to be approximately $11.2 million.

Top estate tax rate	40%	40%
Top gift tax rate	40%	40%

Generation-skipping transfer (GST) tax

Annual GST exclusion	14,000	15,000
Lifetime GST exemption amount	5,490,000	11,200,000***
Flat GST tax rate	40%	40%

Special-use valuation limit	1,120,000	1,140,000
Section 6166 special 2% interest rate	1,490,000	1,520,000

Retirement Plans	2017	2018
Taxpayer or employee contribution limits		
IRA (combined traditional and Roth IRA limit)	5,500	5,500
401(k) plans	18,000	18,500
403(b) plans	18,000	18,500
457 plans	18,000	18,500
SIMPLE plans	12,500	12,500
Catch-up contribution limits		
IRA (combined traditional and Roth IRA limit)	1,000	1,000
401(k) plans	6,000	6,000
403(b) plans	6,000	6,000
457 plans	6,000	6,000
SIMPLE plans	3,000	3,000
Defined-contribution plan limitations		
Participating payroll	25%	25%
Maximum percentage of employee's compensation	100%	100%
Participant's contribution not to exceed	54,000	55,000
Maximum compensation to be considered	270,000	275,000
Defined-benefit plan limitations		
Maximum annual benefit	215,000	220,000
Maximum compensation to be considered	270,000	275,000
SEP plan limitations		
Maximum percentage of employee's compensation	25%	25%
Participant's contribution not to exceed	54,000	55,000
Minimum compensation needed to participate	600	600
Maximum compensation to be considered	270,000	275,000

Qualified plan definitions

Highly-compensated employee		
Any employee who owns 5% or more of the company		
Any employee among the top 20% highest-paid and paid more than	120,000	120,000

Retirement Plans	2017	2018
Key employee		
Any officer earning	175,000	175,000
Any employee who owns 5% or more of the company		
Any employee who owns 1% or more of the company and makes	150,000	150,000
Qualified Longevity Annuity Contract (QLAC)		
Maximum premium invested	125,000	130,000

IRAs	2017	2018
Phaseout of IRA deduction for an active participant at the following amounts:		
Single	62,000 – 72,000	63,000 – 73,000
Married filing jointly or surviving spouse – for the participant spouse	99,000 – 119,000	101,000 – 121,000
Married filing jointly – for a spouse who is not themselves a participant, but the other spouse is a participant	186,000 – 196,000	189,000 – 199,000
Married filing separately	0 – 10,000	0 – 10,000
Head of household	62,000 – 72,000	63,000 – 73,000

Phaseout of Roth IRA contributions at the following amounts:		
Single	118,000 – 133,000	120,000 – 135,000
Married filing jointly or surviving spouse	186,000 – 196,000	189,000 – 199,000
Married filing separately	0 – 10,000	0 – 10,000
Head of household	118,000 – 133,000	120,000 – 135,000

Social Security Benefits	2017	2018
Limit on earnings before the reduction of benefits of $1 for every $2 earnings above limitation ($1 for every $3 in the year of full retirement age)		
Under full retirement age	16,920	17,040
Persons reaching full retirement age	44,880	45,360
Over full retirement age	n/a	n/a
Amount needed to earn one Social Security credit	1,300	1,320

Medicare	2017	2018
Part A deductibles for hospital stays		
Days 1-60 (total deductible for all 60 days)	1,316	1,340
Days 61-90 (deductible per day)	329	335
Days 91-150 (deductible per day)	658	670
Part A deductibles for skilled nursing facility		
Days 1-20	0	0
Days 21-100 (deductible per day)	164.50	167.50
Part B monthly premium (monthly premiums will be higher if AGI exceeds $85,000 for single taxpayers or $170,000 MFJ taxpayers)	134.00	134.00
Part B annual deductible	183	183

TAX TABLES

Income Tax Rate Tables

SCHEDULE X: Single
2018 – TCJA

Taxable Income Over	But Not Over	Pay	+	% on Excess	of the amount over
$ 0 –	9,525	$ 0		10%	$ 0
9,525 –	38,700	952.50		12	9,525
38,700 –	82,500	4,453.50		22	38,700
82,500 –	157,500	14,089.50		24	82,500
157,500 –	200,000	32,089.50		32	157,500
200,000 –	500,000	45,689.50		35	200,000
Over 500,000		150,689.50		37	500,000

SCHEDULE Y-1: Married Filing Jointly and Surviving Spouse
2018 – TCJA

Taxable Income Over	But Not Over	Pay	+	% on Excess	of the amount over
$ 0 –	19,050	$ 0		10%	$ 0
19,050 –	77,400	1,905.00		12	19,050
77,400 –	165,000	8907.00		22	77,400
165,000 –	315,000	28,179.00		24	165,000
315,000 –	400,000	64,179.00		32	315,000
400,000 –	600,000	91,379.00		35	400,000
Over 600,000		161,379.00		37	600,000

SCHEDULE Y-2: Married Filing Separately
2018 – TCJA

Taxable Income Over	But Not Over	Pay	+	% on Excess	of the amount over
$ 0 –	9,525	$ 0		10%	$ 0
9,525 –	38,700	952.50		12	9,525
38,700 –	82,500	4,453.50		22	38,700
82,500 –	157,500	14,089.50		24	82,500
157,500 –	200,000	32,089.50		32	157,500
200,000 –	300,000	45,689.50		35	200,000
Over 300,000		80,689.50		37	300,000

SCHEDULE Z: Head of Household

2018 – TCJA

Taxable Income Over		But Not Over	Pay	+	% on Excess	of the amount over	
$ 0	–	13,600	$ 0		10%	$ 0	
13,600	–	51,800	1,360.00		12	13,600	
51,800	–	82,500	5,944.00		22	51,800	
82,500	–	157,500	12,698.00		24	82,500	
157,500	–	200,000	30,698.00		32	157,500	
200,000	–	500,000	44,298.00		35	200,000	
Over 500,000			149,298.00		37	500,000	

Married filing jointly with income over $250,000 and singles over $200,000 who have net investment income will be subject to an additional 3.8% tax on the lesser of net investment income or the excess of MAGI over the threshold amount, whichever is less.

High income individuals are subject to increased payroll taxes. All wages, bonuses, commissions, and self-employment income are subject to an additional Medicare tax of 0.9% above the thresholds of $200,000 for single filers, $250,000 for joint filers, and $125,000 for spouses filing separately.

CORPORATE INCOME TAX RATES

2018

For tax years beginning after December 31, 2017, the Tax Cuts and Jobs Act permanently changed the corporate tax rate to a flat 21%.

ESTATES AND NONGRANTOR TRUSTS INCOME TAX RATES

2018 – TCJA

Taxable Income Over		But Not Over	Pay	+	% on Excess	of the amount over	
$ 0	–	2,550	$ 0		10%	$ 0	
2,550	–	9,150	255.00		24	2,550	
9,150	–	12,500	1,839.00		35	9,150	
Over 12,500			3,011.50		37	12,500	

2018 ESTATE AND GIFT TAX RATE SCHEDULE

Column A	Column B	Column C	Column D
			Rate of tax on excess over amount in Column A
Taxable amount over	Taxable amount not over	Tax on amount in Column A	Column A Percent
$ 0	$ 10,000	$ 0	18
10,000	20,000	1,800	20
20,000	40,000	3,800	22
40,000	60,000	8,200	24
60,000	80,000	13,000	26
80,000	100,000	18,200	28
100,000	150,000	23,800	30
150,000	250,000	38,800	32
250,000	500,000	70,800	34
500,000	750,000	155,800	37
750,000	1,000,000	248,300	39
Over 1,000,000		345,800	40

Applicable Exclusion/Credit Amount for Estate Tax

Year	Applicable Exclusion	Applicable Credit
2006-2008	2,000,000	780,000
2009	3,500,000	1,455,800
2010-2011	5,000,000	1,730,800
2012	5,120,000	1,772,800
2013	5,250,000	2,045,800
2014	5,340,000	2,081,800
2015	5,430,000	2,117,800
2016	5,450,000	2,125,800
2017	5,490,000	2,141,800
2018	11,200,000	4,425,800

Applicable Exclusion/Credit Amount (Gift Tax)

Year	Applicable Exclusion	Applicable Credit
2006-2009	1,000,000	345,800
2010	1,000,000	330,800
2011	5,000,000	1,730,800
2012	5,120,000	1,772,800
2013	5,250,000	2,045,800
2014	5,340,000	2,081,800
2015	5,430,000	2,117,800
2016	5,450,000	2,125,800
2017	5,490,000	2,141,800
2018	11,200,000	4,425,800

Table VI – Ordinary Joint Life and Last Survivor Annuities; Two Lives – Expected Return Multiples

Ages	65	66	67	68	69	70	71	72	73	74
65	25.0	24.6	24.2	23.8	23.4	23.1	22.8	22.5	22.2	22.0
66	24.6	24.1	23.7	23.3	22.9	22.5	22.2	21.9	21.6	21.4
67	24.2	23.7	23.2	22.8	22.4	22.0	21.7	21.3	21.0	20.8
68	23.8	23.3	22.8	22.3	21.9	21.5	21.2	20.8	20.5	20.2
69	23.4	22.9	22.4	21.9	21.5	21.1	20.7	20.3	20.0	19.6
70	23.1	22.5	22.0	21.5	21.1	20.6	20.2	19.8	19.4	19.1
71	22.8	22.2	21.7	21.2	20.7	20.2	19.8	19.4	19.0	18.6
72	22.5	21.9	21.3	20.8	20.3	19.8	19.4	18.9	18.5	18.2
73	22.2	21.6	21.0	20.5	20.0	19.4	19.0	18.5	18.1	17.7
74	22.0	21.4	20.8	20.2	19.6	19.1	18.6	18.2	17.7	17.3
75	21.8	21.1	20.5	19.9	19.3	18.8	18.3	17.8	17.3	16.9
76	21.6	20.9	20.3	19.7	19.1	18.5	18.0	17.5	17.0	16.5
77	21.4	20.7	20.1	19.4	18.8	18.3	17.7	17.2	16.7	16.2
78	21.2	20.5	19.9	19.2	18.6	18.0	17.5	16.9	16.4	15.9

from Reg. Sec. 1.72-9

One-Life-Expected Return Multiples

Age	Multiples Life Expectancy	Age	Multiples (Life Expectancy)	Age	Multiples (Life Expectancy)
5	76.6	42	40.6	79	10.0
6	75.6	43	39.6	80	9.5
7	74.7	44	38.7	81	8.9
8	73.7	45	37.7	82	8.4
9	72.7	46	36.8	83	7.9
10	71.7	47	35.9	84	7.4
11	70.7	48	34.9	85	6.9
12	69.7	49	34.0	86	6.5
13	68.8	50	33.1	87	6.1
14	67.8	51	32.2	88	5.7
15	66.8	52	31.3	89	5.3
16	65.8	53	30.4	90	5.0
17	64.8	54	29.5	91	4.7
18	63.9	55	28.6	92	4.4
19	62.9	56	27.7	93	4.1
20	61.9	57	26.8	94	3.9
21	60.9	58	25.9	95	3.7
22	59.9	59	25.0	96	3.4
23	59.0	60	24.2	97	3.2
24	58.0	61	23.3	98	3.0
25	57.0	62	22.5	99	2.8
26	56.0	63	21.6	100	2.7
27	55.1	64	20.8	101	2.5
28	54.1	65	20.0	102	2.3
29	53.1	66	19.2	103	2.1
30	52.2	67	18.4	104	1.9
31	51.2	68	17.6	105	1.8
32	50.2	69	16.8	106	1.6
33	49.3	70	16.0	107	1.4
34	48.3	71	15.3	108	1.3
35	47.3	72	14.6	109	1.1
36	46.4	73	13.9	110	1.0
37	45.4	74	13.2	111	0.9
38	44.4	75	12.5	112	0.8
39	43.5	76	11.9	113	0.7
40	42.5	77	11.2	114	0.6
41	41.5	78	10.6	115	0.5

Uniform Table of Applicable Distribution Periods
for Required Minimum Distributions

Age of the Employee	Applicable Divisor	Age of the Employee	Applicable Divisor
70	27.4	93	9.6
71	26.5	94	9.1
72	25.6	95	8.6
73	24.7	96	8.1
74	23.8	97	7.6
75	22.9	98	7.1
76	22.0	99	6.7
77	21.2	100	6.3
78	20.3	101	5.9
79	19.5	102	5.5
80	18.7	103	5.2
81	17.9	104	4.9
82	17.1	105	4.5
83	16.3	106	4.2
84	15.5	107	3.9
85	14.8	108	3.7
86	14.1	109	3.4
87	13.4	110	3.1
88	12.7	111	2.9
89	12.0	112	2.6
90	11.4	113	2.4
91	10.8	114	2.1
92	10.2	115 and older	1.9

2015 Principal Knowledge Topics (72 Topics)

The following Principal Knowledge Topics are based on the results of CFP Board's 2015 Job Analysis Study.

The Principal Knowledge Topics serve as the blueprint for the March 2016 and later administrations of the CFP® Certification Examination. Each exam question will be linked to one of the following Principal Knowledge Topics, in the approximate percentages indicated following the general category headings.

The Principal Knowledge Topics serve as a curricular framework and also represent subject topics that CFP Board accepts for continuing education credit, effective January 2016.

Eight Principal Knowledge Topic Categories

A. **Professional Conduct and Regulation** (7%)

B. **General Financial Planning Principles** (17%)

C. **Education Planning** (6%)

D. **Risk Management and Insurance Planning** (12%)

E. **Investment Planning** (17%)

F. **Tax Planning** (12%)

G. **Retirement Savings and Income Planning** (17%)

H. **Estate Planning** (12%)

A. Professional Conduct and Regulation

A.1. CFP Board's Code of Ethics and Professional Responsibility and Rules of Conduct

A.2. CFP Board's Financial Planning Practice Standards

A.3. CFP Board's Disciplinary Rules and Procedures

A.4. Function, purpose, and regulation of financial institutions

A.5. Financial services regulations and requirements

A.6. Consumer protection laws

A.7. Fiduciary

Professional Conduct & Regulation

1425 K STREET NW #800 ■ WASHINGTON, DC 20005 ■ P 800-487-1497 ■ F 202-379-2299 ■ CFP.NET

B. General Principles of Financial Planning

General Financial Planning Principles

B.8.	Financial planning process
B.9.	Financial statements
B.10.	Cash flow management
B.11.	Financing strategies
B.12.	Economic concepts
B.13.	Time value of money concepts and calculations
B.14.	Client and planner attitudes, values, biases and behavioral finance
B.15.	Principles of communication and counseling
B.16.	Debt management

C. Education Planning

Education Planning

C.17.	Education needs analysis
C.18.	Education savings vehicles
C.19.	Financial aid
C.20.	Gift/income tax strategies
C.21.	Education financing

D. Risk Management and Insurance Planning

Risk Management & Insurance Planning

D.22.	Principles of risk and insurance
D.23.	Analysis and evaluation of risk exposures
D.24.	Health insurance and health care cost management (individual)
D.25.	Disability income insurance (individual)
D.26.	Long-term care insurance (individual)
D.27.	Annuities
D.28.	Life insurance (individual)
D.29.	Business uses of insurance
D.30.	Insurance needs analysis
D.31.	Insurance policy and company selection
D.32.	Property and casualty insurance

E. Investment Planning

E.33.	Characteristics, uses and taxation of investment vehicles
E.34.	Types of investment risk
E.35.	Quantitative investment concepts
E.36.	Measures of investment returns
E.37.	Asset allocation and portfolio diversification
E.38.	Bond and stock valuation concepts
E.39.	Portfolio development and analysis
E.40.	Investment strategies
E.41.	Alternative investments

F. Tax Planning

F.42.	Fundamental tax law
F.43.	Income tax fundamentals and calculations
F.44.	Characteristics and income taxation of business entities
F.45.	Income taxation of trusts and estates
F.46.	Alternative minimum tax (AMT)
F.47.	Tax reduction/management techniques
F.48.	Tax consequences of property transactions
F.49.	Passive activity and at-risk rules
F.50.	Tax implications of special circumstances
F.51.	Charitable/philanthropic contributions and deductions

G. Retirement Savings and Income Planning

G.52.	Retirement needs analysis
G.53.	Social Security and Medicare
G.54.	Medicaid
G.55.	Types of retirement plans
G.56.	Qualified plan rules and options
G.57.	Other tax-advantaged retirement plans
G.58.	Regulatory considerations
G.59.	Key factors affecting plan selection for businesses

G.60.   Distribution rules and taxation

G.61.   Retirement income and distribution strategies

G.62.   Business succession planning

H. Estate Planning

H.63.   Characteristics and consequences of property titling

H.64.   Strategies to transfer property

H.65.   Estate planning documents

H.66.   Gift and estate tax compliance and tax calculation

H.67.   Sources for estate liquidity

H.68.   Types, features, and taxation of trusts

H.69.   Marital deduction

H.70.   Intra-family and other business transfer techniques

H.71.   Postmortem estate planning techniques

H.72.   Estate planning for non-traditional relationships

Estate Planning

Contextual Variables

In addition to the Principal Knowledge Topics, other important variables are to be considered when dealing with specific financial planning situations. These are referred to as "Contextual Variables" and are used as part of content development for the CFP® Certification Examination or other case-based scenarios.

More specifically, financial planning situations require the application of financial planning knowledge for different types of clients. Important client details to consider as part of financial planning situations are:

- **Family Status** (traditional family, single parent, same-sex couples, blended families, widowhood)
- **Net Worth** (ultra-high net worth, high net worth, mass affluent, emerging affluent, mass market)
- **Income Level** (high, medium, low)
- **Life or Professional Stage** (student, starting a career, career transition, pre-retirement, retirement)
- **Other Circumstances** (health issues, divorce, change of employment status, aging parents, special needs children)

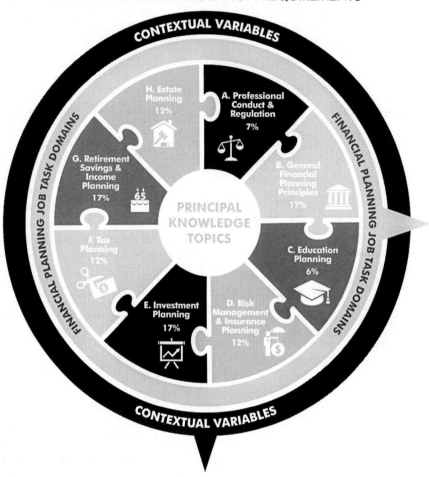

CFP BOARD

2015 JOB TASK ANALYSIS
EXAMINATION AND EDUCATION REQUIREMENTS

CONTEXTUAL VARIABLES

FINANCIAL PLANNING JOB TASK DOMAINS

H. Estate Planning 12%

A. Professional Conduct & Regulation 7%

G. Retirement Savings & Income Planning 17%

B. General Financial Planning Principles 17%

F. Tax Planning 12%

C. Education Planning 6%

E. Investment Planning 17%

D. Risk Management & Insurance Planning 12%

PRINCIPAL KNOWLEDGE TOPICS

FINANCIAL PLANNING JOB TASK DOMAINS

CONTEXTUAL VARIABLES

FINANCIAL PLANNING JOB TASK DOMAINS

 1 Establishing & Defining the Client-Planner Relationship

 2 Gathering Information Necessary to Fulfill the Engagement

 3 Analyzing & Evaluating the Client's Current Financial Status

 4 Developing the Recommendation(s)

 5 Communicating the Recommendation(s)

 6 Implementing the Recommendation(s)

 7 Monitoring the Recommendation(s)

 8 Practicing Within Professional & Regulatory Standards

CONTEXTUAL VARIABLES

FAMILY STATUS	NET WORTH	INCOME LEVEL	LIFE OR PROFESSIONAL STAGE	OTHER CIRCUMSTANCES
Traditional family	Ultra-high net worth	High	Student	Health issues
Single parent	High net worth	Medium	Starting a career	Divorce
Same-sex couples	Mass affluent	Low	Career transition	Change of employment status
Blended families	Emerging affluent		Pre-retirement	Aging parents
Widowhood	Mass market		Retirement	Special needs children

GLOSSARY

INVESTMENT PLANNING

An <u>ACATS (Automated Customer Account Transfer Service)</u> may be used to transfer securities in-kind from one broker-dealer to another without triggering taxation on the holdings.

<u>Accrued interest</u> is that amount of interest earned on a bond since the last date bond interest was paid. The buyer of a bond must pay the seller the price of the bond plus the accrued interest up to the date of settlement.

<u>Active asset allocation</u> refers to periodically revising the allocation of assets within a portfolio among stocks, bonds, cash equivalents, and other asset categories based on market expectations. Market timing is an important part of an active asset allocation strategy.

<u>Activity ratios</u> are numerical measures of the rate at which a business is converting its inventory and accounts receivable into cash during the course of a year.

An <u>adjustable rate fund</u> is a corporate bond fund paying distributions that periodically increase or decrease according to a benchmark such as the rate on 5-year Treasury notes. These funds may also contain some preferred stock.

The <u>advance-decline line</u> measures the daily cumulative net number of stock price increases or decreases on the New York Stock Exchange. It is often referred to as a breadth-of-the-market indicator.

An <u>aggressive growth fund</u> is a mutual fund that invests in risky growth stocks in order to achieve high returns and faster appreciation in the value of its investors' funds.

The <u>alpha</u> is a measure of risk-adjusted performance that will indicate whether a fund's performance is favorable in relation to its risk level. If a fund has an unfavorable return for its risk level, the alpha will be negative; if returns are favorable for the risk level, the alpha is positive. If the fund achieves exactly the expected return for its risk level, the alpha is zero.

<u>Alternative investments</u> include any type of investment that is outside of the traditional asset classes of equities, bonds, or cash. The list of alternative investments is broad, and includes real estate, real estate-backed securities, limited partnership interests, Collateralized Debt Obligations (CDOs), hedge funds, private equity, collectibles, natural resources, and precious metals.

An <u>American Depository Receipt (ADR)</u> is a receipt issued by U.S. banks on foreign securities purchased for them through a foreign correspondent bank and held in trust for the ADR owner.

An <u>annualized return</u> is a rate of return over a full calendar year on an investment that is held for less than a full calendar year. For example, if a stock yields a 6 percent rate of return in 6 months, the annualized rate of return is 12 percent.

Anomalies are documented results in contrast to what one would expect in a totally efficient market. These contrasting results cannot easily be "explained away."

An anticipation note is a short-term security issued by state and local governments in anticipation of tax or revenue receipts in the future. The maturity date is set to coincide with these receipts, which are then used to retire the notes.

Arbitrage is the simultaneous purchase and sale of a particular security in different markets where different prices for the particular security prevail. Profits from arbitrage are possible where markets are inefficient.

Arbitrage pricing theory (APT) is an attempt to explain the role of arbitrage in the determination of returns on securities. Arbitrageurs buy and sell the same security simultaneously in different markets in order to take advantage of price differences in those markets. Arbitrage pricing theory, thus, goes beyond the simple Capital Asset Pricing Model in explaining a stock's rate of return as the model includes multiple macroeconomic and/or company-specific factors.

An ask price is the price at which a dealer of a particular security is willing to sell the security in question to interested investors.

Asset allocation is the determination of the proportions of various types of investment vehicles that will make up an investment portfolio.

An asset allocation fund does not emphasize an investment objective such as growth or income, but seeks to maximize return by investing in many areas pursuant to a total portfolio concept. The assets may be invested in U.S. stocks or bonds, foreign stocks or bonds, real estate, precious metals, or foreign currencies.

Asset classes are general categories of investments that may be used for diversification purposes. Examples are real estate, physical assets, debt, and equity.

Averaging down refers to the process of purchasing more of a security as its price declines, thereby lowering the investor's average cost per unit of the investment.

The bailout provision is the part of an annuity contract that permits the investor to make partial withdrawals or to surrender the annuity contract for its current cash value without imposition of a surrender fee whenever the renewal interest rate declines more than a specified amount below the interest rate the insurance company guaranteed for the first few years.

The balance of payments is an accounting record maintained by national governments of all monetary transactions between a particular country and the rest of the world during a period of time, such as one year. The basic parts of the U.S. balance of payments statement are the current account, the capital account, and the financial account.

The balance of trade of a nation is the difference between the sum of its imports and the sum of its exports within the current account of the nation's balance of payments.

A <u>balanced fund</u> is a mutual fund whose objective is to obtain a balance of income from dividends, interest, and capital appreciation.

<u>Bank loan funds</u> are mutual funds that invest in loans that banks make to corporations. They are a form of alternative investment.

A <u>barbell bond strategy</u> entails allocating approximately equal amounts of the total bond portfolio to short-term bonds and longer-term bonds. The objective is to provide both liquidity from short-term bonds and the opportunity to benefit from the higher yields available on long-term bonds.

<u>Barron's Confidence Index</u> studies the yield differential between Barron's index of yields on high- and intermediate-quality bonds. When the difference between the two yields narrows, it is an indication of a bull market.

A <u>bear spread</u> is a spread in which the investor expects a slight decrease in the price of the underlying stock.

A <u>bearer form</u> of bond is one in which anyone who is the holder of the bond is considered to be the owner. The issuing corporation keeps no record of who owns the bonds. Interest is received by clipping coupons and sending them in to the corporation for payment.

A <u>benchmark portfolio</u> is a portfolio in which the asset mix attempts to duplicate the investment performance of a broadly diversified market index, such as the S&P 500. Benchmark portfolios, then, seek only to match the performance of the market indexes, rather than to beat those indexes.

A <u>best efforts agreement</u> is an agreement between a corporation seeking to raise money and its investment banker in which the investment banker agrees to make its best effort to sell the newly issued securities. Note that the investment banker under this arrangement does not guarantee that a specified amount of money will be raised, so the risk of selling the securities rests with the firm issuing the securities, rather than with the investment banker.

<u>Beta</u> is a measure of volatility versus a benchmark. It measures systematic risk only, as opposed to standard deviation which measures both systematic and unsystematic risk. The benchmark is assigned a beta of 1. A security with a beta greater than 1 will tend to be more volatile than the benchmark, while a security with a beta of less than 1 will tend to be less volatile than the benchmark.

A <u>bid price</u> is the price at which a dealer in a particular security is willing to purchase the security in question from investors.

The <u>Black-Scholes model</u> is a model for valuation of a warrant or call option. The model takes account of five items needed to calculate the value of the option if the stock does not pay a dividend: the stock price, the exercise price, the time to maturity, the risk-free interest rate, and the volatility of the underlying stock, expressed as the standard deviation of the stock's annual return.

A block positioner is a market maker trading large blocks (10,000 shares or more) of stock. The positioner has the responsibility of organizing and executing such trades. These trades emanate largely from institutional investors and are finalized off the floor of the exchange.

Blue Sky laws are state, as contrasted with federal, laws regulating the sale of securities. These laws typically call for the licensing of securities firms and brokers, the filing of financial information about new issues of securities with state regulatory authorities, standards that must be met by new security issues before they may be sold, and the establishment of regulatory bodies to enforce the laws.

Bond swaps refer to selling one type of bond and buying another in order to meet a variety of objectives. Bond swaps may be used to save on taxes, to increase yields, to reduce the risk in a portfolio, or to take advantage of mispricing of certain bonds.

A bull spread is an options spread in which the investor expects a slight increase in the price of the underlying stock.

Bullion is composed of precious metals measured in terms of weight, rather than value. It can take the form of bars, ingots, coins, or plates, all of which can be acquired by an investor.

The business cycle reflects movements in overall economic activity, typically measured in terms of Gross Domestic Product. Business cycles are diverse but have a common framework, beginning with a trough (a low point), building to a peak, and then falling again to a trough. The length of particular business cycles has varied, with a minimum of about three years and a maximum of more than seven years. The mean length of 11 cycles (1945-2009) was 69 months from trough to trough.

Business risk is the uncertainty of the investor's total return associated with the unique problems of a specific industry or a specific company. Some factors that may affect this uncertainty relative to a specific firm are: variations in demand for the firm's products, component supply problems for the firm, variations in the amount of the firm's debt, cost-of-operations problems, and management problems.

A buy/hold strategy is an investment strategy in which an asset mix is established, and the securities are then bought and held for the long term. Transaction costs and risks are minimized in a buy/hold strategy.

A corporation's bylaws are the set of rules by which the company is governed, including such matters as voting rights of the stockholders.

The call provision in a bond indenture allows the issuer to retire the bond before its scheduled maturity date at a designated price. Bonds are often called when the interest rate on the bond is higher than current interest rates.

A call penalty is a monetary amount that an issuing corporation must pay, over and above the par value of a bond, in order to exercise the corporation's right to call or redeem the bond prior to its maturity. A typical call penalty is six months of interest. From the investor's point of view, this extra payment may be referred to as a call premium.

Call risk is the chance the investor takes in purchasing a callable bond. There is a chance that interest rates will fall, and the bond issuer will call the bond (repay the loan and retire the bond), so that the issuer no longer has to pay the high interest rate required by the outstanding bond.

Calls are one of the two types of options, the other being "puts." Each call purchased allows an investor to purchase 100 shares of stock at a specified price at any time during a specified period.

The capital account is a component of a nation's balance of payments that shows all capital investment flows into and out of a country, including direct investment in capital equipment, domestic purchases of foreign securities, and sales of domestic securities to foreigners.

The Capital Asset Pricing Model (CAPM) is essentially an equation that provides the required rate of return for a common stock. It is the basis of much of today's investment analysis. The required rate of return increases as the level of risk increases. This is a breakdown of the equation:

$$r_i = r_f + (r_m - r_f)\beta_i$$

Which may be stated as:

Required return for common stock i = Risk-free return + (Market return – Risk-free return) x Beta of stock i.

A capital gain is the appreciation in the value of an investment (security or real estate). A capital gain may be long-term (a holding period of greater than one year) or short term (a holding period of one year or less).

A capitalization rate, in the context of valuing real estate investments, is a rate that is divided into the investment property's net operating income in order to produce an estimate of the property's value. A seller will prefer a low capitalization rate, whereas a buyer will prefer a high capitalization rate.

A capital loss is depreciation in the value of an investment.

A capital market security is a riskier investment than money market securities because the capital market involves investments of over one year, and they are less easily marketed. Examples of capital market securities include Treasury bonds, corporate bonds, preferred stock, and common stock.

Carried interest is a method of compensating hedge fund and private equity managers via a distribution of a percentage of profits. If the profits are produced from the sale of investments held longer than three years, the carried interest is taxed as a long-term capital gain, making it an attractive method of compensation.

The cash flow of a company refers to the sources and uses of cash for the company in a particular time period. A company's cash flow is contrasted with its accounting revenues and expenses. A company's cash flow is summarized by comparing the difference between the balance sheet cash account at the beginning and end of the period. A statement of cash flows analyzes that change in the cash account by tracing sources and uses of cash in each of three categories: operating activities, investing activities, and financing activities. In another context, cash flow is defined as a company's net earnings, plus its noncash expenses, such as depreciation, minus debt retirement.

The CBOE is the Chicago Board Options Exchange. This is the first organized secondary market for the trading of puts and calls.

A certificate of deposit (CD) is a receipt for a deposit at a bank or savings and loan. Negotiable certificates of deposit that are traded in the money market are in denominations of $100,000 or more.

A certificate of incorporation is a legal document that creates a corporation.

A charter is a document, issued by the state of incorporation, enabling the corporation to be formed and listing the rights of the stockholders, both as individuals and as a group.

Client assessment, in this context, refers to evaluating the ability and willingness of the client to tolerate risk. Client assessment is a part of the data-gathering process in financial planning in which information about the client's goals, liquidity needs, resources, required rates of return, investment attitudes, and tax situation are assembled.

A clone fund is a fund similar to another fund that has been successful but that has been closed to additional investors. The new fund may be similar in name and objectives to the old fund, but it may have a different portfolio manager and may or may not have the same investment success.

A closed-end investment company is an investment company whose shares are listed on a stock exchange and may be traded throughout the day. The company offers a fixed number of shares.

The coefficient of determination (R^2) is the square of the correlation coefficient. It measures the proportion of the movement in one variable that is associated with the movement in another variable. For example, the proportion of the return on an investment in a particular stock may be associated in part with the movement in the market as a whole. The coefficient of determination is a statistical measure of this relationship. When comparing a portfolio to an index, the comparison should be the "best-fit" index, which is the index with the highest R^2 value to portfolio.

The coefficient of variation is a relative measure of the dispersion of data around a mean value. It is computed by dividing the standard deviation by the mean.

Collateralized mortgage obligations (CMOs) are mortgage-backed securities consisting of a pool of mortgages sold as an investment. They are issued by government and private agencies. They resemble bonds because they typically make semiannual interest payments. Principal payments go first to those holding issues with the shortest maturity. CMOs are organized by risk profiles and are sensitive to interest rate changes.

Collectibles are assets that investors accumulate as part of a collection. Examples of collectibles are gems, works of art, and baseball cards.

Commercial paper is a short-term, unsecured, promissory note issued by a business firm. Only large corporations with good credit are able to issue this paper in the money market. The maturity of commercial paper varies but typically does not exceed 270 days.

Commercial real estate includes office buildings, retail stores, shopping centers, and specialty buildings, such as banks, movie theaters, and bowling alleys.

Compound rate of return (IRR). See Glossary term "internal rate of return" below.

A confirmation statement is a statement provided by a brokerage firm to a customer, detailing the sale or purchase of a security and the settlement date on which the sale or purchase was completed.

The Consumer Confidence Index is a monthly report published by the Consumer Research Center of the Conference Board. The Index provides an indicator of consumer sentiment by measuring consumer perceptions of business conditions and of their own financial condition, as well as their willingness to buy durable goods such as automobiles and other "big-ticket" items.

The Consumer Price Index is an index maintained by the Bureau of Labor Statistics to measure inflation. The Index tracks changes in the cost of a given basket of goods and services over time.

The Consumer Sentiment Index is a measure of consumer confidence published by the University of Michigan each month. This Index focuses on consumer perceptions of how the economy is doing and of their own financial condition.

Contractionary monetary policy refers to actions by the Federal Reserve to raise interest rates and restrict growth of the money supply.

Contrarians are investment technicians who contend that the majority of investors are wrong most of the time. Therefore, they analyze the sentiment of the majority of investors. If investors are either very bullish or very bearish, contrarians will trade in the opposite direction.

A conversion premium is the excess of the market price of a common stock over its conversion value. The premium is typically presented as a percentage.

The conversion price is the price at which common stock may be purchased through conversion of a bond or preferred stock. It is determined by dividing the conversion ratio into the par value of the bond or preferred stock.

The <u>conversion ratio</u> is the number of common shares into which a convertible bond or preferred stock may be converted. For example, for a $1,000 face value bond with a $100 conversion price, the conversion ratio is 10 to 1.

The <u>conversion value</u> is the value of a convertible security as determined by the market price of the common stock into which it may be converted. It is derived by multiplying the conversion ratio by the market price of the common stock.

A <u>convertible bond</u> is one that may be exchanged for some other security of the issuing corporation at a specified exchange or conversion rate. For example, convertible bonds and convertible preferred stock are convertible into the common stock of the corporation that issued the bonds or preferred stock.

<u>Convertible preferred stock</u> is preferred stock that may be exchanged in a pre-established ratio for common stock of the same company.

<u>Convertible securities</u> allow the owner to exchange the securities for a specific number of shares of common stock at a set price. They are usually in the form of convertible bonds and convertible preferred stock. The value of a convertible security is based partly on that of the stock into which the security may be converted and partly on that of the security itself.

A <u>corporate bond fund</u> is a mutual fund that invests in debt instruments issued by large corporations. Income from these instruments is passed through to shareholders.

The <u>correlation coefficient</u> is a statistical measure of the relationship between two variables. The numerical values of correlation coefficients range from +1.0 for perfect positive correlation to – 1.0 for perfect negative correlation.

The <u>coupon</u> on a bond is the nominal annual interest rate payable on the bond. The coupon is expressed as a percentage of the bond's par or face value. Hence, an 8 percent coupon bond having a face amount of $1,000 pays $80 per year in interest.

<u>Covariance</u> is a measure as to whether the values associated with two securities generally move in the same direction or in opposite directions. Two securities with a positive covariance move together. Securities with a negative covariance move in opposite directions. A portfolio comprised of securities with a high positive covariance is not diversified.

Writing a <u>covered option</u> refers to writing a call option on a stock that the writer already owns.

<u>Credit rating agencies</u> are organizations that specialize in evaluating the creditworthiness of borrowers, particularly corporate borrowers. Examples of credit rating agencies are Dun & Bradstreet, Moody's, Fitch, and Standard & Poor's.

<u>Cryptocurrency</u> is a digital financial asset that is traded virtually using cryptography, and is theoretically free from government intervention. The most popular cryptocurrencies are: Bitcoin, Litecoin, Namecoin, PPCoin, Ripple, Ethereum, Bitcoin Cash, Iota and Dash. The cryptocurrency

market is a developing market that has been susceptible to computer hacking and fraud. Nevertheless, there are investors who trade these highly speculative currencies, often on a daily basis as their markets are open 24/7. Cryptocurrencies are subject to short-term and long-term capital gains tax.

A cumulative preferred stock carries less risk for the investor than common stock because the preferred shareholders are entitled to the current year's dividend plus any preferred dividends skipped in prior years before the common stock owners are permitted to receive any dividends.

A currency exchange rate is the price at which a particular unit of foreign exchange may be purchased, expressed in the currency of a different country.

Currency futures are contracts calling for the future delivery of a particular foreign exchange or currency.

The current account is a component of a nation's balance of payments that shows the value of imported and exported goods and services, net government spending abroad, and foreign investment income paid out or received.

The current yield for a bond is the amount of current income the bond provides relative to its prevailing market price. Usually, the prevailing market price is assumed to be the closing price for the trading day.

A cyclical industry experiences a pronounced unevenness in the demand for its products caused by factors outside the control of the firm itself, with the main factor being the business cycle. Examples of cyclical industries are: airlines, durable goods manufacturers, construction, and consumer discretionary goods.

The daily price limit is a restriction on the maximum movement of a futures contract price relative to the previous day's settlement price. Each futures contract, except stock index futures, has a daily price limit. The daily price limit for a Treasury bond contract, for example, is 3 points, or $3,000.

The date of record is the date on which an investor must appear on the corporate records as the owner of shares in a company in order to receive the current dividend payment. For example, a company might declare that dividends will be payable on April 15 to stockholders of record on March 31. Consequently, in order to receive the April 15 dividend, one must be shown on the company's books as a stockholder on the record date, March 31.

A day order is a limit order that is good for only one day. In such an order, the investor specifies the price at which he or she is willing to buy or sell, and the trade will be carried out if the price reaches that specified price within one day. Otherwise, the limit order lapses.

A dealer is a financial intermediary who buys and sells securities from his or her own inventory. A dealer is contrasted with a broker, who does not maintain an inventory of the securities being bought and sold but, rather, locates buyers for sellers of securities, and vice versa.

A debenture is an unsecured corporate bond. No specific assets are pledged as collateral or security behind a debenture bond.

The declaration date is the date on which a company first publicly declares that it will be paying a dividend. At this time, the company will announce when the dividend will be paid and also will indicate the holder-of-record date.

A dedicated bond portfolio attempts to match the receipt of cash inflows with the need for funds, both in timing and amount.

Default is the failure of a borrower to live up to one or more of the terms of its loan agreement with the lender(s), for example, failure to make timely payments of loan interest or principal.

A default premium is an add-on to the risk-free rate of return on investments to reflect the possibility that the borrowing organization may fail to make timely payment of principal and interest at some point during the life of the investment.

Default risk is the uncertainty that the debtor will fail to pay interest or principal on its debt obligations on a timely basis. Standard & Poor's, Moody's, and others rate bonds according to this risk of default.

A defensive industry offers investors some protection in that stock market values do not fluctuate greatly during different phases of the business cycle because the revenues and expenses of such firms do not fluctuate significantly. An example of a defensive industry is the retail grocery industry. People must buy groceries during downswings in the business cycle and do not markedly increase their purchases of groceries during upswings in the business cycle. Consequently, stock prices for retail grocery companies tend to be fairly stable.

Deflation means that the general price level is declining. It usually occurs in a time period when business activity is at a low ebb, unemployment tends to be high, and common stock prices are low. High-grade bonds tend to increase in market value because the market rates of interest tend to decline.

A derivative security is an investment in which the value is based upon the value of an underlying security. Derivative securities include options, rights, warrants, convertible bonds, forward contracts, futures contracts, collateralized mortgage obligations, and other convertible securities.

Devaluation refers to a reduction in the value of a particular country's currency as a result of a government's monetary authority's ruling.

Direct investment in real estate refers to the actual purchase of real estate for investment purposes. It is contrasted with indirect investment in real estate, such as by purchasing shares in a real estate investment trust.

A discount bond is a bond whose market price is below its par or face value. A bond will sell at a discount when the market rate of interest for bonds of comparable investment quality is above the coupon rate of the discount bond. Buyers will buy a lower coupon bond only if the market price is low enough to make its yield comparable to the higher market rate of interest.

A discount broker is a securities broker who charges lower-than-normal commissions on security purchases and sales. Often, discount brokers provide fewer services, such as securities research, than do full commission brokers.

Dispersion is the degree to which individual observations vary around or deviate from the average of those observations.

The distribution date is the date on which a dividend that has previously been declared will actually be distributed to holders of the stock on the record date.

Diversification is a means of reducing the risk(s) to which an investment portfolio is exposed. In a diversified portfolio, individual assets are not influenced in the same way by the same variables. For example, if one asset, such as a bond, will decline in value in an inflationary period, another asset that will increase in value during an inflationary period should be included in the portfolio. Diversification can also be by time horizon. Investing in securities of varying maturities, such as a bond ladder, is a method used to compensate for short-term variations in interest rates.

A dividend is a payment to stockholders, usually in the form of cash, but perhaps in the form of stock or other property. Dividends may be regular dividends, which are steady dividend payments distributed at regular intervals. Also, dividends may be irregular, meaning that they do not occur at regular intervals or that they vary substantially in amount. An extra dividend is a dividend that is in addition to the company's regular dividend. In life insurance, a dividend is, in large part, a refund to the policy owner of a deliberate overcharge built into the premium.

The dividend growth rate is the annual expected rate of increase in a company's dividend payments in the foreseeable future. The dividend growth rate is an important part of the common stock dividend-growth valuation model.

A company's dividend policy is its policy with respect to how much, if any, of its earnings are to be paid out as dividends to stockholders, rather than being reinvested in the company.

A dividend reinvestment plan allows an investor in a mutual fund or in a company to use dividends to acquire additional shares automatically, often without sales charge, by reinvesting the dividends.

The dividend valuation model is a commonly used approach for valuing common stock. Future dividend payments are estimated based upon fundamental factors. These dividend payments are discounted at a required rate of return as determined by the risk and yields on other similar investments.

The dividend yield is the stock's current annual dividend per share divided by the stock's market price per share.

Dollar-cost averaging is one of the methods for averaging an investor's purchase prices whereby the investor invests the same dollar amount each time a purchase is made. Accordingly, more shares will be bought when stock prices fall and fewer shares as stock prices rise, leading to a lower average cost of acquiring stock.

A dollar-weighted return is a rate of return calculated by taking into account the amount and timing of each of the cash outflows and inflows associated with an investment. The internal rate of return is a dollar-weighted rate of return.

The Dow Jones Industrial Average is a price-weighted average of 30 large New York Stock Exchange stocks representing major industry sectors.

The Dow Theory is a technical market indicator. If the Dow Jones Industrial Average and the Dow Jones Transportation Average are both declining, the Dow Theory holds that this indicates a strong bear market. If both of the above averages are rising, the Dow Theory signals a bull market.

Due diligence refers to the legal and ethical obligation imposed on those involved in the marketing of securities to assure that all appropriate information has been gathered and disclosed to the client and that the information that has been gathered and disclosed is accurate and reasonable. A registered representative is required to show that he or she has engaged in due diligence in investigating any security that is to be offered to a client.

Durables (or durable goods) are longer-lived products that do not quickly wear out or need immediate replacement. Examples include houses and automobiles.

The duration of a bond is the average number of years it takes to receive the present value of all future payments from the investment, including both interest payments and the repayment of principal. Duration is a weighted average, not an unweighted average, because each of these payments is weighted by the number of years the investor must wait before receiving it.

An earnings multiplier is a multiple applied to the earnings per share of a company's stock that determines the market price of that stock. For example, if a stock is selling for $60 per share and the company's earnings per share are $3, the earnings multiplier is 20, that is, $60 ÷ $3.

Earnings per share (EPS) is calculated by dividing after-tax net income of a company by the average number of its common stock shares outstanding. GAAP accounting allows for possible alternative ways of determining after-tax net income. Earnings per share, therefore, may not be readily comparable over time or for different companies. Earnings per share is the best single indicator of the earnings available to common stockholders.

Earnings retention refers to plowing back the profits of the firm into the company, rather than distributing them as dividends to stockholders.

An efficient frontier is a graphic or arithmetic depiction of an efficient set of portfolios. Any portfolio that offers the highest return possible for a given amount of risk lies on the efficient frontier.

The efficient market hypothesis (EMH) is a theory that the market price of a security fully reflects all relevant and available information, and, therefore, it is difficult for an investor to consistently outperform the market by selecting "undervalued" securities. There are three forms of EMH: weak, semi-strong, and strong.

The equilibrium price is the price at which the quantity demanded of a particular good or service is equal to the quantity supplied, so that there is no inherent incentive for a change in the price.

An equipment trust certificate is a type of corporate bond that is secured by specific equipment. Equipment trust certificates are frequently used to finance such assets as airplanes and rolling stock of railroads. The collateral behind equipment trust certificates consists of the particular assets that are being financed with the proceeds that the issuance of the certificates generates.

An equity income fund is a mutual fund that invests mainly in income-producing common stocks and convertible preferred stocks.

An equity REIT invests in commercial, industrial, or residential properties, and it receives income from renting out these properties.

Equity securities include both common and preferred stock. They represent ownership in the corporation issuing the stock and carry certain rights that differ for preferred and common stockholders.

Eurobonds are corporate bonds that are issued outside the U.S. but denominated in U.S. dollars.

Eurodollars are deposits of U.S. dollars in foreign banks. The Eurodollar market makes up the major part of the international money market.

The Europe, Australia, and Far East Index (EAFE) is a price index made up of stocks in Europe, Australia, and the Far East.

Excess reserves are legal reserves maintained by financial institutions in excess of the reserve requirement imposed on them by the Federal Reserve.

The exchange rate is the ratio of the market value of one currency to the market value of another currency.

Exchange rate risk refers to the potential loss in the value of an investment's principal or income due to fluctuations in the rate of exchange between currencies. For example, if an investment is denominated in pesos and the peso subsequently declines in value relative to the dollar, an American would incur a loss for having invested in the peso-denominated investment.

Exchange traded funds (ETFs) are funds comprised of a market basket of stocks, bonds, foreign currency, industry sectors, commodities, or index, and they trade on an exchange such as the NYSE or Nasdaq. ETFs are passively managed and have lower costs than mutual funds.

The ex-dividend date is the first day on which a stock no longer carries the right to a declared but unpaid dividend. The market price of the common stock will usually decline by the amount of the quarterly dividend per share on the ex-dividend date.

The exercise or strike price is the price at which an option holder may exercise an option. For example, a strike price of $50 means that a call holder may buy 100 shares of common stock, or a put holder may sell 100 shares of common stock, at $50.

Expansionary monetary policy refers to actions by the Federal Reserve to lower interest rates and to accelerate growth in the size of the money supply.

The expected rate of return on an investment is the sum of the anticipated dividend yield and the anticipated return from capital appreciation.

The expense ratio is the ratio found by dividing a mutual fund's annual operating expenses by its average net assets.

The expiration date is the date on which an option contract will expire worthless. It is the last date when an option can be exercised. All puts and calls are designated by their expiration month.

Fannie Maes are securities issued by what was formerly called the Federal National Mortgage Association, a government-sponsored agency of the federal government.

A feasible set is an array of attainable portfolios composed of various combinations of risky securities. Some of the portfolios in a feasible set may be efficient, while others may be inefficient.

Federal agency securities are the debt instruments of agencies of the federal government, as well as of federally sponsored corporations. They are not issued by, nor are they the responsibility of, the federal government.

The federal funds rate is the interest rate that banks charge each other for short-term loans.

The Federal National Mortgage Association (FNMA) is the earlier official name of an agency of the U.S. government that issues debt securities enabling it to operate a mortgage pool. The mortgage pool includes level-payment single-family mortgages that are not guaranteed by the VA or insured by the FHA.

The Federal Reserve System is the executor of the nation's monetary policy, thereby affecting credit and interest rates in the U.S. economy. Its objectives are generally countercyclical in nature. During economic downturns, it typically seeks to foster recovery by expanding the money supply, thereby strengthening credit and reducing the cost of funds. During economic upswings it seeks to maintain momentum while damping inflationary forces, typically by holding a tight rein on the money supply. Its main tools of monetary control are: (a) open market operations, (b) changes in reserve requirements, and (c) changes in the discount rate.

<u>Fiduciary duty</u> refers to the responsibility that the financial planner has to place the clients' interests ahead of his own in the selection of investments for clients. Because of the planner's position of receiving or controlling funds of others, he or she must use a high degree of care in the placement of the funds.

A <u>financial asset</u> is a paper asset. It is a claim on the financial holdings of an individual or organization. Stocks and bonds are examples of financial assets.

<u>Financial futures</u> are futures contracts that have as their underlying commodities financial instruments, currency, or stock indices.

A <u>financial intermediary</u> is an organization that helps bring together individuals and organizations with an excess of funds available to invest with individuals and organizations having a shortage of such funds and wishing to borrow. Examples of financial intermediaries are investment bankers, commercial banks, life insurance companies, and credit unions.

<u>Financial leverage</u> is the use of borrowed funds to acquire an asset. The hope with financial leverage is that the earnings realized on the asset will exceed the cost of the borrowed funds, with the benefit going to the borrowing company's common stockholders.

<u>Financial resources</u> of a client are the client's assets that might be used in achieving financial goals. These assets include currently available lump sums and annual discretionary funds that are available now and in the future.

<u>Financial risk</u> is the uncertainty associated with a security issuer's debt structure. The more a firm borrows to finance the enterprise, the greater the financial risk. Management must pay interest and principal as required. Management's failure to meet its debt obligations may mean bankruptcy and the demise of the firm. Theoretically, a company with no debt would carry no financial risk bearing on the price of the company's common stock.

<u>FINRA</u> is the Financial Industry Regulatory Authority which regulates brokers/dealers in their buying and selling of securities. It was formerly called the <u>NASD</u> (National Association of Security Dealers).

<u>Fiscal policy</u> is the budgetary planning of expenditures and receipts for the implementation of desired economic objectives. It includes the spending, taxing, and borrowing policies of the government.

A <u>fixed-mix portfolio</u> is established with an initial asset allocation and those weightings are consistently maintained.

A <u>foreign bond fund</u> is a mutual fund that invests in bonds issued in foreign currencies, such as bonds issued by foreign companies or foreign governments.

The <u>foreign exchange market</u> is the market for foreign currencies.

Foreign stocks and bonds are stocks and bonds issued by foreign companies, that is, companies headquartered outside the U.S.

A forward contract is a contract for future delivery of a commodity. A forward contract is negotiated on an individual basis. Also, because a forward contract is not standardized, there is no secondary market for it, as there is for a futures contract.

The fourth market is a way in which large institutional investors are able to buy or sell securities that are listed on an organized exchange in the over-the-counter market. In the fourth market, unlike the third market, the financial institutions do not use a brokerage firm. Rather, the institutional investors trade securities through a computerized system.

Freddie Macs are securities issued by what was formerly called the Federal Home Loan Mortgage Corporation, a government-sponsored federal agency.

Fundamental analysis is a type of securities analysis that assumes that the price of a security depends upon the issuing company's financial situation, the outlook for the industry, and the overall condition of the economy. Each security is said to have an intrinsic value at any given time that is determined by expected return and risk. Fundamental analysis is contrasted with technical analysis.

A futures contract is a contract committing one party to deliver something (for example, wheat, corn, currency, or Treasury bonds or bills), at a specified time for a specified price. Typically, the contract is traded before the delivery date for the commodity.

Futures exchanges provide an organized market for the buying and selling of futures contracts. Contracts are regulated and standardized by the exchange, which also facilitates trading and enhances liquidity.

Futures options allow the holder to buy or sell the underlying futures contract for a specified period of time, ending on the expiration date. There is no obligation to exercise a futures option.

The futures price is the price in a futures contract for future delivery of a particular commodity.

A gate (or redemption gate) is a temporary suspension of withdrawals from money market funds for up to 10 days in a 90-day period that may be enacted in times of extreme market volatility.

A general obligation bond is a municipal bond that is secured by the full taxing power of the issuer. Current taxes are available to meet interest and principal payments, and new taxes may be imposed if necessary to raise funds needed to meet contractual obligations.

A general partnership is a form of business ownership in which two or more persons join in a common enterprise for profit. Each general partner is entitled to an equal voice in partnership affairs. Each partner has unlimited liability for partnership obligations.

A geometric average return is a calculation used to determine the average per-period return of an investment that is compounded over multiple periods.

A global fund is an investment company that invests in stocks of both foreign and domestic (U.S.) companies.

Globalization of markets refers to the increasing internationalization of businesses and financial transactions. Businesses raise money in many different countries and spend money in many different countries. They also sell their products or services in many different countries.

GNMA funds, or Ginnie Mae funds, are mutual funds that invest in mortgage-backed securities issued and guaranteed by the Government National Mortgage Association. The monthly mortgage payments of principal and interest from homeowners are passed through to investors, but some GNMA funds reinvest the principal and pay out only interest to shareholders.

A gold fund is a mutual fund or ETF that invests in gold bullion and in stock of gold mining companies, primarily in South African, Canadian, or U.S. companies.

Gold investments take many forms, including direct investment in jewelry, coins, or bullion, as well as investments in stocks of mining companies and in futures contracts.

A good-till-canceled (GTC) order is a limit order that remains in effect until the order is either executed or canceled by the customer of the brokerage firm. It is a type of limit order in that a price is specified at which the investor is willing to buy or sell the security. The order remains on the books of the broker until that price is reached or the order is canceled.

The Government National Mortgage Association (GNMA) is a wholly-owned U.S. government corporation within the Department of Housing and Urban Development. The security underlying GNMA pass-throughs is a pool of FHA-insured or VA-guaranteed level payment mortgage loans. At least 90% of the mortgages must have a 20-year + maturity. The pass-through securities are highly marketable and generally sell at lower yields than other mortgage-backed securities because of their reduced risk.

A government securities fund is a mutual fund that invests in both government-guaranteed bonds and in U.S. government agency debt securities.

Green shoes are options given to an investment banker to sell more than the agreed upon number of shares of a new issue of securities should the issue prove to be highly popular. Note that the investment banker has no obligation to sell any part of the green shoe, but is authorized to do so if he/she is able.

Gross Domestic Product (GDP) is the market value of all final goods and services produced in a given country, regardless of the nationality of those in that country who produced it. For example, the U.S. GDP is made up of the market value of all final goods and services produced in the U.S., even though many of the workers in the U.S. may be citizens of other countries.

A growth and income fund invests assets to achieve both capital appreciation and current income. These funds typically invest in more conservative common stocks of blue-chip companies that have established records of growth and reasonable dividends. The risk is generally lower than with growth funds, and the current income is generally lower than income funds.

A growth fund is a mutual fund that invests primarily in common stocks of companies with above-average potential for capital appreciation. Current income is only an incidental consideration. Growth funds are higher risk as compared to income funds.

A head-and-shoulders pattern is a technical market indicator. When the chart of closing prices forms a pattern that appears in the shape of a person's head and shoulders and then breaks below the resistance line on the right shoulder, this is considered a very bearish sign. If the same pattern occurs, only upside down, and the right shoulder is penetrated on the upside, it is a very bullish sign.

Hedgers are investors who are trying to reduce the risk of holding a certain position in physical commodities, securities, or currencies. They are willing to forgo some profit on their original investment in order to reduce price risk. A futures position opposite to the actual (cash) position is purchased to reduce the risk of the latter.

Hedge positions are positions taken simultaneously but in opposite directions in order to reduce risk. For example, a farmer might take both a long position in a commodity and a short position in the same commodity, thereby reducing his or her risk of loss from a price decline.

High-yield bonds are bonds rated by the rating agencies as lower than BBB or Baa. These so-called "junk bonds" have higher yields because of their lower quality.

The holder-of-record date is intended to determine which stockholders would receive a recently announced dividend. However, according to brokerage house custom, whoever is the owner of record on the fourth business day prior to the company's holder-of-record date receives the dividend.

A holding period return (HPR) is the total return actually realized or expected from holding a specific asset for a specified period of time (typically one year). A stock's HPR can be measured by dividing the capital gain or loss, plus dividends, by the stock's current purchase price.

Immunization represents an investment strategy in which the attempt is made to match the duration of cash receipts with the duration of cash needs. In other words, the bond portfolio's duration is matched with a desired time horizon. The objective of immunization is to achieve the optimal combination of interest rate risk and reinvestment rate risk.

An income bond is a corporate bond in which interest is payable only if it is earned by the firm. If the firm does not have sufficient earnings with which to make the interest payment, failure to make the payment will not constitute a default.

An income fund is a mutual fund that invests assets in bonds and stocks that pay high interest and dividends. The objective is current income, rather than capital appreciation. The risk is generally low.

An increasing rate bond is a bond whose coupon rate increases over time.

A bond indenture is the basic contract between an issuing corporation and the trustee representing the bondholders (the trustee is usually a trust company). The indenture sets forth the important provisions of the borrowing arrangement. An indenture must be used even when no mortgage exists and the bonds are unsecured.

Index arbitrage is the practice whereby an arbitrageur simultaneously buys and sells index futures and securities.

An index fund is a mutual fund that seeks to duplicate the performance of a stock index by buying securities that make up the index, such as the Standard & Poor's 500 Stock Index.

The Index of Consumer Sentiment is a report published monthly by the Survey Research Center at the University of Michigan. Like the Consumer Confidence Index, it attempts to derive information about consumer perceptions of business conditions and of their own financial condition, as well as their willingness to buy durable goods such as automobiles and home appliances. The assumption is that an increase in consumer sentiment is an indicator that consumers will increase their spending, thus leading to enhanced economic growth.

The Index of Leading Economic Indicators is a composite index used to predict near-term directions for economic activity. Among the specific indicators that make up the Index of Leading Economic Indicators are average weekly hours of manufacturing production workers, average weekly new claims for unemployment compensation, building permits for new private-housing units, stock prices, and the size of the money supply.

An indexed portfolio is a portfolio that attempts to duplicate the investment performance of a broadly diversified stock or bond market index, such as the S&P 500. The portfolio consists of the same assets and proportions as does the benchmark index. Consequently, the investment performance of the portfolio should be highly predictable relative to the index itself.

Indifference curves are graphic depictions of various sets of choices that might be made by an individual. The individual has no particular preference as among the various choices offered along the indifference curve. For example, an indifference curve might show that an investor is willing to accept a modest return for a modest amount of risk, but also that the same investor would be willing to bear more risk in order to receive a higher rate of return.

Indirect investment in real estate. See Glossary term "direct investment in real estate" above.

Industrial real estate includes factories, warehouses, utility facilities, and industrial parks.

Industry analysis is the search for those industries that promise the most opportunities for investors in the coming years. The past history and current situation for each industry are reviewed to give a basis for the outlook for that industry.

Industry life cycle. Some observers of industry data have drawn a rough parallel between industry growth and the human life cycle. They believe that industries evolve through at least three, and more typically four, stages: (a) the pioneering stage, (b) the expansion stage, (c) the stabilization or maturity stage, and (d) the declining stage. In general, they describe the industry life cycle as beginning with technological innovation. When new industries are born, demand grows rapidly, competition and new entry are high, and many companies in the pioneering stage will fail (the shakeout period that occurs during the pioneering stage). Eventually, the industry stops growing and often leads a relatively stable existence for an extended period. Then, new technological change brings about a decline.

An inefficient portfolio is a portfolio whose return is not maximized, given the level of risk. Consequently, the portfolio is not on the efficient frontier.

Inelasticity of demand refers to a situation in which the relative change in the quantity of an item demanded is smaller than the relative change in the price of that item.

Inflation refers to a general increase in prices. Various indexes, such as the Consumer Price Index and the Producer Price Index, are used to measure the inflation rate.

The inflation premium (or inflation risk premium) is an addition to the risk-free rate of interest that is designed to compensate an investor for the possible loss of future earning power due to inflation.

Inflation risk is the uncertainty of the future purchasing power of a fixed-income security. As the general level of prices increases, the investor who owns a fixed-income security can purchase fewer goods and services with the interest income received. The principal sum also will have less purchasing power at maturity. In an inflationary period, market rates of interest increase as investors demand a higher yield to compensate them for the loss in purchasing power caused by inflation. This means the market prices of fixed-income securities decline. Thus, the investor experiences a loss of principal if required to sell before the bond matures.

The initial margin on a futures contract is a "good faith" deposit made by the buyer or seller of a futures contract. It represents equity in the contract and is quite small in relationship to the actual value of the contract. The exchange on which the contract is traded sets the minimum initial margin requirement. However, the brokerage house typically requires a higher initial margin.

The initial margin for securities is the amount of funds an investor must have on deposit to purchase marginable securities. Regulation T of the Federal Reserve Board stipulates the federally required margin, but brokerages may set a higher requirement.

Insider trading refers to an individual's use of information, which is not general public knowledge, to benefit himself or herself, either through direct action or through another investor. To avoid this possible situation, officers and directors of companies are required to complete an initial report for the SEC to disclose the extent of their holdings. If one's holdings change, one is required to complete a monthly report.

The Insider Trading Act of 1984 is a federal statute that gave the Securities and Exchange Commission the authority to collect treble damages from one who engages in fraudulent insider trading of securities.

The Insider Trading and Securities Fraud Enforcement Act of 1988 prohibits use of inside information in securities purchases and sales.

An insured fund is an investment company that contains at least some minimum percentage of municipal bond issues that are insured by a private insurer as to timely payment of principal and interest.

Interest rate futures apply to Treasury bills, Treasury bonds, Treasury notes, and GNMAs, among others. They allow investors to speculate on interest rate movements or to hedge existing portfolios subject to the risk of fluctuating interest rates.

Interest rate risk is a systematic risk that exists because of the uncertainty associated with possible future changes in the general level of interest rates. As interest rates increase, the market prices of fixed-income investments decrease. When interest rates decrease, fixed-income investments tend to increase in market price. Of course, at maturity of the fixed-income security, the investor receives the face amount of the bond or other instrument. The risk exists because of the investor's possible need to sell the security prior to maturity.

An intermediate term fund is an investment company that invests in securities with maturities of between 5 and 10 years.

The internal rate of return (IRR) is the rate of return that equates the present value of the cash outflows associated with an investment with the present value of the cash inflows associated with it. Thus, the internal rate of return is the discount rate that produces a net present value of zero for an investment.

An international fund is a mutual fund that invests only in foreign securities. A global fund invests in both domestic U.S. securities and foreign securities. Both international and global funds generally have the investment objective of capital growth.

Call options are said to be in the money when the stock price is greater than the exercise price. Therefore, it is to the option holder's economic advantage to exercise the option since, in the case of the owner of a call, the owner could exercise the call and sell the stock in the open market for a profit. Put options are in the money when the exercise price is greater than the market price.

The intrinsic value:

(a)   Represents what a common stock is really worth to an investor who has a known required rate of return, after considering the likely growth prospects of the common stock.

(b)   Of an option is its minimum value. When a call is in the money, its intrinsic value is the difference between the market price of the stock and the exercise price of the option. For an out-of-the-money option, the intrinsic value is zero. It is never negative because there is no obligation to exercise the option. There may additionally be a speculative value of an option unrelated to its intrinsic value. Therefore, option prices almost always exceed their intrinsic value.

The Investment Advisers Act of 1940 is a federal statute requiring the registration with the SEC of certain persons who are engaged in the business of providing advice about securities for compensation. Although some investment advisers are exempt from the registration requirement, all investment advisers are subject to the antifraud provisions of the Act.

Investment advisory opinions are recommendations to investors produced by professional financial advisers. The advisory opinion theory suggests that financial advisers are often wrong. Consequently, this approach is often referred to as a "contrarian" view since it takes the opposite side of most financial advisers' recommendations.

An investment banker plays the part of middleman for companies that need capital. He or she brings together those who need money with those who have money to invest.

The Investment Company Act of 1940 is a federal statute that gave the SEC authority over publicly owned investment companies, including both closed-end companies and open-end companies, or mutual funds. Public offerings of investment company securities must be registered with the SEC.

An investment-grade fund is a corporate bond mutual fund that invests in corporate bonds rated by the rating agencies as BBB, Baa, or better.

An investment objective is a goal sought in the investment process. For example, a mutual fund may have capital appreciation as its investment objective. Other mutual funds may have as investment objectives a high current income or a balance of appreciation and current income.

Investment policy refers to the broad policy to be followed in light of an investor's particular risk-tolerance level. This risk-tolerance level may suggest investment policies which lie anywhere on the spectrum between extremely conservative and extremely venturesome. Investment policy may also involve setting minimum and maximum limits on the percentage of the total portfolio that is to be allocated to different types of investments.

Investment strategy is the actual selection of assets to meet a client's specific investment goals and requirements. Taken into consideration for such a strategy would be risk tolerance, liquidity, and marketability needs, as well as the client's tax situation.

The investment value of a convertible security is its intrinsic value without the convertible feature. It is the present value of the future stream of earnings and maturity value.

The January effect refers to evidence that there is seasonality in the stock market. Stocks earn higher returns in January than in any other month of the year. One explanation for the January effect is that stocks are bouncing back from depressed levels in December caused by tax-loss selling.

The <u>Jensen performance index (Jensen's alpha)</u> is a statistical measure of a portfolio's return compared to the required return, as calculated by the security market line (SML). A positive alpha indicates that the portfolio return was higher than expected, and a negative alpha indicates that the portfolio return was less than expected.

A <u>junk bond</u> is a high-yield bond that has substantial risk attached to it because of the uncertainty of future interest and principal payments. Junk bonds are rated below BBB or Baa by the rating agencies.

A <u>laddered portfolio</u> is a portfolio of bonds that have maturities distributed over a period of time. Laddering of a portfolio is a way of managing the portfolio's interest rate risk.

<u>Land</u> is real estate. Improved land is land that has been cleared or includes such improvements as gutters, sewer systems, sidewalks, or buildings. Unimproved land is land that has not been cleared and lacks improvements such as the foregoing.

<u>Leverage</u> is the use of borrowed capital for an investment in the expectation that profits will exceed the interest costs. In the context of options, leverage refers to magnification of the potential return on an investment. The magnification arises because of the low price at which options sell in comparison with the price of the underlying securities.

<u>Leverage ratios</u> measure the extent to which a firm uses debt financing and its ability to meet the contractual obligations generated by the use of long-term debt. Debt to owners' equity and total debt to total assets are two leverage ratios. A high return on owners' equity (higher than the return on total assets) and high debt ratios suggest successful use of financial leverage. High financial leverage causes profits to grow faster than sales when sales are rising, but profits will also fall faster than sales when sales decline. Thus, favorable financial leverage offers greater profit potential, but also greater risk. The times-interest-earned ratio and the fixed-charges-coverage ratio are used to see how well the fixed commitments created by the use of debt are covered and, accordingly, indicate whether or not the use of debt is excessive.

A <u>limited partnership</u> is managed by one or more general partners who are fully liable. The remaining investors (also known as limited partners) do not participate actively in management and are liable for actions of the partnership only to the extent of their investment.

A <u>limit order</u> specifies the price at which the investor wants to buy or sell a security. The investor will accept only the specified price or one that is more favorable.

<u>Liquid alternative funds</u> are mutual funds and ETFs that attempt to mimic alternative investment strategies yet provide for daily liquidity and lower minimum purchases than alternative assets. While liquid alternative funds provide more liquidity, they may experience dramatic price declines during periods of market stress.

Liquidity is the ease of quickly converting an investment into cash without a significant loss of invested principal.

The liquidity needs of an investor refer to the investor's need for cash or assets that can readily be converted into cash without significant loss of value.

A liquidity premium is an addition to the rate of return required by investors because of a real or perceived lack of liquidity of the investment in question. The liquidity premium is designed to compensate the investor for the real or perceived inability to convert an investment into cash quickly without significant loss of value.

Liquidity ratios are numerical measures of the ability of a company to meet its short-term obligations. The most commonly used liquidity ratios are the current ratio and the acid-test, or quick ratio.

Liquidity risk is the uncertainty as to the length of time required to convert an asset into cash and the price concession the investor must make to achieve a rapid conversion to cash. Real estate typically has poor liquidity. T-bills have excellent liquidity.

Buying a security is referred to as taking a long position. The investor who is long expects the price of the security to increase in value.

A long-term fund is an investment company that invests in securities with maturities of longer than 10 years.

Loss probability refers to the likelihood of a loss, whether by depreciation in the value of an investment asset or a reduction in the level of income that it provides.

A lump-sum payment or deposit is one that is made at one time only. When a large lump-sum payment occurs after a series of smaller periodic payments, it is called a balloon payment.

The maintenance margin requirement is a level below which the investor's equity in the contract may not drop. The equity will drop when the price of a futures contract moves against the owner's long or short position. When equity drops below the maintenance margin, a margin call will occur.

Managed futures are an alternative investment class consisting of futures contracts managed by professional money managers known as commodity trading advisors (CTAs).

Management fees are fees paid to an investment adviser for the professional management of a fund's investment portfolio. The fee is paid out of the fund's income. Administrative fees are operating expenses such as custodian, accounting, brokerage, and legal fees.

The term "margin" refers to the amount of the investor's own funds that he or she has invested in a security. Margin trading in securities means that the customer is permitted to buy and sell securities by using borrowed funds.

The <u>marginal tax rate</u> is the federal income tax rate at which a taxpayer's last dollar of taxable income is taxed.

A <u>margin call</u> is a requirement imposed by a broker for an investor to provide additional funds or security in an account with the broker as collateral against borrowed funds or as a good faith deposit.

A <u>margin requirement</u> is the proportion of the purchase price of a security that must be paid for by the investor in cash, rather than on credit.

Commodities contracts are <u>marked to the market</u> daily. This means that each day contract profits and losses are calculated. The investor may withdraw gains but will receive a margin call when equity falls below the required maintenance margin.

<u>Market equilibrium</u> is a condition in an economic market such that the quantity demanded and quantity supplied of a good are equal. Consequently, there is no reason for the price of the good in question to change.

A <u>market maker</u> is a dealer or specialist in a particular security. The market maker stands ready at all times to buy a particular security from interested sellers and to sell the particular security to interested investors.

A <u>market order</u> is an order to buy or sell securities at the best price available at the time the order is placed.

The <u>market rate of return</u> is the rate of return provided by an average stock, perhaps as represented by the rate of return on the average of all of the stocks contained in the S&P 500 Index.

<u>Market risk</u> is the uncertainty of the investor's total return because of changes in the market prices of the investor's assets. It is not possible to eliminate the market risk associated with listed common stocks by diversification achieved by purchasing several listed common stocks.

The <u>market sector</u> refers to a specific industry segment, such as oil or tobacco. Portfolios may be diversified or specialize in a market sector.

<u>Market timing</u> is an important part of active asset allocation. Market timing is based on the belief that rates of return can be improved by investors if they switch among asset categories based on timely forecasts of how the markets will change.

The <u>Markowitz model</u> is a mathematical model for constructing a diversified portfolio that maximizes an investor's satisfaction or utility by maximizing returns on the portfolio for a given level of risk.

<u>Master limited partnerships (MLPs)</u> have been formed to make limited partnership interests more liquid and marketable. They acquire or merge limited partnerships and make units available to trade in the secondary market similar to stocks.

The <u>maturity date</u> is the date when a debt issue expires. Principal is repaid at this time if it has not been repaid earlier.

<u>Monetary policy</u> refers to actions to effect changes in the stock of money in the economy with the aim of achieving maximum employment, production, and purchasing power. Observers agree that money influences economic activity, but the direction and amount of influence remain controversial. It is generally agreed that changes in the money supply affect interest rates and, in turn, total spending, output, and prices. The Federal Reserve System has the responsibility of executing monetary policy in the U.S. through the use of several tools, including: open market operations, management of the discount rate, and establishing reserve requirements.

<u>Money market mutual funds</u> are mutual funds that invest in relatively safe, liquid, and high-yield money market instruments. These funds are not federally insured.

The <u>money supply</u> is the amount of money available for use in the economy. There are at least three definitions (M1, M2, and M3). M1, the narrowest definition, measures currency, demand deposits, and other checkable deposits. The slightly broader M2 definition includes money market accounts. M3 includes institutional money market funds as well as M2 and M1.

A <u>mortgage-backed security</u> is a security backed by a collection of mortgages held by an individual or, more commonly, an organization. When homeowners make their monthly mortgage payments, the payments, less administrative fees, are passed on to the investor holding the mortgage-backed security.

A <u>mortgage bond</u> is a bond secured by a mortgage or a pool of mortgages on specific real estate or other fixed assets.

A <u>mortgage REIT</u> invests in construction loans and permanent mortgages and, in some cases, in mortgage-backed securities such as Ginnie Maes.

A <u>moving average</u> is an arithmetic mean or other average that includes a set number of observations and that also moves through time. For instance, if a person is computing a six-month moving average, every time a new month's data become available, he or she would add the most recent month and drop the oldest month. Thus, he or she would continue to take an average of six months, but the observations would move.

A <u>municipal bond</u> is a security issued by a state, county, or city. The coupon payments paid to investors in most municipal bonds are exempt from federal income taxation. Municipal bonds are used to raise funds for the governmental unit for general uses (general obligation bonds) or for a specific purpose that will generate funds to pay interest and, ultimately, the face amount of the bonds (revenue bonds). General obligation bonds are backed by the full faith and taxing power of the municipality. Revenue bonds are only backed by the revenues of the project.

<u>Municipal bond funds</u> invest assets in the debt instruments issued by municipal governments in the U.S. The income from most municipal bonds is tax-free, and the municipal bond funds pass through this tax-free income to investors.

Mutual fund is the more familiar name for an open-end investment company. Investors buy shares of a mutual fund directly from the company and later sell them back to the same mutual fund company. A mutual fund is open-ended because the company may issue additional mutual fund shares at any time.

A naked call is a call option written against stock that the seller or writer does not own.

NASAA is the North American Securities Administrators Association. Its function is to educate its members and to encourage the improvement of laws governing securities issuance and trading in the U.S., Canada, Mexico, and Puerto Rico.

The NASDAQ is the National Association of Security Dealers Automated Quotation System. It is the first electronic quotation system used to report bid and ask prices for over-the-counter securities. The term NASDAQ also refers to the NASDAQ Composite Index. This index tracks a market basket of 4,000 stocks, all of which are traded on the NASDAQ exchange.

The neglected-firm effect is a stock market anomaly that suggests that small firms that are neglected by large financial institutions tend to generate higher rates of return than firms to which the major financial institutions pay a great deal of attention.

A negotiable CD is a certificate of deposit issued by a bank in which the interest rate and terms are tailored to meet the needs of the particular investor. Negotiable CDs are usually issued only in large denominations (typically $100,000) and, unlike other CDs, may be bought and sold but not redeemed prior to their maturity date.

The net asset value (NAV) of a share in an investment company or exchange traded fund is calculated by determining the total value of the investment securities in the investment portfolio, subtracting liabilities, and then dividing by the total number of shares outstanding. Mutual fund shares are redeemed to the company at NAV while ETF shares are sold at fair market value on an exchange.

The net operating income of a piece of investment real estate is computed by adding the gross rental receipts and the non-rental income of the property and subtracting the vacancy and collection losses and the cash operating expenses. Net operating income should be calculated as an average over a period of several years.

A new issue market is a market for new issues of securities. The new issue market for a particular security may consist of segments of the general public with an interest in purchasing it, or it may consist of financial institutions that are interested in buying large portions of the total new issue.

A no-load fund is a mutual fund that does not charge a fee for buying or selling its shares.

The nominal rate on a bond is the coupon rate that the bond carries. The nominal or coupon rate will coincide with the actual rate of return provided by a bond only if the bond is purchased and sold at par value.

The <u>NYSE Composite Index</u> is an index of all stocks, ADRs, REITs, foreign stocks and tracking funds listed on the New York Stock Exchange.

An <u>odd lot</u> is a quantity of securities that is less than a round lot (which is usually 100 shares).

The <u>odd-lot theory</u> is based on the proposition that small investors are usually wrong. A bear market is indicated when the ratio of odd-lot purchases to odd-lot sales is rising.

The usual means of settling a futures contract is through <u>offset</u>. Rather than make or take delivery, option holders will liquidate a futures position by making an offsetting or opposite transaction. Buyers sell their positions at a profit or loss, and sellers buy their position at a profit or loss.

An <u>open-end investment company</u> is a mutual fund. It continuously sells new shares and rebuys outstanding shares that current investors wish to convert to cash.

The <u>open interest</u> is the number of futures contracts in existence for a particular commodity at a particular point in time.

<u>Open market operations</u> are a tool of monetary policy used by the Federal Reserve. Open market operations refer to the purchase and sale of government securities by the Fed in order to expand or contract the size of the country's money supply.

An <u>optimal portfolio</u> provides an investor with the best combination of risk and return.

An <u>option growth fund</u> invests assets in put and call options for capital appreciation. A substantial part of the assets may also be held in money market instruments.

An <u>option income fund</u> is a mutual fund that invests in dividend-paying stocks and enhances its return by writing call options on these stocks.

<u>Organized exchanges</u> are facilities having tangible locations in which securities are bought and sold. Examples of organized exchanges are the New York Stock Exchange and the American Stock Exchange. Organized exchanges are contrasted with the over-the-counter market, which is a network of telephone and computer lines connecting dealers in particular securities.

An <u>originating house</u> is an investment banking firm that agrees with the issuing company to sell a new issue of securities. The originating house forms a syndicate of securities firms assembled to market the securities.

Call options are said to be <u>out of the money</u> when the exercise price is above the market price. Put options are out of the money when the reverse is true. The option holder will not exercise an out-of-the-money option.

The <u>over-the-counter (OTC) market</u> refers to the continuous market for securities that are not listed on one of the national or regional exchanges. The OTC lacks a central marketplace but is connected through computer systems throughout the country.

         www.keirsuccess.com

Paper profits are profits that have been generated by appreciation in the value of a security but have not yet been realized through sale of the appreciated security.

Par value/face value. Par value is the face amount of the security. This is the value usually shown on the books of the corporation. However, preferred stock may be no-par. Also, bonds may be sold at a discount or a premium, rather than at par. The face amount of a bond is the amount the issuer must repay the bond owner at maturity. It is also known as the bond's principal sum.

Passive asset allocation entails regular rebalancing, usually every 6 months or each year, of the portfolio through the buying and selling of specific investments. These purchase and sale decisions are made in order to maintain an initially selected mix of asset categories.

A pass-through security collects the monthly interest and principal from homeowners and then passes them on to the investors in the pass-through (for example, GNMA certificates).

A pay-in-kind (PIK) security is a bond or preferred stock whose interest or dividend may be paid in additional debt or additional shares, instead of in cash. PIKs are appealing to issuers who may need cash for operations in the company and want the option of using cash for other things instead of paying interest or dividends.

The dividend payout ratio is calculated by dividing total dividends paid during a given period by net earnings after taxes for the company during that same period. Alternatively, divide dividends paid per share of common stock by earnings per share of common stock. The ratio measures the portion of earnings paid to stockholders as opposed to the portion retained to finance growth. Stockholders seeking high current income will prefer higher dividend payout ratios, while those emphasizing total gain and long-term growth may well prefer lower dividend payout ratios.

The P/E effect is a stock market anomaly that suggests that portfolios made up of stocks with low price/earnings ratios provide higher average annual rates of return than portfolios made up of stocks with higher price/earnings ratios.

The P/E ratio is typically calculated by dividing the latest twelve months' earnings per share into the current market price of the stock. This offers a crude suggestion of relative value for various stocks. The P/E ratio shows how much the market is currently willing to pay for a given dollar of earnings. The higher the expected growth rate and the lower the volatility of earnings for a firm, other things being equal, the higher will be the P/E ratio awarded by the market. A firm with higher growth prospects and/or less perceived risk, therefore, will show a higher P/E ratio, but it shouldn't be assumed that the stock of the firm with the lower ratio is a better purchase. Investors must ascertain whether the growth prospects and risk warrant the P/E ratio assigned by the market.

Perpetual debt is debt that does not have a maturity date. Hence, the face amount of the debt instrument is never payable. However, these debts typically pay a steady stream of interest payments.

Portfolio construction is the process of creating, through a logical sequence of steps, the optimum combination of investment instruments needed to achieve the stated goals of a client.

<u>Portfolio management</u> is the ongoing maintenance of a portfolio for an individual investor so as to assure that the portfolio will continue to perform in optimal fashion for the achievement of the client's goals.

<u>Portfolio rebalancing</u> entails periodically buying and selling assets and investments in different investment categories in order to restore the initial proportionate mix of asset categories within the total portfolio.

<u>Preemptive rights</u> are the rights of existing common stockholders to purchase additional shares of stock in the same company if a new issue would otherwise diminish the percentage of ownership and voting control held by the present stockholders. An announcement that a company is planning to issue new common stock subject to the preemptive rights of the current stockholders is called a rights offering.

<u>Preferred stock</u> represents equity ownership and is issued without a stated maturity date. It carries a fixed quarterly dividend, which may be paid or passed when the board of directors so decides. However, preferred stockholders receive a claim on income and assets that is prior to that of the common stockholders. Preferred stock carries less risk for the investor than the common stock of a given company but more risk than the bonds of that company.

A <u>premium</u> is the price of an option. It is paid by the buyer to the seller (writer) of the option. It is stated on a per-share basis that is multiplied by 100 to obtain the total cost per contract since each contract represents 100 shares.

A <u>premium bond</u> is one whose market price is above the bond's par value or face amount. A bond will sell at a premium when its coupon rate is above the market rate of interest for bonds of comparable quality. When market rates of interest go down, bond prices will go up, so that the current yields of outstanding bonds are comparable to the yields on newly issued, low-interest bonds. Thus, the market price of these higher coupon bonds will go above their par values.

A <u>premium or discount from NAV (net asset value)</u> refers to the extent to which the price of a closed-end investment company's stock sells above or below the investment company's net asset value.

<u>Prepayment risk</u> refers to a type of risk associated with collateralized mortgage obligations. Homeowners may decide, for a variety of reasons, to pay off their mortgages early. When a mortgage is repaid, the prepayments are passed through to the investors in the CMOs. Any unexpected return of principal early, therefore, subjects the investors in the CMOs to reinvestment risk if interest rates have fallen, which is the most likely scenario when real estate mortgages are paid off early. Prepayment risk also is present in callable bonds.

A <u>price chart</u> is a chart maintained in order to track the movements in price of a security over time, perhaps relative to some other variable, such as trading volume. Price charts are an important tool used in technical analysis of stock markets.

The price-earnings (P/E) ratio is expressed as the current market price of the stock divided by 12 months of earnings per share.

Price fluctuations refer to changes in the market prices of securities.

Price volatility refers to how the price of a security fluctuates in relation to the market as a whole. A very volatile stock will go up or down at a greater rate than the market in general goes up or down.

A private placement is a new issue of securities that is sold entirely to a small number of large, usually institutional, investors. Privately placed securities, then, are not offered to the general public and, therefore, are exempt from registration with the SEC under the terms of the Securities Act of 1933.

A private purpose municipal bond is a debt instrument issued by a governmental unit to finance a private project that is not a government operation, for example, an industrial park. Many private purpose municipal bonds no longer provide tax-free interest income to investors.

Profitability ratios are numerical measures of the amount that a company is earning in relation to some base, such as sales or assets. Typical ratios are return on assets, return on equity, and return on investment.

Programmed trading refers to coordinated buying or selling of large sized portfolios that is triggered by computers and often executed automatically.

A progressive tax is a tax whose rates rise as the income or other measure of ability to pay of the taxpayer rises.

A proportionate tax is a tax whose rates remain the same, regardless of the income or ability to pay of the taxpayer.

A prospectus is a summary of the material contained in the registration statement required by the SEC for sale of new security issues. A copy of the prospectus must be made available to all interested parties before they invest.

A public purpose municipal bond is a bond issued by a governmental unit that is used to finance traditional government functions for which state and local governments must raise money. Public purpose municipal bonds are exempt from federal income taxation.

The Public Utility Holding Company Act of 1935 is a federal statute that reorganized the public utility industry. The statute required improved methods of accounting and more thorough reporting by utilities. It also placed constraints on the use of debt financing by such companies.

Purchasing power risk is the risk that a person's invested assets will not earn enough to keep up with the rate of inflation. For example, if a person's portfolio is earning only 4% per year after taxes, and if the inflation rate is 5%, the investor is losing purchasing power each year.

A put bond allows the investor to sell his or her bond back to the investor at par after a given period of time.

A put option is the right to sell stock at a designated price if the transaction occurs by a designated day.

The quantity demanded is the amount of a particular good or service that purchasers are able and willing to buy at a particular price for that good or service.

The quantity supplied is the amount that producers of a particular good or service are willing and able to make available in the marketplace at a particular price for that good or service.

Random walk is the belief that price changes are unpredictable and random, and as a result, security analysis will not help to predict future prices.

Ratio analysis refers to an analysis of the financial statements of a company by making comparisons of certain accounts with others. For example, ratio analysis might entail estimating the liquidity position of a firm by calculating its current ratio or its quick (acid-test) ratio and comparing these ratios to other firms in the same industry.

A real estate investment trust (REIT) is a publicly traded, closed-end investment company that invests in a diversified portfolio of real estate or real estate mortgages.

The real (inflation-adjusted) return is the rate of return produced by an investment after deducting the impact of inflation. Hence, real rates of return measure the increase in purchasing power that is earned by an investor.

The realized compound yield on a security is the yield that is produced based on an assumption that the periodic income amounts received by the investor from the security are reinvested at a rate that may be greater than or less than the yield-to-maturity rate. Hence, realized compound yield may be greater than yield to maturity if income payments are reinvested at a rate higher than the yield-to-maturity rate. Conversely, realized compound yield on a security may be lower than the yield to maturity if the income provided by the security is reinvested at a rate lower than the yield-to-maturity rate.

Realized return is the actual rate of return an investor earns on his or her invested dollars. Realized return is determined after all the historical facts are arranged, all expenses are deducted, and a final accounting is completed.

Recapitalization is a change in the mix of sources of capital used by a business firm. For example, the issuance of new shares of common stock and the use of the proceeds to retire some of a company's existing bonds would constitute a recapitalization of the company.

Redemption exit fees are sales charges incurred when an investor sells mutual fund shares. Most commonly used in open-end mutual funds, these exit fees may be charged even by no-load funds.

A red herring and a preliminary prospectus are the same. The red lettering on the title page of the preliminary prospectus has led to the use of the term red herring. The red herring announces to prospective buyers that the securities are being registered with the SEC, and, in the near future, they will be offered for sale. The red herring prospectus describes the company in detail. It provides information concerning the company's income, outstanding debt, securities to be offered, current activities, and types of competition. It does not contain information about the planned offering price of the security.

A registered form of bond is one that is issued to a specific owner. The names of all bondholders are formally registered with the issuer, who pays interest to the owners of record by check.

A Registered Investment Adviser is an individual who: (a) gives investment advice about securities, (b) is in the business of giving investment advice, (c) receives compensation for giving investment advice, and (d) has completed the necessary registration with the SEC as an investment adviser.

A regressive tax is a tax whose rates rise as the income or other measure of the taxpayer's ability to pay falls.

A regulated investment company is an investment company, whether open-ended or close-ended, that is subject to the Investment Company Act of 1940. Investment companies that meet the requirements of this Act receive special federal income tax treatment. Their earnings and capital gains are exempt from taxation at the corporate level and, instead, are taxed only to those who hold shares in the investment company.

A reinvestment rate assumption is an assumption as to the rate of return that will be earned on income provided by an asset that is reinvested as it is received. In the calculation of yield to maturity, the reinvestment rate assumption is that the periodic income will be reinvested at the same rate as the yield-to-maturity rate.

Reinvestment rate risk is the uncertainty for the investor with respect to reinvesting the interest and principal amount at the same level of interest at which the initial investment was made.

A repurchase agreement provides for the sale of a money market instrument with a requirement that the buyer sell the instrument back on an agreed date. The seller is in effect receiving a loan on the strength of the collateral being sold temporarily. Repurchase agreements are usually issued to cover holdings of U.S. government securities.

Repurchase of debt refers to a corporation retiring some of its outstanding debt by purchasing it in the open market. Normally, the repurchase of debt would be carried out only if the debt instruments are selling at a discount from their par value.

The required rate of return is the minimum rate of interest that the investor objectively expects to receive and that is needed to induce the investor to commit funds to the particular investment.

Required reserves are reserves that financial institutions must maintain in cash or securities deposited with the Federal Reserve System. The required reserves are established as a percentage of total deposits of the financial institutions subject to the reserve requirement.

Reserve requirements are amounts of legal reserves that must be maintained by financial institutions relative to their deposits subject to reserve requirements. Reserve requirements are established and maintained by the Federal Reserve System.

A reset bond is a bond that does not have a fixed coupon when it is issued. The coupon on a reset bond is adjusted at periodic intervals, such as every six months, based on some specific benchmark like the rate being paid on U.S. Treasury bills. Reset bonds typically have a maximum and minimum coupon.

Residential real estate includes single-family dwellings, multiple-family dwellings, such as apartments and hotels and motels.

Resistance levels are stock prices that do not tend to be penetrated unless there is an unusual wave of selling (on the down side) or buying (on the up side) in the particular security.

Retained earnings are the sum of all of the net profits of a firm since it was formed, less all of the net losses for any year in which they were incurred, less any dividends paid to stockholders. Stated differently, retained earnings are calculated as total assets less total liabilities less capital stock less paid-in capital.

The return on equity ratio is the ratio found by dividing a company's earnings by its stockholders' equity. Return on equity is one of a company's profitability ratios.

Revaluation is an increase in the value of a particular country's currency as a result of government fiat.

A revenue bond is a municipal bond whose principal and interest payments are secured by revenue generated by specific projects, such as water systems, sewer systems, toll roads, or electric utilities. The issuer is not required to use general tax revenues to pay these bonds. Defaults, such as for the West Virginia Turnpike Bonds, have occurred where the project was unable to generate adequate revenues to meet required interest and/or principal payments.

A reverse stock split occurs when a larger number of shares of a company's stock is retired and replaced by a smaller number. For example, a 1-for-2 stock split is a reverse stock split.

Riding the yield curve is an investment technique in which the investor purchases a security with a maturity longer than the anticipated holding period and then sells the security before it matures in order to take advantage of the capital appreciation that results from a stable, upward-sloping yield curve.

A risk-adjusted return is the rate of return on a security adjusted for the degree of risk associated with it. The risk-adjusted return for a security is found by dividing the security's return by its beta coefficient. Risk-adjusted returns facilitate comparisons of the returns from different securities or mutual funds with different degrees of riskiness.

Risk capacity is a measurement of the amount of risk a client can afford to assume. It may be based on the client's ability to adjust goals, on reliability and sources of income, and on ability to absorb losses in the investment portfolio without having a detrimental impact on standard of living. Note the difference between risk capacity and risk tolerance, as defined below.

The risk-free rate is the rate of return (yield) an investor can obtain by investing in such risk-free investments as U.S. Treasury bills and insured money market accounts.

The risk premium is an add-on to the risk-free interest rate, such as the rate on U.S. Treasury bills, to compensate the investor for the fact that the security in question has a variety of risks that are absent in the U.S. Treasury bill.

The risk-return trade-off reflects the fact that, the greater the risk accepted, the greater must be the potential return as a reward for committing one's funds to the uncertain outcome. Generally, as the riskiness rises, the rate of return should also rise, and vice versa. Investors accept a lower rate of return for T-bills because of the low risk. A quiet, restful night's sleep is worth some sacrifice in investment yield!

Risk tolerance is the ability and willingness of a client to accept a given level and type of risk associated with an investment. Note the difference between risk tolerance and risk capacity, as defined above.

A round lot is the minimum number of shares that may be purchased or sold on an organized exchange without having to be treated as an "odd lot." This means that the investor is able to acquire or dispose of the securities at lower commission rates. For most common stocks listed on a national exchange, a round lot is 100 shares.

A sales/front-end load consists of the charges added to fund shares by the underwriter and brokers who sell mutual funds to investors. The sales charges are added to the net asset value of a mutual fund share and may not exceed 8.5% of the offering price.

SEC registration is a requirement imposed on new issues of securities to be sold to the general public. The registration statement provides the SEC with detailed information about the proposed new issue. Only after SEC approval is obtained may the issue be sold to the general public. SEC registration also refers to the requirement imposed by the Investment Advisers Act of 1940 that those who are in the business of providing advice about securities for compensation must register as Investment Advisers with the SEC.

A sector fund concentrates investment of assets in the securities of one industry. For example, an energy fund invests only in the securities of companies in the energy industry. Sector funds may concentrate investments in the health care industry, in technology stocks, in the financial services industry, or in other industries.

The Securities Act of 1933 is a federal statute regulating new issues of securities. The main purpose of the Securities Act of 1933 was to assure that potential investors receive all of the necessary information in order to make an intelligent decision about purchasing a security and that all of the information that is provided is accurate. Hence, the Securities Act of 1933 is a full-disclosure type of law.

The Securities and Exchange Commission (SEC) is the federal agency that enforces the federal securities laws.

The Securities Exchange Act of 1934 is a federal statute that extends the regulation created by the Securities Act of 1933 to existing securities issues. The 1934 Act prohibits manipulation of securities markets, deception and misrepresentation of facts, and fraudulent practices. The Act also created the Securities and Exchange Commission to enforce the 1933 and 1934 laws.

The Securities Investors Protection Act of 1970 is a federal statute creating and empowering the Securities Investor Protection Corporation to provide federal insurance protecting investors from losses resulting from the failure of a securities brokerage firm. Note, of course, that the SIPC does not protect investors against losses due to fluctuation in securities' values.

A security market line (SML) is a graphic representation of the relationship between the risk associated with a particular security, measured by its beta, and the expected rate of return provided by that security.

A selling group is a collection of brokerage firms recruited by an underwriting syndicate to assist the syndicate in selling a new issue of securities.

The semi-strong form of the Efficient Market Hypothesis states that current stock prices reflect all past and public information. Therefore, only private (insider) information may be used to identify mispriced stocks.

A serial bond is a bond issue in which individual bonds within the total issue mature at different periods. For example, perhaps 10 percent of the bonds would have a maturity in the year 2020, another 10 percent in the year 2021, another in 2022, and so on.

Series EE U.S. Savings Bonds are non-marketable bonds that are issued by the U.S. Treasury. The interest is not subject to federal income tax until the bonds mature or are redeemed. There is no secondary market for these bonds.

Series HH U.S. Savings Bonds are debt instruments issued by the U.S. Treasury. These bonds were sold at par, with a minimum of $500 required, and they matured in 20 years, and with interest paid every year. Series HH bonds are no longer available for purchase.

Series I U.S. Savings Bonds are debt instruments issued by the U.S. Treasury which pay both a fixed interest rate and a variable inflation rate. These bonds are intended to protect the buyer's purchasing power through the semi-annual use of the Consumer Price Index to compensate for inflation.

The settlement date is the date on which an investor must complete a security transaction, either by paying for the security he or she has purchased or by receiving payment for a security he or she has sold.

Share averaging means that the same number of shares is bought every time the investor makes a purchase (regardless of the market price of the stock).

The Sharpe performance index calculates the excess return per unit of risk and measures variability. Risk is defined as the standard deviation of the portfolio return. The Sharpe performance index does not assume that the portfolio is well diversified. The formula for calculating the Sharpe index is to take the difference between the portfolio rate of return and the risk-free rate of return and divide that difference by the standard deviation of the return on the portfolio.

The shelf rule is an SEC rule allowing eligible companies to file an abbreviated registration form for a block of securities and place them "on the shelf" for later sale when market conditions are favorable.

The short interest ratio is the ratio between the number of shares sold short and not covered and the average daily trading volume. A high short interest ratio is bullish because it indicates potential demand for stocks by those who sold short.

A short sale is a sale of borrowed securities on the assumption that the price is going to fall. The plan is that, after the security price falls, the security will be purchased by the short seller and returned to the one from whom the security was borrowed.

A short-term fund is an investment company that invests in securities with relatively short maturities, usually 3 to 5 years.

A simple (arithmetic) average is an average produced by adding the number of items in a list and dividing the total by the number of items in that list. For example, if on three successive dates, the prices of a particular stock are $20, $30, and $40, the arithmetic average of those prices is found by adding 20, 30, and 40, for a total of 90, and dividing by 3. The answer is $30.

A single-country fund is a mutual fund that invests in the securities of one country. Most of these funds have an investment objective of capital appreciation.

A single-state fund is a municipal bond fund that invests in the bonds of a specified state to avoid state income tax, as well as federal income tax.

A sinking fund is an investment account of the issuing corporation into which annual payments are made for the purpose of developing a fund to pay off a bond issue prior to maturity. Usually, the sinking fund is utilized by the bond trustee to retire outstanding bonds. The bonds to be retired are typically drawn by lot, and a premium is paid at the time of redemption.

A <u>small company fund (small-cap fund)</u> is a mutual fund or investment company that invests in the stock of companies with a small market capitalization. The funds may be invested either for value or growth.

The <u>small-firm effect</u> is a stock market anomaly suggesting that small-cap (small-capitalization) companies provide higher rates of return than large-cap companies. Size is generally measured by the aggregate market value of the company's stock.

A <u>specialist</u> makes a market for securities listed on an organized exchange. He or she buys and sells securities for his or her own account when there is unusual desire on the part of investors (or traders) to sell or to buy. The specialist stands ready to buy or sell securities at all times to maintain an orderly market. A specialist typically makes a market for 5 to 15 issues. The specialist also makes odd-lot transactions in his or her issues for those people who wish to buy or sell less than a round lot. A <u>dealer</u> performs in the over-the-counter market the same functions performed by the "specialist" on the national exchanges.

<u>Speculators</u> (in the context of futures trading) are investors in futures, derivatives, commodities or currencies, who assume risk in order to profit from movements in prices. They accept risk, rather than try to minimize risk as hedgers do. Speculators add liquidity to the futures market, and, over time, their actions serve to reduce price volatility.

A <u>split-coupon bond</u> is similar to a zero-coupon bond in some ways. During the initial years of the bond issue, typically three to five years, no interest is paid, but is accumulated. After this period, the bond pays a fixed rate of interest.

The <u>spot price</u> of a commodity is the price at which that commodity is selling at the current time.

A <u>spread</u> is an options strategy involving the simultaneous purchase and sale of options on one particular stock that differ only in terms of expiration date or exercise price. It is a popular practice for reducing the risk of an options position. The particular spread strategy used depends on whether the investor is bullish or bearish.

When trading securities, the <u>spread</u> is the difference between the bid and ask price of the security.

A strategy of <u>staggered maturities or laddered bonds</u> entails constructing a portfolio in which the bond holdings have staggered maturity dates. Consequently, some of the total portfolio will mature each year. The rationale for such a strategy is to provide the portfolio with some reinvestment risk protection, spreading reinvestment out over the full interest rate cycle. The effects of overall interest rate changes will thus tend to be averaged, and the extremes of return and risk will be reduced.

The <u>Standard & Poor's 500 Composite Stock Price Index (S&P 500)</u> is a value-weighted index of the stock prices for 500 large companies.

The <u>standard deviation</u> is a measure of the dispersion of individual results around the mean or average of those results. Since it measures the variability of the results, the standard deviation may be used as a measure of risk.

<u>State securities commissions</u> are administrative agencies at the state level that are empowered to administer the Blue Sky laws relating to the issuance of and trading in securities.

A <u>stock dividend</u> is a distribution of additional shares to the current holders of record. The stock dividend is usually expressed as a percentage. For example, a 5% stock dividend would be calculated by multiplying each owner's stock holdings on the record date by 5%. In this example, an owner of 100 shares on the record date would receive 5 more shares as a stock dividend.

<u>Stock index futures</u> are based upon the S&P 500 Index, the NYSE Composite Index, and the Value Line Index. These futures allow investors to hedge against the systematic risk of common stock brought about by movements in the overall market. A short hedge protects against a market decline. A long hedge protects against a market rise before money is available to be invested in the stock market.

A <u>stock index option</u>, like stock index futures, allows investors to profit from movements in the overall stock market. Investors expecting a market rise buy calls, and bearish investors buy puts. Unlike stock index futures, the option buyer knows in advance the maximum loss, which is the option premium. The potential loss for writers, however, is not limited. Stock index options can and are used effectively to hedge stock portfolios.

A <u>stock repurchase</u> is the purchase and retirement of outstanding stock by the issuing corporation.

A <u>stock split</u> is a distribution of additional shares to the current holders of record. Typical stock splits are 2-for-1, 3-for-1, or 3-for-2. The investor could end up owning twice or three times the number of shares previously owned. However, since all stockholders receive the same multiple of shares, the individual stockholder's proportionate interest in the company remains unchanged. Except for differing accounting treatment, there is little practical difference between a stock dividend and a stock split.

A <u>stop order</u> is used to initiate sale of a stock if the price of that stock drops to a specified price or below that price. It is designed to limit the loss an investor might incur when the price of the stock falls after purchase.

A <u>straddle</u> is the simultaneous purchase or sale of a put and a call option for the same stock with the same expiration date and exercise price. The straddle purchaser believes that the stock price will fluctuate significantly so that each option can be exercised separately and profitably. The straddle seller, in contrast, believes that there will be little volatility in the stock price, but it could rise or fall. No likely movement direction is forecast by either the buyer or seller.

<u>Strategic asset allocation</u> is long-range asset allocation based on the asset mix outlined in a client's investment policy. Strategic asset allocation is contrasted with tactical asset allocation, which

involves frequent short-term adjustments in the asset mix as a particular category of assets becomes overvalued or undervalued relative to the other classes.

The street name is the name of the stockbroker with whom securities will be left. Street name refers, then, to the registration of securities in a broker's name, instead of in the name of the buyer of the securities.

The strong form of the Efficient Market Hypothesis states that all past, public and private (insider) information is reflected in current stock prices. According to this theory, there is no information available to help an analyst or investor identify mispriced stocks.

Support levels are resistance levels on the down side of a security's market price. At some point, the decline in the value of the stock will be offset because new purchasers will enter the market at the lower price to obtain the stock, thus stabilizing its price.

A swap dealer is a large institution which, for a fee, acts as a conduit between firms executing swap agreements between each other. Simultaneous exchanges help these firms save on interest costs and may reduce exchange rate risk.

Swaps refer to selling one type of bond and buying another in order to meet a variety of objectives. Bond swaps may be used to save on taxes, to increase yields, to reduce the risk in a portfolio, or to take advantage of mispricing of certain bonds.

A syndicate is a group of investment banking firms assembled by an originating house to market a new issue of securities.

Systematic risk, also called nondiversifiable risk, is found to some degree in nearly all securities because the market prices of similar securities usually move as a group in a systematic way. For example, most common stocks listed on the NYSE tend to respond to the same market psychology. When the general tone is bearish, most stocks tend to move down in market price. Thus, diversifying will not be helpful in eliminating this risk. Systematic risk is that portion of total risk that can't be eliminated by diversification since it is attributed to such broad factors as economic or political changes that affect the price of most similar investments.

Tangible or physical assets are assets that can be touched or seen and have their own intrinsic value. Tangible or physical assets are contrasted with financial assets, such as a life insurance policy or a certificate of stock.

A target fund is a mutual fund that invests in zero-coupon bonds with the same maturity date, such as the year 2020.

A target date fund is a mutual fund whose asset allocation is adjusted periodically based on the anticipated retirement date of the shareholders. Shareholders purchase the target date fund that matches their anticipated year of retirement. For example, the target date may be the year 2035 or 2040.

A taxable equivalent yield is the yield that a tax-exempt municipal security must produce to be equivalent to a taxable investment. The comparison can be made by using the following formula:

$$\text{Tax equivalent yield} = \frac{\text{Tax-exempt yield}}{(1 - \text{Marginal tax rate})}$$

A tax anticipation note is a short-term debt obligation issued by a state or local government against anticipated future receipts from taxes. When the tax revenues are received, the notes are retired. The maturity date of the note is set to coincide with the anticipated timing of the receipts.

A tax-exempt bond is a debt instrument issued by a state, county, or local government whose income is free of federal income taxes.

Technical analysis is analysis of past volume and/or price behavior in the stock market to identify which securities to purchase and when to buy them. Technical analysis also is used to determine which securities to sell and when to sell them.

The terminal value of proceeds from an investment is the future value of those proceeds, compounded at a specified annual rate of interest, as of the maturity date of the investment.

A term premium is an add-on to the risk-free rate of return on a security to reflect investor uncertainties associated with the length of time until the maturity of a security. In general, longer-term securities carry higher term premiums than shorter-term securities, all other things being equal.

The term structure of interest rates refers to the relationship between a security's interest rate and its term to maturity. The term structure of interest rates is sometimes presented graphically, in which case it is called a yield curve.

A thin issue is an issue that consists of a small number of securities in the hands of the general public or a small volume of transactions carried on by the public.

The third market is the market in which securities listed on an organized exchange are traded in the over-the-counter market. In the third market, large institutional investors wishing to buy or sell listed securities at reduced commission rates work through large brokerage firms that complete the transaction for them.

The time horizon refers to the length of the planning period for purposes of formulating an investment policy and strategy for a client.

The time premium paid for an option is the amount by which an option's price exceeds its intrinsic value.

A time-weighted return is a rate of return in which the inflows and outflows are weighted, depending on how soon the outflows must be undertaken and how the long the investor must wait for each of the inflows. Time-weighting is an important part of the calculation of a bond's duration.

Total portfolio risk is the entire risk associated with owning a portfolio. Total portfolio risk is made up of two components: the systematic risk and the unsystematic risk.

The total return on an investment is the sum of the return represented by the income from the investment and the return represented by capital appreciation between the time the asset is bought and later sold.

A tranche is a classification of collateralized mortgage obligation bonds with a stated maturity, such as 3 years, 5 years, or 10 years. Issues of CMOs may have up to 10 to 12 classes, or tranches. Individual tranches have varying degrees of interest rate risk and prepayment risk.

A Treasury bill (T-bill) is a short-term, non-interest-bearing debt instrument issued by the U.S. government. It is sold at a discount and redeemed at face value, the difference providing the return to the investor. T-bills have a maturity of less than one.

A Treasury bond is a long-term debt security, with a maturity of greater than ten years, which are sold in $100 to $1,000,000 denominations. These bonds have fixed semi-annual interest payments and are readily marketable and moderately liquid. Their market prices are, however, subject to interest rate risk.

A Treasury Floating Rate Note is a Treasury note with a minimum denomination of $100, a 2-year maturity, and an interest rate that is adjusted weekly and paid quarterly. These notes can be held until maturity or resold.

A Treasury note is an intermediate term, fixed-rate debt instrument with a maturity of two to ten years. Treasury notes are issued by the U.S. government in $100 to $1,000,000 denominations.

The Treynor performance index is similar to the Sharpe performance index in that it calculates the excess return per unit of risk and measures volatility. However, risk is defined as the portfolio beta in the Treynor performance index. The formula for calculating the Treynor index is to take the difference between the portfolio rate of return and the risk-free rate of return and divide that difference by the beta of the portfolio. In contrast, in the Sharpe performance index, the difference is divided by the standard deviation of the return on the portfolio. Therefore, the higher the Treynor index, the greater the excess return generated by a portfolio per unit of risk.

A 12b-1 fee is an annual marketing and distribution fee imposed by some mutual funds to pay for advertising and marketing costs. The fee is imposed under a plan of distribution adopted pursuant to SEC Rule 12b-1.

Underwriting refers to an investment banker purchasing or guaranteeing the sale of securities. Typically, the underwriter must absorb any of the unsold securities. The underwriter accepts varying degrees of risk with respect to the new issue, depending on the terms of the underwriting agreement.

A unit investment trust (UIT) is an investment company formed under a trust document to administer specified assets. The unit trust maintains a fixed portfolio of assets that does not change, so active management by an investment adviser is not required.

Unsystematic risk is that portion of total risk that can be reduced by diversification since it is attributable to specific factors unique to a firm or industry. Examples of these factors include: labor strikes, management capabilities, or market demand for the firm's products. The degree of uncertainty associated with a firm's earnings prospects (business risk) and the way it is financed (financial risk) have an impact on unsystematic risk.

The uptick rule is a rule governing the conduct of short sales of securities. Short sales may be executed only if the previous change in the price of the stock in question was an uptick, that is, an increase in the price from the preceding trade. As of July 2007, the uptick rule no longer applies to short sales.

Utility is usefulness or satisfaction derived from a particular choice. For example, an investor may prefer to invest in a riskier security in order to obtain a higher rate of return. If so, investing in the riskier security will provide greater utility to the investor.

The Value Line effect is one of the documented results that contrasts with what one would expect in a totally efficient market. The Value Line ranking system has had an impressive record of outperforming the market indicators.

The Value Line Index is an equal-weighted index of approximately 1,700 stocks followed by the Value Line Investment Service.

Value-weighted refers to a method of weighting a stock market index where each stock is weighted by its market capitalization (current market price x number of shares outstanding). Thus, changes in the market price of the larger companies carry more weight in the index than do price changes of the smaller companies' securities.

A variable-interest-rate bond has two unique features. First, the coupon rate changes at prescribed intervals of time based on the interest rate offered on some specified kind of investment medium, such as the average yield on 10-year Treasury obligations. Second, an option is granted to the investor to require the issuer to redeem the issue at par prior to maturity.

Voting rights are rights held by common stockholders of a company to elect members of the company's board of directors and to vote on other corporate issues.

A warrant is an option to purchase a stated number of shares of common stock at a specified price within a specified time period. Warrants typically expire from 3 to 10 years in the future. However, the terms of a warrant are not standardized. Warrants are typically issued by a corporation as an inducement to investors to buy a new bond or preferred stock issue. They are "sweeteners" to make the new issue attractive for investors.

A <u>wash sale</u> is the sale of a particular security at a loss, immediately followed by the repurchase of the same or a "substantially identical" security. In a wash sale, the investor is not allowed to take credit for the loss for tax purposes, although a wash sale is by no means illegal. In order to avoid the wash sale restriction for tax purposes, the investor must wait at least 31 days before repurchasing the security. If he or she does so, then the loss may be deducted for federal income tax purposes.

The <u>weak-form of the Efficient Market Hypothesis</u> speculates that current stock prices reflect all past information. Proponents of this theory believe that fundamental analysis can be used to identify mispriced or underperforming stocks.

A <u>weighted average</u> is an average computed by giving more emphasis to certain components of the average than others. For example, if the rate of return on one stock in a portfolio is 4 percent and another stock in the portfolio is 7 percent, and if the 7 percent stock constitutes twice as much of the portfolio as the 4 percent stock, then the weighted average would be found by multiplying 4 percent by 1, and 7 percent by 2. The sum of these products would be 18 percent, which, when divided by 3, the sum of the weights, produces an average of 6 percent.

The <u>weighted-average expected return</u> on an investment is determined by weighting the return expected for each security by the percentage it will represent in the total investment portfolio and then adding these weighted percentages together.

The <u>weighted beta coefficient</u> measures the risk of a given portfolio compared to that of the overall market. It is specifically the summation of all the betas in a portfolio weighted by the proportion of each asset in the portfolio.

<u>Writing a naked option</u> refers to writing an option on stock that the writer does not own.

A <u>yield curve</u> shows the relationship between yield to maturity and time to maturity for a group of similar securities at a certain point in time. Yield is plotted on the vertical axis and time to maturity is plotted on the horizontal axis. One would expect interest rates to be higher for long-term issues than for short-term issues. This would be expected because of the risk factor. However, there have been instances in which short-term rates have been higher than long-term rates. A yield curve may be constructed to show the term structure of interest rates at a given moment of time for a particular type of security. For example, the yield curve for Treasury securities is different from the yield curve for AA corporate bonds or AA municipal bonds.

The <u>yield to call</u> is similar to a bond's yield to maturity. The only difference is that the security's expected call date is substituted for the bond's maturity date. Thus, the yield to call is the fully compounded rate of return for the investor if the investor receives the bond's call price (usually, a premium above par) on the earliest call date.

<u>Yield to maturity</u> is the fully compounded rate of return when a bond is held to maturity. This rate is the internal rate of return that equates its present market price with the present value of its future interest income and capital appreciation.

A zero-coupon bond pays no interest from issue date to maturity date. The full amount of accumulated interest is paid at date of maturity. Thus, in effect, the investor is purchasing a very deep discount bond. There are two disadvantages of the zero-coupon bond for the investor: (a) he or she is deprived of annual cash flow during the investment period; and (b) he or she is taxed annually on the assumed interest income, although he or she does not receive any income. To avoid taxation of imputed interest, some investors purchase zero coupon municipal bonds, which may be triple tax free (federal, state and local) in the state of issue. Taxes can also be deferred by buying zero coupon bonds in IRAs or qualified plans.

A zero-coupon Treasury security is a security on which no interest is paid annually. Rather, interest accrues until maturity, when the security pays its full face value. The security is sold at a discount from face value. U.S. Treasury bills are examples of zero-coupon Treasury securities.

INDEX

Iowa Book LLC
8 S. Clinton St.
Iowa City, IA 52240
Phone 319-337-4188
WWW.IOWABOOK.COM

Sale

Receipt: RC0350220-6 001 002   Register_6
Cashier: CASHIER21   09/11/18 17:03

                                    Sale
    Discount
----

  1 KEIR EDUCATIONAL RESOURCES

    14539350
    978-1-945276-48-4   Y $95.00

                  Subtotal: $95.00
Tax:
 6% SALES AND OP $5.70

                    Total: $100.70
Tender:

 DEBIT CARD $100.70
 XXXXXXXXXXXX3972

Change Due: $0.00

            Thank You!

* R C 0 3 5 0 2 2 0 - 6 *